ADh-3847

DATE		

The Selected Essays of Gore Vidal

Also by Gore Vidal

The

Selected Essays

of

GORE VIDAL

By Gore Vidal

Edited by Jay Parini

DOUBLEDAY

New York   London   Toronto   Sydney   Auckland

DD

DOUBLEDAY

Published in the United States by Doubleday, an imprint of The Doubleday Publishing
Group, a division of Random House, Inc., New York.
www.doubleday.com

DOUBLEDAY is a registered trademark
and the DD colophon is a trademark of Random House, Inc.

"Novelists and Critics of the 1940s," "Tarzan Revisited," "The Top Ten Best-Sellers," "French
Letters: Theories of the New Novel," "American Plastic," "Calvino's Novels," "The Hacks of
Academe," "Some Memories of the Glorious Bird and an Earlier Self," "Edmund Wilson: This
Critic and This Gin and These Shoes," "William Dean Howells," "Dawn Powell: The American
Writer," "Montaigne," "Passage to Egypt" (originally published as "Nassar's Egypt"), "Pornography,"
"The Holy Family," "Homage to Daniel Shays," "Pink Triangle and Yellow Star," "Theodore
Roosevelt: An American Sissy," "The Second American Revolution," "The National Security State,"
and "Monotheism and Its Discontents" were published in *United States: Essays 1952–1992* by
Gore Vidal (Random House: New York), 1993

"Rabbit's Own Burrow" was published in *The Last Empire: Essays 1992–2000*
by Gore Vidal (Doubleday: New York), 2001.

"Black Tuesday" was originally published as "September 11, 2001 (A Tuesday)" in *Perpetual War
for Perpetual Peace* (Nation Books: New York), 2002.

"State of the Union, 2004" was originally published in the September 13, 2004,
issue of *The Nation*.

Book design by Jennifer Ann Daddio

Library of Congress Cataloging-in-Publication Data

Vidal, Gore, 1925–
[Essays. Selections]
The selected essays of Gore Vidal / by Gore Vidal ; edited by Jay Parini. — 1st ed.
p.   cm.
I. Parini, Jay. II. Title.
PS3543.I26A6 2008
814'.54—dc22
2008013517

ISBN 978-0-385-52484-1

PRINTED IN THE UNITED STATES OF AMERICA

1 3 5 7 9 10 8 6 4 2

First Edition

CONTENTS

PART TWO: READING THE WORLD

INTRODUCTION

By Jay Parini

Gore Vidal is America's premier man of letters. His twenty-five novels reveal an imagination that can inhabit the past (*Julian, Burr, Lincoln, Creation, Empire*) or embody the dizzying present (*Myra Breckinridge, Duluth, Live from Golgotha*). In *The City and the Pillar* (1948), one of the earliest American novels to deal frankly with a gay theme, he opened a fresh vein in American fiction. He has written witty plays for Broadway, including *Visit to a Small Planet* and *The Best Man*, as well as countless plays for television during its Golden Age. As a screenwriter, he has written or contributed to many scripts, with *Suddenly, Last Summer* and *Ben-Hur* among his many credits. His absorbing memoir, *Palimpsest*, appeared in 1995, with its sequel—*Point to Point Navigation*—just published. On top of this, his shrewd, elegantly written, and relentlessly brilliant essays must be considered among the finest examples of the genre.

Vidal began writing essays in the late 1940s and has never stopped. These have been gathered at regular intervals in more than a dozen editions, with the most comprehensive collection being *United States: Essays 1952–1992*. This vast book offers a vast treasury of good reading, but it should have been published with little wheels and a retractable handle. This *Selected Essays* attempts to whittle down the contents of that volume, adding a sampling of recent work. It shows the range of Vidal's work in this genre, with subjects ranging from history and autobiography to literature and politics. These are landmark essays, reflecting the author's insatiable interest in the world as he found it. They represent both a response to his times and, in fact, a consistent effort to change hearts and minds.

At least half of these essays fall into the category of literary criticism, what Vidal has derisively called "book-chat," while the others meditate on historical or cultural issues. There is almost always an autobiographical thread as well, and whether Vidal is reading a writer's work or the world at large, he does so from a distinctive perch. A compulsive autodidact, he demonstrates an enviable catholicity of taste and range of association. Nobody else writes like him, as in his essay on the novelists of the 1940s, where he reflects on the foibles of critics past and present: "One could invent a most agreeable game," he says, "of drawing analogies between the fourth century and today. F. R. Leavis and Saint Jerome are perfectly matched, while John Chrysostom and John Crowe Ransom suggest a possibility. The analogy works amusingly on all levels save one: the church fathers had a Christ to provide them with a primary source of revelation, while our own dogmatists must depend either upon private systems or else upon those proposed by such slender reeds as Matthew Arnold and T. S. Eliot, each, despite his genius, a ritual victim as well as a hero of literary fashion."

Like all great critics, Vidal makes pronouncements that ring true and, finally, become true. "Carson McCullers, Paul Bowles, Tennessee Williams are, at this moment at least, the three most interesting writers in the United States. Each is engaged in the task of truth-saying (as opposed to saying the truth, which is not possible this side of revelation). Each has gone further into the rich interior of the human drama than any of our immediate predecessors with the possible exception of William Faulkner, whose recent work has unfortunately resembled bad translations from Pindar." As ever, his choices—the essay appeared in 1953—are astute, astonishingly so. The distinction between "truth-saying" and "saying the truth" is at once provocative and illuminating. The remark about Faulkner, who was fresh from his Nobel Prize, is both challenging and, in retrospect, accurate; it's also amusing, which is one of the main things one must say about Vidal. He has (like Noel Coward, who coined the phrase) a "talent to amuse." But he also has a talent to instruct. One repeatedly comes away from his essays knowing more than when one began.

While some of these essays, such as his review of the top ten best-sellers of 1973, are hilarious, there is also a wise knowingness in these pages. For instance, when dismissing Solzhenitsyn's tedious *August 1914,* he writes: "I daresay as an expression of one man's indomitable spirit in a tyrannous society we must honor if not the art the author. Fortunately the Nobel Prize is designed for just such a purpose." Elsewhere, he says with a typical droll aside: "A peculiarity of American sexual mores is that those men who like to think of themselves as exclusively and triumphantly het-erosexual are convinced that the most masculine of all activities is not tending to the sexual needs of women but watching other men play games." Indeed.

His survey of the French New Novel is a classic, introducing Ameri-can readers to a range of recent French writers, including Nathalie Sar-raute and Alain Robbe-Grillet. Vidal explores the philosophic origins of the New Novel with an easy knowledge of the field: utterly unpedantic yet deeply learned (and therefore a model from which academics could learn a thing or two). And there is, always, that nonprofessorial wisdom: "The portentous theorizings of the New Novelists are of no more use to us than the self-conscious avant-gardism of those who are forever trying to figure out what the next 'really serious' thing will be when it is plain that there is not going to be a next serious thing in the novel. Our lovely vulgar and most human art is at an end, if not the end. Yet that is no rea-son not to want to practice it, or even to read it. In any case, rather like priests who have forgotten the meaning of the prayers they chant, we shall go on for quite a long time talking of books and writing books, pre-tending all the while not to notice that the church is empty and the parishioners have gone elsewhere to attend other gods, perhaps in silence or with new words."

Vidal is often scathing about academics, as in "The Hacks of Aca-deme." "Professor Halperin has not an easy way with our rich language," he writes of one such. The essay is side-splittingly funny and dismissive. Vidal, as a critic once observed, pisses from a great height, and that lofti-ness may well dizzy the uninitiated reader. But the height is necessary for the sort of thing he does here. It's a delight to be lifted so high, so easily, by an eagle of our time. He scans the world of letters with his large, hooded eyes, and the shadow of his wingspan leaves a distinct mark on the earth below.

Vidal's reading spreads wide, as in "American Plastic: The Matter of Fiction," where he takes on several esteemed American writers of the Sixties and early Seventies, including Donald Barthelme, John Barth, Grace Paley, William Gass, and Thomas Pynchon. His iconoclastic reading of these writers seems, in retrospect, amazingly astute. "The meager rattling prose of all these writers, excepting Gass, depresses me," he concludes, seeing these novelists as products of the academy, without a real audience. He would, for himself, prefer to have voluntary readers, not students with an assignment.

When Vidal takes on an assignment himself, however, he makes a splendid student. One could not hope for a better introduction to William Dean Howells, Edmund Wilson, Dawn Powell, Italo Calvino, or Montaigne. These essays are peerless examples of exposition. In the case of Powell and Calvino, he was—in effect—introducing these writers to a wide audience. His yeoman's work in the field of criticism has, I think, been underestimated, in part because it's so fiercely unacademic, even anti-academic. There is not a trace of jargon anywhere, unless held up for derision. Clarity and common sense reign. Vidal's intelligence, with its intense wattage, shines brightly everywhere, and when the beam narrows onto a passage, the passage glows. This is illuminating criticism, quite literally. When Vidal takes on a writer who disappoints him, as in the withering essay on Updike called "Rabbit's Own Burrow," he does so more in sorrow than anger. "Although I've never taken Updike seriously as a writer," he says, "I now find him the unexpectedly relevant laureate of the way we would like to live now, if we have the money, the credentials, and the sort of faith in our country and its big God that passes all understanding."

The essay on Tennessee Williams ranks among the best things Vidal has written. An excursion in autobiography, it arose from the author's close personal knowledge of the playwright. He met Williams in Rome in 1948, when Vidal had just published *The City and the Pillar*. Williams had recently scored a huge hit on Broadway with *A Streetcar Named Desire*. The friendship prospered, and this essay describes the arc of their relations. The playwright himself is summoned vividly into being, his conversation recalled verbatim, and poignant moments caught in the Vidalian shimmer. At the core of the essay lies an acute understanding of what made Williams a major playwright. He observes, for example, that Williams is "not the sort of writer who sees words on the page; rather he hears them in his head and when he is plugged into the right character, the wrong word never sounds."

On matters of sexual politics, and politics in general, Vidal is equally astute. His groundbreaking essay on intolerance called "Pink Triangle and Yellow Star" appeared in 1981. "Like it or not," he writes, "Jews and homosexualists are in the same fragile boat, and one would have to be pretty obtuse not to see the common danger." His essay assails the "shrill fag-baiting of Joseph Epstein, Norman Podhoretz, Alfred Kazin, and the Hilton Kramer Hotel." In "Pornography," another seminal essay, he skewers those who regard homosexuality as a "pernicious sickness," as a writer in *Time* had recently done. With a keen sense of history, he reminds us that "in the great world of pre-Christian cities, it never occurred to anyone that a homosexual act was less 'natural' than a heterosexual one. It was simply a matter of taste." Here, as elsewhere, Vidal argues that "we are bisexual," all of us. "Opportunity and habit incline us toward this or that sexual object. Since additional children are no longer needed, it is impossible to say that some acts are 'right' and others 'wrong.'" Radical common sense permeates these essays, and they are worth rereading carefully.

Vidal is always willing—even eager—to call a pothole in the road a pothole. He says exactly what he sees, however unpopular, willing to risk offense, as in "The Holy Family," his ironic look at the Kennedy clan. A skeptical tone pervades his historical essays and makes his writing on the past both amusing and informative. In one example included here, he gleefully dissects the macho presidency of Theodore Roosevelt, whom he calls "an American sissy." He can be a passionate advocate of a point of view as well, as in "Homage to Daniel Shays," where he takes on the American tax system, as did the eponymous rebel to whom this essay is dedicated. Shays remains a relatively unknown figure, though he created a good deal of mayhem in 1786, when he led a revolt of small farmers who hated the disproportionate taxes they had been asked to bear. Their fledgling government was still paying off the Revolutionary War, and the regressive tax system of the time proved intolerable. Whole farms had to be sold to pay taxes, and families fell into abysmal debt. Shays and his men, calling themselves the Regulators, forced important changes, and Vidal would do the same. "Why do we allow our governors to take so much of our money and spend it in ways that not only fail to benefit us but do great damage to others as we prosecute undeclared wars?" he wonders. "The taxpayers' revolt has begun."

This was written during the Vietnam War, which Vidal tirelessly protested in many venues. With Dr. Benjamin Spock, he co-chaired the People's Party. He was a fixture on American television talk shows, decrying the prosecution of this illegal and immoral war. (Not surprisingly, Vidal has been equally vehement against George W. Bush and the Iraq War, which he has opposed vocally in fierce political essays and, of course, on talk shows—one of his favorite venues.) What Vidal brought to the table in the Sixties and early Seventies was a deeply meditated sense of history and a visceral understanding of politics, which he acquired in Washington, D.C., where he grew up in the Thirties in the large home on Rock Creek Park owned by his grandfather, Senator Thomas P. Gore, a major figure in Democratic politics.

Vidal spent a good deal of time on the floor of the U.S. Senate with his grandfather, seeing firsthand how the democratic process in the United States actually worked (or didn't). His own father, Eugene Vidal, was a member of the Roosevelt administration, in charge of air commerce during the earliest years of the airline industry. Vidal himself ran (unsuccessfully) for both the House and the Senate, and he has campaigned for many others. Perhaps his most successful political role was that of the aging senator in the film *Bob Roberts*—one of many parts he has played in the movies. In any case, Vidal comes by his political interests honestly, and when he writes about the political life, he does so with the passion and knowledge of an insider.

"The Second American Revolution" was the title essay of a collection that appeared in 1982, two years into the era of Ronald Reagan, whom Vidal called "our acting President." "The people of the United States," he writes, "are deeply displeased with their government as it now malfunctions." Vidal does not accept the myth that the framers of the U.S.

Constitution were a group of world-class geniuses who gathered in Philadelphia to create an eternal and sacrosanct document, which must never be altered. According to Vidal, the Founding Fathers "feared monarchy and democracy," inventing a system of checks and balances that would "keep the people and their passions away from government and the would-be dictator hedged 'round with prohibitions." Quite sensibly, he calls for rethinking this ancient document, revising its contents in the direction of greater democracy. He would put further limits on executive power, as the presidency has increasingly over recent decades allowed the President to behave like an elected monarch.

In "The National Security State," Vidal takes on the military-industrial complex, as Eisenhower once dubbed the lethal combination of government, military, and the weapons industry that still consumes a large portion of the annual budget of the United States. He notes here the vast mobilization that began soon after the end of the Second World War, with the National Security Act of 1947. In essence, the United States committed itself to perpetual war, hurling immense quantities of cash and energy into the creation of lethal weaponry and a standing army as powerful as anything before it in human history. It was important to have an enemy, and one could hardly imagine anything better than godless Communism, which represented everything that the American republic wasn't. For three decades, it presented a fierce and Hydra-headed enemy that made it "necessary" for the U.S. government to order large quantities of tanks, planes, warships, and bombs. Vidal argues for lifting the "imperial burden" and taking back the country, *our* country, as he calls it.

Always the iconoclast, Vidal has a particular distaste for piety in its American manifestations. "From the beginning," he writes in "Monotheism and Its Discontents," "sky-godders have always exerted great pressure in our secular republic." Sky-godders are Jews and Christians: nomadic people of the desert, who discerned the presence of an omnipotent God in the endless undivided blue overhead. The monotheists are different from more primitive polytheists, who live in jungles, where many gods flash their smiles and frowns. Vidal retains a lofty detachment through much of this essay, but he can barely control his rage when he writes about the Christian evangelicals who "feel it necessary to convert everyone on earth," who have forced "their superstitions and hatreds upon all of us through the civil law and through general prohibitions." Vidal himself declares "an all-out war on the monotheists."

A true son of the Enlightenment, Vidal prizes tolerance. He would normally say "live and let live," allowing the monotheists to practice their faiths as they see fit. But they won't let him be, he argues. "They have a divine mission to take away our rights as private citizens." And so they forbid abortion, gambling, homosexuality, and so forth: all things that Vidal would leave to the individual. Like his hero, Tom Paine, Vidal subscribes to the "religion of humanity," he says, arguing that the time has come to "re-establish a representative government firmly based upon the Bill of Rights."

It should be noticed that Vidal is conservative in many respects, asking only for liberty in the eighteenth-century sense of that term. He stands behind individual choice, the limitation of executive power, and the preservation of the environment. Like his grandfather, he dislikes the drive for empire (which he has analyzed in his later novels, such as *Empire*, *Hollywood*, and *The Golden Age*). He would return us, if possible, to the pure republicanism of early America. When Ronald Reagan asked to get the government "off our backs," Vidal countered that we should get them "off our fronts" as well. He supports the freedom to worship as one pleases, as long as one does not try to stop others from worshiping in a different way. He frequently points out the obvious truth that the American government has only one political party, the party of business, which has two wings, Republican and Democrat. In writing like this, he is very much in a tradition of American dissent that reaches back to Tom Paine and moves through such figures as Thoreau, Randolph Bourne, and others. But Vidal retains his Enlightenment perch, wry and ready to flash his wit, to unmask what is pretentious or foolish or self-serving. If his temper has grown short in recent times, one can hardly blame him, as in many ways his worst nightmares have come true under the regime of George W. Bush.

With preternatural inventiveness, Vidal has recently revived the political pamphlet as a genre. First came *Perpetual War for Perpetual Peace*, in 2002—his visceral response to 9/11, which drew an enthusiastic response from a wide audience looking around in desperation for clarity and common sense in a time of sheer madness. The essay called "Black Tuesday" opens this pamphlet, and it begins with Vidalian gusto: "According to the Koran, it was on a Tuesday that Allah created darkness." The author catches our eye, and ear, from the outset, and he rivets our attention as he looks at the "perpetual war" that the United States has waged for the past half century in pursuit of "perpetual peace." Seven or so trillion dollars have gone into what is euphemistically called "defense," he notes. Yet there was no advance warning about 9/11 (or, if there was, it was ignored). Vidal sweeps through contemporary American history, observing that the United States always needs "a new horrendous enemy" who must be struck down for the empire to survive. He appends a list of the wars that have absorbed American taxpayer dollars since the Berlin Airlift of 1948. (Compiled by the Federation of American Scientists, it makes for compelling reading, and is included here.)

This book comes right up to the present century with Vidal's ferocious "State of the Union, 2004"—the opening salvo of a recent pamphlet called *Dreaming War*. As America's perpetual Shadow President, Vidal has periodically delivered a mock-version of the president's annual speech to the assembled House and Senate. Here he casts a cold eye on the efforts of the Bush administration to protect the nation from various Third World enemies, the "Axis of Evil." His assessment of the current state of affairs in "The United States of Amnesia" is devastating, though he delivers the bad news with a wry smile. Needless to say, the willingness of George Bush and Dick Cheney to trade blood for oil infuriates him. That Bush has "nearly banished truth entirely" in his efforts to remain in power is more than merely annoying to Vidal; it is downright illegal and threatens the very fabric of democracy.

Dark times have befallen the republic, which has never before been so much in need of Gore Vidal. He afflicts the comfortable with a dazzling array of facts and arguments, in a style that compels the attention of readers by its wit and eloquence. Now in his eighties, he remains a figure of immense poise, a unique voice whose luminous, excoriating, funny, and informative essays may well be regarded by future generations as the pinnacle of his achievement.

Part One

READING

THE

WRITERS

NOVELISTS AND CRITICS

OF THE 1940s

It is a rare and lucky physician who can predict accurately at birth whether a child is to become a dwarf or a giant or an ordinary adult, since most babies look alike and the curious arrangements of chromosomes which govern stature are inscrutable and do not yield their secret order even to the shrewdest eye. Time alone gives definition. Nevertheless, interested readers and writers, like anxious parents and midwives, forever speculate upon the direction and meaning of current literary trends, and professional commentators with grave authority make analyses which the briefest interval often declares invalid. But despite their long historic record of bad guesses, bookish men continue to make judgments, and the recorded derelictions of taste and the erratic judgments of earlier times tend only to confirm in them a sense of complacency: *they* are not we, and did not know; *we* know. To disturb this complacency is occasionally worthwhile, and one way of doing it is to exhume significant critical texts from the recent past. Those of the last century, in particular, provide us with fine warnings.

For instance: "We do not believe any good end is to be effected by fictions which fill the mind with details of imaginary vice and distress and crime, or which teach it instead of endeavoring after the fulfillment of simple and ordinary duty to aim at the assurance of superiority by creating for itself fanciful and incomprehensible perplexities. Rather we believe that the effect of such fictions tends to render those who fall under their influence unfit for practical exertion by intruding on minds which ought to be guarded from impurity the unnecessary knowledge of evil." This was the *Quarterly Review* on George Eliot's *The Mill on the Floss*, and it is really quite well said: the perennial complaint of the professional reviewers and the governors of lending libraries ("enough unpleasant things in the world without reading about them in books").

Or the following attack on preciosity and obscurantism (*Blackwood's Magazine*, 1817): "Mr. Coleridge conceives himself to be a far greater man than the public is likely to admit; and we wish to waken him from what seems to us a most ludicrous delusion. He seems to believe that every tongue is wagging in his praise. . . . The truth is that Mr. Coleridge is but an obscure name in English literature." [Coleridge was forty-five years old at this time and his major work was long since done.] "In London he is well known in literary society for his extraordinary loquacity . . ." And there follows a prolix attack upon the *Biographia Literaria*.

Or this excerpt from an 1848 *Quarterly Review*, deploring the pagan, the sexual, and the vicious:

> At all events there can be no interest attached to the writer of Wuthering Heights—*a novel succeeding* Jane Eyre *and purporting to be written by Ellis Bell—unless it were for the sake of more individual reprobation. For though there is a decided resemblance between the two, yet the aspect of the Jane and Rochester animals in their native state, as Catherine and Heatfield [sic], is too odiously and abominably pagan to be palatable even to the most vitiated class of English readers. With all the unscrupulousness of the French school of novels it combines that repulsive vulgarity in the choice of its vice which supplies its own antidote.*

Differently worded, these complaints still sound in our press. The Luce editors who cry for an "affirmative" literature echo voices once raised against George Eliot. When middlebrow reviewers deplore "morbidity" in our best writers, they only paraphrase the outrage of those who found the Brontës repellent. And the twitterings of an Orville Prescott when he has discovered a nice and busy book echo the same homely song of those long-dead reviewers who found in the three-volume novels of forgotten lady writers so much warm comfort.

As the essential problems of life remain the same from generation to generation, despite altered conditions, so the problems of literary recognition remain, for contemporaries, peculiarly difficult. Despite the warnings of other times, the impetuous and the confident continue their indiscriminate cultivation of weeds at the expense of occasional flowers.

To consider the writing of any period, including the present, it is perhaps of some importance to examine the climate in which the work is done, to chart if possible the prevailing winds, the weather of the day.

Today there is a significant distinction between the reviewers for popular newspapers and magazines, whom no one interested in literature reads, and the serious critics of the Academy, who write for one another in the quarterlies and, occasionally, for the public in the Sunday supplements. The reviewers are not sufficiently relevant or important to be considered in any but a social sense: they reflect the commonest prejudices and aspirations of the middle class for whom they write, and they need not concern us here.

The critics, however, are significant. They are dedicated men; they are serious; their learning is often respectable. They have turned to the analysis of literature with the same intensity that, born in an earlier time, they might have brought to formal philosophy, to the law, to the ministry. They tend, generically and inevitably, to be absolutists. They believe that by a close examination of "the text," the laws and the crafty "strategies" of its composition will be made clear and the findings will provide "touchstones" for a comparative criticism of other works. So far so good. They have constructed some ingenious and perhaps valuable analyses of metaphysical verse whose order is often precise and whose most disparate images proceed with a calculable wit and logic.

Unfortunately, the novel is not so easily explicated. It is a loose form, and although there is an inherent logic in those books we are accustomed to call great, the deducible "laws" which governed the execution of *Emma* are not going to be of much use in defining *The Idiot*. The best that a serious analyst can hope to do is comment intelligently from his vantage point in time on the way a work appears to him in a contemporary, a comparative, or a historic light; in which case, his opinion is no more valuable than his own subtlety and knowledge. He must be, as T. S. Eliot put it so demurely, "very intelligent." The point, finally, is that he is not an empiricist dealing with measurable quantities and calculable powers. Rather, he is a man dealing with the private vision of another, with a substance as elusive and amorphous as life itself. To *pretend* that there are absolutes is necessary in making relative judgments (Faulkner writes better than Taylor Caldwell), but to *believe* that there are absolutes and to order one's judgments accordingly is folly and disastrous. One is reminded of Matthew Arnold and his touchstones; it was his conviction that certain lines from a poet by all conceded great might be compared to those of lesser poets to determine their value. Arnold selected Dante as his great poet, an irreproachable choice, but then he misread the Italian, which naturally caused some confusion. Arnold's heirs also demand order, tidiness, labels, ultimate assurance that this work is "good" and that work is "bad," but sooner or later someone misreads the Italian and the system breaks down. In our time there are nearly as many critical systems as there are major critics, which is a pleasing anarchy. The "new critics," as they have been termed (*they* at least dislike being labeled and few will now answer when called), are fundamentally mechanics. They go about dismantling the text with the same rapture that their simpler brothers experience while taking apart combustion engines: inveterate tinkerers both, solemnly playing with what has been invented by others for use, not analysis.

Today's quarterlies are largely house organs for the academic world. They seldom publish imaginative work and one of their most distinguished editors has declared himself more interested in commentaries on writing than in the writing itself. Their quarrels and schisms and heresies do not in the least resemble the Alexandrians whom they occasionally mention, with involuted pride, as spiritual ancestors. Rather, one is reminded of the semantic and doctrinal quarrels of the church fathers in the fourth century, when a diphthong was able to break the civilized world in half and spin civilization into nearly a millennium of darkness. One could invent a most agreeable game of drawing analogies between the fourth century and today. F. R. Leavis and Saint Jerome are perfectly matched, while John Chrysostom and John Crowe Ransom suggest a possibility. The analogy works amusingly on all levels save one: the church fathers had a Christ to provide them with a primary source of revelation, while our own dogmatists must depend either upon private systems or else upon those proposed by such slender reeds as Matthew Arnold and T. S. Eliot, each, despite his genius, a ritual victim as well as a hero of literary fashion.

But the critics are indefatigable and their game is in earnest, for it is deeply involved not only with literature but with such concrete things as careers in the Academy, where frequent and prestigious publication is important. Yet for all their busyness they are by no means eclectic. In a Henry James year not one will write an analysis of George Meredith. They tend to ignore the contemporary writers, not advancing much later than F. Scott Fitzgerald, whose chief attraction is that he exploded before he could be great, providing a grim lesson in failure that, in its completeness, must be awfully heartening when contemplated on the safe green campus of some secluded school.

Of the critics today, Edmund Wilson, the most interesting and the most important, has shown virtually no interest in the writing of the last fifteen years, his talents engaged elsewhere in the construction of heroic sepulchers for old friends like Fitzgerald and Millay, a likable loyalty but a not entirely useful one. He can of course still make a fine point during a Peacock flurry and he has been startling brilliant in recent essays on Grant and Lincoln, but one can search the pages of that book of his which he calls a "Literary Chronicle of the Forties" without coming upon any but the most cursory mention of the decade's chief talents.

Malcolm Cowley, a good professional literary man, had some sharp things to say recently about the young writers. Although he made almost no reference to the better writing of the day, he did say some accurate things about the university-trained writers, whose work, he feels, is done with too reverent an eye upon their old teachers, the new critics. Cowley speaks out for a hearty freedom from university influence, citing his own generation (the men of the 1920s are loyal to their time if not to one another: *everyone* was a genius then, and liquor was cheap abroad) as being singularly independent of formal instruction. Yet McCullers, Bowles,

Capote, etc. (like Hemingway, Faulkner, O'Neill, etc.) are not graduates of universities, and many of the other young lions have had enough war to wash them clean of academicism. Mr. Cowley, like most commentators, tends to bend whatever he finds to his premise. To him there is no single genius who can set the tone for a generation but one wonders if he would recognize that great writer any more than Lord Jeffrey, a century ago, was able to recognize *his* time's greatness? For the Cowleys, the novel stopped at *Gatsby*. That Carson McCullers (whom he does not mention) has influenced many works, that Tennessee Williams has influenced the theater of the world, that Paul Bowles, among others, has reshaped the short story—none of these things impinges on him.

Mr. Cowley's gloom is supported by the young John W. Aldridge, Jr. In his amusing novel *After the Lost Generation* he got onto the subject of "values" (by way of Lionel Trilling and perhaps V. S. Pritchett). After discussing a number of fictitious characters who were writing books (using real, if unlikely, names like Truman Capote and Gore Vidal), he "proved," by the evidence of their works, that they had all failed of greatness because, except for "a pocket or two of manners" (the Army; the South; here and there in New England), there was really nothing left to write about, none of that social conflict out of which comes art, like sparks from a stone grinding metal. His coda indicated that a young writer of singular genius is at this moment hovering in the wings awaiting his cue. It will be interesting to read Mr. Aldridge's next novel.

Yet Mr. Aldridge does have a case: the old authority of church, of settled Puritan morality, *has* broken down, and if one's vision is historically limited to only a few generations in time it might seem that today's novelists are not having the fun their predecessors in the 1920s had, breaking cultural furniture. But to take a longer view, one must recall that the great times for literature and life were those of transition: from the Middle Ages to modern times by way of the Renaissance, from dying paganism to militant Christianity by way of the Antonines, and so on back to Aristophanes. The opportunity for the novelist when Mr. Aldridge's "values" are in the discard is fabulous: to create without wasting one's substance in political or social opposition. What could be more marvelous! Neither Virgil nor Shakespeare had to attack their day's morality or those in authority. They were morally free to write of life, of Henry James's "the main thing."

There were certainly inequities and barbarities in sixteenth-century England and first-century Rome, but the writers, affected partly by convention (not to mention the Star Chamber), did not address themselves to attacks upon the government or the time's morality, which, apparently, did not obsess them. Writers, after all, are valuable in spite of their neuroses, obsessions, and rebellions, not because of them. It is a poor period indeed which must assess its men of letters in terms of their opposition to their society. Opposition to life's essential conditions perhaps, or to death's implacable tyranny, is something else again, and universal; but novels, no matter how clever, which attempt to change statutes or moral attitudes are, though useful at the moment, not literature at all. In fact, if Mr. Aldridge were right in his proposition we would have *not* a barren, "subjectless" world for literature but the exact opposite: a time of flowering, of creation without waste and irrelevancy. Unhappily, American society has not changed that much in the last thirty years. There is as much to satirize, as much to protest as ever before, and it will always be the task of the secondary figures to create those useful public books whose momentary effect is as stunning as their literary value is not.

There is no doubt but that the West has come to Malraux's "twilight of the absolute." One awaits with hope the period between when, unencumbered by the junk of dogma, writers can turn to the great things with confidence and delight. Loss of authority by removing targets does not destroy the true novelist, though it eliminates the doctrinaire and those busy critics who use the peculiar yardstick of social usefulness to determine merit. (It is no accident that the few works admired by Mr. Aldridge are those compositions which sturdily and loudly discuss the social scene, or some "pocket" of it—interesting books, certainly, whose public effect is often admirable; though the noise they create seldom persists long enough to enjoy even a first echo.) Actually, one might say that it is only the critic who suffers unduly from the lack of authority. A critic, to criticize, must, very simply, have standards. To have standards he must pretend there is some optimum against which like creations can be measured. By the nature of his own process he is eventually forced, often inadvertently, to accept as absolute those conditions for analysis which he has only tentatively proposed. To be himself significant he needs law and revealed order; without them he is only a civilized man commenting for others upon given works which, temperamentally, he may or may not like without altering the value, if any, of the work examined. With a law, with authority, with faith he becomes something more grand and meaningful; the pythoness through whom passes Apollo's word.

Much of the despondency and apparent confusion in the world of peripheral letters today derives partly from the nervous, bloody age in which we live and partly from that hunger for the absolute which, in our own immediate experience, delivered two great nations into the hands of tyrants, while in our own country the terror of being man alone, unsupported by a general religious belief and undirected by central authority, has reduced many intellectuals either to a bleak nihilism or, worse, to the acceptance of some external authority (Rome, Marx, Freud). One is reminded of Flaubert's comment nearly a century ago: "The melancholy of the ancients seems to me deeper than that of the moderns, who all more or less assume an immortality on the far side of the black pit. For the ancients the black pit was infinity itself; their dreams take shape and pass against a background of unchanging ebony. No cries, no struggles, only the fixity of the pensive gaze. The gods being dead and Christ not yet born [sic], there was between Cicero and Marcus Aurelius one unique moment in which there was man."

Our own age is one of man alone, but there are still cries, still struggles against our condition, against the knowledge that our works and days have value only on the human scale; and those who most clearly remember the secure authority of other times, the ordered universe, the immutable moral hierarchies, are the ones who most protest the black pit. While it is perfectly true that any instant in human history is one of transition, ours more than most seems to be marked by a startling variety of conflicting absolutes, none sufficiently great at this moment to impose itself upon the majority whose lives are acted out within an unhuman universe which some still prefer to fill with a vast manlike shadow containing stars, while others behold only a luminous dust which *is* stars, and us as well. This division between those who recognize the unhumanity of creation and those who protest the unchanging ebony sets the tone of our literature, with the imaginative writers inclining (each in his own way) to the first view and their critics to the second. The sense of man not being king of creation (nor even the work of a king of creation) is the burden, directly and indirectly, of modern literature. For the writers there is no reality for man except in his relations with his own kind. Much of the stuff of earlier centuries—like fate, high tragedy, the interventions of *dei ex machina*—have been discarded as brave but outworn devices, not applicable in a world where kings and commoners occupy the same sinking boat.

Those of our writers who might yet enjoy the adjective "affirmative" are the ones who tend to devote themselves to the dramas within the boat, the encompassing cold sea ignored in the passions of the human moment. Most of the worst and a number of the best writers belong to this category. The key words here are "love" and "compassion." And though, like most such devices, they have grown indistinct with use, one can still see them at work, and marvelously so, in the novels of Carson McCullers and certain (though not all) of the plays of Tennessee Williams. Christopher Isherwood once said that to his mind the finest single line in modern letters was: "I have always depended upon the kindness of strangers," from *A Streetcar Named Desire*. At such moments, in such works, the human drama becomes so unbearably intense that time and the sea are blotted out and only the human beings are illuminated as they cease, through the high magic of art, to be mere residents in a time which stops and become, instead, archetypes—elemental figures like those wild gods our ancestors peopled heaven with.

Then there are the writers to whom neither sea nor boat exists. They have accepted some huge fantasy wherein they need never drown, where death is life, and the doings of human beings on a social and ethical level are of much consequence to some brooding source of creation who dispenses his justice along strictly party lines at the end of a gloomy day. To this category belong such talented writers as Graham Greene and Evelyn Waugh. In theory at least, speculation has ended for them; dogma supports them in all things. Yet it is odd to find that the tone of their works differs very little from that of the other mariners adrift. They are, if anything, perhaps a bit more lugubrious, since for them is not the principality of this world.

Finally, there are those who see human lives as the lunatic workings of compulsive animals no sooner born than dead, no sooner dead than replaced by similar creatures born of that proliferating seed which too will die. Paul Bowles is a striking example of this sort of writer as he coolly creates nightmare visions in which his specimens struggle and drown in fantasy, in madness, in death. His short stories with their plain lines of monochromatic prose exploit extreme situations with a chilling resourcefulness; he says, in short, "Let it sink; let us drown."

Carson McCullers, Paul Bowles, Tennessee Williams are, at this moment at least, the three most interesting writers in the United States. Each is engaged in the task of truth-saying (as opposed to saying the truth, which is not possible this side of revelation). Each has gone further into the rich interior of the human drama than any of our immediate predecessors with the possible exception of William Faulkner, whose recent work has unfortunately resembled bad translations from Pindar. On a social level, the hostility shown these essential artists is more significant than their occasional worldly successes, for it is traditional that he who attempts to define man's condition demoralizes the majority, whether relativist or absolutist. We do not want ever to hear that we will die but that first we must live; and those ways of living which are the fullest, the most intense, are the very ones which social man traditionally dreads, summoning all his superstition and malice to combat strangers and lovers, the eternal victims.

The obsessive concern with sexuality which informs most contemporary writing is not entirely the result of a wish *épater le bourgeois* but, more, the reflection of a serious battle between the society man has constructed so illogically and confusedly and the nature of the human being, which needs a considerably fuller expression sexually and emotionally than either the economics or morality of this time will permit. The sea is close. Two may find the interval between awareness and death more meaningful than one alone. Yet while ours is a society where mass murder and violence are perfectly ordinary and their expression in the most popular novels and comic books is accepted with aplomb, any love between two people which does not conform is attacked.

Malcolm Cowley has complained that writers no longer handle some of the more interesting social relationships of man, that there is no good stock-market novel, no Balzacian concern among the better writers with economic motive. His point is valid. The public range of the novel has been narrowed. It would be good to have well-written accounts of the way we live now, yet our important writers eschew, almost deliberately it would seem, the kind of book which provided not only Trollope but Tolstoi with so much power. Mr. Cowley catches quite well the tone of the second-rate good writers (a phenomenon peculiar to this moment; it seems as if a whole generation writes well, though not often to any point); they are concerned with the small scale, and goodness as exemplified by characters resembling the actress Shirley Booth holding out valiantly against villainous forces, usually represented by someone in business. But Mr. Cowley does not mention the novelist from whom these apotheosis-in-the-kitchen writers derive. Carson McCullers, using the small scale, the relations of human beings at their most ordinary, transcends her milieu and shows, in bright glimpses, the potentiality which exists in even the most banal of human relationships, the "we" as opposed to the meager "I."

The Match-maker

Or again, in Tennessee Williams's remarkable play *Camino Real*, though the world is shown in a nightmare glass, a vision of those already drowned, there are still moments of private triumphs . . . in Kilroy's love with (not for) the gypsy's daughter and in Lord Byron's proud departure through the gate to *terra incognita*, his last words a reproach and an exhortation: "Make voyages! Make voyages!"

And, finally, most starkly, we have a deliberate act of murder, Gide's *l'acte gratuite*, which occurs at the end of Paul Bowles's *Let It Come Down*. Here the faceless, directionless protagonist, in a sudden storm of rage against his life, all life, commits a murder without reason or passion, and in this one terrible moment (similar perhaps to that of a nation gone to war) he at last finds "a place in the world, a definite status, a precise relationship with the rest of men. Even if it had to be one of open hostility, it was his, created by him." In each of these three writers man acts, through love, through hate, through despair. Though the act in each is different, the common emotion is sufficiently intense to dispel, for a time at least, the knowledge of that cold drowning which awaits us all.

The malady of civilized man is his knowledge of death. The good artist, like the wise man, addresses himself to life and invests with his private vision the deeds and thoughts of men. The creation of a work of art, like an act of love, is our one small "yes" at the center of a vast "no."

The lesser writers whose works do not impress Mr. Cowley despite their correctness possess the same vision as those of the major writers, but their power of illusion is not so great and their magic is only fitful: too often their creatures are only automatons acted upon. Though they may shed light on interesting aspects of ordinary life they do not, in the best sense, illuminate, flood with brilliance, our strange estate.

Among the distinguished second rank of younger writers there is much virtuosity and potentiality. The coolly observant short stories of Louis Auchincloss provide wise social comment of the sort which the Cowleys would probably admire but never seem to read in their haste to generalize. Eudora Welty fashions a subtle line and Jean Stafford, though currently obsessed with literary interior decoration, has in such stories as "The Echo and the Nemesis" displayed a talent which makes all the more irritating her recent catalogues of bric-a-brac, actual and symbolic. John Kelly, whose two novels have been neglected, has created a perverse, operatic world like nothing else in our literature, while the late John Horne Burns, out of fashion for some years, was a brilliant satirist in a time when satire is necessary but difficult to write since to attack successfully one must have a complacent, massive enemy—and though there are numerous villains today, none is entirely complacent.

The serious writers have been attacked by the reviewers for their contempt of narrative and their neglect to fashion "real live characters" (which means familiar stereotypes from Victorian fiction masquerading in contemporary clothes). The reviewers have recognized that a good deal of writing now being done doesn't resemble anything they are used to (although in almost a century there has been a royal line of which they are ignorant . . . from *The Temptation of Saint Anthony* to *The Golden Bowl* to *Mrs. Dalloway*); they still feel most at home with *The Newcomes*, or, if they came to maturity in the 1920s, with *The Sun Also Rises*. When the technique of a play like *Camino Real* seems bizarre and difficult to follow for those accustomed to the imitators of Ibsen, there must be a genuine reason for the change in technique, other than the author's presumed perversity. The change from the exterior to the interior world which has been taking place in literature for at least a century is due not only to a general dissatisfaction with the limitations of naturalism but also to the rise of a new medium, the movies, which, properly used, are infinitely superior to the old novel and to the naturalistic play, especially in the rendering of plain narrative.

The Quiet One, a movie, was far superior as a social document (as "art," too, for that matter) to any book published so far in this country dealing with Negro problems. Instinctively, the writers have reacted to the camera. If another medium can handle narrative and social comment so skillfully, even on their lowest aesthetic levels, then the novelist must go deeper, must turn into the maze of consciousness where the camera cannot follow. He must also become wise, and wisdom even in its relative sense was never a notable characteristic of novelists in our language. One can anticipate the direction of the novel by studying that of the painters who, about the time of the still camera's invention, began instinctively to withdraw into a less literal world where they might do work which a machine could not imitate. It is a possibility, perhaps even a probability, that as the novel moves toward a purer, more private expression it will cease altogether to be a popular medium, becoming, like poetry, a cloistered avocation—in which case those who in earlier times might have written great public novels will be engaged to write good public movies, redressing the balance. In our language the novel is but three centuries old and its absorption by the movies, at least the vulgar line of it, is not necessarily a bad thing. In any event, it is already happening.

For the present, however, the tone of the contemporary novel, though not cheerful, is precise. Man is on his own. In certain human actions, in love, in violence, he can communicate with others, touch and be touched, act and in the act forget his fate. The scale is often small. Kings are neglected because, to relativists, all men are the same within eternity. Or rather their crisis is the same. The concern in modern letters is with that crisis which defines the prospect.

In general, the novelists have rejected authority, parting company with their cousins-german the serious critics. To the creative man, religious dogma and political doctrine, when stated in ultimate terms, represent the last enemy, the protean Lucifer in our race's bloody progress.

The artist speaks from that awareness of life, that secret knowledge of life in death the absolutists are driven to obscure and to distort, to shape, if possible, to tidy ends.

The interior drama at its most bitterly human comes into sharp focus in the writings of Williams and McCullers, and there are signs that other writers, undismayed by the hostility of the absolutists, may soon provide us with some strength in these last days before the sure if temporary victory of that authoritarian society which, thanks to science, now has every weapon with which to make even the most inspired lover of freedom conform to the official madness.

The thought of heaven, a perennial state of mind, a cheerful conception of what might be in life, in art (if not in death), may yet save our suicidally inclined race—if only because heaven is as various as there are men in the world who dream of it, and writers to evoke that dream. One recalls Constantine (to refer again to the image of the early church) when he teased a dissenting bishop at one of the synods: "Acesius, take a ladder and get up to heaven by yourself." We are fortunate in our time to have so many ladders going up. Each ladder is raised in hope, which is heaven enough.

New World Writing #4
1953

TARZAN REVISITED

There are so many things that people who take polls never get around to asking. Fascinated as we all are to know what our countrymen think of great issues (approving, disapproving, don't-knowing, with that native shrewdness which made a primeval wilderness bloom with Howard Johnson signs), the pollsters never get around to asking the sort of interesting personal questions our new Romans might be able to answer knowledgeably. For instance, how many adults have an adventure serial running in their heads? How many consciously daydream, turning on a story in which the dreamer ceases to be an employee of IBM and becomes a handsome demigod moving through splendid palaces, saving maidens from monsters (or monsters from maidens: this is a jaded time). Most children tell themselves stories in which they figure as powerful figures, enjoying the pleasures not only of the adult world as they conceive it but of a world of wonders unlike dull reality. Although this sort of Mittyesque daydreaming is supposed to cease in maturity, I suggest that more adults than we suspect are dazedly wandering about with a full Technicolor extravaganza going on in their heads. Clad in tights, rapier in hand, the daydreamers drive their Jaguars at fantastic speeds through a glittering world of adoring love objects, mingling anachronistic historic worlds with science fiction. "Captain, the time-warp's been closed! We are now trapped in a parallel world, inhabited entirely by women with three breasts!"

Though from what we can gather about these imaginary worlds, they tend to be more Adlerian than Freudian: the motor drive is the desire not for sex (other briefer fantasies take care of that) but for power, for the ability to dominate one's environment through physical strength, best demonstrated in the works of Edgar Rice Burroughs, whose books are enjoying a huge revival.

When I was growing up, I read all twenty-three Tarzan books, as well as the ten Mars books. My own inner story-telling mechanism was vivid. At any one time, I had at least three serials going as well as a number of tried and true reruns. I mined Burroughs largely for source material. When he went to the center of the earth à la Jules Verne (much too fancy a writer for one's taste), I immediately worked up a thirteen-part series, with myself as lead and various friends as guest stars. Sometimes I used the master's material, but more often I adapted it freely to suit myself. One's daydreams tended to be Tarzanish pre-puberty (physical strength and freedom) and Martian post-puberty (exotic worlds and subtle *combinazione* to be worked out). After adolescence, if one's life is sufficiently interesting, the desire to tell oneself stories diminishes. My last serial ran into sponsor trouble when I was in the Second World War, and it was never renewed.

Until recently I assumed that most people were like myself: daydreaming ceases when the real world becomes interesting and reasonably manageable. Now I am not so certain. The life and success of Burroughs lead one to believe that a good many people find their lives so unsatisfactory that they go right on year after year telling themselves stories in which they are able to dominate their environment in a way that is not possible in the overorganized society.

According to Edgar Rice Burroughs, "Most of the stories I wrote were the stories I told myself just before I went to sleep." He is a fascinating figure to contemplate, an archetypal American dreamer. Born in 1875 in Chicago, he was a drifter until he was thirty-six. He served briefly in the U.S. Cavalry; then he was a gold miner in Oregon, a cowboy in Idaho, a railroad policeman in Salt Lake City; he attempted several businesses that failed. He was perfectly in the old-American grain: the man who could take on almost any job, who liked to keep moving, who tried to get rich quick but could never pull it off. And while he was drifting through the unsatisfactory real world, he consoled himself with an inner world where he was strong and handsome, adored by beautiful women and worshiped by exotic races. His principal source of fantasy was Rider Haggard. But even that rich field was limited, and so, searching for new veins to tap, he took to reading the pulp magazines, only to find that none of the stories could compare for excitement with his own imaginings. Since the magazine writers could not please him, he had no choice but to please himself, and the public. He composed a serial about Mars and sold it to *Munsey's*. The rest was easy, for his fellow daydreamers recognized at once a master dreamer.

In 1914 Burroughs published *Tarzan of the Apes* (Rousseau's noble savage reborn in Africa), and history was made. To date the Tarzan books have sold over twenty-five million copies in fifty-six languages. There is hardly an American male of my generation who has not at one time or another tried to master the victory cry of the great ape as it issued from the voluptuous chest of Johnny Weissmuller, to the accompaniment of thousands of arms and legs snapping during attempts to swing from tree to tree in the backyards of the Republic. Between 1914 and his death in 1950, the squire of Tarzana, California (a prophet more than honored in his own land), produced over sixty books, while enjoying the unique status of being the first American writer to be a corporation. Burroughs is said to have been a pleasant, unpretentious man who liked to ride and play golf. Not one to compromise a vivid unconscious with dim reality, he never set foot in Africa.

With a sense of recapturing childhood, I have just reread several Tarzan books. It is fascinating to see how much one recalls after a quarter century. At times the sense of *déjà vu* is overpowering. It is equally interesting to discover that one's memories of Tarzan of the Apes are mostly action scenes. The plot had slipped one's mind . . . and a lot of plot there is. The beginning is worthy of Conrad. "I had this story from one who had no business to tell it to me, or to any other. I may credit the seductive influence of an old vintage upon the narrator for the beginning of it, and my own skeptical incredulity during the days that followed for the balance of the strange tale." It is 1888. The young Lord and Lady Greystoke are involved in a ship mutiny ("there was in the whole atmosphere of the craft that undefinable something which presages disaster"). The peer and peeress are put ashore on the west coast of Africa, where they promptly build a tree house. Here Burroughs is at his best. He tells you the size of the logs, the way to hang a door when you have no hinges, the problems of roofing. One of the best things about his books is the descriptions of making things. The Greystokes have a child, and conveniently die. The "man-child" is discovered by Kala, a Great Ape, who brings him up as a member of her tribe. As anthropologist, Burroughs is pleasantly vague. His apes are carnivorous, and they are able, he darkly suspects, to mate with human beings.

Tarzan grows up as an ape, kills his first lion (with a full nelson), teaches himself to read and write English by studying some books found in the cabin. The method he used, sad to say, is the currently fashionable "look-say." Though he can read and write, he cannot speak any language except that of the apes. He also gets on well with other members of the animal kingdom, with Tantor the elephant, Ska the vulture, Numa the lion (Kipling was also grist for the Burroughs dream mill). Then white folks arrive: Professor Archimedes Q. Porter and his daughter Jane. Also, a Frenchman named D'Arnot who teaches Tarzan to speak French, which is confusing. By an extraordinary coincidence, Jane's suitor is the current Lord Greystoke, who thinks the Greystoke baby is dead. Tarzan saves Jane from an ape. Then he puts on clothes and goes to Paris, where he drinks absinthe. Next stop, America. In Wisconsin, he saves Jane Porter from a forest fire: only to give her up nobly to Lord Greystoke, not revealing the fact that *he* is the real Lord Greystoke. Fortunately in the next volume, *The Return of Tarzan*, he marries Jane and they live happily ever after in Africa, raising a son John, who in turn grows up and has a son. Yet even as a grandfather, Tarzan continues to have adventures with people a foot high, with descendants of Atlantis, with the heirs of a Roman legion who think that Rome is still a success. All through these stories one gets the sense that one is daydreaming, too. Episode follows episode with no particular urgency. Tarzan is always knocked on the head and taken captive; he always escapes; there is always a beautiful princess or high priestess who loves him and assists him; there is always a loyal friend who fights beside him, very much in that Queequeg tradition which, Professor Leslie Fiedler assures us, is the urning in the fuel supply of the American psyche. But no matter how difficult the adventure, Tarzan, clad only in a loincloth with no weapon save a knife (the style is comforting to imitate), wins against all odds and returns to his shadowy wife.

Stylistically, Burroughs is—how shall I put it?—uneven. He has moments of ornate pomp, when the darkness is "Cimmerian"; of redundancy, "she was hideous and ugly"; of extraordinary dialogue: "Name of a name," shrieked Rokoff. "Pig, but you shall die for this!" Or Lady Greystoke to Lord G.: "Duty is duty, my husband, and no amount of sophistries may change it. I would be a poor wife for an English lord were I to be responsible for his shirking a plain duty." Or the grandchild: "Muvver," he cried, "Dackie doe? Dackie doe?" "Let him come along," urged Tarzan. "Dare!" exclaimed the boy, turning triumphantly upon the governess, "Dackie do doe yalk!" Burroughs's use of coincidence is shameless even for a pulp writer. In one book he has three sets of characters shipwrecked at exactly the same point on the shore of Africa. Even Burroughs finds this a bit much. "Could it be possible [muses Tarzan] that fate had thrown him up at the very threshold of his own beloved jungle?" It was possible since anything can happen in a daydream.

Though Burroughs is innocent of literature and cannot reproduce human speech, he does have a gift very few writers of any kind possess: he can describe action vividly. I give away no trade secrets when I say that this is as difficult for a Tolstoi as it is for a Burroughs (even William). Because it is so hard, the craftier contemporary novelists usually prefer to tell their stories in the first person, which is simply writing dialogue. In character, as it were, the writer settles for an impression of what happened rather than creating the sense of the thing happening. In action Tarzan is excellent.

There is something basic in the appeal of the 1914 Tarzan which makes me think that he can still hold his own as a daydream figure, despite the sophisticated challenge of his two young competitors, James Bond and Mike Hammer. For most adults, Tarzan (and John Carter of Mars) can hardly compete with the conspicuous consumer consumption of James Bond or the sickly violence of Mike Hammer, but for children and adolescents the old appeal continues. All of us need the idea of a world alternative to this one. From Plato's Republic to Opar to Bondland, at every level, the human imagination has tried to imagine something better for itself than the existing society. Man left Eden when he got up off all fours, endowing his descendants with nostalgia as well as chronic backache. In its naïve way, the Tarzan legend returns us to that Eden where, free of clothes and the inhibitions of an oppressive society, a man is able, as William Faulkner put it in his high Confederate style, to prevail as well as endure. The current fascination with LSD and drugs—not to mention alcohol—is all a result of a general sense of boredom. Since the individual's desire to dominate his environment is not a desirable trait in a society that every day grows more and more confining, the average man must take to daydreaming. James Bond, Mike Hammer, and Tarzan are all dream selves, and the aim of each is to establish personal primacy in a world that, more and more, diminishes the individual. Among adults, the current popularity of these lively fictions strikes me as a most significant and unbearably sad phenomenon.

Esquire
December 1963

THE TOP TEN BEST-SELLERS

ACCORDING TO THE

SUNDAY *NEW YORK TIMES*

AS OF JANUARY 7, 1973

"Shit has its own integrity." The Wise Hack at the Writers' Table in the MGM commissary used regularly to affirm this axiom for the benefit of us alien integers from the world of Quality Lit. It was plain to him (if not to the front office) that since we had come to Hollywood only to make money, our pictures would entirely lack the one basic homely ingredient that spells boffo world-wide grosses. The Wise Hack was not far wrong. He knew that the sort of exuberant badness which so often achieves perfect popularity cannot be faked even though, as he was quick to admit, no one ever lost a penny underestimating the intelligence of the American public. He was cynical (so were we); yet he also truly believed that children in jeopardy *always* hooked an audience, that Lana Turner was convincing when she rejected the advances of Edmund Purdom in *The Prodigal* "because I'm a priestess of Baal," and he thought that Irving Thalberg was a genius of Leonardo proportion because he had made such tasteful "products" as *The Barretts of Wimpole Street* and *Marie Antoinette*.

In my day at the Writers' Table (mid-Fifties) television had shaken the industry and the shit-dispensers could now . . . well, flush their products into every home without having to worry about booking a theater. In desperation, the front office started hiring alien integers whose lack of reverence for the industry distressed the Wise Hack who daily lectured us as we sat at our long table eating the specialty of the studio, top-billed as the *Louis B. Mayer Chicken Soup with Matzoh Balls* (yes, invariably, the dumb starlet would ask, What do they do with the rest of the matzoh?). Christopher Isherwood and I sat on one side of the table; John O'Hara on the other. Aldous Huxley worked at home. Dorothy Parker drank at home.

The last time I saw Dorothy Parker, Los Angeles had been on fire for three days. As I took a taxi from the studio I asked the driver, "How's the fire doing?" "You mean," said the Hollywoodian, "the holocaust." The style, you see, must come as easily and naturally as that. I found Dorothy standing in front of her house, gazing at the smoky sky; in one hand she held a drink, in the other a comb which absently she was passing through her short straight hair. As I came toward her, she gave me a secret smile. "I am combing," she whispered, "Los Angeles out of my hair." But of course that was not possible. The ashes of Hollywood are still very much in our hair, as the ten best-sellers I have just read demonstrate.

The bad movies we made twenty years ago are now regarded in altogether too many circles as important aspects of what the new illiterates want to believe is the only significant art form of the twentieth century. An entire generation has been brought up to admire the product of that era. Like so many dinosaur droppings, the old Hollywood films have petrified into something rich, strange, numinous—golden. For any survivor of the Writers' Table (alien or indigenous integer), it is astonishing to find young directors like Bertolucci, Bogdanovich, Truffaut reverently repeating or echoing or paying homage to the sort of kitsch we created first time around with a good deal of "help" from our producers and practically none at all from the directors—if one may quickly set aside the myth of the director as *auteur*. Golden-age movies were the work of producer(s) and writer(s). The director was given a finished shooting script with each shot clearly marked, and woe to him if he changed MED CLOSE SHOT to MED SHOT without permission from the front office, which each evening, in serried ranks, watched the day's rushes with script in hand ("We've got some good pages today," they would say; never good film). The director, as the Wise Hack liked to observe, is the brother-in-law.

I think it is necessary to make these remarks about the movies of the Thirties, Forties, and Fifties as a preface to the ten best-selling novels under review since most of these books reflect to some degree the films each author saw in his formative years, while at least seven of the novels appear to me to be deliberate attempts not so much to re-create new film product as to suggest old movies that will make the reader (and publisher and reprinter and, to come full circle, film-maker) recall past success and respond accordingly. Certainly none of the ten writers (save the noble engineer Solzhenitsyn and the classicist Mary Renault) is in any way rooted in literature. For the eight, storytelling began with *The Birth of a Nation.* Came to high noon with, well, *High Noon* and *Mrs. Miniver* and *Rebecca* and *A Farewell to Arms.* Except for the influence of the dead Ian Fleming (whose own work was a curious amalgam of old movies in the Eric Ambler–Hitchcock style with some sado-masochist games added), these books connect not at all with other books. But with the movies . . . ah, the movies!

Let us begin with number ten on your Hit Parade of Fiction, *Two from Galilee,* by Marjorie Holmes. Marjorie is also the author of *I've Got to Talk to Somebody, God* and *Who Am I, God? Two from Galilee* is subtitled significantly, "*A Love Story of Mary and Joseph.*" Since the film *Love Story* really took off, what about a love story starring the Mother and the Stepfather of Our Lord? A super idea. And Marjorie has written it. We open with the thirteen-year-old Mary menstruating ("a bloody hand had smitten her in the night"). " 'I am almost fourteen, Father,' she said, 'and I have become nubile this day.' " She is "mad for" Joseph, a carpenter's son; he is mad for her.

Shrewdly Marjorie has taken two young Americans of the lower middle class and placed them in old Galilee. I recognize some of the descriptions as being from the last version of *Ben-Hur* to which I made a considerable contribution. "The couches covered with a silken stuff threaded with gold. The glow from a hanging alabaster lamp. . . ." Luckily, I was on the set at the beginning of the shooting and so was able to persuade the art director to remove tomatoes from Mrs. Ben-Hur Senior's kitchen. Otherwise, Marjorie might have had Hannah prepare a tomato and bacon sandwich for her daughter Mary.

Since Miss Holmes is not an experienced writer, it is difficult to know what, if anything, she had in mind when she decided to tell the Age-Old Story with nothing new to add. True, there are some domestic crises and folksy wrinkles like Joseph's father being a drunk. Incidentally, Joseph and Mary are known by their English names while the other characters keep their Hebrew names. Mary's mother Hannah is fun: a Jewish mother as observed by a gentile housewife in McLean, Virginia, who has seen some recent movies on the subject and heard all the jokes on television.

Hannah worries for her daughter. Will Joseph get into Mary *before* the wedding? "Hannah had no idea what it was like to be a man—this waiting. No woman could comprehend physical passion." Helen Gurley Brown and Germaine Greer will no doubt set Miss Holmes straight on that sexist point. But perhaps the author is reflecting her audience (Who are they, by the way? *Where* are they? Baptists in Oklahoma City? Catholics in Duluth suburbs?) when she writes that Hannah "did not have the faintest concept of the demon-god that entered a youth's loins at puberty and gave him no peace thereafter." Yes, I checked the last noun for spelling. Joseph, incidentally, is such a stud that when Mary is with him "the thing that was between them chimed and quivered and lent discomfort to all."

Suddenly between that chiming, quivering thing and Mary falls the shadow of the Holy Ghost. "Mary's flesh sang," as she experienced "the singing silence of God:" Miss Holmes rises to lyricism. "The Holy Spirit came upon her, invaded her body, and her bowels stirred and her loins melted." Obviously entry was not made through the ear as those Renaissance painters who lacked Miss Holmes's powerful realism believed. Mary soon starts wondering why "the blood pumps so painfully in my breast and my bowels run so thin?" She finds out in due course. Joseph has a hard time believing her story until the Holy Spirit tells him to get it together and accept his peculiar role as the antlered saint of a new cult.

At census time the young marrieds set out for Bethlehem, where the local Holiday Inn is full up or, as a passer-by says, " 'The Inn? You'll be lucky to find a corner for the ass at the inn.' " As these quotations demonstrate, Miss Holmes's style is beyond cliché. But when it comes to scene-making, she is sometimes betrayed by the familiarity of her subject matter. If the Story is to be told truly there must be a birth scene, and so she is obliged to write. " 'Some hot water if you can get it,' " adding, " 'Go no further even to fetch a midwife.' " To which a helpful stranger replies, " 'I'll send one of them for one,' " reminding us of the Joan Crawford interview some decades ago when the living legend asked with quiet majesty, "Whom is fooling whom?" Finally, "Each night the great star stood over the stable's entrance. Joseph had never seen such a star, flaming now purple, now white. . . ."

I am told that religioso fiction has a wide audience around the country, and though these books rarely appear on best-seller lists in sinks of corruption like New York City, their overall sales in the country remind us that the enormous audience which flocked to see *Ben-Hur, The Robe, The Ten Commandments* is still waiting to have its simple faith renewed and stimulated with, as the sage at the Writers' Table would say, teats and sand.

Number nine, *The Eiger Sanction*, by Trevanian (just one name) is light years distant from *Two from Galilee*. For one thing, it is sometimes well-written, though hardly, as the blurb tells us, "vintage Huxley." Actually *The Eiger Sanction* is an Ian Fleming byblow and of its too numerous kind pretty good. Fleming once remarked that he wrote his books for warm-blooded heterosexuals. I suspect that Mr. Trevanian (Ms. Trevanian?) is writing for tepid-blooded bisexuals—that is to say, a majority of those who prefer reading kinky thrillers to watching that television set before whose busy screen 90 percent of all Americans spend a third of their waking hours.

Mr. Trevanian's James Bond is called Dr. Jonathan Hemlock. A professor of art, he "moonlights" as a paid assassin for the Search and Sanction Division of CII, an aspect (presumably invented) of the CIA. Dr. Hemlock is engaged to kill those who kill CII agents. With the proceeds from these murders, he buys paintings to hang in the renovated church where he lives on Long Island. He drinks Pichon-Longueville-Baron, worships his "beloved Impressionists" (his taste in pictures is duller than the author suspects), and as for sex, well, he's a tough cookie and finds it temporarily satisfying, "like urination" or "a termination of discomfort, not an achievement of pleasure." This drives women mad.

Mr. Trevanian has a nice gift for bizarre characters. The chief of Search and Sanction is an albino who lives in darkness; he must also undergo periodic changes of blood because he is "one of nature's rarest genealogical phenomena," presumably related to a cadet branch of the Plantagenet family. It seems only yesterday that Sidney Greenstreet was growing orchids in a most sinister greenhouse and chuckling mirthlessly. Actually, that was thirty years ago and writers are now having a difficult time thinking up unlikely traits . . . not to mention names. Unhappily the mind that created Pussy Galore cloned before it went to ashes, and Mr. Trevanian brightly offers us Felicity Arce, Jean-Paul Bidet, Randie Nickers, and a host of other cute names.

But he is also capable of writing most engagingly. "His line of thought was severed by the paternal and the plebeian voice of the pilot assuring him that he knew where they were going." Or, "He intended to give [the book] a handsome review in obedience to his theory that the surest way to maintain position at the top of the field was to advance and support men of clearly inferior capacities." More of this and Mr. Trevanian will write himself out of the genre and into Quality Lit, Satire Division. But he must refrain from writing beautifully: "mountain stars still crisp and cold despite the threat of dawn to mute their brilliance," not to mention "organic viscosity of the dark around him"—an inapplicable description of a night in the high Alps worthy of Nathalie Sarraute, as is "Time had been viscous for Ben, too."

It is sad to report that Mr. Trevanian cannot resist presenting in thin disguise Mr. and Mrs. Burton and Mr. and Mrs. Onassis. There is nothing wrong with this if you have a point to make about them. But he has nothing to say; he simply mentions them in order to express disdain. No doubt they deserve his Olympian disgust, but he should leave to Suzy the record of their doings and to the really bad writers the exploitation of their famous legends. It is interesting, incidentally, to observe the curiously incestuous feedback of the so-called media. About a dozen people are known to nearly everyone capable of reading a simply written book. Therefore the golden dozen keep cropping up in popular books with the same insistence that their doings dominate the press, and the most successful exploiters of these legends are the very primitive writers like Harold Robbins who not only do not know the golden dozen at first or even second hand but, inexcusably, lack the imagination to think up anything exciting to add to what the reader has already learned from gossip columns and magazine interviews. At times while reading these bestsellers I had the odd sensation that I was actually reading a batch of old Leonard Lyons gossip columns or a copy of Photoplay or anything except a book. But then it is a characteristic of today's writers (serious as well as commercial) to want their books to resemble "facts" rather than fiction. *The Odessa File, August 1914, The Eiger Sanction* are nonfiction titles.

Mr. Trevanian has recourse to that staple of recent fiction the Fag Villain. Since kikes and niggers can no longer be shown as bad people, only commies (pre-Nixon) and fags are certain to arouse the loathing of all decent fiction addicts. I will say for Mr. Trevanian that his Fag Villain is pretty funny—an exquisite killer named Miles Mellough with a poodle named Faggot. In fact, Mr. Trevanian in his comic mood is almost always beguiling, and this bright scenario ought to put new life into the Bond product. I think even the Wise Hack would have applauded the screenplay I automatically started preparing in my head. LONG SHOT the Eiger mountain. DAY. As titles begin, CUT TO . . .

On the Night of the Seventh Moon belongs to a genre I know very little about: the Gothic novel for ladies. But I do recall the films made from the novels of Daphne du Maurier, the queen of this sort of writing. In fact, I once wrote the screenplay for one of her most powerful works, *The Scapegoat*, in which the dogged (and in this case hounded) Alec Guinness played two people. Although Miss du Maurier had written an up-to-date variation on *The Prisoner of Zenda*, she had somehow got the notion that she had written the passion of St. Theresa. She used to send me helpful memos; and though she could not spell the simplest words or adhere to any agreed-upon grammar, her prose surged with vulgar invention and powerful feeling of the sort that cannot be faked.

I suspect Victoria Holt is also serious about her work. The publishers tell us that she is very popular; certainly she has written many books with magical titles. This one starts rather like *Rebecca*: "Now that I have reached the mature age of twenty-seven I look back on the fantastic adventure of my youth and can almost convince myself that it did not happen. . . ." A sense of warm security begins to engulf the reader at this point. Even the heroine's name inspires confidence: Helena Trant . . . so reminiscent of Helen Trent, whose vicissitudes on radio kept my generation enthralled, not to mention the ever so slight similarity to the name Trapp and all that that truly box-office name suggests; we are almost in the same neck of the woods, too, the Black Forest, 1860. And here is Helen, I mean Helena, asking herself a series of fascinating questions.

"Did I suffer some mental aberration? Was it really true—as they tried to convince me—that I, a romantic and rather feckless girl, had been betrayed as so many had before? . . ."

Helena's mother was German (noble); her father English (donnish). Mother dies; girl goes to school in Germany. On a misty day she gets lost in the Black Forest. She is nubile, as Marjorie Holmes would say. Suddenly, riding toward her, "like a hero of the forest on his big white horse," was a godlike young man. He was "tall, broad, and immediately I was aware of what I could only describe then as authority." (How right she was! Though Maximilian is incognito he is really the heir to the local Grand Duchy and—but we are ahead of our story.)

He offers to take her to his hunting lodge. She sits in front of him on his horse ("He held me tightly against him which aroused in me a strange emotion which I had never felt before and which should, of course, have been a warning"). A nice old woman retainer gets her into dry things ("my hair fell about my shoulders; it was thick, dark and straight"). She wants to go back to school but "the mist is too thick." Supper. " 'Allow me to serve you some of this meat,' " says the randy prince. "He did so and I took a piece of rye bread which was hot and crusty and delicious. There was a mixture of spicy pickle and a kind of sauerkraut such as I had never tasted before." Miss Holt knows her readers like a good din from time to time along with romance, and terror. As it turns out, Max doesn't lay Helena despite the demon-god in his loins. A virgin, Helena departs not knowing whom it was she met.

Back to England. Father dead, Helena lives with two aunts. A couple arrive from Germany; they say that they are cousins of her late mother. She goes back to Germany with them. Festival in a small town known as The Night of the Seventh Moon. *He* appears; takes her away with him into the forest. He sends for the couple. They witness his marriage to Helena. She is in a state of ecstasy. For one thing, she is well-groomed. "My best dress; it was of a green silky material with a monk's collar of velvet of a slightly darker shade of green." Remember Joan Fontaine at Manderley? The new clothes? And, ah, the mystery? But Helena has done better than Joan's Max de Winter. She is now Countess Lokenburg. She gloats: "I wondered what the aunts would say when they heard that I had become the wife of a count."

But almost as good as social climbing, there is lust. Max's kiss "made me feel exalted and expectant all at once. It was cruel and yet tender; it was passionate and caressing." Can such happiness last? Certainly not. A mysterious illness; she is out of her head. When she recovers, she is told that on the night of the seventh moon she was taken into the forest and . . . "there criminally assaulted." Those blissful days with Max were all a dream, brought on by a doctor's drug. Meanwhile, she is knocked up. She has the baby; goes back to England. A clergyman falls in love with her and wants to marry her but Helena feels that her past will ruin his career. He is noble: " 'I'd rather have a wife than a bishopric.' "

The plot becomes very complex. Hired to be governess to children of what turns out to be a princely cousin of Max who is married to Wil- helmina because he thinks Helena dead because Wilhelmina's col- leagues the supposed cousins of Helena were in a plot to . . . Enough! All turns out well, though it is touch-and-go for a while when her child, the heir to the principality, is kidnapped by the wicked cousin (Raymond Massey in *The Prisoner of Zenda*) who then attacks her. " 'You *are* mad,' I said." He cackles: " 'You will not live to see me rule Rochenstein, but be- fore you die I am going to show you what kind of lover you turned your back on.' " (Mailer's *American Dream*?)

Finally, Helena takes her place at Maximilian's side as consort. Each year they celebrate the night of the seventh moon, and in the year Cousin Victoria Regina dies, "What a beautiful night! With the full moon high in the sky paling the stars to insignificance . . ." Those stars keep cropping up in these books, but then as Bette Davis said to Paul Henreid in the last but one frame of *Now Voyager*, "Don't ask for the moon when we have" (a beat) "the stars!" FADE OUT on night sky filled with stars.

I have never before read a book by Herman Wouk on the sensible ground that I could imagine what it must be like: solid, uninspired, and filled with rabbinical lore. After all, one knows of his deep and abiding religious sense, his hatred of sex outside marriage, his love for the Amer- ican ruling class. I did see the film of *The Caine Mutiny* (from Queequeg to Queeg, or the decline of American narrative); and I found the moral- ity disturbing. Mr. Wouk has an embarrassing passion for the American goyim, particularly the West Point–Annapolis crowd who stand, he would seem to believe, between him and the Cossacks. In his lowbrow way he reflects what one has come to think of as the *Commentary* syndrome or: all's right with America if you're not in a gas chamber, and making money.

I did see the film *Youngblood Hawke* four times, finding something new to delight in at each visit. When James Franciscus, playing a raw provincial genius like Thomas Wolfe, meets Suzanne Pleshette in a publisher's office, he is told, "She will be your editor and stylist." Well, she pushes these heavy glasses up on her forehead and, my God, she's pretty as well as brilliant and witty, which she proves by saying, "Shall I call you Youngy or Bloody?" The Wise Hack at the Writers' Table always maintained that when boy meets girl they've *got* to meet cute.

The Winds of War: 885 pages of small type in which Herman Wouk describes the family of a naval captain just before America enters the Second World War (there is to be a sequel). As I picked up the heavy book, I knew terror, for I am that rarest of reviewers who actually reads every word, and rather slowly. What I saw on the first page was disquieting. The protagonist's name, Victor Henry, put me off. It sounded as if he had changed it from something longer, more exotic, more, shall we say, *Eastern*. But then Henry was the family name of the hero of *A Farewell to Arms* so perhaps Mr. Wouk is just having a little fun with us. Mrs. Henry is called Rhoda; the sort of name someone in New York would think one of *them* would be called out there west of the Hudson. "At forty-five, Rhoda Henry remained a singularly attractive woman, but she was rather a crab." This means that she is destined for extramarital high jinks. "In casual talk [Rhoda] used the swooping high notes of smart Washington women." I grew up in Washington at exactly the same period Mr. Wouk is writing about and I must demur: smart Washington ladies sounded no different from smart New York ladies (no swooping in either city).

Captain Henry is stationed at the War Department. He is "a squat Navy fullback from California, of no means or family." Mr. Wouk quotes from the letter he wrote his congressman asking for an appointment to the Naval Academy. "My life aim is to serve as an officer in the U.S. Navy." We are told he speaks Russian learned from "Czarist settlers in Fort Ross, California." Anyway he got appointed; has risen; is gung ho and wants to command a battleship. The marriage? "Rhoda returned an arch glance redolent of married sex." Elsewhere—the Nazis are on the march.

There are three children. Son Warren was involved in "an escapade involving an older woman and a midnight car crash. The parents had never raised the topic of women, partly from bashfulness—they were both prudish churchgoers, ill at ease with such a topic. . . ." Son Byron is in Siena carrying on with one Nathalie, niece of a famed American Jewish writer, author of *A Jew's Jesus*. Byron has recently turned against his Renaissance studies because " 'I don't believe David looked like Apollo, or Moses like Jupiter.' " Further, " 'The poor idealistic Jewish preacher from the back hills. That's the Lord I grew up with. My father's a religious man; we had to read a chapter of the Bible every morning at home.' "

At this point my worst fears about Mr. Wouk seemed justified. The Russian-speaking Victor Henry who reads a chapter of the Bible every morning to his family and is prudish about sexual matters is, Mr. Wouk wants us to believe, a typical gallant prewar goyisher American naval officer. If I may speak from a certain small knowledge (I was born at West Point, son of an instructor and graduate), I find Mr. Wouk's naval officer incredible—or "incredulous," as they say in best-seller land. There may have been a few religious nuts here and there in the fleet but certainly a naval officer who is about to be posted as an attaché to the American embassy in Berlin would not be one of them. In those days Annapolis was notoriously snobbish and no matter how simple and fundamentalist the background of its graduates, they tended toward worldliness; in fact, a surprising number married rich women. West Pointers were more square but also rowdier. Mr. Wouk's failure to come to terms with the American gentile is not unusual. Few American Jewish writers have been able to put themselves into gentile skins—much less foreskins. With ecumenical relish, Mr. Wouk tells us that son Byron (who marries a Jewish girl) is circumcised.

With an obviously bogus protagonist, Mr. Wouk must now depend upon the cunning of his narrative gift to propel these characters through great events: Berlin under Hitler, Poland during the Nazi invasion, London in the Blitz, Pearl Harbor on December 7, 1941; and not only must he describe the sweep of military and political action but also give us close-ups of Roosevelt, Churchill, Stalin, Hitler, Mussolini. It is Upton Sinclair all over again and, to my astonishment, it is splendid stuff. The detail is painstaking and generally authentic. The naïve portraits of the great men convince rather more than subtler work might have done.

Henry's reports from Berlin attract Roosevelt's attention. Mr. Wouk's portrait of FDR is by no means as sycophantish as one might expect. No doubt the recent revelations of the late president's sexual irregularities have forced the puritan Mr. Wouk to revise his estimate of a man I am sure he regarded at the time as a god, not to mention shield against the Cossacks. With hindsight he now writes, "Behind the jolly aristocratic surface, there loomed a grim ill-defined personality of distant visions and hard purpose, a tough son of a bitch to whom nobody meant very much, except perhaps his family; and maybe not they either." This is not at all bad, except as prose. Unfortunately, Mr. Wouk has no ear for "jolly aristocratic" speech patterns. I doubt if FDR would have called Pug "old top" (though when my father was in the administration the president used to address him, for some obscure reason, as "Brother Vidal").

Also, Mr. Wouk makes strange assumptions. For instance, FDR "wore pince-nez glasses in imitation of his great relative, President Teddy Roosevelt, and he also imitated his booming manly manner; but a prissy Harvard accent made this heartiness somewhat ridiculous." The pince-nez was worn by a good many people in those days, but if FDR was consciously imitating anyone it would have been his mentor, the pince-nezed Woodrow Wilson. T. Roosevelt's voice was not booming but thin and shrill. FDR's accent was neither prissy nor Harvard but Dutchess County and can still be heard among the American nobles now, thank God, out of higher politics.

With extraordinary ease, Mr. Wouk moves from husband to wife to sons to daughter, and the narrative never falters. His reconstruction of history is painless and, I should think, most useful to simple readers curious about the Second War. Yet there is a good deal of pop-writing silliness. We get the Mirror Scene (used by all pop-writers to tell us what the characters look like): "the mirror told her a different story, but even it seemed friendly to her that night: it showed . . ." We get the Fag Villain. In this case an American consul at Florence who will not give the good Jew Jastrow a passport because "people don't see departmental circulars about consuls who've been recalled and whose careers have gone *poof!*" Sumner Welles is briefly glimpsed as a villian (and those who recall the gossip of the period will know why).

Then, of course, there is the problem of Mr. Wouk and sex. Daughter Madeline rooms with two girls and "both were having affairs—one with a joke writer, the other with an actor working as a bellhop. Madeline had found herself being asked to skulk around, stay out late, or remain in her room while one or another pair copulated. . . . She was disgusted. Both girls had good jobs, both dressed with taste, both were college graduates. Yet they behaved like sluts. . . ." But then to Madeline, "sex was a delightful matter of playing with fire, but enjoying the blaze from a safe distance, until she could leap into the hallowed white conflagration of a bridal night. She was a middle class good girl, and not in the least ashamed of it."

Incidentally, Mr. Wouk perpetuates the myth that the SS were all fags. This is now an article of faith with many uneducated Americans on the ground that to be a fag is the worst thing that could befall anyone next to falling into the hands of a fag sadist, particularly the SS guards who were as "alike as chorus boys . . . with blond waved hair, white teeth, bronzed skin, and blue eyes." Actually the SS guards in 1939 were not particularly pretty; they were also not fags. Hitler had eliminated that element.

Mr. Wouk's prose is generally correct if uninspired. The use of the ugly verb "shrill" crops up in at least half the best-sellers under review and is plainly here to stay. Also, I suppose we must stop making any distinction between "nauseous" and "nauseated." The book ends with Pearl Harbor in flames and . . . yes, you've guessed it. The stars! "Overhead a clear starry black sky arched" (at least the sky was overhead and not underfoot), "with Orion setting in the west, and Venus sparkling in the east. . . . The familiar religious awe came over him, the sense of a Presence above this pitiful little earth. He could almost picture God the Father looking down with sad wonder at this mischief."

The films *Since You Went Away* and *The Best Years of Our Life* come to mind; not to mention all those *March of Times* in the Trans-Lux theaters of the old republic as it girded itself for war. But for all Mr. Wouk's idiocies and idiosyncrasies, his competence is most impressive and his professionalism awe-inspiring in a world of lazy writers and TV-stunned readers. I did not in the least regret reading every word of his book, though I suspect he is a writer best read swiftly by the page in order to get the sweep of his narrative while overlooking the infelicities of style and the shallowness of mind. I realize my sort of slow reading does a dis-service to this kind of a book. But then I hope the author will be pleased to know that at least one person has actually read his very long best-seller. Few people will. There is evidence that a recent best-seller by a well-known writer was never read by its publisher or by the book club that took it or by the film company that optioned it. Certainly writers of book-chat for newspapers *never* read long books and seldom do more than glance at short ones.

Number six on the best-seller list, *The Camerons*, by Robert Crich-ton, is a mystifying work. One understands the sincerity of Herman Wouk, number seven, as he tries to impose his stern morality on an alien culture, or even that of the dread Marjorie Holmes, number ten, exploit-ing Bible Belt religiosity with what I trust is some degree of seriousness (all those chats with God must have made her a fan). But Mr. Crichton has elected to address himself to characters that seem to be infinitely re-mote from him, not to mention his readers. A UK mining town in what I take to be the 1870s (there is a reference to Keir Hardie, the trade union-ist). With considerable fluency Mr. Crichton tells the story of a miner's sixteen-year-old daughter who goes to the Highlands to find herself a golden youth to give her children. She captures a Highland fisherman, locks him up in the mines for twenty years, and has a number of children by him who more or less fulfill her "genealogical" (as Trevanian would say) dream.

Of all these books this one is closest to the movies. The characters all speak with the singing cadences of Burbank's *How Green Was My Valley*. Another inspiration is *None But the Lonely Heart*, in which Ethel Barry-more said to Cary Grant, "Love's not for the poor, son." Mr. Cameron plays a number of variations on that theme, among them "Love, in every-day life, is a luxury."

One reads page after page, recalling movies. As always the Mirror Scene. The Food Scene (a good recipe for finnan haddie). There is the Fever Breaks Scene (during this episode I *knew* that there would have to be a tracheotomy and sure enough the doctor said that it was sometimes necessary but that in this case . . .). The Confrontation between Mr. Big and the Hero. Cameron has been injured while at work; the mine owner will give him no compensation. Cameron sues; the miners strike. He wins but not before the Confrontation with the Mob Scene when the miners turn on him for being the cause of their hunger. There is even the Illiterate Learning about Literature Scene, inspired by *The Corn Is Green*, in which Bette Davis taught the young Welsh miner John Dall to read Quality Lit so that he could grow up to be Emlyn Williams. Well, Cameron goes to the library and asks for *Macbeth* and reads it to the amazement of the bitter drunken librarian (Thomas Mitchell).

There is the Nubile Scene ("For a small girl she had large breasts and the shirt was tight and made her breasts stand out, and she kept the jacket near at hand because she didn't want to embarrass her father if he came into the room. She had only recently become that way and both she and her father weren't quite sure how to act about it"). Young Love Scene (the son's girl friend is named Allison—from *Peyton Place*). At the end, the Camerons sail for the New World. The first night out Cameron "wouldn't go down to her then and so he stayed at the rail and watched the phosphorescent waves wash up against the sides of the ship and explode in stars."

There is something drastically wrong with this smoothly executed novel and I cannot figure out what it is other than to suspect that the author lacks the integrity the Wise Hack insists upon. Mr. Crichton has decided to tell a story that does not seem to interest him very much. At those moments when the book almost comes alive (the conflict between labor and management), the author backs away from his true subject because socialism cannot be mentioned in best-seller land except as something innately wicked. Yet technically Mr. Crichton is a good writer and he ought to do a lot better than this since plainly he lacks the "integrity" to do worse.

Can your average beautiful teen-age Persian eunuch find happiness with your average Greek world conqueror who is also a dish and aged only twenty-six? The answer Mary Renault triumphantly gives us in *The Persian Boy* is *ne!* Twenty-five years ago *The City and the Pillar* was considered shocking because it showed what two nubile boys did together on a hot summer afternoon in McLean, Virginia. Worse, one of them went right on doing that sort of thing for the rest of his life. The scandal! The shame! In 1973 the only true love story on the best-seller list is about two homosexuals, and their monstrous aberration (so upsetting to moralists like Mr. Wouk) is apparently taken for granted by those ladies who buy hardcover novels.

At this point I find myself wishing that one had some way of knowing just who buys and who reads what sort of books. I am particularly puzzled (and pleased) by the success of Mary Renault. Americans have always disliked history (of some fifty subjects offered in high school the students recently listed history fiftieth and least popular) and know nothing at all of the classical world. Yet in a dozen popular books Mary Renault has made the classical era alive, forcing even the dullest of book-chat writers to recognize that bisexuality was once our culture's norm and that Christianity's perversion of this human fact is the aberration and not the other way around. I cannot think how Miss Renault has managed to do what she has done, but the culture is the better for her work.

I am predisposed to like the novel dealing with history and find it hard to understand why this valuable genre should be so much disdained. After all, every realistic novel is historical. But somehow, describing what happened last summer at Rutgers is for our solemn writers a serious subject, while to re-create Alexander the Great is simply frivolous. Incidentally, I am here concerned only with the traditional novel as practiced by Updike, Tolstoi, George Eliot, Nabokov, the Caldwells (Taylor and Erskine) as well as by the ten writers under review. I leave for another and graver occasion the matter of experimental high literature and its signs.

In *The Persian Boy* Miss Renault presents us with Alexander at the height of his glory as seen through the eyes of the boy eunuch Bagoas. Miss Renault is good at projecting herself and us into strange cultures. With ease she becomes her narrator Bagoas; the book is told in the first person (a device *not* invented by Robert Graves as innocent commentators like to tell us but a classroom exercise going back more than two millennia: write as if you were Alexander the Great addressing your troops before Tyre). Bagoas's father is murdered by political enemies; the boy is enslaved; castrated; rented out as a whore by his first master. Because of his beauty he ends up in the bed of the Great King of Persia, Darius. Alexander conquers Persia; sets fire to Persepolis. The Great King is killed by his own people and Bagoas is presented by one of the murderers to Alexander, who, according to historical account, never took advantage sexually of those he captured. Bagoas falls in love with the conqueror and, finally, seduces him. The love affair continues happily to the end, although there is constant jealousy on Bagoas's side because of Alexander's permanent attachment to his boyhood friend Hephaestion, not to mention the wives he picks up en route.

The effect of the book is phantasmagoric. Marvelous cities, strange landscapes, colliding cultures, and at the center the golden conqueror of the earth as he drives on and on past the endurance of his men, past his own strength. Today when a revulsion against war is normal, the usual commercialite would be inclined to depict Alexander as a Fag Villain-Killer, but in a note Miss Renault makes the point: "It needs to be borne in mind today that not till more than a century later did a handful of philosophers even start to question the morality of war." Alexander was doing what he thought a man in his place ought to do. The world was there to be conquered.

The device of observing the conqueror entirely through the eyes of an Oriental is excellent and rather novel. We are able to see the Macedonian troops as they appeared to the Persians: crude gangsters smashing to bits an old and subtle culture they cannot understand, like today's Americans in Asia. But, finally, *hubris* is the theme; and the fire returns to heaven. I am not at all certain that what we have here is the "right" Alexander, but right or not, Miss Renault has drawn the portrait of someone who *seems* real yet unlike anyone else, and that divinity the commercialites are forever trying for in their leaden works really does gleam from time to time in the pages of this nice invention.

As a fiction, *August 1914* is not as well managed as Mr. Wouk's *Winds of War*. I daresay as an expression of one man's indomitable spirit in a tyrannous society we must honor if not the art the author. Fortunately the Nobel Prize is designed for just such a purpose. Certainly it is seldom bestowed for literary merit; if it were, Nabokov and not the noble engineer Solzhenitsyn would have received it when the Swedes decided it was Holy Russia's turn to be honored.

Solzhenitsyn is rooted most ambitiously in literature as well as in films. Tolstoi appears on page 3 and Tolstoi hangs over the work like a mushroom cloud. In a sense the novel is to be taken as a dialogue between the creator of *War and Peace* and Solzhenitsyn; with the engineer opposing Tolstoi's view of history as a series of great tides in which the actions of individuals matter not at all. I'm on Solzhenitsyn's side in this debate but cannot get much worked up over his long and wearisome account of Russian military bungling at the beginning of the First World War. The characters are impossible to keep straight, though perhaps future volumes will clarify things. Like *Winds of War*, this is the first of a series.

The book begins with dawn on the Caucasus, towering "so vast above petty human creation, so elemental . . ." The word "vast" is repeated in the next paragraph to get us in the mood for a superspectacle. Then we learn that one of the characters has actually met Tolstoi, and their meeting is recalled on page 17. " 'What is the aim of man's life on earth?' " asks the young man. Tolstoi's reply is prompt: " 'To serve good and thereby to build the Kingdom of Heaven on earth.' " How? " 'Only through love! Nothing else. No one will discover anything better.' " This is best-seller writing with a vengeance.

In due course we arrive at the Mirror Scene: "She was not even comforted by the sight of her naturally rosy skin, her round shoulders, the hair which fell down to her hips and took four buckets of rain water to wash." The Nubile Scene: "She had always avoided undressing even in front of other women, because she was ashamed of her breasts, which were large, big and generous even for a woman of her build." Wisdom Phrases: "The dangers of beauty are well known: narcissism, irresponsibility, selfishness." Or "Evil people always support each other; that is their chief strength." Like Hitler and Stalin? Also, *Christian* Wisdom Phrases: "There is a justice which existed before us, without us and for its own sake. And our task is to *divine* what it is." Not since Charles Morgan's last novel has there been so much profundity in a best-seller.

As for the movies, the best Russian product is recalled, particularly *Battleship Potemkin*. Also, boldly acknowledging the cinema's primacy, Solzhenitsyn has rendered his battle scenes in screenplay form with "=" meaning CUT TO. These passages are particularly inept. *"Mad tearing sound of rifle fire, machine-gun fire, artillery fire!/ Reddened by fire, THE WHEEL still rolls./ = The firelight glitters with savage joy!"* and so on. The Wise Hack would have been deeply disturbed by the presumption of this member of the audience who ought to be eating popcorn in the second balcony and not parodying the century's one true art form that also makes money. From time to time Solzhenitsyn employs the Dos Passos device of random newspaper cuttings to give us a sense of what is going on in August 1914. This works a bit better than the mock screenplay.

At the book's core there is nothing beyond the author's crypto-Christianity, which is obviously not going to please his masters; they will also dislike his astonishing discovery that "the best social order is not susceptible to being arbitrarily constructed, or even to being scientifically constructed." To give the noble engineer his due he is good at describing how things work, and it is plain that nature destined him to write manuals of artillery or instructions on how to take apart a threshing machine. Many people who do not ordinarily read books have bought this book and mention rather proudly that they are reading it, but so far I have yet to meet anyone who has finished it. I fear that the best one can say of Solzhenitsyn is *goré vidal* (a Russian phrase meaning "he has seen grief").

A peculiarity of American sexual mores is that those men who like to think of themselves as exclusively and triumphantly heterosexual are convinced that the most masculine of all activities is not tending to the sexual needs of women but watching other men play games. I have never understood this aspect of my countrymen but I suppose there is a need for it (bonding?), just as the Romans had a need to see people being murdered. Perhaps there is a connection between the American male's need to watch athletes and his fatness: according to a W.H.O. report the American male is the world's fattest and softest; this might explain why he also loves guns—you can always get your revolver up.

I fear that I am not the audience Mr. Dan Jenkins had in mind when he wrote his amiable book *Semi-Tough*, but I found it pleasant enough, and particularly interesting for what it does *not* go into. The narrator is a pro football player who has been persuaded "that it might be good for a pro football stud to have a book which might have a healthy influence on kids." Question: Do young people watch football games nowadays? It seems to me that "jock-sniffers" (as Mr. Jenkins calls them) are of Nixonian age and type—though few have the thirty-seventh president's nose for such pleasures. The unfat and the unsoft young must have other diversions. One wonders, too, if they believe that "a man makes himself a man by whatever he does with himself, and in pro football that means busting his ass for his team."

Semi-Tough tells of the preparation for the big game. Apparently, training involves an astonishing amount of drink, pot, and what the narrator refers to as "wool," meaning cunt. There is one black player who may or may not like boys and the narrator clams up on what is a very delicate subject in jock circles. I am not sure Mr. Jenkins is aware of all the reverberations set off by the jokes of one of his white players. Asked why he is an athlete, the stud says, " 'Mainly, we just like to take showers with niggers.' " It is a pity Mary Renault did not write this book. And a pity, come to think of it, that Mr. Jenkins did not write *August 1914*, a subject suitable for his kind of farce. No movie in *Semi-Tough*. As the Wise Hack knows all too well, sports movies bomb at the box office. Perhaps the Warhol factory will succeed where the majors have failed. SHOWER ROOM— LONG SHOT. CUT TO: CLOSE SHOT—SOAP.

At first glance *The Odessa File*, by Frederick Forsyth, looks to be just another bold hard-hitting attack on the Nazis in the form of a thriller masked as a pseudo-documentary. But the proportions of this particular bit of nonsense are very peculiarly balanced. First, the book is dedicated "to all press reporters." The dust jacket tells us that the author worked for Reuters in the early 1960s; it does not give us his nationality but from the odd prose that he writes I suspect his first language is not English. Also the book's copyright is in the name of a company: a tax dodge not possible for American citizens. Next there is an Author's Note. Mr. Forsyth tells us that although he gives "heartfelt thanks" to all those who helped him in his task he cannot name any of them for three reasons. Apparently some were former members of the SS and "were not aware at the time either whom they were talking to, or that what they said would end up in a book." Others asked not to be mentioned; still others are omitted "for their sakes rather than for mine." This takes care of the sources for what he would like us to believe is a true account of the way Odessa (an organization of former SS officers) continues to help its members in South America and the Federal Republic.

After the Author's Note there is a Foreword (by the author). We are told who Adolf Hitler was and how he and the Nazis ruled Germany from 1933 to 1945 and how they organized the SS in order to kill fourteen million "so-called enemies of the Reich," of which six million were Jews. When Germany began to lose the war, "vast sums of gold were smuggled out and deposited in numbered bank accounts, false identity papers were prepared, escape channels opened up. When the Allies finally conquered Germany, the bulk of the mass-murderers had gone."

Well, one knows about Eichmann, and of course Martin Bormann is a minor industry among bad journalists; so presumably there are other "important" SS officers growing old in Paraguay. But do they, as Mr. Forsyth assures us, have an organization called Odessa whose aim is "five-fold"? Firstfold is "to rehabilitate former SS men *into the professions* of the Federal Republic"; second, "to infiltrate at least the lower echelons of political party activity"; third, to provide "legal defense" for any SS killer hauled before a court and in every way possible to stultify the course of justice in West Germany; fourth, to promote the fortunes of former SS members (this seems to be a repeat of the first of the fivefolds); and, five, "to propagandize the German people to the viewpoint that the SS killers were in fact none other than ordinary patriotic soldiers."

This is food for thought. Yet why has one never heard of Odessa? Mr. Forsyth anticipates that question: "changing its name several times" (highly important for a completely secret society), "the Odessa has sought to deny its own existence as an organization, with the result that many Germans are inclined to say that Odessa does not exist. The short answer is: it exists. . . ." We are then assured that the tale he is about to tell represents one of their failures. Obviously fun and games; presumably, there is no such thing as the Odessa but in the interest of making a thriller look like a document (today's fashion in novels) the author is mingling true with "false facts," as Thomas Jefferson would say.

Now for the story. But, no, after the Dedication and the Author's Note and the Foreword there comes a Publisher's Note. Apparently many of the characters in the book are "real people" but "the publishers do not wish to elucidate further because it is in this ability to perplex the reader as to how much is true and how much false that much of the grip of the story lies." The publishers, Viking, write suspiciously like Mr. Forsyth. "Nevertheless, the publishers feel the reader may be interested or assisted to know that the story of former SS Captain Eduard Roschmann, the commandant of the concentration camp at Riga from 1941 to 1944, from his birth in Graz, Austria, in 1908, to his present exile in South America, is completely factual and drawn from SS and West German records." So let us bear this Publisher's Note in mind as we contemplate the story Mr. Forsyth tells.

After the fall of Hitler, Roschmann was harbored at "the enormous Franciscan Monastery in Rome in Via Sicilia." There is no such establishment according to my spies in the order. "Bishop Alois Hudal, the German Bishop in Rome" (Mr. Forsyth seems to think that this is some sort of post) "spirited thousands [of SS] to safety." "The SS men traveled on Red Cross travel documents, issued through the intervention of the Vatican." After a period in Egypt, Roschmann returns to Germany in 1955 under a pseudonym. Thanks to Odessa, he becomes the head of an important firm. He conducts secret research "aimed at devising a tele-guidance system for those rockets [he] is now working on in West Germany. His code name is Vulkan."

Why is Roschmann at work on the rockets? Because Odessa and its evil scientists "have proposed to President Nasser" (whose predecessor Mr. Forsyth thinks was named Naguil), and he "accepted with alacrity, that these warheads on the Kahiras and Zafiras be of a different type. Some will contain concentrated cultures of bubonic plague, and the others will explode high above the ground, showering the entire territory of Israel with irradiated cobalt-sixty. Within hours they will all be dying of the pest or of gamma-ray sickness."

This is splendid Fu Manchu nonsense (infecting the Israelis with bubonic plague would of course start a world epidemic killing the Egyptians, too, while spreading radioactive cobalt in the air would probably kill off a large percentage of the world's population, as any story conference at Universal would quickly conclude). Next Mr. Forsyth presents us with the classic thriller cliché: only one man holds this operation together. Roschmann. Destroy him and Israel is saved.

The plot of course is foiled by a West German newspaperman and its details need not concern us: it is the sort of storytelling that propels the hero from one person to the next person, asking questions. As a stylist, Mr. Forsyth is addicted to the freight-car sentence: "This time his destination was Bonn, the small and boring town on the river's edge that Konrad Adenauer had chosen as the capital of the Federal Republic, because he came from it." (Adenauer came from Cologne but Mr. Forsyth is not one to be deterred by small details: after all, he is under the impression that it was Martin Bormann "on whom the mantle of the Führer had fallen after 1945.") What is important is that Mr. Forsyth and Viking Press want us to believe that the Vatican knowingly saved thousands of SS men after 1945, that six of the ten high-ranking Hamburg police officers in 1964 were former SS men, that President Nasser authorized a clandestine SS organization to provide him with the means to attack Israel with bubonic plague, and that when this plot failed, the Argentine government presumably offered asylum to Captain Roschmann. *Caveat emptor.*

The boldness of author and publisher commands . . . well, awe and alarm. Is it possible now to write a novel in which Franklin Roosevelt secretly finances the German American Bund because he had been made mad by infantile paralysis? Can one write a novel in which Brezhnev is arranging with the American army defectors in Canada to poison Lake Michigan (assuming this is not a redundancy)? Viking would probably say, yes, why not? And for good measure, to ensure success, exploit the prejudices, if possible, of American Jewish readers, never letting them forget that the guilt of the Germans ("dreaming only in the dark hours of the ancient gods of strength and lust and power") for having produced Hitler is now as eternal in the works of bad writers and greedy publishers as is the guilt of the Jews for the death of Jesus in the minds of altogether too many simple Christians. Exploitation of either of these myths strikes me as an absolute evil and not permissible even in the cheapest of fiction brought out by the most opportunist of publishers.

The number one best-seller is called *Jonathan Livingston Seagull.* It is a greeting card bound like a book with a number of photographs of seagulls in flight. The brief text celebrates the desire for excellence of a seagull who does not want simply to fly in order to eat but to fly beautifully for its own sake. He is much disliked for this by his peers; in fact, he is ostracized. Later he is translated to higher and higher spheres where he can spend eternity practicing new flight techniques. It is touching that this little story should be so very popular because it is actually celebrating art for art's sake as well as the virtues of nonconformity; and so, paradoxically, it gives pleasure to the artless and to the conforming, to the drones who dream of honey-making in their unchanging hive.

Unlike the other best-sellers this work is not so much a reflection of the age of movies as it is a tribute to Charles Darwin and his high priestess, the incomparable creatrix of *The Fountainhead* (starring Gary Cooper and Patricia Neal), Ayn Rand.

There is not much point in generalizing further about these bestsellers. The authors prefer fact or its appearance to actual invention. This suggests that contemporary historians are not doing their job if to Wouk and Solzhenitsyn falls the task of telling today's reader about two world wars and to Forsyth and Trevanian current tales of the cold war. As Christianity and Judaism sink into decadence, religioso fictions still exert a certain appeal. It will surprise certain politicians to learn that sex is of no great interest to best-selling authors. Only *Semi-Tough* tries to be sexy, and fails. Too much deodorant.

Reading these ten books one after the other was like being trapped in the "Late Late Show," staggering from one half-remembered movie scene to another, all the while beginning to suspect with a certain horror that the Wise Hack at the Writers' Table will be honored and remembered for his many credits on numerous profitable pix long after Isherwood (adapted "The Gambler," with Gregory Peck), Faulkner (adapted *The Big Sleep*, with Humphrey Bogart), Huxley (adapted *Pride and Prejudice*, with Greer Garson), Vidal (adapted *Suddenly, Last Summer*, with Elizabeth Taylor) take their humble places below the salt, as it were, for none of us regarded with sufficient seriousness the greatest art form of all time. By preferring perversely to write books that reflected not the movies we had seen but life itself, not as observed by that sterile machine the camera but as it is netted by a beautiful if diminishing and polluted language, we were, all in all, kind of dumb. Like Sam, one should've played it again.

The New York Review of Books
May 17 and May 31, 1973

FRENCH LETTERS: THEORIES OF THE NEW NOVEL

To say that no one now much likes novels is to exaggerate very little. The large public which used to find pleasure in prose fictions prefers movies, television, journalism, and books of "fact." But then, Americans have never been enthusiastic readers. According to Dr. Gallup, only five percent of our population can be regarded as habitual readers. This five percent is probably a constant minority from generation to generation, despite the fact that at the end of the nineteenth century there were as many bookstores in the United States as there are today. It is true that novels in paperback often reach a very large audience. But that public is hardly serious, if one is to believe a recent *New York Times* symposium on paperback publishing. Apparently novels sell not according to who wrote them but according to how they are presented, which means that *Boys and Girls Together* will outsell *Pale Fire*, something it did not do in hard cover. Except for a handful of entertainers like the late Ian Fleming, the mass audience knows nothing of authors. They buy titles, and most of those titles are not of novels but of nonfiction: books about the Kennedys, doctors, and vivid murders are preferred to the work of anyone's imagination no matter how agreeably debased.

In this, if nothing else, the large public resembles the clerks, one of whom, Norman Podhoretz, observed nine years ago that "A feeling of dissatisfaction and impatience, irritation and boredom with contemporary

serious fiction is very widespread," and he made the point that the magazine article is preferred to the novel because the article is useful, specific, relevant—something that most novels are not. This liking for fact
may explain why some of our best-known novelists are read with attention only when they comment on literary or social matters. In the highest intellectual circles, a new novel by James Baldwin or William Gass or
Norman Mailer—to name at random three celebrated novelists—is apt
to be regarded with a certain embarrassment, hostage to a fortune often
too crudely gained, and bearing little relation to its author's distinguished
commentaries.

An even odder situation exists in the academy. At a time when the
works of living writers are used promiscuously as classroom texts, the
students themselves do little voluntary reading. "I hate to read," said a
Harvard senior to a *New York Times* reporter, "and I never buy any paper-
backs." The undergraduates' dislike of reading novels is partly due to the
laborious way in which novels are taught: the slow killing of the work
through a close textual analysis. Between the work and the reader comes
the explication, and the explicator is prone to regard the object of analysis as being somehow inferior to the analysis itself.

In fact, according to Saul Bellow, "Critics and professors have declared themselves the true heirs and successors of the modern classic authors." And so, in order to maintain their usurped dignity, they are given
"to redescribing everything downward, blackening the present age and
denying creative scope to their contemporaries." Although Mr. Bellow
overstates the case, the fact remains that the novel as currently practiced
does not appeal to the intellectuals any more than it does to the large
public, and it may well be that the form will become extinct now that we
have entered the age which Professor Marshall McLuhan has termed
post-Gutenberg. Whether or not the Professor's engaging generalities are
true (that linear type, for centuries a shaper of our thought, has been superseded by electronic devices), it is a fact that the generation now in
college is the first to be brought up entirely within the tradition of television and differs significantly from its predecessors. Quick to learn
through sight and sound, today's student often experiences difficulty in
reading and writing. Linear type's warm glow, so comforting to Gutenberg
man, makes his successors uncomfortably hot. Needless to say, that

bright minority which continues the literary culture exists as always, but it is no secret that even they prefer watching movies to reading novels. John Barth ought to interest them more than Antonioni, but he doesn't.

For the serious novelist, however, the loss of the audience should not be disturbing. "I write," declared one of them serenely. "Let the reader learn to read." And contrary to Whitman, great audiences are not necessary for the creation of a high literature. The last fifty years have been a particularly good time for poetry in English, but even that public which can read intelligently knows very little of what has been done. Ideally, the writer needs no audience other than the few who understand. It is immodest and greedy to want more. Unhappily, the novelist, by the very nature of his coarse art, is greedy and immodest; unless he is read by everyone, he cannot delight, instruct, reform, destroy a world he wants, at the least, to be different for his having lived in it. Writers as various as Dickens and Joyce, as George Eliot and Proust, have suffered from this madness. It is the nature of the beast. But now the beast is caged, confined by old forms that have ceased to attract. And so the question is: can those forms be changed, and the beast set free?

Since the Second World War, Alain Robbe-Grillet, Nathalie Sarraute, Michel Butor, Claude Simon, and Robert Pinget, among others, have attempted to change not only the form of the novel but the relationship between book and reader, and though their experiments are taken most seriously on the Continent, they are still too little known and thought about in those countries the late General de Gaulle believed to be largely populated by Anglo-Saxons. Among American commentators, only Susan Sontag in *Against Interpretation, and Other Essays*, published in 1966, has made a sustained effort to understand what the French are doing, and her occasional essays on their work are well worth reading, not only as reflections of an interesting and interested mind but also because she shares with the New Novelists (as they loosely describe themselves) a desire for the novel to become "what it is not in England and America, with rare and unrelated exceptions: a form of art which people with serious and sophisticated [sic] taste in the other arts can take seriously." Certainly Miss Sontag finds nothing adventurous or serious in "the work of the American writers most admired today: for example, Saul Bellow, Norman Mailer, James Baldwin, William Styron, Philip Roth, Bernard

Malamud." They are "essentially unconcerned with the problems of the novel as an art form. Their main concern is with their 'subjects.' " And because of this, she finds them "essentially unserious and unambitious." By this criterion, to be serious and ambitious in the novel, the writer must create works of prose comparable to those experiments in painting which have brought us to Pop and Op art and in music to the strategic silences of John Cage. Whether or not these experiments succeed or fail is irrelevant. It is enough, if the artist is serious, to attempt new forms; certainly he must not repeat old ones.

The two chief theorists of the New Novel are Alain Robbe-Grillet and Nathalie Sarraute. As novelists, their works do not much resemble one another or, for that matter, conform to each other's strictures. But it is as theorists not as novelists that they shall concern us here. Of the two, Alain Robbe-Grillet has done the most to explain what he thinks the New Novel is and is not, in *Snapshots* and *For a New Novel*, translated by Richard Howard (1965). To begin with, he believes that any attempt at controlling the world by assigning it a meaning (the accepted task of the traditional novelist) is no longer possible. At best, meaning was

> *an illusory simplification; and far from becoming clearer and clearer because of it, the world has only, little by little, lost all its life. Since it is chiefly in its presence that the world's reality resides, our task is now to create a literature which takes that presence into account.*

He then attacks the idea of psychological "depth" as a myth. From the Comtesse de La Fayette to Gide, the novelist's role was to burrow "deeper and deeper to reach some ever more intimate strata." Since then, however, "something" has been "changing totally, definitively in our relations with the universe." Though he does not define that ominous "something," its principal effect is that "we no longer consider the world as our own, our private property, designed according to our needs and readily domesticated." Consequently:

> *the novel of characters belongs entirely to the past; it describes a period: and that which marked the apogee of the individual. Perhaps this is not an advance, but it is evident that the present period is rather one of administra-*

tive numbers. The world's destiny has ceased, for us, to be identified with the rise or fall of certain men, of certain families.

Nathalie Sarraute is also concerned with the idea of man the administrative number in *Tropisms* and in *The Age of Suspicion*, translated by Maria Jolas (1964). She quotes Claude-Edmonde Magny: "Modern man, overwhelmed by mechanical civilization, is reduced to the triple determinism of hunger, sexuality and social status: Freud, Marx and Pavlov." (Surely in the wrong order.) She, too, rejects the idea of human depth: "The deep uncovered by Proust's analyses had already proved to be nothing but a surface."

Like Robbe-Grillet, she sees the modern novel as an evolution from Dostoevsky-Flaubert to Proust-Kafka; and each agrees (in essays written by her in 1947 and by him in 1958) that one of its principal touchstones is Camus's *The Stranger*, a work which she feels "came at the appointed time," when the old psychological novel was bankrupt because, paradoxically, psychology itself, having gone deeper than ever before, "inspired doubts as to the ultimate value of all methods of research." *Homo absurdus*, therefore, was Noah's dove, the messenger of deliverance. Camus's stranger is shown entirely from the inside, "all sentiment or thought whatsoever appears to have been completely abolished." He has been created without psychology or memory; he exists in a perpetual present. Robbe-Grillet goes even further in his analysis:

> *It is no exaggeration to claim that it is things quite specifically which ultimately lead this man to crime: the sun, the sea, the brilliant sand, the gleaming knife, the spring among the rocks, the revolver . . . as, of course, among these things, the leading role is taken by Nature.*

Only the absolute presence of things can be recorded; certainly the depiction of human character is no longer possible. In fact, Miss Sarraute believes that for both author and reader, character is "the converging point of their mutual distrust," and she makes of Stendhal's "The genius of suspicion has appeared on the scene" a leitmotiv for an age in which "the reader has grown wary of practically everything. The reason being that for some time now he has been learning too many things and he is unable to forget entirely all he had learned." Perhaps the most vivid thing he has learned (or at least it was vivid when she was writing in 1947) is the fact of genocide in the concentration camps:

> *Beyond these furthermost limits to which Kafka did not follow them but to where he had the superhuman courage to precede them, all feeling disappears, even contempt and hatred; there remains only vast, empty stupefaction, definitive total, don't understand.*
>
> *To remain at the point where he left off or to attempt to go on from there are equally impossible. Those who live in a world of human beings can only retrace their steps.*

The proof that human life can be as perfectly meaningless in the scale of a human society as it is in eternity stunned a generation, and the shock of this knowledge, more than anything else (certainly more than the discoveries of the mental therapists or the new techniques of industrial automation), caused a dislocation of human values which in turn made something like the New Novel inevitable.

Although Nathalie Sarraute and Alain Robbe-Grillet are formidable theorists, neither is entirely free of those rhetorical plangencies the French so often revert to when their best aperçus are about to slip the net of logic. Each is very much a part of that French intellectual tradition so wickedly described in *Tristes Tropiques* by Lévi-Strauss (1964, translated by John Russell):

> *First you establish the traditional "two views" of the question. You then put forward a common-sensical justification of the one, only to refute it by the other. Finally, you send them both packing by the use of a third interpretation, in which both the others are shown to be equally unsatisfactory. Certain verbal maneuvers enable you, that is, to line up the traditional "antitheses" as complementary aspects of a single reality: form and substance, content and container, appearance and reality, essence and existence, continuity and discontinuity, and so on. Before long the exercise becomes the merest verbalizing, reflection gives place to a kind of superior punning, and the "accomplished philosopher" may be recognized by the in-*

genuity with which he makes ever-bolder play with assonance, ambiguity, and the use of those words which sound alike and yet bear quite different meanings.

Miss Sarraute is not above this sort of juggling, particularly when she redefines literary categories, maintaining that the traditional novelists are formalists, while the New Novelists, by eschewing old forms, are the true realists because

their works, which seek to break away from all that is prescribed, conventional and dead, to turn towards what is free, sincere and alive, will necessarily, sooner or later, become ferments of emancipation and progress.

This fine demagoguery does not obscure the fact that she is obsessed with form in a way that the traditional writer seldom is. It is she, not he, who dreams

of a technique that might succeed in plunging the reader into the stream of those subterranean dreams of which Proust only had time to obtain a rapid aerial view, and concerning which he observed and reproduced nothing but the broad motionless lines. This technique would give the reader the illusion of repeating these actions himself, in a more clearly aware, more orderly, distinct and forceful manner than he can do in life, without their losing that element of indetermination, of opacity and mystery, that one's own actions always have for the one who lives them.

This is perilously close to fine lady-writing (Miss Sarraute is addicted to the triad, particularly of adjectives), but despite all protestations, she is totally absorbed with form; and though she dislikes being called a formalist, she can hardly hope to avoid the label, since she has set herself the superb task of continuing consciously those prose experiments that made the early part of the twentieth century one of the great ages of the novel.

In regard to the modern masters, both Robbe-Grillet and Miss Sarraute remark with a certain wonder that there have been no true heirs to

Proust, Joyce, and Kafka; the main line of the realistic novel simply resumed as though they had never existed. Yet, as Robbe-Grillet remarks:

> *Flaubert wrote the new novel of 1860, Proust the new novel of 1910. The writer must proudly consent to bear his own date, knowing that there are no masterpieces in eternity, but only works in history, and that they have survived only to the degree that they have left the past behind them and heralded the future.*

Here, as so often in Robbe-Grillet's theorizing, one is offered a sensible statement, followed by a dubious observation about survival (many conventional, even reactionary works have survived nicely), ending with a look-to-the-dawn-of-a-new-age chord, played fortissimo. Yet the desire to continue the modern tradition is perfectly valid. And even if the New Novelists do not succeed (in science most experiments fail), they are at least "really serious," as Miss Sontag would say.

There is, however, something very odd about a literary movement so radical in its pronouncements yet so traditional in its references. Both Miss Sarraute and Robbe-Grillet continually relate themselves to great predecessors, giving rise to the suspicion that, like Saul Bellow's literary usurpers, they are assuming for themselves the accomplishments of Dostoevsky, Flaubert, Proust, Joyce, and Beckett. In this, at least, they are significantly more modest than their heroes. One cannot imagine the Joyce of *Finnegans Wake* acknowledging a literary debt to anyone or Flaubert admitting—as Robbe-Grillet does—that his work is "merely pursuing a constant evolution of a genre." Curiously enough, the writers whom Robbe-Grillet and Miss Sarraute most resemble wrote books which were described by Arthur Symons for the *Encyclopaedia Britannica* as being

> *made up of an infinite number of details, set side by side, every detail equally prominent. . . . [the authors] do not search further than "the physical basis of life," and they find everything that can be known of that unknown force written visibly upon the sudden faces of little incidents, little expressive movements. . . . It is their distinction—the finest of their inven-*

tions—that, in order to render new sensations, a new vision of things, they invented a new language.

They, of course, are the presently unfashionable brothers Edmond and Jules de Goncourt, whose collaboration ended in 1870.

In attacking the traditional novel, both Robbe-Grillet and Miss Sarraute are on safe ground. Miss Sarraute is particularly effective when she observes that even the least aware of the traditionalists seems "unable to escape a certain feeling of uneasiness as regards dialogue." She remarks upon the self-conscious way in which contemporary writers sprinkle their pages with "he saids" and "she replieds," and she makes gentle fun of Henry Green's hopeful comment that perhaps the novel of the future will be largely composed in dialogue since, as she quotes him, people don't write letters any more: they use the telephone.

But the dialogue novel does not appeal to her, for it brings "the novel dangerously near the domain of the theater, where it is bound to be in a position of inferiority"—on the ground that the nuances of dialogue in the theater are supplied by actors while in the novel the writer himself must provide, somehow, the sub-conversation which is the true meaning. Opposed to the dialogue novel is the one of Proustian analysis. Miss Sarraute finds much fault with this method (no meaningful depths left to plumb in the wake of Freud), but concedes that "In spite of the rather serious charges that may be brought against analysis, it is difficult to turn from it today without turning one's back on progress."

"Progress," "*New* Novel," "permanent creation of tomorrow's world," "the discovery of reality will continue only if we abandon outward forms," "general evolution of the genre" . . . again and again one is reminded in reading the manifestos of these two explorers that we are living (one might even say that we are trapped) in the age of science. Miss Sarraute particularly delights in using quasi-scientific references. She refers to her first collection of pieces as "Tropisms." (According to authority, a tropism is "the turning of an organism, or part of one, in a particular direction in response to some special external stimulus.") She is also addicted to words like "larval" and "magma," and her analogies are often clinical: "Suspicion, which is by way of destroying the character and the entire

outmoded mechanism that guaranteed its force, is one of the morbid reactions by which an organism defends itself and seeks another equilib-
rium. . . ."

Yet she does not like to be called a "laboratory novelist" any more than
she likes to be called a formalist. One wonders why. For it is obvious that
both she and Robbe-Grillet see themselves in white smocks working out
new formulas for a new fiction. Underlying all their theories is the assumption that if scientists can break the atom with an equation, a dedicated writer ought to be able to find a new form in which to redefine the
"unchanging human heart," as Bouvard might have said to Pécuchet.
Since the old formulas have lost their efficacy, the novel, if it is to survive, must become something new; and so, to create that something new,
they believe that writers must resort to calculated invention and bold
experiment.

It is an interesting comment on the age that both Miss Sarraute and
Robbe-Grillet take for granted that the highest literature has always been
made by self-conscious avant-gardists. Although this was certainly true of
Flaubert, whose letters show him in the laboratory, agonizing over that
double genitive which nearly soured the recipe for *Madame Bovary*, and
of Joyce, who spent a third of his life making a language for the night,
Dostoevsky, Conrad, and Tolstoi—to name three novelists quite as great—
were not much concerned with laboratory experiments. Their interest
was in what Miss Sontag calls "the subject"; and though it is true they did
not leave the form of the novel as they found it, their art was not the
product of calculated experiments with form so much as it was the result
of their ability, by virtue of what they were, to transmute the familiar and
make it rare. They were men of genius unobsessed by what Goethe once
referred to as "an eccentric desire for originality." Or as Saul Bellow puts
it: "Genius is always, without strain, avant-garde. Its departure from tradition is not the result of caprice or of policy but of an inner necessity."

Absorbed by his subject, the genius is a natural innovator—a fact
which must be maddening to the ordinary writer, who, because he is
merely ambitious, is forced to approach literature from the outside, hoping by the study of a masterpiece's form and by an analysis of its content
to reconstruct the principle of its composition in order that he may cre-

ate either simulacra or, if he is furiously ambitious, by rearranging the component parts, something "new." This approach from the outside is of course the natural way of the critic, and it is significant that the New Novelists tend to blur the boundary between critic and novelist. "Critical preoccupation," writes Robbe-Grillet, "far from sterilizing creation, can on the contrary serve it as a driving force."

In the present age the methods of the scientist, who deals only in what can be measured, demonstrated, and proved, are central. Consequently, anything as unverifiable as a novel is suspect. Or, as Miss Sarraute quotes Paul Tournier:

> There is nobody left who is willing to admit that he invents. The only thing that matters is the document, which must be precise, dated, proven, authentic. Works of the imagination are banned, because they are invented. . . . The public, in order to believe what it is told, must be convinced that it is not being "taken in." All that counts now is the "true fact."

This may explain why so many contemporary novelists feel they must apologize for effects which seem unduly extravagant or made up ("but that's the way it really happened!"). Nor is it to make a scandal to observe that most "serious" American novels are autobiographies, usually composed to pay off grudges. But then the novelist can hardly be held responsible for the society he reflects. After all, much of the world's reading consists of those weekly news magazines in which actual people are dealt with in fictional terms. It is the spirit of the age to believe that any fact, no matter how suspect, is superior to any imaginative exercise, no matter how true. The result of this attitude has been particularly harrowing in the universities, where English departments now do their best to pretend that they are every bit as fact-minded as the physical scientists (to whom the largest appropriations go). Doggedly, English teachers do research, publish learned findings, make breakthroughs in F. Scott Fitzgerald and, in their search for facts, behave as if no work of literature can be called complete until each character has been satisfactorily identified as someone who actually lived and had a history known to the author. It is no wonder that the ambitious writer is tempted to re-create the novel along what he believes to be scientific lines. With admiration, Miss Son-tag quotes William Burroughs:

> *I think there's going to be more and more merging of art and science. Sci-entists are already studying the creative process, and I think that the whole line between art and science will break down and that scientists, I hope, will become more creative and writers more scientific.*

Recently in France the matter of science and the novel was much de-bated. In an essay called *Nouvelle Critique ou Nouvelle Imposture*, Ray-mond Picard attacked the new critic Roland Barthes, who promptly defended himself on the ground that a concern with form is only natural since structure precedes creation (an insight appropriated from anthro-pology, a discipline recently become fashionable). Picard then returned to the attack, mocking those writers who pretend to be scientists, point-ing out that they

> *improperly apply to the literary domain methods which have proved fruitful elsewhere but which here lose their efficiency and rigor. . . . These critical approaches have a scientific air to them, but the resemblance is pure cari-cature. The new critics use science roughly as someone ignorant of electric-ity might use electronics. What they're after is its prestige: in other respects they are at opposite poles to the scientific spirit. Their statements generally sound more like oracles than useful hypotheses: categorical, unverifiable, unilluminating.*

Picard is perhaps too harsh, but no one can deny that Robbe-Grillet and Nathalie Sarraute often appropriate the language of science without understanding its spirit—for instance, one can verify the law of physics which states that there is no action without reaction, but how to prove the critical assertion that things in themselves are what caused Camus's creature to kill? Yet if to revive a moribund art form writers find it help-ful to pretend to be physicists, then one ought not to tease them unduly for donning so solemnly mask and rubber gloves. After all, Count Tolstoi thought he was a philosopher. But whether pseudo-scientists or original thinkers, neither Robbe-Grillet nor Miss Sarraute finds it easy to put theory into practice. As Robbe-Grillet says disarmingly: "It is easier to indicate a new form than to follow it without failure." And he must be said to fail a good deal of the time: is there anything more incantatory than the repetition of the word *"lugubre"* in *Last Year at Marienbad*? Or more visceral than the repetition of the killing of the centipede in *Jealousy*? While Miss Sarraute finds that her later essays are "far removed from the conception and composition of my first book"—which, nevertheless, she includes in the same volume as the essays, with the somewhat puzzling comment that "this first book contains *in nuce* all the raw material that I have continued to develop in my later works."

For Robbe-Grillet, the problem of the novel is—obviously—the problem of man in relation to his environment, a relationship which he believes has changed radically in the last fifty years. In the past, man attempted to personalize the universe. In prose, this is revealed by metaphor: "majestic peaks," "huddled villages," "pitiless sun." "These anthropomorphic analogies are repeated too insistently, too coherently, not to reveal an entire metaphysical system." And he attacks what he holds to be the humanistic view: "On the pretext that man can achieve only a subjective knowledge of the world, humanism decides to elect man the justification of everything." In fact, he believes that humanists will go so far as to maintain that "it is not enough to show man where he is: it must further be proclaimed that man is everywhere." Quite shrewdly he observes: "If I say 'the world is man,' I shall always gain absolution; while if I say things are things, and man is only man, I am immediately charged with a crime against humanity."

It is this desire to remove the falsely human from the nature of things that is at the basis of Robbe-Grillet's theory. He is arguing not so much against what Ruskin called "the pathetic fallacy," as against our race's tendency to console itself by making human what is plainly nonhuman. To those who accuse him of trying to dehumanize the novel, he replies that since any book is written by a man "animated by torments and passion," it cannot help but be human. Nevertheless, "suppose the eyes of this man rest on things without indulgence, insistently: he sees them but he refuses to appropriate them." Finally, "man looks at the world but the world does not look back at him, and so, if he rejects communion, he also rejects tragedy." Inconsistently, he later quotes with admiration Joé

Bousquet's "We watch things pass by in order to forget that they are watching us die."

Do those things watch or not? At times Miss Sarraute writes as if she thought they did. Her *Tropisms* are full of things invested with human response ("The crouched houses standing watch all along the gray streets"), but then she is not so strict as Robbe-Grillet in her apprehension of reality. She will accept "those analogies which are limited to the instinctive irresistible nature of the movements . . . produced in us by the presence of others, or by objects from the outside world." For Robbe-Grillet, however, "All analogies are dangerous."

Man's consciousness has now been separated from his environment. He lives in a perpetual present. He possesses memory but it is not chronological. Therefore the best that the writer can hope to do is to impart a precise sense of man's being in the present. To achieve this immediacy, Miss Sarraute favors "some precise dramatic action shown in slow motion"; a world in which "time was no longer the time of real life but of a hugely amplified present." While Robbe-Grillet, in commenting upon his film *Last Year at Marienbad*, declares:

> *The Universe in which the entire film occurs is, characteristically, in a perpetual present which makes all recourse to memory impossible. This is a world without a past, a world which is self-sufficient at every moment and which obliterates itself as it proceeds.*

To him, the film is a ninety-minute fact without antecedents. "The only important 'character' is the spectator. In his mind unfolds the whole story which is precisely imagined by him." The verb "imagine" is of course incorrect, while the adverb means nothing. The spectator is *not* imagining the film; he is watching a creation which was made in a precise historic past by a writer, a director, actors, cameramen, etc. Yet to have the spectator or reader involve himself directly and temporally in the act of creation continues to be Robbe-Grillet's goal. He wants "a present which constantly invents itself" with "the reader's creative assistance," participating "in a creation, to invent in his turn the work—and the world—and thus to learn to invent his own life." This is most ambitious. But the ingredients of the formula keep varying. For instance, in praising Raymond Roussel, Robbe-Grillet admires the author's *"investigation* which destroys, in the writing itself, its own object." Elsewhere: "The work must seem necessary but necessary for nothing; its architecture is without use; its strength is untried." And again: "The genuine writer has nothing to say. He has only a way of speaking. He must create a world but starting from nothing, from the dust. . . ." It would not seem to be possible, on the one hand, to invent a world that would cause the reader to "invent his own life" while, on the other hand, the world in question is being destroyed as it is being created. Perhaps he means for the reader to turn to dust, gradually, page by page: not the worst of solutions.

No doubt there are those who regard the contradictions in Robbe-Grillet's critical writing as the point to them—rather in the way that the boredom of certain plays or the incompetence of certain pictures are, we are assured, their achievement. Yet it is worrisome to be told that a man can create a world from nothing when that is the one thing he cannot begin to do, simply because, no matter how hard he tries, he cannot dispose of himself. Even if what he writes is no more than nouns and adjectives, who and what he is will subconsciously dictate order. Nothing human is random and it is nonsense to say:

> Art is based on no truth that exists before it; and one may say that it ex-. presses nothing but itself. It creates its own equilibrium and its own meaning. It stands all by itself . . . or else it falls.

Which reminds us of Professor Herzog's plaintive response to the philosophic proposition that modern man at a given moment fell into the quotidian: so where was he standing before the fall? In any case, how can something unique, in Robbe-Grillet's sense, rise or fall or be anything except itself? As for reflecting "no truth that existed before it," this is not possible. The fact that the author is a man "filled with torments and passion" means that all sorts of "truths" are going to occur in the course of the writing. The act of composing prose is a demonstration not only of human will but of the desire to reflect truth—particularly if one's instinct is messianic, and Robbe-Grillet is very much in that tradition. Not only does he want man "to invent his own life" (by reading Robbe-Grillet), but he proposes that today's art is "a way of living in the present world, and of participating in the permanent creation of tomorrow's world." It also seems odd that a theory of the novel which demands total existence in a self-devouring present should be concerned at all with the idea of future time since man exists, demonstrably, only in the present—the future tense is a human conceit, on the order of "majestic peaks." As for the use of the adjective "permanent," one suspects that rhetoric, not thought, forced this unfortunate word from the author's unconscious mind.

The ideal work, according to Robbe-Grillet, is

> *A text both "dense and irreducible"; so perfect that it does not seem "to have touched," an object so perfect that it would obliterate our tracks. . . . Do we not recognize here the highest ambition of every writer?*

Further, the only meaning for the novel is the invention of the world. "In dreams, in memory, as in the sense of sight, our imagination is the organizing force of our life, of *our* world. Each man, in his turn, must reinvent the things around him." Yet, referring to things, he writes a few pages later,

> *They refer to no other world. They are the sign of nothing but themselves. And the only contact man can make with them is to imagine them.*

But how is one to be loyal to the actual fact of things if they must be reinvented? Either they are *there* or they are not. In any case, by filtering them through the imagination (reinvention), true objectivity is lost, as he himself admits in a further snarling of his argument: "Objectivity in the ordinary sense of the word—total impersonality of observation—is all too obviously an illusion. But freedom of observation should be possible and yet it is not"—because a "continuous fringe of culture (psychology, ethics, metaphysics, etc.) is added to things, giving them a less alien aspect." But he believes that "humanizing" can be kept to a minimum, if we try "to construct a world both more solid and more immediate. Let it be first of all by their presence that objects and gestures establish themselves and let this presence continue to prevail over the subjective." Consequently, the task of the New Novel is nothing less than to seek *new forms for the novel . . . forms capable of expressing (or of creating) new relations between man and the world, to all those who have determined to invent the novel, in other words, to invent man. Such writers know that the systematic repetition of the forms of the past is not only absurd and futile, but that it can even become harmful: blinding us to our real situation in the world today, it keeps us, ultimately, from constructing the world and man of tomorrow.*

With the change of a noun or two, this could easily be the coda of an address on American foreign policy, delivered by Professor Arthur Schlesinger, Jr., to the ADA.

Like Robbe-Grillet, Nathalie Sarraute regards Camus's *The Stranger* as a point of departure. She sees the book's immediate predecessors as "The promising art of the cinema" and "the wholesome simplicity of the new American novel." Incidentally, she is quite amusing when she describes just what the effect of these "wholesome" novels was upon the French during the years immediately after the war:

By transporting the French reader into a foreign universe in which he had no foothold, [they] lulled his wariness, aroused in him the kind of credulous curiosity that travel books inspire, and gave him a delightful impression of escape into an unknown world.

It is reassuring to learn that these works were not regarded with any great seriousness by the French and that Horace McCoy was not finally the master they once hailed him. Apparently the American novel was simply a vigorous tonic for an old literature gone stale. Miss Sarraute is, however, sincerely admiring of Faulkner's ability to involve the reader in his own world. To her the most necessary thing of all is "to dispossess the reader and entice him, at all costs, into the author's territory. To achieve this the device that consists in referring to the leading characters as 'I' constitutes a means." The use of the first person seems to her to be the emblem of modern art. ("Since Impressionism all pictures have been painted in the first person.") And so, just as photography drove painters away from representing nature (ending such ancient arts as that of the

miniaturist and the maker of portrait busts), the cinema "garners and per-
fects what is left of it by the novel." The novel must now go where the
camera may not follow. In this new country the reader has been aided by
such modern writers as Proust and Joyce; they have so awakened his sen-
sibilities that he is now able to respond to what is beneath the interior
monologue, that "immense profusion of sensations, images, sentiments,
memories, impulses, little larval actions that no inner language can convey." For her, emphasis falls upon what she calls the sub-conversation,
that which is sensed and not said, the hidden counterpoint to the stated
theme (obviously a very difficult thing to suggest, much less write, since
"no inner language can convey it").

   "Bosquet's universe—ours—is a universe of signs," writes Robbe-
Grillet. "Everything in it is a sign; and not the sign of something else,
something more perfect, situated out of reach, but a sign of itself, of that
reality which asks only to be revealed." This answer to Baudelaire's *The
Salon of 1859* is reasonable (although it is anthropomorphic to suggest
that reality *asks* to be revealed). Robbe-Grillet is equally reasonable in his
desire for things to be shown, as much as possible, as they are.

> *In the future universe of the novel, gestures and objects will be there before
> being something; and they will still be there afterwards, hard, unalterably,
> eternally present, mocking their own "meaning," that meaning which vainly
> tries to reduce them to the role of precarious tools, etc.*

One agrees with him that the integrity of the nonhuman world should
be honored. But what does he mean (that proscribed verb!) when he says
that the objects will be *there*, after meaning has attempted to rape them?
Does he mean that they will still exist on the page, in some way inviolate
in their thing-ness? If he does, surely he is mistaken. What exists on the
page is ink; or, if one wishes to give the ink designs their agreed-upon human meaning, letters have been formed to make words in order to suggest things not present. What is on the page are not real things but their
word-shadows. Yet even if the things were there, it is most unlikely that
they would be so human as to "mock their own meaning." In an eerie way,
Robbe-Grillet's highly rhetorical style has a tendency to destroy his argu-

ments even as he makes them; critically, this technique complements ideally the self-obliterating anecdote.

On the question of how to establish the separateness, the autonomy of things, Robbe-Grillet and Miss Sarraute part company. In contemplating her method, she ceases altogether to be "scientific." Instead she alarmingly intones a hymn to words—all words—for they "possess the qualities needed to seize upon, protect and bring out into the open those subterranean movements that are at once impatient and afraid." (Are those subterranean movements really "impatient and afraid"?) For her, words possess suppleness, freedom, iridescent richness of shading, and by their nature they are protected "from suspicion and from minute examination." (In an age of suspicion, to let words off scot-free is an act of singular trust.) Consequently, once words have entered the other person, they swell, explode, and "by virtue of this game of actions and reactions . . . they constitute a most valuable tool for the novelist." Which, as the French say, goes without saying.

But of course words are not at all what she believes they are. All words lie. Or as Professor Frank Kermode put it in *Literary Fiction and Reality*: "Words, thoughts, patterns of word and thought, are enemies of truth, if you identify that with what may be had by phenomenological reductions." Nevertheless, Miss Sarraute likes to think that subterranean movements (tropisms) can be captured by words, which might explain why her attitude toward things is so much more conventional than that of Robbe-Grillet, who writes:

> *Perhaps Kafka's staircases lead* elsewhere, *but they are* there, *and we look at them step by step following the details of the banisters and the risers.*

This is untrue. First, we do not look at the staircases; we look at a number of words arranged upon a page by a conscious human intelligence which would like us to consider, among a thousand other things, the fact of those staircases. Since a primary concern of the human mind is cause and effect, the reader is bound to speculate upon why those staircases have been shown him; also, since staircases are usually built to connect one man-made level with another, the mind will naturally speculate as to what those two levels are like. Only a far-gone schizophrenic (or an LSD tripper) would find entirely absorbing the description of a banister.

Perhaps the most naïve aspect of Robbe-Grillet's theory of fiction is his assumption that words can ever describe with absolute precision anything. At no point does he acknowledge that words are simply fiat for real things; by their nature, words are imprecise and layered with meanings—the signs of things, not the things themselves. Therefore, even if Robbe-Grillet's goal of achieving a total reality for the world of things was desirable, it would not be possible to do it with language, since the author (that man full of torments and passions) is bound to betray his attitude to the sequence of signs he offered us; he has an "interest" in the matter, or else he would not write. Certainly if he means to reinvent man, then he will want to find a way of defining man through human (yes, psychological) relations as well as through a catalogue of things observed and gestures coolly noted. Wanting to play God, ambition is bound to dictate the order of words, and so the subjective will prevail just as it does in the traditional novel. To follow Robbe-Grillet's theory to its logical terminus, the only sort of book which might be said to be *not* a collection of signs of absent things but the actual things themselves would be a collection of ink, paper, cardboard, glue, and typeface, to be assembled or not by the reader-spectator. If this be too heavy a joke, then the ambitious writer must devise a new language which might give the appearance of maintaining the autonomy of things, since the words, new-minted, will possess a minimum of associations of a subjective or anthropomorphic sort. No existing language will be of any use to him, unless it be that of the Trobriand Islanders: those happy people have no words for "why" or "because"; for them, things just happen. Needless to say, they do not write novels or speculate on the nature of things.

The philosophic origins of the New Novel can be found (like most things French) in Descartes, whose dualism was the reflection of a split between the subjective and the objective, between the irrational and the rational, between the physical and the metaphysical. In the last century Auguste Comte, accepting this dualism, conceived of a logical empiricism which would emphasize the "purely" objective at the expense of the subjective or metaphysical. An optimist who believed in human progress,

Comte saw history as an evolution toward a better society. For him the age of religion and metaphysics ended with the French Revolution. Since that time the human race was living in what he termed "the age of science," and he was confident that the methods of the positive sciences would enrich and transform human life. At last things were coming into their own. But not until the twentieth century did the methods of science entirely overwhelm the arts of the traditional humanists. To the scientific-minded, all things, including human personality, must in time yield their secrets to orderly experiment. Meanwhile, only that which is verifiable is to be taken seriously, emotive meaning must yield to cognitive meaning. Since the opacity of human character has so far defeated all objective attempts at illumination, the New Novelists prefer, as much as possible, to replace the human with objects closely observed and simple gestures noted but not explained.

In many ways, the New Novel appears to be approaching the "pure" state of music. In fact, there are many like Miss Sontag who look forward to "a kind of total structuring" of the novel, analogous to music. This is an old dream of the novelist. Nearly half a century ago, Joyce wrote (in a letter to his brother), "Why should not a modern literature be as unsparing and as direct as song?" Why not indeed? And again, why? The answer to the second "why" is easy enough. In the age of science, the objective is preferred to the subjective. Since human behavior is notoriously irrational and mysterious, it can be demonstrated only in the most impressionistic and unscientific way; it yields few secrets to objective analysis. Mathematics, on the other hand, is rational and verifiable, and music is a form of mathematics. Therefore, if one were to eliminate as much as possible the human from the novel, one might, through "a kind of total structuring," come close to the state of mathematics or music—in short, achieve that perfect irreducible artifact Robbe-Grillet dreams of.

The dates of Miss Sarraute's essays range from 1947 to 1956, those of Robbe-Grillet from 1955 to 1963. To categorize in the French manner, it might be said that their views are particularly representative of the Fifties, a period in which the traditional-minded (among whom they must be counted) still believed it possible to salvage the novel—or anything—by new techniques. With a certain grimness, they experimented. But though some of their books are good (even very good) and some are bad, they did not make a "new" novel, if only because art forms do not evolve—in literature at least—from the top down. Despite Robbe-Grillet's tendency to self-congratulation ("Although these descriptions—motionless arguments or fragments of scene—have acted on the readers in a satisfactory fashion, the judgment many specialists make of them remains pejorative"), there is not much in what he has so far written that will interest anyone except the specialist. It is, however, a convention of the avant-garde that to be in advance of the majority is to be "right." But the New Novelists are not in advance of anyone. Their works derive from what they believe to be a need for experiment and the imposition of certain of the methods of science upon the making of novels. Fair enough. Yet in this they resemble everyone, since to have a liking for the new is to be with the dull majority. In the arts, the obviously experimental is almost never denounced *because* it is new: if anything, our taste-makers tend to be altogether too permissive in the presence of what looks to be an experiment, as anyone who reads New York art criticism knows. There is not much likelihood that Robbe-Grillet will be able to reinvent man as a result of his exercises in prose. Rather he himself is in the process of being reinvented (along with the rest of us) by the new world in which we are living.

At the moment, advance culture scouts are reporting with a certain awe that those men and women who were brought up as television-watchers respond, predictably, to pictures that move and talk but not at all to prose fictions; and though fashion might dictate the presence of an occasional irreducible artifact in a room, no one is about to be reinvented by it. Yet the old avant-garde continues worriedly to putter with form.

Surveying the literary output for 1965, Miss Sontag found it "hard to think of any one book [in English] that exemplifies in a *central* way the possibilities for enlarging and complicating the forms of prose literature." This desire to "enlarge" and "complicate" the novel has an air of madness to it. Why not minimize and simplify? One suspects that out of desperation she is picking verbs at random. But then, like so many at present, she has a taste for the random. Referring to William Burroughs's resolutely random work *The Soft Machine*, she writes: "In the end, the voices come together and sound what is to my mind the most serious, urgent and original voice in American letters to be heard for many years." It is, how-

ever, the point to Mr. Burroughs's method that the voices *don't* come together: he is essentially a sport who is (blessedly) not serious, not urgent,
and original only in the sense that no other American writer has been so
relentlessly ill-humored in his send-up of the serious. He is the Grand
Guy Grand of American letters. But whether or not Miss Sontag is right
or wrong in her analyses of specific works and general trends, there is
something old-fashioned and touching in her assumption (shared with the
New Novelists) that if only we all try hard enough in a "really serious" way,
we can come up with the better novel. This attitude reflects not so much
the spirit of art as it does that of Detroit.

No one today can predict what games post-Gutenberg man will want
to play. The only certainty is that his mind will work differently from
ours; just as ours works differently from that of pre-Gutenberg man, as
Miss Frances Yates demonstrated so dramatically in *The Art of Memory*.
Perhaps there will be more Happenings in the future. Perhaps the random will take the place of the calculated. Perhaps the ephemeral will be
preferred to the permanent: we stop in time, so why should works of art
endure? Also, as the shadow of atomic catastrophe continues to fall
across our merry games, the ephemeral will necessarily be valued to the
extent it gives pleasure in the present and makes no pretense of having a
future life. Since nothing will survive the firewind, the ashes of one thing
will be very like those of another, and so what matters excellence?

One interesting result of today's passion for the immediate and the
casual has been the decline, in all the arts, of the idea of technical virtuosity as being in any way desirable. The culture (*kitsch* as well as camp)
enjoys singers who sing no better than the average listener, actors who do
not act yet are, in Andy Warhol's happy phrase, "super-stars," painters
whose effects are too easily achieved, writers whose swift flow of words
across the page is not submitted to the rigors of grammar or shaped by
conscious thought. There is a general Zen-ish sense of why bother? If a
natural fall of pebbles can "say" as much as any shaping of paint on canvas or cutting of stone, why go to the trouble of recording what is there
for all to see? In any case, if the world should become, as predicted, a village united by an electronic buzzing, our ideas of what is art will seem as
curious to those gregarious villagers as the works of what we used to call
the Dark Ages appear to us.

Regardless of what games men in the future will want to play, the matter of fiction seems to be closed. Reading skills—as the educational-ists say—continue to decline with each new generation. Novel reading is not a pastime of the young now being educated, nor, for that matter, is it a preoccupation of any but a very few of those who came of age in the last warm years of linear type's hegemony. It is possible that fashion may from time to time bring back a book or produce a book which arouses something like general interest (Miss Sontag darkly suspects that "the nineteenth-century novel has a much better chance for a comeback than verse drama, the sonnet, or landscape painting"). Yet it is literature itself which seems on the verge of obsolescence, and not so much because the new people will prefer watching to reading as because the language in which books are written has become corrupt from misuse.

In fact, George Steiner believes that there is a definite possibility that "The political inhumanity of the twentieth century and certain elements in the technological mass-society which has followed on the erosion of European bourgeois values have done injury to language. . . ." He even goes so far as to suggest that for now at least silence may be a virtue for the writer—when

> language simply ceases, and the motion of spirit gives no further outward manifestation of its being. The poet enters into silence. Here the word bor-ders not on radiance or music, but on night.

Although Mr. Steiner does not himself take this romantic position ("I am not saying that writers should stop writing. This would be fatuous"), he does propose silence as a proud alternative for those who have lived at the time of Belsen and of Vietnam, and have witnessed the perversion of so many words by publicists and political clowns. The credibility gap is now an abyss, separating even the most honorable words from their an-cient meanings. Fortunately, ways of communication are now changing, and though none of us understands exactly what is happening, language is bound to be affected.

But no matter what happens to language, the novel is not apt to be revived by electronics. The portentous theorizings of the New Novelists are of no more use to us than the self-conscious avant-gardism of those who are forever trying to figure out what the next "really serious" thing will be when it is plain that there is not going to be a next serious thing in the novel. Our lovely vulgar and most human art is at an end, if not the end. Yet that is no reason not to want to practice it, or even to read it. In any case, rather like priests who have forgotten the meaning of the prayers they chant, we shall go on for quite a long time talking of books and writing books, pretending all the while not to notice that the church is empty and the parishioners have gone elsewhere to attend other gods, perhaps in silence or with new words.

Encounter
December 1967

AMERICAN PLASTIC:

THE MATTER OF FICTION

The New Novel is close to forty years old. Although forty is young for an American presidential candidate or a Chinese buried egg, it is very old indeed for a literary movement, particularly a French literary movement. But then what, recently, *has* one heard of the New Novel, whose official *vernissage* occurred in 1938 with Nathalie Sarraute's publication of *Tropismes*? The answer is not much directly from the founders but a good deal indirectly, for, with characteristic torpor, America's departments of English have begun slowly, slowly to absorb the stern aesthetics of Sarraute and Robbe-Grillet, not so much through the actual writing of these masters as through their most brilliant interpreter, the witty, meta-camp sign-master and analyst of *le degré zéro de l'écriture* Roland Barthes, whose amused and amusing saurian face peers like some near-sighted chameleon from the back of a half-dozen slim volumes now being laboriously read in Academe.

Barthes has also had a significant (or signifying) effect on a number of American writers, among them Mr. Donald Barthelme. Two years ago Mr. Barthelme was quoted as saying that the only American writers worth reading are John Barth, Grace Paley, William Gass, and Thomas Pynchon. Dutifully, I have read all the writers on Mr. Barthelme's list, and presently I will make my report on them. But first, a look at M. Barthes.

For over twenty years Barthes has been a fascinating high critic who writes with equal verve about Charlie Chaplin, detergents, Marx, toys, Balzac, structuralism, and semiology. He has also put the theory of the New Novelists rather better than they have themselves, a considerable achievement since it is as theoreticians and not as practitioners that these writers excel. Unlike Sarraute, Robbe-Grillet, and Butor, Professor Barthes is much too clever actually to write novels himself, assuming that such things exist, new or old, full of signs or not, with or without sequential narratives. Rather, Barthes has remained a commentator and a theoretician, and he is often pleasurable to read though never blissful, to appropriate his own terminology.

Unlike the weather, theories of the novel tend to travel from east to west. But then, as we have always heard (sometimes from the French themselves), the French mind is addicted to the postulating of elaborate systems in order to explain everything, while the Anglo-American mind tends to shy away from unified-field theories. We chart our courses point to point; they sight from the stars. The fact that neither really gets much of anywhere doesn't mean that we haven't all had some nice outings over the years.

Nine years ago I wrote an exhaustive and, no doubt, exhausting account of the theory or theories of the French New Novel. Rejected by the American literary paper for which I had written it (subject not all that interesting), I was obliged to publish in England at the CIA's expense. Things have changed since 1967. Today one can hardly pick up a Serious literary review without noting at least one obligatory reference to Barthes, or look at any list of those novelists currently admired by American English departments without realizing that although none of these writers approaches zero degree, quite a few are on the chilly side. This is not such a bad thing. Twice, by the way, I have used the word "thing" in this paragraph. I grow suspicious, as one ought to be in zero-land, of all *things* and their shadows, words.

Barthes's American admirers are particularly fascinated by semiology, a quasi-science of signs first postulated by Ferdinand de Saussure in his *Course in General Linguistics* (1916). For some years the school of Paris and its American annex have made much of signs and signification, linguistic and otherwise. Barthes's *Elements of Semiology* (1964) is a key work and not easy to understand. It is full of graphs and theorems as well as definitions and puzzles. Fortunately, Susan Sontag provides a useful preface to the American edition of *Writing Degree Zero*, reminding us that Barthes "simply takes for granted a great deal that we do not." Zero degree writing is that colorless "white" writing (first defined and named by Sartre in his description of Camus's *L'Étranger*). It is a language in which, among other things and nothings, metaphor and anthropomorphizing are eliminated. According to Sontag, Barthes is reasonable enough to admit that this kind of writing is but "*one* solution to the disintegration of literary language."

As for semiology or the "science" of signs, Barthes concedes that "this term, *sign*, which is found in very different vocabularies . . . is for these very reasons very ambiguous." He categorizes various uses of the word "from the Gospels to Cybernetics." I should like to give him a use of the word he seems not to know. The word for "sign" in Sanskrit is "lingam," which also means "phallus," the holy emblem of our Lord Shiva.

In *S/Z* (1970) Barthes took "Sarrasine," a Balzac short story, and subjected it to a line-by-line, even a word-by-word analysis. In the course of this assault, Barthes makes a distinction between what he calls the "readerly text" and the "writerly text" (I am using Mr. Richard Miller's translation of these phrases). Barthes believes that "the goal of literary work (of literature as work) is to make the reader no longer a consumer, but a producer of the text. Our literature is characterized by the pitiless divorce . . . between the producer of the text and its user, between its owner and its customer, between its author and its reader. This reader is thereby plunged into a kind of idleness—he is intransitive; he is, in short, *serious*. Opposite the writerly text, then, is its counter-value, its negative, reactive value: what can be read but not written: the *readerly*. We call any readerly text a classic text." Then "the writerly is the novelistic without the novel, poetry without the poem. . . . But the readerly texts? They are products (and not productions), they make up the mass of our literature. How [to] differentiate this mass once again?"

Barthes believes that this can be done through "*interpretation* (in the Nietzschean sense of the word)." He has a passion, incidentally, for lizardlike dodges from the direct statement by invoking some great reverberating name as an adjective, causing the reader's brow to contract. But then the lunges and dodges are pretty much the matter as well as the manner of Barthes's technique as he goes to work on Balzac's short story of a man who falls in love with a famous Italian singer who turns out to be not the beautiful woman of his dreams but a castrated Neapolitan boy.

I do not intend to deal with Barthes's "interpretation" of the text. It is a very elaborate and close reading in a style that seems willfully complicated. I say willfully because the text of itself is a plain and readerly one in no need of this sort of assistance, not that Barthes wants to assist either text or reader. Rather he means to make for his own delectation or bliss a writerly text of his own. I hope that he has succeeded.

Like so many of today's academic critics, Barthes resorts to formulas, diagrams; the result, no doubt, of teaching in classrooms equipped with blackboards and chalk. Envious of the half-erased theorems—the prestigious *signs*—of the physicists, English teachers now compete by chalking up theorems and theories of their own, words having failed them yet again.

Fair stood the wind for America. For twenty years from the east have come these thoughts, words, signs. Let us now look and see what our own writers have made of so much exciting heavy weather, particularly the writers Mr. Donald Barthelme has named. Do they show signs of the French Pox?

Two years ago, I had read some of Gass, tried and failed to read Barth and Pynchon. I had never read Mr. Barthelme and I had never heard of Grace Paley. I have now made my way through the collected published works of the listed writers as well as through Mr. Barthelme's own enormous output. I was greatly helped in my journey through these texts by Mr. Joe David Bellamy's *The New Fiction*, a volume containing interviews with most of the principals and their peers.

Over the years I have seen but not read Donald Barthelme's short stories in *The New Yorker*. I suppose I was put off by the pictures. Barthelme's texts are usually decorated with perspective drawings, ominous faces, funny-looking odds and ends. Let the prose do it, I would think severely, and turn the page, looking for S. J. Perelman. I was not aware that I was *not* reading one who is described in *The New Fiction* as, "according to Philip Stevick . . . 'the most imitated fictionist in the United States today.'" Mr. Stevick is plainly authority to the interviewer, who then gets Barthelme to say a number of intelligent things about the life of a "fictionist" today. Mr. Barthelme tells us that his father was "a 'modern' architect." Incidentally, it is now the fashion to put quotes around any statement or word that might be challenged. This means that the questionable word or statement was not meant literally but ironically or "ironically." Another way of saying, "Don't hit me. I didn't really 'mean' it." As son of a School of Barnstone architect, Barthelme came naturally by those perspective drawings that so annoyed (and still annoy) me. He has worked as an editor and "I enjoy editing and enjoy doing layout-problems of design. I could very cheerfully be a typographer."

Barthelme's first book, *Come Back, Dr. Caligari*, contains short stories written between 1961 and 1964. This was the period during which Sarraute and Robbe-Grillet and Barthes were being translated into English. Although Robbe-Grillet's *For a New Novel* was not translated until 1965, Nathalie Sarraute's *Tropismes* was translated in 1963 as were such essential novels as *Le Planétarium, Fruits d'or, Jalousie*, and *Le Voyeur*. I note the fact of translation only because Barthelme admits to our common "American lack-of-language." Most American and English writers know foreign literature only through translation. This is bad enough when it comes to literature but peculiarly dangerous when it comes to theory. One might put the case that without a French education there is no way of comprehending, say, Roland Barthes (Sontag suggests as much). One can only take a piece here, a piece there, relate it to the tradition that one knows, and hope for the best. There is comfort, however, in knowing that the French do not get the point to us either.

The stories in *Come Back, Dr. Caligari* are fairly random affairs. Barthelme often indulges in a chilling heterosexual camp that is, nevertheless, quite a bit warmer than zero degree centigrade. There are funny names and cute names. Miss Mandible. Numerous non sequiturs. Dialogue in the manner not only of Ionesco but of Terry Southern (another Texas master). One can read any number of Barthelme's lines with a certain low-keyed pleasure. But then silliness stops the eye cold. " 'You're supposed to be curing a ham.' 'The ham died,' she said." The Marx Brothers could get a big laugh on this exchange because they would already have given us a dozen other gags in as many minutes. Unhappily one small gag on its own shrivels and dies. " '*You* may not be interested in absurdity,' she said firmly, 'but absurdity is interested in *you*.' "

Three years later came *Snow White*. This fiction was billed by the publisher as "a perverse fairy tale." The book is composed of fairly short passages. Quotation marks are used to enclose dialogue and there are the usual number of "he saids," and "she replieds." This is an important point. *Truly* new writing eliminates quotation marks and "he saids." Barthelme is still cooking on a warm stove. The seven dwarfs are indistinguishable from one another and from the heroine. But the somewhat plodding tone of this work holds the attention rather better than did any of those fragments in the first volume. Yet Barthelme is compelled always to go for the easy twist. "Those cruel words remain locked in his lack of heart." Also, he writes about the writing he is writing:

> *We like books that have a lot of* dreck *in them, matter which presents itself as not wholly relevant (or indeed at all relevant) but which, carefully attended to, can supply a kind of "sense" of what is going on. This kind of "sense" is not to be obtained by reading between the lines (for there is nothing there, in those white spaces) but by reading the lines themselves. . . .*

Roland Barthes, his mark.

Unspeakable Practices, Unnatural Acts (1968) contains fifteen pieces mostly published in *The New Yorker*. Occasionally the text is broken with headlines in the Brechtian manner. With film subtitles. With lists. One list called *Italian Novel* names sixteen Italian writers "she" was reading. Most are fashionable; some are good; but the premier Sciascia has been omitted. *What can this mean?*

Many proper names from *real* life appear in these texts. Paul Goodman, J. B. Priestley, Julia Ward Howe, Anthony Powell, Godard. Also *Time, Newsweek*, the Museum of Modern Art. Curiously enough those names that are already invested with an *a priori* reality help the texts which, as usual, maunder, talking to themselves, keeping a dull eye out for the odd joke as the author tries not to be himself a maker of dreck but an arranger of dreck.

The most successful of the lot is "Robert Kennedy Saved from Drowning." The reader brings to the story an altogether too vivid memory of the subject. We learn from the interview in Bellamy's book that, though the story "is, like, made up," Barthelme did use a remark that he heard Kennedy make about a geometric painter (" 'Well, at least we know he has a ruler' " . . . high wit from Camelot). Yet the parts that are not, like, made up are shrewd and amusing and truthful (relatively, of course). Also, the see-Jane-run style is highly suited to a parody of a contemporary politician on the make as he calculates his inanities and holds back his truths (relative—and relatives, too) and rage. Mr. William Gass takes an opposite view of this story. "Here Barthelme's method fails; for the idea is to *use* dreck, not write about it." But surely one can do both. Or neither. Or one. Or the other. But then Mr. Gass thinks that Barthelme at his best "has the art to make a treasure out of trash. . . ."

Throughout Barthelme's work one notes various *hommages* to this writer or that (who lives at Montreux? and where will one hear the ultimate message *Trink?*); some are a bit too close. For instance, the famous opening scene of Beckett's *Molloy* in which a father is carrying his son becomes in "A Picture History of the War": "Kellerman, gigantic with gin, runs through the park at noon with his naked father slung under one arm."

City Life (1970). Fourteen short stories, much as before except that now Barthelme is very deep into fiction's R and D (Research and Development) as opposed to the old-fashioned R and R (Rest and Recuperation). There are, galore, graphics. Big black squares occupy the center of white pages. Elaborate studies in perspective. Lots of funny old pictures. There are wide white margins, nice margins, too. There are pages of questions and answers (Q and A). Father returns. In fact, the first paragraph of the first story is: "An aristocrat was riding down the street in his carriage. He ran over my father."

It must be said that America's most imitated young writer is also not only the most imitable but one of the most imitative. *Hommage* to Robbe-Grillet:

> *Or a long sentence moving at a certain pace down the page aiming for the bottom—if not the bottom of this page then of some other page—where it can rest, or stop for a moment to think about the questions raised by its own (temporary) existence, which ends when the page is turned, or the sentence falls out of the mind that holds it (temporarily) in some kind of an embrace*

and so on for eight whole pages with *not one full stop*, only a breaking off of the text, which is called "Sentence." The only development in "Sentence" is that what looks to be Robbe-Grillet at work in the first lines turns gradually (temporarily) into something like Raymond Roussel. Not quite zero degree: at the frozen pole no sentence ever thinks or even "thinks."

Sadness (1972). More stories. More graphics. The pictures are getting better all the time. There is a good one of a volcano in eruption. The prose . . . as before. Simple sentences. "Any writer in the country can write a beautiful sentence," Barthelme has declared. But he does not want to be like any writer in the country: "I'm very interested in awkwardness: sentences that are awkward in a particular way." What is "beauty," one wonders, suspicious of words. What, for that matter, is "awkward" or "particular"? But we do know all about sentences and occasionally among the various tributes to European modern masters (in translation), certain themes (or words) reoccur. One is the father. Of that more later. Also, drunkenness. In fact, alcohol runs like a torrent through most of the writers I have been reading. From Barthelme to Pynchon there is a sense of booziness, nausea, hangover.

> I say: "I'm forty. I have bad eyes. An enlarged liver."
> "That's the alcohol," he says.
> "Yes," I say.
> "You're very much like your father, there."

The only pages to hold me were autobiographical. Early dust-jacket pictures of Barthelme show an amiable-looking young man upon whose full upper lip there is a slight shadow at the beginning of the lip's bow. The dust jacket of *Sadness* shows a bearded man with what appears to be a harelip. Barthelme explains that he has had an operation for a "basal-cell malignancy" on his upper lip. True graphics, ultimately, are not old drawings of volcanoes or of perspective but of the author's actual face on the various dust jackets, aging in a definitely serial way with, in Barthelme's case, the drama of an operation thrown in, very much in the R and R tradition, and interesting for the reader though no doubt traumatizing for the author.

Guilty Pleasures (1974). This writer cannot stop making sentences. I have stopped reading a lot of them. I feel guilty. It is not pleasurable to feel guilty about not reading every one of those sentences. I do like the pictures more and more. In this volume there are more than thirty pictures. In the prose I spotted *hommages* to Calvino, Borges, early Ionesco. I am now saving myself for *The Dead Father*, the big one, as they say on Publisher's Row, the first big novel, long awaited, even heralded.

In *The Pleasure of the Text*, published just before *The Dead Father* (and by the same American publisher), Roland Barthes observes: "Death of the Father would deprive literature of many of its pleasures. If there is no longer a Father, why tell stories? Doesn't every narrative lead back to Oedipus? Isn't storytelling always a way of searching for one's origin. . . . As fiction, Oedipus was at least good for something: to make good novels. . . ." Apparently Barthelme took the hint. In *The Dead Father* a number of people are lugging about the huge remains of something called The Dead Father. Only this monster is not very dead because he talks quite a bit. The people want to bury him but he is not all that eager to be buried. Barthelme ends his book by deliberately burying the eponymous hero and, perhaps, fiction too. All of this is very ambitious.

Barthelme's narrative is reasonably sequential if lacking in urgency. There is, as always, Beckett: "said Julie, let us proceed. / They proceeded." Within the book is A Manual for Sons, written in a splendid run-on style quite at odds with the most imitated imitable writing that surrounds this unexpectedly fine burst of good writing on the nature of fathers, sons. For the record: there are no quotation marks. And no pictures. There is one diagram of a *placement*; but it is not much fun.

I am not sure that my progress through all these dull little sentences has been entirely justified by A Manual for Sons, but there is no doubt that beneath the mannerisms, the infantile chic, the ill-digested culture of an alien world, Barthelme does have a talent for, of all things in this era, writing. Shall I quote an example? I think not. Meanwhile, Barthelme himself says, "I have trouble reading, in these days. I would rather drink, talk or listen to music. . . . I now listen to rock constantly." Yes.

I can only assume that Grace Paley is a friend of Mr. Barthelme because she does not belong to what a certain Hack of Academe named Harry T. Moore likes, mistakenly, to call a *galère*. Paley is a plain short-story writer of the R and R school, and I got a good deal of pleasure from reading her two collections of short stories, *The Little Disturbances of Man* (with the nice subtitle: "Stories of Men and Women at Love") and *Enormous Changes at the Last Minute*. She works from something very like life . . . I mean "life"; she has an extraordinary ear for the way people sound. She do the ethnics in different voices. Although she tends, at times, to the plain-Jane or see-Jane-run kind of writing, her prose has such a natural energy that one is not distracted, a sign of good writing if not of a blissful text (she is close to boiling, in any case, and will never freeze).

With William Gass we are back in R and D country. I read Gass's first novel *Omensetter's Luck* in 1966 and found much to admire in it. Gass's essays are often eerily good. At his best, he can inhabit a subject in a way that no other critic now writing can do (see, in particular, his commentaries on Gertrude Stein). He seems not to have enjoyed being interviewed in Bellamy's collection, and his tone is unusually truculent (of New York quality lit. types: "I snub them"). It should be noted that of the writers admired by Barthelme only William Gass is an intellectual in the usual sense (I put no quotes around the words "intellectual," "usual," or "sense"). Gass's mind is not only first-rate but far too complex to settle for the easy effects of, say, Mr. Barthelme. But then: "As a student of philosophy, I've put in a great deal of time on the nature of language and belong, rather vaguely, to a school of linguistic philosophy which is extremely skeptical about the nature of language itself."

Gass has a complaint about Barth, Borges, and Beckett: "occasionally their fictions, conceived as establishing a metaphorical relationship between the reader and the world they are creating, leave the reader too passive." This is fair comment, though open to the question: just what is passive in this context? Ought the reader to be dancing about the room? blood pressure elevated? adrenaline flowing as he and the text battle one another? But then Gass shifts ground in his next sentence but one: "I have little patience with the 'creative reader.'" In other words the ideal reader is active but not creative. Quotation marks are now in order to protect these adjectives from becoming meaningless.

"I rarely read fiction and generally don't enjoy it." Gass is as one with the other R and D writers of fiction today. Although they do not read with any pleasure what anyone else is doing, they would like, naturally, to be themselves read with pleasure . . . by whom? Perhaps a college of writerly texts, grave as cardinals.

Gass himself is a curious case. Essentially, he is a traditional prose writer, capable of all sorts of virtuoso effects on the inner ear as well as on the reading eye. Yet he appears to have fallen victim to the R and D mentality. Speaking of a work in progress, "I hope that it will be really original in form and in effect, although mere originality is not what I'm after." This is worthy of Jimmy Carter.

> *Fiction has traditionally and characteristically borrowed its form from let-ters, journals, diaries, autobiographies, histories, travelogues, news stories, backyard gossip, etc. It has simply pretended to be one or other of them. The history of fiction is in part a record of the efforts of its authors to create for fiction in its own forms. Poetry has its own. It didn't borrow the ode from somebody. Now the novel is imagined news, imagined psychological or soci-ological case studies, imagined history . . . feigned, I should say, not imag-ined. As Rilke shattered the journal form with* Malte, *and Joyce created his own for* Ulysses *and* Finnegan, *I should like to create mine.*

There seems to me to be a good deal wrong not only logically but aes-thetically and historically with this analysis. First, poetry has never *had* its form. The origins of the ode are ancient but it was once created if not by a single ambitious schoolteacher, then by a number of poets roving like Terence's rose down the centuries. Certainly in this century poetry has gone off in as many directions as the novel, an art form whose tute-lary deity is Proteus. The more like something else the novel is, the more like its true self it is. And since we do not *have* it, we can go on making it. Finally, whether or not a work of art is feigned or imagined is irrele-vant if the art is good.

Like many good books, *Omensetter's Luck* is not easy to describe. What one comes away with is the agreeable memory of a flow of language that ranges from demotic Midwest ("I just up and screams at him—thump thump thump, he'd been going, die die die—I yell . . .") to incan-tatory ("For knowledge, for good and evil, would Eve have set her will against her Father's? Ah, Horatio . . ."). In his interview the author tells

us that he knows nothing of the setting (an Ohio river town); that everything is made up. He also confesses, "I haven't the dramatic imagination
at all. Even my characters tend to turn away from one another and talk
to the void. This, along with my inability to narrate, is my most serious
defect (I think) as a writer and incidentally as a person."

The stories in *In the Heart of the Heart of the Country* seem to me to
be more adventurous and often more successful than the novel. "The
Pedersen Kid" is beautiful work. In a curious way the look of those short
sentences on pages uncluttered with quotation marks gives the text a visual purity and coldness that perfectly complements the subject of the
story, and compels the reader to know the icy winter at the country's
heart. In most of these stories the prevailing image is winter.

> *Billy closes his door and carries coal or wood to his fire and closes his eyes,*
> *and there's simply no way of knowing how lonely and empty he is or whether*
> *he's as vacant and barren and loveless as the rest of us are—here in the heart*
> *of the country.*

At actual zero degree, Gass, perversely, blazes with energy.

The title story is the most interesting of the collection. Despite a sign
or two that the French virus may have struck: "as I write this page, it is
eleven days since I have seen the sun," the whole of the story (told in
fragments) is a satisfying description of the world the narrator finds himself in, and he makes art of the quotidian:

> *My window is a grave, and all that lies within it's dead. No snow is falling.*
> *There's no haze. It's not still, not silent. Its images are not an animal that*
> *waits, for movement is no demonstration.*

What is art?

Art is energy shaped by intelligence. The energy that the text of
Madame Bovary generates for the right reader is equal to that which sus-
tains the consumer of *Rebecca*. The ordering intelligence of each writer
is, of course, different in kind and intention. Gass's problem as an artist
is not so much his inability to come up with some brand-new Henry
Ford–type invention that will prove to be a breakthrough in world fiction

(this is never going to happen) as what he calls his weak point—a lack of dramatic gift—which is nothing more than low or rather intermittent energy. He can write a dozen passages in which the words pile up without effect. Then, suddenly, the current, as it were, turns on again and the text comes to beautiful life (in a manner of speaking of course . . . who does not like a living novel? particularly one that is literate).

I have seen the sea slack, life bubble through a body without a trace, its spheres impervious as soda's.

For a dozen years I have been trying to read *The Sot-Weed Factor*. I have never entirely completed this astonishingly dull book but I have read most of John Barth's published work and I feel that I have done him, I hope, justice. There is a black cloth on my head as I write.

First, it should be noted that Barth, like Gass, is a professional schoolteacher. He is a professor of English *and* Creative Writing. He is extremely knowledgeable about what is going on in R and D land and he is certainly eager to make his contribution. Interviewed, Barth notes "the inescapable fact that literature—because it's made of the common stuff of language—seems more refractory to change in general than the other arts." He makes the obligatory reference to the music of John Cage. Then he adds, sensibly, that "the permanent changes in fiction from generation to generation more often have been, and are more likely to be, modifications of sensibility and attitude rather than dramatic innovations in form and technique."

Barth mentions his own favorite writers. Apparently "Borges, Beckett and Nabokov, among the living grand masters (and writers like Italo Calvino, Robbe-Grillet, John Hawkes, William Gass, Donald Barthelme)— *have* experimented with form and technique and even with the *means* of fiction, working with graphics and tapes and things. . . ." What these writers have in common (excepting Robbe-Grillet) "is a more or less fantastical, or as Borges would say, 'irrealist,' view of reality. . . ." Barth thinks—hopes— that this sort of writing will characterize the Seventies.

What is "irrealism"? Something that cannot be realized. This is a curious goal for a writer though it is by no means an unfamiliar terminus for many an ambitious work. Further, Barth believes that realism is "a kind of aberration in the history of literature." I am not exactly sure what he means by realism. After all, the Greek myths that he likes to play around with were once a "reality" to those who used them as stuff for narrative. But then Barth broods. "Perhaps we should *accept* the fact that writing and reading are essentially linear activities and devote our attention as writers to those aspects of experience that can best be rendered linearly—with words that go left to right across the page; subjects, verbs and objects; punctuation!" He ends with the rather plaintive, "The trick, I guess, in any of the arts at this hour of the world, is to have it both ways." How true!

The Floating Opera (1956) and *The End of the Road* (1958) are two novels of a kind and that kind is strictly R and R, and fairly superior R and R at that. The author tells us that they were written in his twenty-fourth year, and a good year it was for him. Publishers meddled with the ending of the first novel. He has since revised the book and that is the version I read. It is written in first-person demotic (Eastern Shore of Maryland, Barth's place of origin). The style is garrulous but not unattractive. "I was just thirty-seven then, and as was my practice, I greeted the new day with a slug of Sherbrook from the quart on my window sill. I've a quart sitting there now, but it's not the same one. . . ."

There is a tendency to put too much in, recalling Barthes's "The Prattle of Meaning" (S/Z): certain storytellers

> *impose a dense plenitude of meaning or, if one prefers, a certain redundancy, a kind of semantic prattle typical of the archaic—or infantile—era of modern discourse, marked by the excessive fear of failing to communicate meaning (its basis); while, in reaction, in our latest—or "new" novels,*

the action or event is set forth "without accompanying it with its signification."

Certainly Barth began as an old-fashioned writer who wanted us to know all about the adulteries, money-hassling, and boozing on what sounded like a very real Eastern Shore of a very real Maryland, as lacking in bears as the seacoast of Illyria: "Charley was Charley Parks, an attorney whose office was next door to ours. He was an old friend and poker partner of mine, and currently we were on opposite sides in a complicated litigation. . . ."

In 1960 Barth published *The Sot-Weed Factor*. The paperback edition is adorned with the following quotation from *The New York Times Book Review*: "Outrageously funny, villainously slanderous. . . . The book is a brass-knuckled satire of humanity at large. . . ." I am usually quick, even eager, to respond to the outrageously funny, the villainously slanderous . . . in short, to *The New York Times* itself. But as I read on and on, I could not so much as summon up a smile at the lazy jokes and the horrendous pastiche of what Barth takes to be eighteenth-century English (" ' 'Tis not that which distresses me; 'tis Andrew's notion that I had vicious designs on the girl. 'Sheart, if anything be improbable, 'tis . . .' "). I stopped at page 412 with 407 pages yet to go. The sentences would not stop unfurling; as Peter Handke puts it in *Kaspar*: "Every sentence helps you along: you get over every object with a sentence: a sentence helps you get over an object when you can't really get over it, so that you really get over it," etc.

To read Barth on the subject of his own work and then to read the work itself is a puzzling business. He talks a good deal of sense. He is obviously intelligent. Yet he tells us that when he turned from the R and R of his first two novels to the megalo-R and R of *The Sot-Weed Factor*, he moved from "a merely comic mode to a variety of farce, which frees your hands even more than comedy does." Certainly there are comic aspects to the first two books. But the ponderous jocosity of the third book is neither farce nor satire nor much of anything except English-teacher-writing at a pretty low level. I can only assume that the book's admirers are as ignorant of the eighteenth century as the author (or, to be fair, the author's imagination) and that neither author nor admiring reader has a sense of humor, a fact duly noted about Americans in general—and their serious ponderous novelists in particular—by many peoples in other lands. It still takes a lot of civilization gone slightly high to make a wit.

Giles Goat-Boy arrived on the scene in 1966. Another 800 pages of ambitious schoolteacher-writing: a book to be taught rather than read. I shall not try to encapsulate it here, other than to say that the central metaphor is the universe is the university is the universe. I suspect that this will prove to be one of the essential American university novels and to dismiss it is to dismiss those departments of English that have made such a book possible. The writing is more than usually clumsy. A verse play has been included. "*Agnora:* for Pete's sake, simmer down, boys. Don't you think / I've been a dean's wife long enough to stink / my public image up?"

Barth thinks that the word "human" is a noun; he also thinks that Giles is pronounced with a hard "g" as in "guile" instead of a soft "g" as in "giant." But then the unlearned learned teachers of English are the new barbarians, serenely restoring the Dark Ages.

By 1968 Barth was responding to the French New Novel. *Lost in the Funhouse* is the result. A collection (or, as he calls it, a "series") of "Fiction for Print, Tape, Live Voice." Barth is not about to miss a trick now that he has moved into R and D country. The first of the series, "Night-Sea Journey," should—or could—be on tape. This is the first-person narrative of a sperm heading, it would appear, toward an ovum, though some of its eschatological musings suggest that a blow-job may be in progress. Woody Allen has dealt more rigorously with this theme.

The "story" "Lost in the Funhouse" is most writerly and self-conscious; it chats with the author who chats with it and with us. "Description of physical appearance and mannerisms is one of several standard methods of characterization used by writers of fiction." Thus Barth distances the reader from the text. A boy goes to the funhouse and . . . "The more closely an author identifies with the narrator, literally or metaphorically, the less advisable it is, as a rule, to use the first-person narrative viewpoint." Some of this schoolteacherly commentary is amusing. But the ultimate effect is one of an ambitious but somewhat uneasy writer out to do something brand-new in a territory already inhabited by, among other texts that can read and write, the sinister *Locus Solus*, the immor(t)al *Tlooth* and the dexterous *A Nest of Ninnies*.

It is seldom wise for a born R and R writer to make himself over into an R and D writer unless he has something truly formidable and new to show us. Barth just has books. And sentences. And a fairly clear idea of just how far up the creek he is without a paddle. "I believe literature's not likely ever to manage abstraction successfully, like sculpture for example, is that a fact, what a time to bring up that subject. . . ." What a time! And what is the subject, Alice? Incidentally, Barth always uses quotation marks and "he saids."

In 1972 Barth published three long stories in a volume called *Chimera*. Two of the stories are based on Greek myths, for are they not, as admirers of Jung declare, part of the racial memory, the common stock of all our dreams and narratives? Well, no, they are not. The Greek myths are just barely relevant to those Mediterranean people who still live in a landscape where the *anima* of a lost world has not yet been entirely covered with cement. The myths are useful but not essential to those brought up on the classics, the generation to which Dr. Jung (and T. S. Eliot) belonged; and of course they are necessary to anyone who would like to understand those works of literature in which myth plays a part. Otherwise they are of no real use to Americans born in this century. For us Oedipus is not the doomed king of Thebes but Dr. Freud's depressing protagonist, who bears no relation at all to the numinous figure that Sophocles and Euripides portrayed. Thebes is another country, where we may not dwell.

Joyce's *Ulysses* is often regarded as a successful attempt to use Greek myth to shore up a contemporary narrative. But it is plain to most non-creative readers that the myth does not work at all in Joyce's creation and were it not for his glorious blarney and fine naturalistic gifts, the book's classical structure alone could not have supported the novel. Since Joyce, alas, the incorporation of Greek myth into modern narrative has been irresistible to those who have difficulty composing narrative, and no Greek. These ambitious writers simply want to give unearned resonance to their tales of adultery on the Eastern Shore of Maryland, of misbehavior in faculty rooms, of massive occlusions in the heart of the country. But the results are deeply irritating to those who have some sense of the classical world and puzzling, I would think, to those taking English courses where the novel is supposed to have started with Richardson.

Barth has browsed through Robert Graves's *The Greek Myths* (and gives due acknowledgment to that brilliantly eccentric custodian of the old world). At random, I would guess, Barth selected the story of Bellerophon (tamer of Pegasus) for modernizing; also, more to his point, Perseus, the slayer of Medusa. The first story is taken from Arabian mythology, a narrative called "Dunyazadiad," as told by the "kid sister of Scheherazade." It should also be noted that two of the stories in *Lost in the Funhouse* were wacky versions of certain well-known high jinks in old Mycenae.

The kid sister of Scheherazade is a gabby co-ed who mentions with awe the academic gifts of her sister "Sherry," "an undergraduate arts-and-sciences major at Banu Sasan University. Besides being Homecoming Queen, valedictorian-elect, and a four-letter varsity athlete. . . . Every graduate department in the East was after her with fellowships." This unbearable cuteness has a sinister side. Since Barth's experience of literature and the world is entirely that of a schoolteacher, he appears to take it for granted that the prevailing metaphor for his own life (and why not all life itself?) is the university. There is also an underlying acceptance of the fact that since no one is ever going to read him except undergraduates in American universities, he had better take into account that their reading skills are somewhat underdeveloped, their knowledge of the way society works vague, and their culture thin.

Barth's *Hamlet* would no doubt begin, "Well, I guess flunking out of Rutgers is no big deal when I got this family up in Wilmington where we make these plastics that, like, kill people but I'm changing all that or I was going to up until my mother went and married this asshole uncle of mine. . . ." Perhaps this is the only way to get the classics into young television-shrunk minds. But the exercise debases both classics and young minds. Of course Barth is no fool. He is often quick to jump in and forestall criticism. Sherry's kid sister remarks: "currently, however, the only readers of artful fiction were critics, other writers, and unwilling students who, left to themselves, preferred music and pictures to words."

Sherry is helped in her literary efforts to think up 1001 stories by a genie who is, like so many of Barth's male protagonists, a *thoroughly good person*: his policy "was to share beds with no woman who did not reciprocate his feelings." For a United Statesman (posing as an Arabian genie), this is true heterosexual maturity. In case we missed Barth's first testimonial to the genie's niceness, we are later told that "he was no more tempted to infidelity than to incest or pederasty." I guess this makes him about the best genie on campus. Between Genie and Sherry there is a lot of talk about the nature of fiction, which is of course the only reason for writing university fiction. There is not a glimmer of intelligence in this jaunty tale.

Barth was born and grew up a traditional cracker-barrelly sort of American writer, very much in the mainstream—a stream by no means polluted or at an end. But he chose not to continue in the vein that was most natural to him. Obviously he has read a good deal about Novel Theory. He has the standard American passion not only to be original but to be great, and this means creating one of Richard Poirier's "worlds elsewhere": an alternative imaginative structure to the mess that we have made of our portion of the Western Hemisphere. Aware of French theories about literature (but ignorant of the culture that has produced those theories), superficially acquainted with Greek myth, deeply involved in the academic life of the American university, Barth is exactly the sort of writer our departments of English were bound, sooner or later, to produce. Since he is a writer with no great gift for language either demotic or mandarin, Barth's narratives tend to lack energy; and the currently fashionable technique of stopping to take a look at the story as it is being told simply draws attention to the meagerness of what is there.

I am obliged to remark upon the sense of suffocation one experiences reading so much bad writing. As the weary eyes flick from sentence to sentence, one starts *willing* the author to be good. Either I have become shell-shocked by overexposure to the rockets' red glare and bombs bursting in air or Barth has managed a decent narrative in "Perseid." As usual, the language is jangling everyday speech: "Just then I'd've swapped Mycenae for a cold draught and a spot of shade to dip it in. . . ." The gods and demigods are straight from Thorne Smith, who ought to be regarded, in Harry T. Moore's *galère*, as the American Dante. But the story of the middle-aged Perseus and his problems of erection (and love) with a young girl seems at times authentic, even true . . . despite Barth's unremitting jocosity: " 'Were you always psychosexually weak, or is that Andromeda's doing?' "

In some ways, the writers' interviews are more revealing about the state of fiction than the books they write. The twelve writers interviewed for Joe David Bellamy's book often sound truculent; also, uneasy. For instance, John Gardner (whose *Grendel* I much admired) is very truculent, but then Mr. Barthelme is on record as not admiring him; this cannot help but hurt. Gardner is as much his own man as anyone can be who teaches school and wants to get good reviews from his fellow teachers in *The New York Times Book Review*. Yet he dares to say of *The Sot-Weed Factor*: "nothing but a big joke. It's a philosophical joke; it might even be argued that it's a philosophical advance. But it ain't like Victor Hugo." It also ain't an advance of any kind. Although Gardner is myth-minded, he is much more intuitive and authentic than the usual academic browser in Robert Graves's compendium. Gardner also knows where proto-myths are to be found: Walt Disney's work, for one.

Gardner tells us that "most writers today are academicians: they have writing or teaching jobs with universities. In the last ten years the tone of university life and of intellectuals' responses to the world have changed. During the Cold War there was a great deal of fear and cynicism on account of the Bomb." Gardner then makes the astonishing suggestion that when the other Americans (those somewhat unreal millions condemned to live off-campus) turned against the Vietnam war (after eight years of defeat), the mood changed in the universities as the academicians realized that "the people around you are all working hard to make the world better." A startling observation. In any case, the writers of University or U-novels will now become more life-affirming than they were in the sad Sixties; "notable exceptions are writers who very carefully stay out of the mainstream and therefore can't be influenced by the general feeling of people around them."

At first I thought Gardner was joking. But I was wrong. He really believes that the mainstream of the world is the American university and that a writer outside this warm and social-meliorizing ambience will fall prey to old-fashioned cynicism and hardness of heart. For instance, "Pynchon stays out of universities. He doesn't know what chemists and physicists are doing; he knows only the pedantry of chemistry and physics. When good chemists and physicists talk about, say, the possibility of extraterrestrial life, they agree that for life to be evolved beyond our stage, creators on other planets must have reached decisions we now face." Removed from the academic mainstream and its extraterrestrial connections, Pynchon's *Gravity's Rainbow* is just an apocalyptic "whine."

Fortunately, Gardner's imagination is fabulous; otherwise, he would be fully exposed in his work as being not only *not* in the mainstream of

American society but perfectly irrelevant in his academic *cul de sac*. Yet if he is right that most contemporary writers are also teaching school and listening in on warm-hearted life-enhancing physicists and chemists as they talk of their peers on other planets, then literature has indeed had its day and there will be no more books except those that teachers write to teach.

Although Barthelme has mentioned Pynchon as one of the writers he admires, neither Gass nor Barth refers to him and Gardner thinks him a "whiner" because he no longer spawns in the mainstream of Academe. I daresay that it will come as news to these relatively young writers that American literature, such as it is, has never been the work of school-teachers. Admittedly, each year it is harder and harder for a writer to make a living from writing, and many writers must find the temptation to teach overwhelming. Nevertheless, those of us who emerged in the Forties (Roosevelt's children) regarded the university (as did our predecessors) as a kind of skid row far worse than a seven-year writer's contract at Columbia (the studio, not the university). Except for Saul Bellow, I can think of no important novelist who has taught on a regular basis throughout a career.

I find it admirable that of the nonacademics Pynchon did not follow the usual lazy course of going for tenure as did so many writers—no, "writers"—of his generation. He is thirty-nine years old and attended Cornell (took a class from former Professor V. Nabokov); he is eminently *academebile*. The fact that he has got out into the world (somewhere) is to his credit. Certainly he has not, it would seem, missed a trick; and he never whines.

Pynchon's first novel, *V.*, was published in 1963. There is some similarity to other R and D works. Cute names abound. Benny Profane, Dewey Gland, Rachel Owlglass. Booze flows through scene after scene involving members of a gang known as The Whole Sick Crew. The writing is standard American. "Kilroy was possibly the only objective onlooker in Valletta that night. Common legend had it he'd been born in the U.S. right before the war, on a fence or latrine wall." Above this passage is a reproduction of the classic Kilroy sketch; below this passage there is a broken-line Kilroy. These are the only graphics in a long book that also contains the usual quotation marks and "he saids." All in all, a naturalistic rendering of an essentially surrealist or perhaps irrealist subject, depending on one's apprehension of the work.

Benny Profane is described as "a schlemihl and human yo-yo." He is a former sailor. On Christmas Eve 1955 he is in Norfolk, Virginia. He goes into a bar, "his old tin can's tavern on East Main Street." People with funny names sing songs at each other (lyrics provided in full by the author) and everyone drinks a lot. There is vomiting. Scene with a girl: "What sort of Catholic was she? Profane, who was only half Catholic (mother Jewish), whose morality was fragmentary (being derived from experience and not much of it). . . ." Profane is "girl-shy" and fat. " 'If I was God . . .' " begins a fantasy. Definitely a clue to the state of mind of the creator of the three books I have been reading.

A shift from Profane to "Young Stencil, the world adventurer" and the mystery woman V. Elliptical conversation (1946) between a margravine and Stencil (whose father Sidney was in the British foreign office; he died in Malta "while investigating the June Disturbances"). They sit on a terrace overlooking the Mediterranean. "Perhaps they may have felt like the last two gods." Reference to an entry in father's journal, " 'There is more behind and inside V. than any of us had suspected. Not who, but what: what is she.' " Stencil pursues the idea of V. A quest: "in the tradition of *The Golden Bough* or *The White Goddess*."

From various references to Henry Adams and to physics in Pynchon's work, I take it that he has been influenced by Henry Adams's theory of history as set forth in *The Education of Henry Adams* and in the posthumously published "The Rule of Phase Applied to History." For Adams, a given human society in time was an organism like any other in the universe and he favored Clausius's speculation that "the entropy of the universe tends to a maximum" (an early Pynchon short story is called "Entropy").

Maximum entropy is that state at which no heat/energy enters or leaves a given system. But nothing known is constant. The Second Law of Thermodynamics appears to be absolute: everything in time loses energy to something else and, finally, drops to zero (centigrade) and dies or, perhaps, ceases to be matter as it was and becomes anti-matter. Question: to anti-matter are we anti-anti-matter or no matter at all?

I have little competence in the other of Lord Snow's celebrated two cultures. Like so many other writers I flunked physics. But I know my Adams and I can grasp general principles (without understanding how they have been arrived at); in any case, to make literature, a small amount of theory is enough to provide commanding metaphors. Pynchon's use of physics is exhilarating and as an artist he appears to be gaining more energy than he is losing. Unlike the zero writers, he is usually at the boil. From Adams he has not only appropriated the image of history as Dynamo but the attractive image of the Virgin. Now armed with these concepts he embarks in *V.* on a quest, a classic form of narrative, and the result is mixed, to say the least.

To my ear, the prose is pretty bad, full of all the rattle and buzz that were in the air when the author was growing up, an era in which only the television commercial was demonically acquiring energy, leaked to it by a declining Western civilization. Happily, Pynchon is unaffected by the French disease, except for one passage: "Let me describe the room. The room measures 17 by 11½ feet by 7 feet. The walls are lathe and plaster. . . . The room is oriented so that its diagonals fall NNE/SSW, and NW/SE." As another ex-seaman, I appreciate Pynchon's ability to box the compass, something no French ice-cream vendor could ever do. With this satisfying send-up, Pynchon abandons the New Novel for his own worlds and anti-worlds.

The quest for V. (the Virgin? or nothing much?) takes Stencil to Valletta, capital of Malta, a matriarchal island, we are told, where manhood must identify itself with the massive rock. There are clues. False scents. Faust is on the scene. And Profane is also in Malta. The prose is very close to that of the comic books of the Fifties:

"Thirteen of us rule the world in secret."

"Yes, yes. Stencil went out of his way to bring Profane here. He should have been more careful; he wasn't. Is it really his own extermination he's after?"

Maijstral turned smiling to him. Gestured behind his back at the ramparts of Valletta. "Ask her," he whispered. "Ask the rock."

Energy nicely maintained; controlling intelligence uneven.

With *The Crying of Lot 49* (1966) Pynchon returns to the quest, to conspiracy. Cute names like Genghis Cohen, an ancient Hollywood joke. Bad grammar: "San Narcisco lay further south," "some whirlwind rotating too slow for her heated skin." A lot of booze. Homophobia. Mysteries. It would appear that most of the courses Pynchon took at Cornell are being used: first-year physics, psychology, Jacobean tragedy—but then his art is no doubt derived "from experience and not much of that."

This time the grail is an alternative postal service. Haunting the narrative is the noble house of Thurn and Taxis (the wife of a descendant was a literary agent in the United States: known to Pynchon? Also, Rilke's patroness was a princess of that house). Jokes: " 'I was in the little boys' room,' he said. 'The men's room was full.' " There are numerous images of paranoia, the lurking "they" who dominate the phantom postal service of the Tristero (sometimes spelled Trystero), a mirror-alternative in earlier times to the Thurn and Taxis postal monopoly. "While the Pony Express is defying deserts, savages and sidewinders, Tristero's giving its employees crash courses in Siouan and Athapascan dialects. Disguised as Indians their messengers mosey westward. Reach the coast every time, zero attrition rate, not a scratch on them. The entire emphasis now toward silence, impersonation, opposition masquerading as allegiance.' " Well, Joyce also chose exile, cunning, silence, but eschewed allegiance's mask. Lot 49 has been cried. Who will bid?

Gravity's Rainbow (1973) contains close to 900 densely printed pages. For a year I have been reading in and at the text. Naturally, I am impressed that a clear-cut majority of the departments of English throughout North America believe this to be the perfect teachers' novel. I am sure that they are right. Certainly no young writer's book has been so praised since Colin Wilson's *The Outsider*.

The first section of *Gravity's Rainbow* is called "Beyond the Zero." Plainly a challenge not only to *l'écriture blanche* but to proud entropy itself. Pynchon has now aimed himself at anti-matter, at what takes place beyond, beneath the zero of freezing, and death. This is superbly ambitious and throughout the text energy hums like a . . . well, dynamo.

The narrative begins during the Second War, in London. Although Pynchon works hard for verisimilitude and fills his pages with period jabber, anachronisms occasionally jar (there were no "Skinnerites" in that happy time of mass death). The controlling image is that of the V-2, a guided missile developed by the Germans and used toward the end of the war (has Pynchon finally found V.? and is she a bomb?). There is an interesting epigraph from Werner von Braun: "Nature does not know extinction; all it knows is transformation." Braun believes "in the continuity of our spiritual existence after death." So much then for zero degree. This quasi-Hindu sentiment is beguiling and comforting and, no doubt, as concerns matter, true: in time or phases, energy is always lost but matter continues in new arrangements. Personally, I find it somber indeed to think that individual personality goes on and on beyond zero, time. But I am in a minority: this generation of Americans is god-hungry and craves reassurance of personal immortality. If Pynchon can provide it, he will be as a god—rather his intention, I would guess.

It is curious to read a work that excites the imagination but disturbs the aesthetic sense. A British critic no longer in fashion recently made the entirely unfashionable observation that prose has everywhere declined in quality as a result of mass education. To compare Pynchon with Joyce, say, is to compare a kindergartener to a graduate student (the permanent majority of the culturally inadequate will promptly respond that the kindergartener *sees* more clearly than the graduate student and that his incompetence with language is a sign of innocence not ignorance and hence grace). Pynchon's prose rattles on and on, broken by occasional lengthy songs every bit as bad, lyrically, as those of Bob Dylan.

> *Light-up, and-shine, you—in-candescent Bulb Ba-bies!*
> *Looks-like ya got ra-bies*
> *Just lay there foamin' and a-screamin' like a buncha little demons,*
> *I'm deliv'rin' unto you a king-dom of roa-ches. . . .*

England. Germany. Past. Present. War. Science. Telltale images of approaching . . . deity? Two characters with hangovers "are wasted gods urging on a tardy glacier." Of sandbags at a door, "provisional pyramids erected to gratify curious gods' offspring." And "slicks of nighttime vomit, pale yellow, clear as the fluids of gods." Under deity, sex is central to this work of transformation. A character's erections achieve a mysterious symbiosis with the V-2s. A sadist abuses a young man and woman. "Every true god must be both organizer and destroyer." A character declaims:

" 'If only S and M could be established universally, at the family level, the state would wither away.' " This is a nice joke (although I thought S and M was already universal at the family level). " 'Submit, Gottfried. Give it all up. See where she takes you. Think of the first time I fucked you. . . . Your little rosebud bloomed.' " Hard to believe that it is close to a decade since that pretty moss tea-rose was first forced, as it were, in my green-house.

Eventually, the text exhausts patience and energy. In fact, I suspect that the energy expended in reading *Gravity's Rainbow* is, for anyone, rather greater than that expended by Pynchon in the actual writing. This is entropy with a vengeance. The writer's text is ablaze with the heat/energy that his readers have lost to him. Yet the result of this exchange is neither a readerly nor a writerly text but an uneasy combination of both. Energy and intelligence are not in balance, and the writer fails in his ambition to be a god of creation. Yet his ambition and his failure are very much in the cranky, solipsistic American vein, and though I doubt if anyone will ever want to read all of this book, it will certainly be taught for a very long (delta) time: "approaching zero, eternally approaching, the slices of time growing thinner and thinner, a succession of rooms each with walls more silver, transparent, as the pure light of the zero comes nearer. . . ." Everything is running down. We shall freeze. Then what? A film by Stanley Kubrick?

Richard Poirier is more satisfied than I with Pynchon's latest work. For one thing, he is awed by the use of science. Approvingly, he quotes Wordsworth's hope that the poet would one day "be ready to follow the steps of the Man of science, not only in those general indirect effects, but he will be at his side, carrying sensation into the midst of science itself." Pynchon would appear to fulfill Wordsworth's reverie. He is as immersed in contemporary physics and cybernetics as Henry Adams was in the scientific theories of *his* day. But the scientific aspects of Pynchon's work will eventually become as out-of-date as those of Henry Adams. Science changes: one day we are monists, the next day pluralists. Proofs are always being disproven by other proofs. At the end, there are only words and their arrangement.

Poirier compares Pynchon to the Faulkner of *Absalom, Absalom* and finds both likeness and a significant difference, for "this genius of our day is shaped by thermodynamics and the media, by Captain Marvel rather than by Colonel Sartoris." This is no doubt a true description, but is the result as good? or good? What I find to be tedious and random in Pynchon's list-making, Poirier sees as so many

> *Dreiserian catalogues of the waste materials of our world that only by remaining resolutely on the periphery, without ever intruding himself into the plotting that emanates from his material, only then can he see what most humanly matters.*

"Matter," a verb. "Matter," a noun. The matter of fiction has been expanded by Pynchon's ascent from zero degree (writing as well as centigrade); nevertheless, entropy is sovereign. That which gains energy/heat does so at the expense of that which is losing energy/heat to it. At the end there is only the cold and no sublunary creatures will ever know what songs the quasars sing in their dark pits of anti-matter.

I cannot help but feel a certain depression after reading Mr. Barthelme's chosen writers. I realize that language changes from generation to generation. But it does not, necessarily, improve. The meager rattling prose of all these writers, excepting Gass, depresses me. Beautiful sentences are not easy to write, despite Mr. Barthelme's demur. Since beauty is relative only to intention, there are doubtless those who find beauty in the pages of books where I find "a flocculent appearance, something opaque, creamy and curdled, something powerless ever to achieve the triumphant smoothness of Nature. But what best reveals it for what it is is the sound it gives, at once hollow and flat; its noise is its undoing, as are its colors, for it seems capable of retaining only the most chemical-looking ones. Of yellow, red and green, it keeps only the aggressive quality. . . ." What is "it"? The work of the new American formalists? No, "it" is plastic, as described by Barthes in *Mythologies*.

The division between what I have elsewhere called the Public-novel and the University-novel is now too great to be bridged by any but the occasional writer who is able to appeal, first to one side, then to the other, fulfilling the expectations (more or less) of each. I find it hard to take seriously the novel that is written to be taught, nor can I see how the American university can provide a base for the making of "new" writing when the American university is, at best, culturally and intellectually conservative and, at worst, reactionary.

Academics tell me that I am wrong. They assure me that if it were not for them, the young would never read the Public-novels of even the recent past (Faulkner, Fitzgerald). If this is true, then I would prefer for these works decently to die rather than to become teaching-tools, artifacts stinking of formaldehyde in a classroom (original annotated text with six essays by the author and eight critical articles examining the parameters of the author's vision). But the academic bureaucracy, unlike the novel, will not wither away, and the future is dark for literature. Certainly the young in general are not going to take up reading when they have such easy alternatives as television, movies, rock. The occasional student who might have an interest in reading will not survive a course in English, unless of course he himself intends to become an academic bureaucrat.

As for Thomas Pynchon, one can applaud his deliberate ascent from Academe into that dangerous rainbow sky in which he will make his parabola and fall as gravity pulls him back to where he started, to Academe, to zero, or to (my first graphic, ever) O.

The New York Review of Books
July 15, 1974

CALVINO'S NOVELS

Between the end of the Second World War in 1945 and the beginning of the Korean War in 1950, there was a burst of creative activity throughout the American empire as well as in our client states of Western Europe. From Auden's *Age of Anxiety* to Carson McCuller's *Reflections in a Golden Eye* to Paul Bowles's *The Sheltering Sky* to Tennessee Williams's *A Streetcar Named Desire* to Tudor's ballets and to Bernstein's enthusiasms, it was an exciting time. The cold war was no more than a nip in the air while the junior senator from Wisconsin was just another genial pol with a drinking problem and an eye for the boys. In that happy time the young American writer was able to reel in triumph through the old cities of Europe—the exchange rate entirely in his favor.

Twenty-six years ago this spring I arrived in Rome. First impressions: Acid-yellow forsythia on the Janiculum. Purple wisteria in the Forum. Chunks of goat on a plate in a trattoria. Samuel Barber at the American Academy, talking Italian accurately. Harold Acton politely deploring our barbarous presence in *his* Europe. Frederic Prokosch at Doney's, eating cakes. Streets empty of cars. Had there been traffic of any kind, Tennessee Williams would have been planted long since in the Protestant cemetery, for he drove a jeep although "I am practically *blind* in one eye," he would say proudly, going through the occasional red light, treating sidewalk and street as one.

I visited George Santayana in his hospital cell at the Convent of the Blue Nuns. He wore a dressing gown; Lord Byron collar open at the withered neck; faded mauve waistcoat. He was genial; made a virtue of his deafness. "*I* will talk. *You* will listen." A sly smile; black glittering eyes—he looked exactly like my grandmother gone dramatically bald.

"Have you met my young *new* friend Robert Lowell?" I said no. "He will have a difficult life. To be a Lowell. From Boston. A Catholic *convert*." The black eyes shone with a lovely malice. "And a poet, too! Oh, dear. Now tell me who is a Mr. Edmund Wilson? He came to see me. I think that he must be very important. In fact, I believe he *said* that he was very important. You sent me a book, he said. I said that I had not. He said but you did, and got very angry. I tried to tell him that I do not *send* books. But later I recalled that when we were rescued by the American army—and how *glad* we were to see you!" A fond glance at me (one still wore khakis, frayed army belt). "A major, a very forceful man, came to see me, with a number of my books. He stood over me and *made* me sign them . . . for this one, for that one. I was terrified and did as he requested. Perhaps one of those books was for Mr. Wilson."

The only books in Santayana's cell were his own—and a set of Toynbee's recently published history, which he was reading characteristically; that is, he first broke (or foxed) the spine of the book and undid the sections; then, as he finished reading each section, he would throw it in the wastebasket. "Some sort of preacher, I should think," he said of Toynbee. "But the footnotes are not entirely worthless."

Santayana signed a copy of *The Middle Span* for me; he wrote "from" before his name. "I almost never do that," he said. An appraising look. "You look younger than you are because your head is somewhat small in proportion to your body." That was in 1948, when the conquering Americans lived in Rome and Paris and strolled streets as yet uncrowded with automobiles or with the billion or so human beings who have since joined us.

In that far-off time, the people one met talked about novels and novelists the way they now talk of movies and directors. Young people today think that I am exaggerating. But novelists mattered then and the Italian novel, in particular, was having a fine flowering. Yet the American writers in Rome and Paris saw little of their counterparts. For one thing, the Italians were just getting around to reading Dos Passos and Steinbeck—the generation that had gone untranslated during the Fascist era. Also, few Italian writers then (or now) spoke or read English with any ease while the American writers then (though not so much now) proudly spoke no language but English.

I do remember in 1948 coming across a book by Italo Calvino. An Italian Calvin, I said to myself, fixing permanently his name in my memory. Idly, I wondered what a man called Italo Calvino would write about. I glanced at his first novel, *Il sentiero dei nidi di ragno* (1947). Something about partisans in Liguria. A fellow war novelist. No, I thought; and put it down. I did note that he was two years older than I, worked for the publisher Einaudi, lived in Turin.

During the last year, I have read Calvino straight through, starting with the book I only glanced at in 1948, now translated as *The Path to the Nest of Spiders*.

Calvino's first novel is a plainly told, exuberant sort of book. Although the writing is conventional, there is an odd intensity in the way Calvino sees things, a closeness of scrutiny much like that of William Golding. Like Golding he knows how and when to occupy entirely, with all senses functioning, landscape, state of mind, act. In *The Spire* Golding makes the flawed church so real that one smells the mortar, sees the motes of dust, fears for the ill-placed stones. Calvino does the same in the story of Pin, a boy living on the Ligurian coast of Italy, near San Remo (although Calvino was brought up in San Remo, he was actually born in Cuba, a detail given by none of his American publishers; no doubt in deference to our recent attempted conquest of that unfortunate island).

Pin lives with his sister, a prostitute. He spends his days at a low-life bar where he amuses with songs and taunts the grown-ups, a race of monsters as far as he is concerned, but he has no other companions, for "Pin is a boy who does not know how to play games, and cannot take part in the games either of children or grown-ups." Pin dreams, however, of "a friend, a real friend who understands him and whom he can understand, and then to him, and only to him, will he show the place where the spiders have their lairs."

It's on a stony little path which winds down to the torrent between earthy grassy slopes. There, in the grass, the spiders make their nests, in tunnels lined with dry grass. But the wonderful thing is that the nests have tiny doors, also made of dried grass, tiny round doors which can open and shut.

This sort of precise, quasi-scientific observation keeps Calvino from the sort of sentimentality that was prevalent in the Forties, when wise children learned compassion from a black mammy as she deep-fried chitlins and Jesus in equal parts south of the Mason-Dixon line.

Pin joins the partisans in the hills above the Ligurian coast. I have a suspicion that Calvino is dreaming all this, for he writes like a bookish, near-sighted man who has mislaid his glasses: objects held close-to are vividly described but the middle and far distances of landscape and war tend to blur. It makes no difference, however, for the dreams of a near-sighted young man at the beginning of a literary career can be more real to the reader than the busy reportage of those journalist-novelists who were so entirely there and, seeing it all, saw nothing.

Although Calvino manages to inhabit the skin of the outraged and outrageous child, his men and women are almost always shadowy. Later in his career, Calvino will eliminate men and women altogether as he re-creates the cosmos. Meanwhile, as a beginning, he is a vivid, if occasionally clumsy, writer. Two thirds of the way through the narrative he shifts the point of view from Pin to a pair of commissars who would have been more effective had he observed them from outside. Then, confusingly, he shifts again, briefly, into the mind of a traitor who is about to be shot. Finally, he returns to Pin just as the boy finds the longed-for friend, a young partisan called Cousin who takes him in hand not only literally but, presumably, for the rest of the time Pin will need to grow up. Calvino's last paragraphs are almost always jubilant—the sort of cheerful codas that only a deep pessimist about human matters could write. But then Calvino, like one of Pin's friends, Red Wolf, "belongs to the generation brought up on strip cartoons; he has taken them all seriously and life has not disproved them so far."

In 1952 Calvino published *The Cloven Viscount*, one of the three short novels he has since collected under the title *Our Ancestors*. They are engaging works, written in a style somewhat like that of T. H. White's

Arthurian novels. The narrator of *The Cloven Viscount* is, again, an orphan boy. During a war between Austria and Turkey (1716) the boy's uncle Viscount Medardo was cloven from pate to crotch by a cannonball. Saved by doctors on the battlefield, the half Viscount was sent home with one leg, one arm, one eye, half a nose, mouth, etc. En route, Calvino pays homage (ironic?) to Malaparte ("The patch of plain they were crossing was covered with horses' carcasses, some supine with hooves to the sky, others prone with muzzles dug into the earth"—a nice reprise of those dead horses in *The Skin*).

The story is cheerfully, briskly told. The half Viscount is a perfect bastard and takes pleasure in murder, fire, torture. He burns down part of his own castle, hoping to incinerate his old nurse Sebastiana; finally, he packs her off to a leper colony. He tries to poison his nephew. He never stops slashing living creatures in half. He has a thing about halfness.

> *"If only I could have every thing like this," said my uncle, lying face down on the rocks, stroking the convulsive half of an octopus, "so that everyone could escape from his obtuse and ignorant wholeness. I was whole and all things were natural and confused to me, stupid as the air; I thought I was seeing all and it was only the outside rind. If you ever become a half of yourself, and I hope you do for your own sake, my boy, you'll understand things beyond the common intelligence of brains that are whole. You'll have lost half of yourself and of the world, but the remaining half will be a thousand times deeper and more precious."*

I note that the publisher's blurb would have us believe that this is "an allegory of modern man—alienated and mutilated—this novel has profound overtones. As a parody of the Christian parables of good and evil, it is both witty and refreshing." Well, at least the book is witty and refreshing. Actually the story is less Christian than a send-up of Plato and his ideas of the whole.

In due course the other half of the Viscount hits town; this half is unbearably good and deeply boring. He, too, is given to celebrating halfness because "One understands the sorrow of every person and thing in the world at its own incompleteness. I was whole and did not understand. . . ." A charming young girl named Pamela (homage to Richardson)

is beloved by both halves of the Viscount; but she has serious reserva-
tions about each. "Doing good together is the only way to love," intones
the good half. To which the irritable girl responds, "A pity. I thought there
were other ways." When the two halves are finally united, the resulting
whole Viscount is the usual not very interesting human mixture. In a
happy ending, he marries Pamela. But the boy-narrator is not content.
"Amid all this fervor of wholeness, [I] felt myself growing sadder and
more lacking. Sometimes one who thinks himself incomplete is merely
young."

The Cloven Viscount is filled with many closely observed natural images like "The subsoil was so full of ants that a hand put down anywhere
came up all black and swarming with them." I don't know which was
written first, The Cloven Viscount (1952) or "The Argentine Ant," published in Botteghe Oscure (1952), but Calvino's nightmare of an ant-
infested world touched on in the novel becomes the subject of "The
Argentine Ant" and I fear that I must now trot out that so often misused
word "masterpiece." Or, put another way, if "The Argentine Ant" is not a
masterpiece of twentieth-century prose writing, I cannot think of anything better. Certainly it is as minatory and strange as anything by Kafka.
It is also hideously funny. In some forty pages Calvino gives us "the human condition," as the blurb writers would say, in spades. That is, the human condition today. Or the dilemma of modern man. Or the disrupted
environment. Or nature's revenge. Or an allegory of grace. Whatever . . .
But a story is, finally, what it tells and no more.

Calvino's first sentence is rather better than God's "in the beginning
was the word." God (as told to Saint John) has always had a penchant for
cloudy abstractions of the sort favored by American novelists, heavy-
weight division—unlike Calvino, who simply tells us what's what: "When
we came to settle here we did not know about the ants." No nonsense
about "here" or "we." Here is a place infested with ants and we are the nuclear family: father, mother, child. No names.

"We" have rented a house in a town "where our Uncle Augusto used
to hang out. Uncle Augusto rather liked the place, though he did say, 'You
should see the ants over there . . . they're not like the ones here, those
ants. . . .' But we paid no attention at the time." As the local landlady
Signora Mauro shows the young couple about the house they have just

rented from her, she distracts their attention from the walls with a long dissertation on the gas meter. When she has gone, the baby is put to bed and the young couple take a stroll outside. Their next-door neighbor is spraying the plants in his garden with a bellows. The ants, he explains, "as if not wanting to make it sound important."

The young couple return to their house and find it infested with ants. The Argentine ants. The husband-narrator suddenly recalls that this country is known for them. "It comes from South America," he adds, helpfully, to his distraught wife. Finally, they go to bed without "the feeling we were starting a new life, only a sense of dragging on into a future full of new troubles."

The rest of the story deals with the way that the others in the valley cope with the ants. Some go in for poisons; others make fantastic contraptions to confuse or kill the insects while for twenty years the Argentine Ant Control Corporation's representative has been putting out molasses ostensibly to control (kill) the ants but many believe that this is done to *feed* the ants. The frantic young couple pay a call on Signora Mauro in her dim palatial drawing room. She is firm; ants do not exist in well-tended houses, but from the way she squirms in her chair it is plain that the ants are crawling about under her clothes.

Methodically, Calvino describes the various human responses to The Condition. There is the Christian Scientist ignoring of all evidence; the Manichaean acceptance of evil; the relentless Darwinian faith that genetic superiority will prevail. But the ants prove indestructible and the story ends with the family going down to the seaside where there are no ants; where

> The water was calm, with just a slight continual change of color, blue and black, darker farthest away. I thought of the expanses of water like this, of the infinite grains of soft sand down there at the bottom of the sea where the currents leave white shells washed clean by the waves.

I don't know what this coda means. I also see no reason for it to mean. A contrast has been made between the ant-infested valley and the cool serenity of mineral and of shell beneath the sea, that other air we can no longer breathe since our ancestors chose to live upon the land.

In 1956 Calvino edited a volume of Italian fables, and the local critics decided that he was true heir to Grimm. Certainly the bright, deadly
fairy tale attracts him and he returned to it with *The Baron in the Trees*
(1957). Like the other two tales in the trilogy, the story is related in the
first person: this time by the eponymous baron's brother. The year is
1767. The place Liguria. The Baron is Cosimo Piovasco di Rondò, who
after an argument at dinner on June 15 decides to live in the trees. The
response of family and friends to this decision is varied. But Cosimo
is content. Later he goes in for politics; deals with Napoleon himself;
becomes legend.

Calvino has now developed two ways of writing. One is literally fabulous. The other makes use of a dry, rather didactic style in which the detail is as precisely observed as if the author were writing a manual for the
construction of a solar heating unit. Yet the premises of the "dry" stories
are often quite as fantastic as those of the fairy tales.*

"Smog" was published in 1958, a long time before the current preoccupation with man's systematic destruction of the environment. The
narrator comes to a large city to take over a small magazine called
Purification. The owner of the magazine, Commendatore Cordà, is an
important manufacturer who produces the sort of air pollution that his
magazine would like to eliminate. Cordà has it both ways and his new editor settles in nicely. The prevailing image of the story is smog: gray dust
covers everything; nothing is ever clean. The city is very like the valley of
the Argentine ants but on a larger scale, for now a vast population is
slowly strangling in the fumes of its industry, of the combustion engine.

Calvino is finely comic as he shows us the publisher instructing his
editor in how to strike the right tone. "We are not utopians, mind you, we
are practical men." Or, "It's a battle for an ideal." Or, "There will not be
(nor has there ever been) any contradiction between an economy in free,
natural expansion and the hygiene necessary to the human organism . . .
between the smoke of our productive factories and the green of our incomparable natural beauty. . . ." Finally, the editorial policy is set. "We

*I have not read *La speculazione edilizia* (1957). From the description of it in *Dizionario
della letteratura italiana contemporanea*, it is a general indictment of Italy's postwar building boom and of the helplessness of the intellectual Quinto Anfossi to come to terms with
"cement fever."

are one of the cities where the problem of air pollution is most serious, but at the same time we are the city where most is being done to
counteract the situation. At the same time, you understand!" By some
fifteen years, Calvino anticipated Exxon's double-talk ads on American
television.

This is the first of Calvino's stories where a realistic affair takes place
between a man and a woman—well, fairly realistic. We never know how
the elegant and wealthy Claudia came to meet the narrator or what she
sees in him; yet, periodically, she descends upon him, confuses him ("to
embrace her, I had removed my glasses"). One day they drive out of the
city. The narrator comments on the ugliness of the city and the ubiquitous smog. Claudia says that "people have lost the sense of beauty." He
answers, "Beauty has to be constantly invented." They argue; he finds
everything cruel. Later, he meets a proletarian who is in arms against
Cordà. The narrator admires the worker Omar, admires "the stubborn
ones, the tough ones." But Calvino does not really *engage*, in Sartre's
sense. He suspects that the trap we are in is too great for mere politics
to spring.

The narrator begins to write about atomic radiation in the atmosphere; about the way the weather is changing in the world. Is there a
connection? Even Cordà is momentarily alarmed. But then life goes on,
for is not Cordà himself "the smog's master? It was he who blew it out
constantly over the city," and his magazine was "born of the need to give
those working to produce the smog some hope of a life that was not all
smog, and yet, at the same time, to celebrate its power."

The story's coda resembles that of "The Argentine Ant." The narrator
goes to the outskirts of the city where the women are doing laundry. The
sight is cheering. "It wasn't much, but for me, seeking only images to re-
tain in my eyes, perhaps it was enough."

The next year Calvino switched to his other manner. *The Nonexistent
Knight* is the last of the Our Ancestors trilogy though it comes first
chronologically, in the age of Charlemagne. Again a war is going on. We
are not introduced to the narrator until page 34—Sister Theodora is a
nun in a convent who has been assigned to tell this story "for the health
of the soul." Unfortunately, the plot is giving her a good deal of trouble
because "we nuns have few occasions to speak with soldiers. . . . Apart

from religious ceremonies, triduums, novenas, gardening, harvesting, vintaging, whippings, slavery, incest, fires, hangings, invasions, sacking, rape and pestilence, we have had no experience."

Sister Theodora does her best with the tale of Agiluf, a knight who does not exist. What does exist is a suit of white armor from which comes the voice of Agiluf. He is a devoted knight in the service of Charlemagne who thinks him a bit much but graciously concedes, "for someone who doesn't exist, you seem in fine form." Since Agiluf has no appetites or weaknesses, he is the perfect soldier and so disliked by all. As for Agiluf, "people's bodies gave him a disagreeable feeling resembling envy, but also a stab of pride of contemptuous superiority." A young man (an older version of Pin, of the cloven Viscount's nephew) named Raimbaut joins the army to avenge his father's death. Agiluf gives him dull advice. There are battles. General observations. "What is war, after all, but this passing of more and more dented objects from hand to hand?" Then a meeting with a man who confuses himself with things outside himself. When he drinks soup, he becomes soup; thinks he is soup to be drunk in turn: "the world being nothing but a vast shapeless mass of soup in which all things dissolved."

Calvino now strikes a theme which will be developed in later works. The confusion between "I"/"it"; "I"/"you"; the arbitrariness of naming things, of categorizing, and of setting apart, particularly when "World conditions were still confused in the era when this book took place. It was not rare then to find names and thoughts and forms and institutions that corresponded to nothing in existence. But at the same time the world was polluted with objects and capacities and persons who lacked any name or distinguishing mark."

A triangle occurs. Raimbaut falls in love with a knight who proves to be a young woman, Bradamante. Unfortunately, *she* falls in love with Agiluf, the nonexistent knight. At this point there is rather too much plot for Sister Theodora, who strikes the professional writer's saddest note. "One starts off writing with a certain zest, but a time comes when the pen merely grates in dusty ink, and not a drop of life flows, and life is all outside, outside the window, outside oneself, and it seems that never more can one escape into a page one is writing, open out another world, leap the gap."

But the teller finally gets a grip on the tale; closes the gap. Knightly quests are conducted, concluded. Agiluf surrenders his armor and ceases to be; Raimbaut is allowed to inhabit the armor. Bradamante has vanished, but with a fine *coup de théâtre* Sister Theodora reveals to us that *she* is Bradamante, who is now rushing the narrative to its end so that she can take the beloved white armor in her arms: aware that it now contains the young and passionate Raimbaut, her true love. "That is why my pen at a certain point began running on so. I rush to meet him. . . . A page is good only when we turn it and find life urging along. . . ."

With the completion of the trilogy, Calvino took to his other manner and wrote "The Watcher," the most realistic of his stories and the most overtly political. The narrator has a name, Amerigo Ormea. He is a poll watcher in Turin for the Communist party during the national election of 1953. Amerigo's poll is inside the vast "Cottolengo Hospital for Incurables." Apparently the mad and the senile and even the comatose are allowed to vote ("hospitals, asylums and convents had served as great reservoirs of votes for the Christian Democrat party"). Amerigo is a serene observer of democracy's confusions, having "learned that change, in politics, comes through long and complex processes"; he also confesses that "acquiring experience had meant becoming slightly pessimistic."

In the course of the day, Amerigo observes with fine dispassion the priests and nuns as they herd their charges into the polling booths that have been set up inside the hospital. Despite the grotesqueries of the situation, Amerigo takes some pleasure in the matter-of-factness of the voting, for "in Italy, which had always bowed and scraped before every form of pomp, display, sumptuousness, ornament, this seemed to him finally the lesson of an honest, austere morality, and a perpetual, silent revenge on the Fascists . . . ; now they had fallen into dust with all their gold fringe and their ribbons, while democracy, with its stark ceremony of pieces of paper folded over like telegrams, of pencils given to callused or shaky hands, went ahead."

But for the watcher boredom eventually sets in; it is a long day. "Amerigo felt a yearning need for beauty, which became focused in the thought of his mistress Lia." He contemplates Lia in reverie. "What is this need of ours for beauty? Amerigo asks himself." Apparently Calvino has not advanced much beyond the last dialogue in "Smog." He contemplates the perfection of classical Greece but recalls that the Greeks destroyed deformed children, redundant girls. Obviously placing beauty too high in the scale of values is "a step toward an inhuman civilization, which will then sentence the deformed to be thrown off a cliff."

When another poll watcher remarks to Amerigo that the mad all must recognize one another in Cottolengo, he slips into reverie: "They would remember that humanity could be a different thing, as in fables, a world of giants, an Olympus. . . . As we do: and perhaps, without realizing it, we are deformed, backward, compared to a different, forgotten form of existence. . . ." What is human, what is real?

Calvino's vision is usually presented in fantastic terms but now he becomes unusually concrete. Since he has elected to illuminate an actual time and place (Italy between 1945 and the election of 1953), he is able to spell it out. "In those years the Italian Communist party, among its many other tasks, had also assumed the position of an ideal liberal party, which had never really existed. And so the bosom of each individual communist could house two personalities at once: an intransigent revolutionary and an Olympian liberal." Amerigo's pessimism derives from the obvious fact that the two do not go together. I am reminded of Alexander Herzen's comment about the Latins: they do not want liberty, they want to sue for liberty.

Amerigo goes home to lunch (he has a maid who cooks and serves! Written in 1963 about the events of 1953, this is plainly a historical novel). He looks for a book to read. "Pure literature" is out. "Personal literature now seemed to him a row of tombstones in a cemetery; the literature of the living as well as of the dead. Now he sought something else from books: the wisdom of the ages or simply something that helped to understand something." He takes a stab at Marx's *Youthful Writings*. "Man's universality appears, practically speaking, in that same universe that makes all nature man's *inorganic body*. . . . Nature is man's *inorganic body* precisely because it is not his human body." Thus genius turns everything into itself. As Marx invented *Kapital* from capitalism, so Calvino turns a passage of Marx into Calvino himself: the man who drinks soup is the soup that drinks him. Wholeness is all.

Fortified with this reassuring text, Amerigo endures a telephone conversation with Lia. It is the usual quibbling conversation between Calvino protagonist and Calvino mistress. She tells him that she is pregnant. "Amerigo was an ardent supporter of birth control, even though his party's attitude on the subject was either agnostic or hostile. Nothing shocked him so much as the ease with which people multiply, and the more hungry and backward, the more they keep having children. . . ." In the land of Margaret Sanger this point of view is not exactly startling, but for an Italian Communist a dozen years ago, the sense of a world dying of too many children, of too much "smog" was a monstrous revelation. At this point, Amerigo rounds on both the Bible and Marx as demented celebrators of human fecundity.

Amerigo returns to the hospital; observes children shaped like fish and again wonders at what point is a human being human. Finally the day ends; the voting is done. Amerigo looks out over the complex of hospital buildings and notes that the reddish sun appeared to open "perspectives of a city that had never been seen." Thus the Calvino coda strikes its first familiar chord. Laughing women cross the courtyard with a cauldron, "perhaps the evening soup. Even the ultimate city of imperfection has its perfect hour, the watcher thought, the hour, the moment, when every city is the City." In Italian the plural for the word "city" is also the singular.

Most realistic and specific of Calvino's works, "The Watcher" has proved (to date) to be the last of the "dry" narratives. In 1965 Calvino published *Cosmicomics*: twelve brief stories dealing in a fantastic way with the creation of the universe, man, society. Like Pin's young friend who decided that life indeed resembles the strip cartoon, Calvino has deployed his complex prose in order to compose in words a super strip cartoon narrated by Qfwfq whose progress from life inside the first atom to mollusk on the earth's sea floor to social-climbing amphibian to dinosaur to moon-farmer is told in a dozen episodes that are entirely unlike anything that anyone else has written since, well, let us say Lucian.

"At Daybreak" is the story of the creation of the universe as viewed by Qfwfq and his mysterious tribe consisting of a father, mother, sister, brother, Granny, as well as acquaintances—formless sentiencies who inhabit the universal dust that is on the verge of becoming the nebula which will contain our solar system. Where and who *they* are is, literally, obscure, since light has not yet been invented. So "there was nothing to do but wait, keep covered as best we could, doze, speak out now and then to make sure we were all still there; and, naturally, scratch ourselves; because—they can say what they like—all those particles spinning around had only one effect, a troublesome itching." That itch starts to change things. Condensation begins. Also, confusion: Granny loses her cushion, "a little ellipsoid of galactic matter." Things clot; nickel is formed; members of the tribe start flying off in all directions. Suddenly the condensation is complete and light breaks. The sun is now in its place and the planets begin their orbits "and, above all, it was deathly hot."

As the earth starts to jell, Qfwfq's sister takes fright and vanishes inside the planet and is not heard from again "until I met her, much later, at Canberra in 1912, married to a certain Sullivan, a retired railroad man, so changed I hardly recognized her."

The early Calvino was much like his peers Pavese and Vittorini—writers who tended to reflect the realistic storytelling of Hemingway and Dos Passos. Then Calvino moved to Paris, where he found his own voice or voices and became, to a degree, infected by the French. Since the writing of *Our Ancestors* and the three stories that make up *The Watcher*, Calvino has been influenced, variously, by Barthes and the semiologists, by Borges, and by the now old New Novel. In *Cosmicomics* these influences are generally benign, since Calvino is too formidable and original an artist to be derailed by theoreticians or undone by the example of another creator. Nevertheless the story "A Sign in Space" comes perilously close to being altogether too reverent an obeisance to semiology.

As the sun takes two hundred million years to revolve around the galaxy, Qfwfq becomes obsessed with making a sign in space, something peculiarly his own to mark his passage as well as something that would impress anyone who might be watching. His ambition is the result of a desire to think because "to think something had never been possible, first because there were no things to think about, and second because signs to think of them by were lacking, but from the moment there was that sign, it was possible for someone thinking to think of a sign, and therefore that one, in the sense that the sign was the thing you could think about and also the sign of the thing thought, namely, itself." So he makes his sign ("I felt I was going forth to conquer the only thing that mattered to me, sign and dominion and name . . .").

Unfortunately, a spiteful contemporary named Kgwgk erases Qfwfq's sign and replaces it with his own. In a rage, Qfwfq wants "to make a new sign in space, a real sign that would make Kgwgk die of envy." So, out of competitiveness, art is born. But the task of sign-making is becoming more difficult because the world "was beginning to produce an image of itself, and in everything a form was beginning to correspond to a function" (a theme from *The Nonexistent Knight*) and "in this new sign of mine you could perceive the influence of our new way of looking at things, call it style if you like. . . ."

Qfwfq is delighted with his new sign but as time passes he likes it less and less, thinks it is a bit pretentious, old-fashioned; decides he must erase it before his rival sees it (so writers revise old books or make new ones that obliterate earlier works—yes, call it style if you like). Finally, Qfwfq erases the inadequate sign. For a time he is pleased that there is nothing in space which might make him look idiotic to a rival—in this, he resembles so many would-be writers who contrive to vanish into universities and, each year, by not publishing that novel or poem, increase their reputations.

But doing nothing is, finally, abhorrent to the real artist: Qfwfq starts to amuse himself by making *false* signs, "to annoy Kgwgk . . . notches in space, holes, stains, little tricks that only an incompetent creature like Kgwgk could mistake for signs." So the artist masochistically mocks his own art, shatters form (the sign) itself, makes jokes to confuse and exploit 57th Street. But then things get out of hand. To Qfwfq's horror, every time he passes what he thinks was one of his false signs, there are a dozen other signs, all scribbled over his.

Finally, everything was now so obscured by a crisscross of meaningless signs that "world and space seemed the mirror of each other, both minutely adorned with hieroglyphics and ideograms" including the badly inked tail of the letter *R* in an evening newspaper joined to a thready imperfection in the paper, one among the eight hundred thousand flakings of a tarred wall in the Melbourne docks. . . . In the universe now there was no longer a container and a thing contained, but only a general thickness of signs superimposed and coagulated."

Qfwfq gives up. There is no longer a point of reference "because it was clear that, independent of signs, space didn't exist and perhaps had never existed." So the story concludes; and the rest is the solipsism of art. To the old debate about being and non-being, Calvino adds his own vision of the multiplicity of signs which obliterates *all* meaning. Too many names for a thing is like no name for a thing; therefore, no thing, nothing.

"How Much Shall We Bet?" continues the theme. At the beginning Qfwfq "bet that there was going to be a universe, and I hit the nail on the head." This was the first bet he won with Dean (k)yK. Through the ages the two continue to make bets and Qfwfq usually wins because "I bet on the possibility of a certain event's taking place, whereas the Dean almost always bet against it."

Qfwfq kept on winning until he began to take wild leaps into the future. "On February 28, 1926, at Santhia, in the Province of Vercelli—got that? At number 18 in Via Garibaldi—you follow me? Signorina Giuseppina Pensotti, aged twenty-two, leaves her home at quarter to six in the afternoon; does she turn right or left?" Qfwfq starts losing. Then they begin to bet about characters in unwritten novels . . . will Balzac make Lucien de Rubempré kill himself at the end of *Les illusions perdues*? The Dean wins that one.

The two bettors end up in charge of vast research foundations which contain innumerable reference libraries. Finally, like man's universe itself, they begin to drown in signs and Qfwfq looks back nostalgically to the beginning, "How beautiful it was then, through that void, to draw lines and parabolas, pick out the precise point, the intersection between space and time when the event would spring forth, undeniable in the prominence of its glow; whereas now events come flowing down without interruption, like cement being poured, one column next to the other . . . a doughy mass of events without form or direction, which surrounds, submerges, crushes all reasoning."

In another story the last of the dinosaurs turns out to be Qfwfq, who meets and moves in with the next race. The New Ones don't realize that he is one of their dread enemies from the past. They think him remarkably ugly but not unduly alien. Qfwfq's attitude is like that of the protagonist in William Golding's *The Inheritors* except that in Calvino's version the last of the Old Ones merges with the inheritors. Amused, Qfwfq listens to the monstrous, conflicting legends about his race, tribute to the power of man's imagination, to the words he uses, to the signs he recognizes.

Finally, "I knew that the more the Dinosaurs disappear, the more they extend their dominion, and over forests far more vast than those that cover the continents: in the labyrinth of the survivors' thoughts." But Qfwfq was not at all sentimental about being the last dinosaur and at the story's end he left the New Ones and "travelled through valleys and plains. I came to a station, caught the first train, and was lost in the crowd."

In "The Spiral," the last of the *Cosmicomics*, Qfwfq is a mollusk on a rock in the primeval sea. The theme is again *in ovo omnes*. Calvino describes with minuteness the sensations of the mollusk on the rock, "damp and happy. . . . I was what they call a narcissist to a slight extent; I mean I stayed there observing myself all the time, I saw all my good points and all my defects, and I liked myself for the former and for the latter; I had no terms of comparison, you must remember that, too." Such was Eden. But then the heat of the sun started altering things; there were vibrations from another sex; there were eggs to be fertilized: love.

In response to the new things, Qfwfq expresses himself by making a shell which turns out to be a spiral that is not only very good for defense but unusually beautiful. Yet Qfwfq takes no credit for the beauty: "My shell made itself, without my taking any special pains to have it come out one way rather than another." But then the instinctive artist in the mollusk asserts itself: "This doesn't mean that I was absent-minded during that time; I applied myself instead, to the act of secreting. . . ." Meanwhile, *she*, the beloved, is making *her* shell, identical with his.

Ages pass. The shell-Qfwfq is on a railroad embankment as a train passes by. A party of Dutch girls looks out the window. Qfwfq is not startled by anything, for "I feel as if, in making the shell, I had also made the rest." But one new element has entered the equation. "I had failed to foresee one thing: the eyes that finally opened to see us didn't belong to us but to others." So dies Narcissus. "They developed eyes at our expense. So sight, *our* sight, which we were obscurely waiting for, was the sight that the others had of us."

But the artist who made the spiral-shaped shell is not to be outdone by miscalculation or by fate. Proudly he concludes: "All these eyes were mine. I had made them possible; I had had the active part; I furnished them the raw material, the image." Again the gallant coda, for fixed in the watcher's eye is not only the fact of the beautiful shell that *he* made but also "the most faithful image of her" who had inspired the shell and was the shell: thus male and female are at last united in the retina of a stranger's eye.

In 1967, Calvino published more of Qfwfq's adventures in *Time and the Hunter*. For the most part they are engaging cartoons, but one is disconcerted to encounter altogether too many bits of Sarraute, of Robbe-Grillet, of Borges (far too much of Borges) incorporated in the prose of what I have come to regard as a true modern master. On page 6 occurs "viscous"; on page 11 "acid mucus." I started to feel queasy: these are Sarraute words. I decided that their use was simply a matter of coincidence. But when, on page 29, I saw the dread word "magma" I knew that Calvino has been too long in Paris, for only Sarrautistes use "magma," a word the great theoretician of the old New Novel so arbitrarily and uniquely appropriated from the discipline of science. Elsewhere in the stories, Robbe-Grillet's technique of recording the minutiae of a banal situation stops cold some of Calvino's best effects.

"The Chase," in fact, could have been written by Robbe-Grillet. This is not a compliment. Take the beginning:

> That car chasing me is faster than mine; inside there is one man, alone, armed with a pistol, a good shot. . . . We have stopped at a traffic signal, in a long column. The signal is regulated in such a way that on our side the red light lasts a hundred and eighty seconds and the green light a hundred and twenty, no doubt based on the premise that the perpendicular traffic is heavier and slower.

And so on for sixteen pages, like a movie in slow motion.

The theory behind this sort of enervating prose is as follows, since to write is to describe, with words, why not then describe words themselves (with other words)? Or, glory be! words describing words describing an action of no importance (the corner of that room in Robbe-Grillet's

Jalousie). This sort of "experiment" has always seemed to me to be of more use to students of language than to readers of writing. On his own and at his best, Calvino does what very few writers can do: he describes imaginary worlds with the most extraordinary precision and beauty (a word he has single-handedly removed from that sphere of suspicion which the old New Novelists maintain surrounds all words and any narrative).

In *Cosmicomics* Calvino makes it possible for the reader to inhabit a meson, a mollusk, a dinosaur; makes him for the first time see light ending a dark universe. Since this is a unique gift, I find all the more alarming the "literariness" of *Time and the Hunter*. I was particularly put off by the central story "t zero," which could have been written (and rather better) by Borges.

With a bow and arrow, Qfwfq confronts a charging lion. In his head he makes an equation: Time zero is where he Qfwfq is; where the Lion-o is. All combinations of a series which may be finite or infinite pass through Qo's head, exactly like the man before the firing squad in Borges's celebrated story. Now it is possible that these stories will appeal to minds more convergent than mine (students of mathematics, engineers, Young Republicans are supposed to think convergently while novelists, gourmets, and non-Christian humanists think divergently) but to me this pseudo-scientific rendering of a series of possibilities is deeply boring.

But there are also pleasures in this collection. Particularly "The Origin of the Birds." "Now these stories can be told better with strip drawings than with a story composed of sentences one after the other." So the crafty Calvino by placing one sentence after another *describes* a strip cartoon and the effect is charming even though Qfwfq's adventure among the birds is not really a strip cartoon but the description of a cartoon *in words*.

The narrator's technique is like that of *The Nonexistent Knight*. He starts to draw a scene; then erases it the way Sister Theodora used to eliminate oceans and forests as she hurried her lovers to their inevitable rendezvous. Calvino also comes as close as any writer can to saying that which is sensed about creation but may not be put into words or drawn in pictures.

"I managed to embrace in a single thought the world of things as they were and of things as they could have been, and I realized that a single system included all." In the arms of Or, the queen of the birds, Qfwfq begins to *see* that "the world is single and what exists can't be explained without . . ." But he has gone too far. As he is about to say the unsayable, Or tries to smother him. But he is still able to blurt out, "There's no difference. Monsters and non-monsters have always been close to one another! What hasn't been continues to be. . . ." At that point, the birds expel him from their paradise; and like a dreamer rudely awakened, he forgets his vision of unity. "(The last strip is all photographs: a bird, the same bird in close-up, the head of the bird enlarged, a detail of the head, the eye. . . .)" It is the same eye that occurs at the end of *Cosmicomics*, the eye of—cosmic consciousness for those who recall that guru of a past generation, Dr. Richard M. Bucke.

Calvino ends these tales with his own *The Count of Monte Cristo*. The problem he sets himself is how to get out of Château d'If. Faria keeps making plans and tunneling his way through an endless, exitless fortress. Dantès, on the other hand, broods on the nature of the fortress as well as on the various drafts of the novel that Dumas is writing. In some drafts, Dantès will escape and find a treasure and get revenge on his enemies. In other drafts, he suffers a different fate. The narrator contemplates the possibilities of escape by considering the way a fortress (or a work of art) is made. "To plan a book—or an escape—the first thing to know is what to exclude." This particular story is Borges at his very best and, taking into account the essential unity of the multiplicity of all things, one cannot rule out that Calvino's version of *The Count of Monte Cristo* by Alexandre Dumas is indeed the finest achievement of Jorge Luis Borges as imagined by Italo Calvino.

Calvino's seventh and latest novel (or work or meditation or poem), *Invisible Cities*, is perhaps his most beautiful work. In a garden sit the aged Kublai Khan and the young Marco Polo—Tartar emperor and Venetian traveler. The mood is sunset. Prospero is holding up for the last time his magic wand: Kublai Khan has sensed the end of his empire, of his cities, of himself.

Marco Polo, however, diverts the emperor with tales of cities that he has seen within the empire and Kublai Khan listens, searches for a pattern in Marco Polo's Cities and memory, Cities and desire, Cities and signs, Thin Cities, Trading Cities, Cities and eyes, Cities and names, Cities and the dead, Cities and the sky, Continuous Cities, Hidden Cities. The emperor soon determines that each of these fantastic places is really the same place.

Marco Polo agrees: " 'Memory's images, once they are fixed in words, are erased,' Polo said. 'Perhaps I am afraid of losing Venice all at once, if I speak of it, or perhaps, speaking of other cities, I have already lost it, little by little.' " Again the theme of multiplicity and wholeness, "when every city," as Calvino wrote at the end of "The Watcher," "is the City."

Of all tasks, describing the contents of a book is the most difficult and in the case of a marvelous creation like *Invisible Cities*, perfectly irrelevant. I shall spare myself the labor; noting, however, that something new and wise has begun to enter the Calvino canon. The artist seems to have made a peace with the tension between man's idea of the many and of the one. He could now, if he wanted, stop.

Yet Calvino is obliged to go on writing just as his Marco Polo goes on traveling because

> *he cannot stop; he must go on to another city, where another of his pasts awaits him, or something perhaps that had been a possible future of his and is now someone else's present. Futures not achieved are only branches of the past: dead branches.*
>
> *"Journeys to relive your past?" was the Khan's question at this point, a question which could also have been formulated: "Journeys to recover your future?"*
>
> *And Marco's answer was: "Elsewhere is a negative mirror. The traveler recognizes the little that is his, discovering the much he has not had and will never have."*

Later, after more descriptions of his cities, Kublai Khan decides that "the empire is nothing but a zodiac of the mind's phantasms."

> *"On the day when I know all the emblems," he asked Marco, "shall I be able to possess my empire, at last?"*

And the Venetian answered, "Sire, do not believe it. On that day you will be an emblem among emblems."

Finally, Kublai Khan recognizes that all cities are tending toward the concentric circles of Dante's hell.

He said: "It is all useless, if the last landing place can only be the infernal city, and it is there that, in ever-narrowing circles, the current is drawing us."

And Polo said: "The inferno of the living is not something that will be; if there is one, it is what is already here, the inferno where we live every day, that we form by being together. There are two ways to escape suffering it. The first is easy for many: accept the inferno and become such a part of it that you can no longer see it. The second is risky and demands constant vigilance and apprehension; seek and learn to recognize who and what, in the midst of the inferno, are not inferno, then make them endure, give them space."

During the last quarter century Italo Calvino has advanced far beyond his American and English contemporaries. As they continue to look for the place where the spiders make their nests, Calvino has not only found that special place, but learned how himself to make fantastic webs of prose to which all things adhere. In fact, reading Calvino, I had the unnerving sense that I was also writing what he had written; thus does his art prove his case as writer and reader become one, or One.

The New York Review of Books
May 30, 1974

THE HACKS OF ACADEME

The Theory of the Novel: New Essays, edited by John Halperin. The two articles arouse suspicion. *The* theory? *The* novel? Since there is no such thing as the novel, how can there be a single theory? Or is the editor some sort of monist? Blinkered hedgehog in wild fox country? The jacket identifies Mr. Halperin as "Associate Professor and Director of Graduate Studies in the Department of English at the University of Southern California." This is true academic weight. "He is also the author of *The Language of Meditation: Four Studies in Nineteenth-Century Fiction* and *Egoism and Self-Discovery in the Victorian Novel*." Well, meditation if not language is big in Southern California, where many an avocado tree shades its smogbound Zen master, while the Victorian novel continues to be a growth industry in Academe. Eagerly, one turns to Professor Halperin's "A Critical Introduction" to nineteen essays by as many professors of English. Most are American; most teach school in the land of the creative writing course.

"Christ left home at twelve." Professor Halperin's first sentence is startlingly resonant, to use an adjective much favored by the contributors, who also like "mythopoeic," "parameter" (almost always misused), "existential" (often misused), "linear," "schematic" and "spatial." Professor Halperin tells us that during the lifetime of Nazareth's gift to the joy of nations,

poetry's age . . . was in the thousands of years and drama's in the hundreds.
It was not until a millennium and a half later that the gestation period of
the novel began. Thus it is not surprising, three quarters of the way through
the twentieth century, that we find ourselves with a growing but still rela-
tively small body of critical theory pertaining to the novel . . .

This is sweet innocence; also, ignorance. Two very good novels (*Satyri-*
con, Golden Ass) were written by near-contemporaries of the gentle
Nazarene. Later, during the so-called long "gestation," other cultures
were lightened (as William Faulkner would put it) of novels as distinguished as the Lady Murasaki's *Tale of Genji* (c. A.D. 1005).

But Professor Halperin is not very interested in novels. Rather:

It is the purpose of the present volume to reflect and hopefully to deal with
some of the more radical issues of contemporary novel-theory. . . . This col-
lection, containing original essays of theoretical cast written especially for
this volume by some of the most distinguished critics of our time, hopefully
will be a major addition to the growing corpus of theoretical approaches to
fiction.

Professor Halperin has not an easy way with our rich language. Nevertheless, one opens his book in the hope that the prose of "some of the
most distinguished critics of our time" will be better than his own. Certainly the great names are all here: Meir Sternberg, Robert Bernard Martin, Irving H. Buchen, Alan Warren Friedman, Max F. Schulz, Alice R.
Kaminsky, George Levine, John W. Loofourow, Marvin Mudrick, Walter
F. Wright, Robert B. Heilman, Richard Harter Fogle, Dorothea Krook.
Also Leon Edel, Leslie. A. Fiedler, Walter Allen, and Frank Kermode. *Un*
sac mixte, as Bouvard might have said to Pécuchet.

Professor Halperin quotes approvingly Barthes's

Flaubert . . . finally established Literature as an object, through promoting
literary labour to the status of a value; form became the end-product of
craftsmanship, like a piece of pottery or a jewel . . . [The] whole of Litera-
ture, from Flaubert to the present day, became the problematics of language.

Professor Halperin adds his own gloss.

> *Modern theoretical novel-criticism . . . is occupied less with the novel as a mimetic and moral performance than with the novel as an autonomous creation independent of or at least not wholly dependent on the real world. The world of the autonomous novel may inevitably resemble our own, but it is not created as a conscious representation of anything outside itself.*

American professors of English have never had an easy time with French theoreticians of the novel (close scrutiny of the quotation from Barthes reveals that it was taken from an English not an American translation). Nevertheless, despite various hedges like "may inevitably," Professor Halperin has recklessly enrolled himself in the school of Paris (class of '56). As a result, he believes that the autonomous novel "is not created as a conscious representation of anything outside itself." Aside from the presumption of pretending to know what any writer has in mind (is he inevitably but not consciously describing or mimicking the real world?), it is naïve to assume that a man-made novel can ever resemble a meteor fallen from outer space, a perfectly autonomous artifact whose *raison d'être* is "with the relationships among the various structural elements within the work of fiction itself" rather than "between reader and text." Apparently the novel is no longer what James conceived it, a story told, in Professor Halperin's happy phrase, from "the limited perspective of a single sentient consciousness." And so, in dubious battle, unconscious sentiencies clash in the English departments of the West with insentient consciousnesses.

The first essay is called "What Is Exposition?" This subject plainly troubles Professor Meir Sternberg. At a loss for the right words, he resorts to graphics. An inverted "V" occupies the top of one page. At the foot of the left leg is the word "introduction"; then "exciting force"; then "rise." The apex of the inverted "V" is labeled "climax." Partway down the right leg is the word "fall," while at the base occurs the somber word "catastrophe." This treasure-seeker's map to tragedy is something called "Freytag's pyramid," which the eponymous architect set up in the desert of novel-theory to show how "time-honored" exposition works in tragedy.

Professor Sternberg then adds his own markings to the sand. "Suppose an author wishes to compose a narrative which is to consist of three motifs: a1, a2, a3. These motifs, arranged in an order in which a2 follows a1 in a time and a3 follows a2, will form the *fabula* of his story." The sequence of numbered a's is then arranged vertically on the page, and casts almost as minatory a shadow as Freytag's pyramid. Later Professor Sternberg assembles a positively Cheopsean structure with such parallel headings as "story," "*fabula*," "plot," "*sujet*," a monster Rosetta stone with which to confound strawman Freytag. The resulting *agon* (or duel or *lutte*) in the desert is very elaborate and not easy to follow. Occasionally there is a simple sentence like: "A work of fiction presents characters in action during a certain period of time." But, by and large, sentences are as elaborate as the ideas that they wish to express are simple. And so, as the sun sinks behind the last tautology, our guide sums up: "As my definition of it clearly implies, exposition is a time problem *par excellence*." (Instructor's note: Transpose "it" and "exposition.")

Further on in the Sahelian wilderness we meet Professor Irving H. Buchen. At first, one is charmed: "Critics may need novels to be critics but novels do not need critics to be novels." This is fine stuff. The pathetic fallacy is at last able to define for us that mysterious entity "the living novel." Professor Buchen likes his literature lean.

> Almost all novelistic failures, especially significant ones, are the result of crushing richness. Plenitude swelled to bursting Fielding's Tom Jones, deluged Conrad's Nostromo, over-refined Proust's sensibility, and transformed Joyce in Finnegans Wake into a self parodist.

Solution? "The key to the artistry of the novel is managing fecundity." The late Margaret Sanger could not have put it better.

Although Professor Buchen's "The Aesthetics of the Supra-Novel" deals only in the obvious, his footnotes are often interesting. Occasionally a shy aphorism gleams like a scarab in the sand. "The novel is not a given form; it is given to be formed." Pondering the vast amount of novel-theory" written for classrooms, he notes that this process of over-explicating texts produces

new novelists who, like the re-issue of older novelists, seemed to be but-
tressed both in front and in back. Finally, virtually every facet of the novel
has been subjected to structural, stylistic, formalistic, epistemological pro-
cessing. Aside from some outstanding seminal pieces, what is instructive
about the entire theoretical enterprise is that it has created a Frankenstein.

I assume that he means the monster and not the baron. In any case, relieved of those confining "parameters" of "novel-theory" (also known as
"book-chat"), Professor Buchen's footnotes betray glimmers of true intelligence.

In general, Professor Halperin's novel-theorists have nothing very urgent or interesting to say about literature. Why then do they write when
they have nothing to say? Because the ambitious teacher can only rise in
the academic bureaucracy by writing at complicated length about writing
that has already been much written about. The result of all this book-chat
cannot interest anyone who knows literature while those who would like
to learn something about books can only be mystified and discouraged by
these commentaries. Certainly it is no accident that the number of students taking English courses has been in decline for some years. But that
is beside the point. What matters is that the efforts of the teachers now
under review add up to at least a half millennium of academic tenure.

Although The Novel is not defined by Professor Halperin's col-
leagues, some interesting things are said about novels. Professor Frank
Kermode's "Novel and Narrative" is characteristically elegant. In fact, so
fine-meshed is his prose that one often has to reread whole pages but
then, as Kant instructs us, "comprehension is only a knowledge adequate
to our intention." Kermode is particularly good on the virtues and demer-
its of Roland Barthes, no doubt because he has actually read Barthes and
not relied upon the odd quotation picked up here and there in translation. Kermode tends to pluralism and he is unimpressed by the so-called
great divide between the mimetic fiction of the past and the autonomous
fiction of the present. "It seems doubtful, then, whether we need to
speak of some great divide—a strict historical *coupure*—between the old
and new." Minor complaint: I do wish Kermode would not feel obliged
always to drag in the foreign word whose meaning is no different from

the English equivalent. Also, my heart sinks every time he fashions a critical category and then announces firmly: "I shall call it, hermeneutic activity." As for the great divide:

> There are differences of emphasis, certainly, as to what it is to read; and there are, within the narratives themselves, rearrangement of emphasis and interest. Perhaps, as metacritics often allege, these are to be attributed to a major shift in our structures of thought; but although this may be an efficient cause of the mutation of interests it does not appear that the object of those interests—narrative—imitates the shift.

Phrased like a lawyer and, to my mind, demonstrably true. Nevertheless, the other "most distinguished critics" seem to believe that there has indeed been at least a gap or split or *coupure* between old and new writing, requiring, if not a critical bridge, an academic's bandage.

Professor Leon Edel chats amiably about "Novel and Camera," reminding us that Robbe-Grillet's reliance on the close-shot in his novels might have something to do with his early training as an agronomist where the use of a microscope is essential. Professor Edel notes that the audience for the novel is dwindling while the audience for films, television, comic books continues to grow; he echoes Saul Bellow:

> Perhaps we have had too many novels. People no longer seem to need them. On the other hand, pictorial biographies—real pictures of real lives—exist in abundance, and there will be more of these in the coming year. The camera is ubiquitous.

In "Realism Reconsidered," Professor George Levine has a number of intelligent things to say about writing. Although limited by a certain conceit about his own place in time ("Reality has become problematic in ways the Victorians could only barely imagine"), he is aware that the word "reality" is protean: even the French ex-agronomist wants to be absolutely realistic. Buttressed by Auerbach, Gombrich and Frye, Professor Levine's meditation on realism in the novel is not only sensible but his sentences are rather better than those of his fellow most-distinguished critics. There is a plainness reminiscent of Edmund Wilson. Possibly because:

My bias, then, is historical. . . . What is interesting here is that at one point in European history writers should have become so self-conscious about truth-telling in art [which I take to imply the growth of doubt about art in society] that they were led to raise truth-telling to the level of doctrine and to imply that previous literatures had not been telling it.

Then Levine states the profound truth that "fiction is fiction," ruling out Truth if not truth. Or as Calvin Coolidge said in a not too dissimilar context: "In public life it is sometimes necessary in order to appear really natural to be actually artificial."

"The Death and Rebirth of the Novel." The confident ring of the title could only have been sounded by America's liveliest full-time professor and seducer of the *Zeitgeist* (no proper English equivalent), Leslie A. Fiedler. A redskin most at home in white clown makeup, Fiedler has given many splendid performances over the years. From a secure heterosexual base, he has turned a bright amused eye on the classic American *goyim* and finds them not only homoerotic to a man (or person as they say nowadays) but given to guilty pleasures with injuns like Queequeg, with niggers like Jim. As far as I know, Fiedler has yet to finger an American-Jewish author as a would-be reveler in the savage Arcadia of Sodom-America, but then that hedge of burning bushes no doubt keeps pure the American Jewish writer/person.

Fiedler reminds us that for a "century or more" the leading novelists and a good many critics have forgotten "that at its most authentic the novel is a form of popular art." But he shares the academic delusion that the novel was invented in the middle of the eighteenth century by "that extraordinary anti-elitist genius" Samuel Richardson, who launched "the first successful form of Pop Art." For Fiedler, Richardson reflects little of what preceded him (the epic, the ballad) but he made possible a great deal that has come since: "the comic strip, the comic book, cinema, TV." After the Second World War, the appearance of mass-production paperback books in the supermarkets of the West was insurance against the main line of the novel becoming elitist, for "the machine-produced commodity novel is, therefore, dream literature, mythic literature, as surely as any tale told over the tribal fire." Consequently, "form and content, in the traditional sense, are secondary, optional if not irrelevant—since it is, in the first instance, primordial images and archetypal narrative structures that the novel is called on to provide." Fiedler believes that dream-literature (*Pickwick Papers, Valley of the Dolls*) is peculiarly "immune to formalist criticism." Further, "it sometimes seems as if all such novels want to metamorphose into movies . . . a kind of chrysalis yearning to be a butterfly."

Certainly Pop narratives reveal the society's literally vulgar daydreams. Over and over again occur and recur the sex lives and the murders of various Kennedys, the sphinx-like loneliness of Greta Garbo, the disintegration of Judy Garland or, closer to the heart of Academe, the crack-up of Scott Fitzgerald in Hollywood, the principal factory of this century's proto-myths. Until recently no Art Novelist (Fiedler's phrase) would go near a subject as melodramatic as the collapse of a film star or the murder of a president. Contemporary practitioners of the Art Novel ("beginning with, perhaps, Flaubert, and reaching a climax in the work of Proust, Mann and Joyce") are doggedly at work creating "fiction intended not for the market-place but the library and classroom; or its sub-variety, the Avant-Garde Novel, which foresees immediate contempt followed eventually by an even securer status in future Museums of Literary Culture."

> *To put it as bluntly as possible, it is incumbent on all who write fiction or criticism in the disappearing twentieth century to realize that the Art Novel or Avant-Garde Novel is in the process of being abandoned wherever fiction remains most alive, which means that that sub-genre of the novel is dying if not dead.*

Although Fiedler's funeral oration ought to alarm those teachers who require a certain quantity of serious "novel writing" so that they can practice "novel criticism," I suspect that they will, secretly, agree with him. If all the Art Novels have been written, then no one need ever run the risk of missing the point to something new. After all, a lot can still be written about the old Modern masterpieces.

As always, Fiedler makes some good sense. He can actually see what is in front of him and this is what makes him such a useful figure. Briskly, he names four present-day practitioners of the Art Novel of yesteryear:

Bellow, Updike, Moravia, Robbe-Grillet. This is an odd grouping, but one sees what he means. Then he gives two examples of what he calls, approvingly, "the Anti-art Art Novel." One is Nabokov's *Pale Fire*. The other is John Barth's *Giles Goat-Boy*: "a strange pair of books really"—note the first sign of unease—

> *the former not quite American and the latter absolutely provincial American. Yet they have in common a way of using typical devices of the Modernist Art Novel, like irony, parody, travesty, exhibitionistic allusion, redundant erudition, and dogged experimentalism, not to extend the possibilities of the form but to destroy it.*

This is nonsense. Professor (Emeritus) Nabokov's bright clever works are very much in the elitist Art-Novel tradition. It is true that the Black Swan of Lac Léman makes fun of American academics and their ghastly explications, but his own pretty constructions are meant to last forever. They are not autonomous artifacts designed to "self-destruct."

Giles Goat-Boy is a very bad prose-work by Professor John Barth. Certainly the book is not, as Fiedler claims,

> *a comic novel, a satire intended to mock everything which comes before it . . . it is itself it mocks, along with the writer capable of producing one more example of so obsolescent a form, and especially us who are foolish enough to be reading it. It is as if the Art Novel, aware that it must die, has determined to die laughing.*

With that, Professor Fiedler goes over the side of Huck's raft. Whatever Professor Barth's gifts, humor, irony, wit are entirely lacking from his ambitious, garrulous, jocose productions. If this is the Anti-art Art Novel, then I predict that it will soon be superseded by the Anti-Anti-art Art Novel, which will doubtless prove to be our moribund friend the Art Novel. I suspect that the works of Professor Barth are written not so much to be read as to be taught. If this is the case then, according to Fiedler's own definition, they are Art Novels. Certainly they are not destined for the mass marketplace where daydreams of sex and of money, of movie stars and of murdered presidents are not apt to be displaced by a leaden narrative whose burden is (oh, wit, oh, irony) the universe is the university is the universe.

Happily, Fiedler soon abandons the highlands of culture for those lowlands where thrive science fiction and the Western, two genres that appear to reflect the night mind of the race. Fiedler mentions with approval some recent "neo-Pop Novels." *Little Big Man* excites him and he is soon back on his familiar warpath as white skin confronts redskin. Yet why the "neo" in front of Pop? Surely what used to be called "commercial fiction" has never ceased to reflect the dreams and prejudices of those still able to read. Fiedler does not quite deal with this. He goes off at a tangent. "At the moment of the rebirth of the novel, all order and distinction seem lost, as High Art and Low merge into each other, as books become films. . . ." Fiedler ends with an analysis of a novel turned into film called *Drive, He Said*, and he suggests that "therapeutic" madness may be the next chapter in our collective dreaming: injuns, niggers, subversives . . . or something.

Rebirth of the novel? That seems unlikely. The University-novel tends to be stillborn, suitable only for classroom biopsy. The Public-novel continues to be written but the audience for it is drifting away. Those brought up on the passive pleasures of films and television find the act of reading anything at all difficult and unrewarding. Ambitious novelists are poignantly aware of the general decline in what Professor Halperin would call "reading skills." Much of Mr. Donald Barthelme's latest novel, *The Dead Father*, is written in a kind of numbing baby talk reminiscent of the "see Jane run" primary school textbooks. Of course Mr. Barthelme means to be ironic. Of course he knows his book is not very interesting to read, but then life is not very interesting to live either. Hopefully, as Professor Halperin would say, the book will self-destruct once it has been ritually praised wherever English is taught but not learned.

Obviously what Fiedler calls the Art Novel is in more trouble than the Pop novel. Movies still need larvae to metamorphose into moths. The Anti-art Art Novel does not exist despite the nervous attempts of teachers to find a way of making the novel if not news, really and truly new. I think it unlikely that Barthes, Barth, and Barthelme will ever produce that unified field theory of Art-Novel writing and theory so long dreamed of by students of Freytag's pyramid.

Meanwhile, the caravans bark, and the dogs move on. Last December the Modern Language Association met in San Francisco. According to a reliable authority, the most advanced of the young bureaucrats of literature were all reading and praising the works of Burroughs. Not William, Edgar Rice.

Times Literary Supplement
February 20, 1976

SOME MEMORIES

OF THE GLORIOUS BIRD

AND AN EARLIER SELF

"I particularly like New York on hot summer nights when all the . . . uh, superfluous people are off the streets." Those were, I think, the first words Tennessee addressed to me; then the foggy blue eyes blinked, and a nervous chuckle filled the moment's silence before I said whatever I said.

Curtain rising. The place: an apartment at the American Academy in Rome. Occasion: a party for some newly arrived Americans, among them Frederic Prokosch, Samuel Barber. The month: March 1948. The day: glittering. What else could a March day be in the golden age?

I am pleased that I can remember so clearly my first meeting with the Glorious Bird, as I almost immediately called him for reasons long since forgotten (premonition, perhaps, of the eventual take-off and flight of youth's sweet bird?). Usually, I forget first meetings, excepting always those solemn audiences granted by the old and famous when I was young and green. I recall vividly every detail of André Gide's conversation and appearance, including the dark velvet beret he wore in his study at 1-bis rue Vaneau. I recall even more vividly my visits to George Santayana in his cell at the Convent of the Blue Nuns. All these audiences, meetings, introductions took place in that *anno mirabilis* 1948, a year that proved to be the exact midpoint between the end of the Second World War and the beginning of what looks to be a permanent cold war. At the time, of course, none of us knew where history had placed us.

At that first meeting I thought Tennessee every bit as ancient as Gide and Santayana. After all, I was twenty-two. He was thirty-seven; but claimed to be thirty-three on the sensible ground that the four years he had spent working for a shoe company did not count. Now he was the most celebrated American playwright. *A Streetcar Named Desire* was still running in New York when we met that evening in a flat overlooking what was, in those days, a quiet city where hardly anyone was superfluous unless it was us, the first group of American writers and artists to arrive in Rome after the war.

In 1946 and 1947 Europe was still out-of-bounds for foreigners. But by 1948 the Italians had begun to pull themselves together, demonstrating once more their astonishing ability to cope with disaster which is so perfectly balanced by their absolute inability to deal with success.

Rome was strange to all of us. For one thing, Italy had been sealed off not only by war but by Fascism. Since the early thirties few English or American artists knew Italy well. Those who did included mad Ezra, gentle Max, spurious B.B., and, of course, the Anglo-American historian Harold (now Sir Harold) Acton, in stately residence at Florence. By 1948 Acton had written supremely well about both the Bourbons of Naples and the later Medici of Florence; unfortunately, he was—is—prone to the writing of memoirs. And so, wanting no doubt to flesh out yet another chapter in the ongoing story of a long and marvelously uninteresting life, Acton came down to Rome to look at the new invaders. What he believed he saw and heard, he subsequently published in a little volume called *More Memoirs of an Aesthete*, a work to be cherished for its quite remarkable number of unaesthetic misprints and misspellings.

"After the First World War American writers and artists had emigrated to Paris; now they pitched upon Rome." So Acton begins. "According to Stendhal, the climate was enough to gladden anybody, but this was not the reason: one of them explained to me that it was the facility of finding taxis, and very little of Rome can be seen from a taxi. Classical and Romantic Rome was no more to them than a picturesque background. Tennessee Williams, Victor [he means Frederic] Prokosch and Gore Vidal created a bohemian annexe to the American Academy. . . ." Liking Rome for its many taxis is splendid stuff and I wish I had said it. Certainly whoever did was putting Acton on, since the charm of Rome—

1948—was the lack of automobiles of any kind. But Acton is just getting into stride. More to come.

Toward the end of March Tennessee gave a party to inaugurate his new flat in the Via Aurora (in the golden age even the street names were apt). Somehow or other, Acton got himself invited to the party. I remember him floating like some large pale fish through the crowded room; from time to time, he would make a sudden lunge at this or that promising bit of bait while Tennessee, he tells us, "wandered as a lost soul among the guests he assembled in an apartment which might have been in New York. . . . Neither he nor any of the group I met with him spoke Italian, yet he had a typically Neapolitan protégé who could speak no English."

At this time Tennessee and I had been in Rome for only a few weeks and French, not Italian, was the second language of the reasonably well-educated American of that era. On the other hand, Prokosch knew Italian, German, and French; he also bore with becoming grace the heavy weight of a Yale doctorate in Middle English. But to Acton the author of *The Asiatics*, the translator of Hölderlin and Louise Labé was just another barbarian whose works "fell short of his perfervid imagination, [he] had the dark good looks of an advertiser of razor blades. . . ." Happily, "Gore Vidal, the youngest in age, aggressively handsome in a clean-limbed sophomore style, had success written all over him. . . . His candour was engaging but he was slightly on the defensive, as if he anticipated an attack on his writings or his virtue." Well, the young G.V. wasn't so dumb: seeing the old one-two plainly in the middle distance, he kept sensibly out of reach.

"A pudgy, taciturn, moustached little man without any obvious distinction." Thus Acton describes Tennessee. He then zeroes in on the "protégé" from Naples, a young man whom Acton calls "Pierino." Acton tells us that Pierino had many complaints about Tennessee and his friends, mostly due to the language barrier. The boy was also eager to go to America. Acton tried to discourage him. Even so, Pierino was enthralled. " 'You are the first *galantuomo* who has spoken to me this evening.' " After making a date to see the *galantuomo* later on that evening, Pierino split. Acton then told Tennessee, "as tactfully as I could, that his young protégé felt neglected. . . . [Tennessee] rubbed his chin

thoughtfully and said nothing, a little perplexed. There was something in-
nocently childish about his expression." It does not occur to the memoirist that Tennessee might have been alarmed at his strange guest's bad
manners. "Evidently he was not aware that Pierino wanted to be taken to
America and I have wondered since whether he took him there, for that
was my last meeting with Tennessee Williams." It must be said that Acton managed to extract quite a lot of copy out of a single meeting. To put
his mind at rest, Tennessee did take Pierino to America and Pierino is
now a married man and doing, as they say, well.

"This trifling episode illustrated the casual yet condescending attitude of certain foreigners towards the young Italians they cultivated on
account of their Latin charm without any interest in their character, aspirations, or desires." This sentiment or sentimentality could be put just
as well the other way around and with far more accuracy. Italian trade has
never had much interest in the character, aspirations, or desires of those
to whom they rent their ass. When Acton meditates upon The Italian
Boy, a sweet and sickly hypocrisy clouds his usually sharp prose and we
are in E. M. Forsterland where the lower orders (male) are worshiped,
and entirely misunderstood. But magnum of sour grapes to one side, Acton is by no means inaccurate. Certainly he got right Tennessee's indifference to place, art, history. The Bird seldom reads a book and the only
history he knows is his own; he depends, finally, on a romantic genius to
get him through life. Above all, he is a survivor, never more so than now
in what he calls his "crocodile years."

I picked up Tennessee's *Memoirs* with a certain apprehension. I
looked myself up in the Index; read the entries and found some errors,
none grave. I started to read; was startled by the technique he had chosen. Some years ago, Tennessee told me that he had been reading (that
is to say, looking at) my "memoir in the form of a novel" *Two Sisters*. In
this book I alternated sections describing certain events in 1948 with my
everyday life while writing the book. Memory sections I called *Then*. The
day-by-day descriptions I called *Now*. At the time Tennessee found *Two
Sisters* interesting because he figured in it. He must also have found it
technically interesting because he has serenely appropriated my form
and has now no doubt forgotten just how the idea first came to him to

describe the day-to-day life of a famous beleaguered playwright acting in an off-Broadway production of the failing play *Small Craft Warnings* while, in alternating sections, he recalls the early days not only of Tennessee Williams but of one Thomas Lanier Williams, who bears only a faint familial resemblance to the playwright we all know from a thousand and one altogether too candid interviews.

There is a foreword and, like all forewords, it is meant to disarm. Unfortunately, it armed me to the teeth. During the 1973 tryout of a play in New Haven, Tennessee was asked to address some Yale drama students. Incidentally, the style of the foreword is unusually seductive, the old master at his most beguiling: self-pity and self-serving kept in exquisite balance by the finest comic style since S. L. Clemens.

"I found myself entering (through a door marked EXIT) an auditorium considerably smaller than the Shubert but containing a more than proportionately small audience. I would say roughly about two-score and ten, not including a large black dog which was resting in the lap of a male student in the front row. . . . The young faces before me were uniformly inexpressive of any kind of emotional reaction to my entrance. . . ." I am surprised that Tennessee was surprised. The arrogance and self-satisfaction of drama students throughout Academe are among the few constants in a changing world. Any student who has read Sophocles in translation is, demonstrably, superior to Tennessee Williams in the untidy flesh. These dummies reflect of course the proud mediocrity of their teachers, who range, magisterially, through something called "world drama" where evolution works only backward. Teachers and taught are to be avoided.

"I am not much good at disguising my feelings, and after a few moments I abandoned all pretense of feeling less dejection than I felt." The jokes did not work. So "I heard myself describing an encounter, then quite recent, with a fellow playwright in the Oak Room Bar at Manhattan's Plaza Hotel." It was with "my old friend Gore Vidal. I had embraced him warmly. However, Mr. Vidal is not a gentleman to be disarmed by a cordial embrace, and when, in response to his perfunctory inquiries about the progress of rehearsals . . . I told him . . . all seemed a dream come true after many precedent nightmares, he smiled at me with a sort of rueful benevolence and said 'Well, Bird, it won't do much good, I'm afraid, you've had too much bad personal exposure for anything to help you much anymore.'

"Well, then, for the first time, I could see a flicker of interest in the young faces before me. It may have been the magic word Vidal or it may have been his prophecy of my professional doom." Asked if the prognosis was accurate, Tennessee looked at the black dog and said, "Ask the dog."

An unsettling anecdote. I have no memory of the Plaza meeting. I am also prone, when dining late, to suffer from what Dorothy Parker used grimly to refer to as "the frankies," or straight talk for the other person's good like frankly-that-child-would-not-have-been-born-mongoloid-if-you-hadn't. . . . An eyewitness, however, assures me that I did not say what Tennessee attributes to me. Yet his paranoia always has some basis in reality. I have an uncomfortable feeling that I was probably thinking what I did not say and what he later thought I did say. When it comes to something unspoken, the Bird has a sharp ear.

It is hard now to realize what a bad time of it Tennessee used to have from the American press. During the Forties and Fifties the anti-fag battalions were everywhere on the march. From the high lands of *Partisan Review* to the middle ground of *Time* magazine, envenomed attacks on real or suspected fags never let up. A *Time* cover story on Auden was killed when the managing editor of the day was told that Auden was a fag. From 1945 to 1961 *Time* attacked with unusual ferocity everything produced or published by Tennessee Williams. "Fetid swamp" was the phrase most used to describe his work. But, in *Time*, as well as in time, all things will come to pass. The Bird is now a beloved institution.

Today, at sixty-four, Tennessee has the same voracious appetite for work and for applause that he had at twenty-four. More so, I would suspect, since glory is a drug more addictive than any other as heroes have known from Achilles on (Donald Windham's *roman à clef* about Tennessee bore the apt title *The Hero Continues*). But fashions in the theater change. The superstar of the Forties and Fifties fell on bad times, and that is the burden of these memoirs. In sharp detail we are told how the hero came into being. Less sharply, Tennessee describes the bad days when the booze and the pills caused him to hallucinate; to slip out of a world quite bad enough as it is into nightmare land. "I said to my friend Gore, 'I slept through the Sixties,' and he said, 'You didn't miss a thing.' " Tennessee often quotes this exchange. But he leaves out the accompanying caveat: "If you missed the Sixties, Bird, God knows what you are going to do with the Seventies."

But of course life is not divided into good and bad decades; it is simply living. For a writer, life is, again simply, writing and in these memoirs the old magician can still create a world. But since it is hardly news to the Bird that we are for the night, the world he shows us is no longer the Romantic's lost Eden but Prospero's island where, at sunset, magicians often enjoy revealing the sources of their rude magic, the tricks of a trade.

Not that a magician is honor-bound to tell the whole truth. For instance: "I want to admit to you that I undertook this memoir for mercenary reasons. It is actually the first piece of work, in the line of writing, that I have undertaken for material profit." The sniffy tone is very much that of St. Theresa scrubbing floors. Actually, Tennessee is one of the richest of living writers. After all, a successful play will earn its author a million or more dollars and Tennessee has written quite a few successful plays. Also, thirteen of his works have been made into films.

Why the poor-mouthing? Because it has always been the Bird's tactic to appear in public flapping what looks to be a pathetically broken wing. By arousing universal pity, he hopes to escape predators. In the old days before a play opened on Broadway, the author would be asked to write a piece for the Sunday *New York Times* drama section. Tennessee's pieces were always thrilling; sometimes horrendous. He would reveal how that very morning he had coughed up blood with his sputum. But, valiantly, he had gone on writing, knowing the new play would be his last work, ever . . . By the time the Bird had finished working us over, only Louis Kronenberger at *Time* had the heart to attack him.

But now that Tennessee's physical and mental health are good (he would deny this instantly; "I have had, in recent days, a series of palpitations of the variety known as terminal"), only the cry of poverty will, he thinks, act as lightning conductor and insure him a good press for the

Memoirs. Certainly he did not write this book for the $50,000 advance. As always, fame is the spur. Incidentally, he has forgotten that in the past he *did* write for money when he was under contract to MGM and worked on a film called *Marriage Is a Private Affair*, starring Lana Turner and James Craig (unless of course Tennessee now sees in this movie that awesome moral grandeur first detected by the film critic Myra Breckinridge).

The *Memoirs* start briskly. Tennessee is a guest at a country house in Wiltshire near Stonehenge. On the grounds of the estate is a "stone which didn't quite make it to Henge." He looks himself up in *Who's Who*. Broods on his past; shifts back and forth in time. *Now* and *Then*. The early days are fascinating to read about even though the Williams family is already known to every playgoer not only from *The Glass Menagerie* but also from the many other plays and stories in which appear, inexorably, Rose the Sister, Edwina the Mother, Dakin the Brother, Cornelius the Father, Reverend Dakin the Grandfather, as well as various other relatives now identified for the first time. He also tells us how he was hooked by the theater when some St. Louis amateurs put on a play he had written. "I knew that writing was my life, and its failure would be my death. . . ."

I have never known any writer with the exception of the artistically gifted and humanly appalling Carson McCullers who cared so much about the opinion of those condemned to write for newspapers. Uneasily confronting a truly remarkable hunger for absolute praise and total notice, Tennessee admits that, when being interviewed, he instinctively "hams it up in order to provide 'good copy.' The reason? I guess a need to convince the world that I do indeed still exist and to make this fact a matter of public interest and amusement." Fair enough, Bird. But leave your old friends out.

"This book is a sort of catharsis of puritanical guilt feelings, I suppose. 'All good art is an indiscretion.' Well, I can't assure you that this book will be art, but it is bound to be an indiscretion, since it deals with my adult life. . . .

"Of course I could devote this whole book to a discussion of the art of drama, but wouldn't that be a bore?

"It would bore me to extinction, I'm afraid, and it would be a very,

very short book, about three sentences to the page with extremely wide margins. The plays speak for themselves."

A wise choice: the plays do speak for themselves and Tennessee's mind is not, to say the least, at home with theory. Most beautifully, the plays speak for themselves. Not only does Tennessee have a marvelous comedic sense but his gloriously outrageous dramatic effects can be enormously satisfying. He makes poetic (without quotes) the speech of those half-educated would-be genteel folk who still maintain their babble in his head. Only on those rare occasions when he tries to depict educated or upper-class people does he falter. Somewhat reproachfully, he told me that he had been forced several times to use a dictionary while reading *Two Sisters*.

What, I asked, was one of the words you had to look up? "Solipsistic," he said. Tennessee's vocabulary has never been large (I note that he still thinks "eclectic" means "esoteric"). But then he is not the sort of writer who sees words on the page; rather he hears them in his head and when he is plugged into the right character, the wrong word never sounds.

"Life that winter in Rome: a golden dream, and I don't just mean Raffaello [Acton's 'Pierino'] and the mimosa and total freedom of life. Stop there: What I do mean is the total freedom of life and Raffaello and the mimosa. . . ." That season we were, all of us, symbolically, out of jail. Free of poverty and hack work, Tennessee had metamorphosed into the Glorious Bird while I had left behind me three years in the wartime army and a near-fatal bout with hepatitis. So it was, at the beginning of that golden dream, we met.

Tennessee's version: "[Gore] had just published a best-seller, called *The City and the Pillar*, which was one of the first homosexual novels of consequence. I had not read it but I knew that it had made the best-seller lists and that it dealt with a 'forbidden subject.' " Later, Tennessee actually read the book (the only novel of mine he has ever been able to get through) and said, "You know you spoiled it with that ending. You didn't know what a good book you had." Fair comment.

"Gore was a handsome kid, about twenty-four [*sic*], and I was quite taken by his wit as well as his appearance." Incidentally, I am mesmerized by the tributes to my beauty that keep cropping up in the memoirs of the period. At the time nobody reliable thought to tell me. In fact, it was my impression that I was not making out as well as most people because, with characteristic malice, Nature had allowed Guy Madison and not me to look like Guy Madison.

"We found that we had interests in common and we spent a lot of time together. Please don't imagine that I am suggesting that there was a romance." I don't remember whether or not I ever told Tennessee that I had actually seen but not met him the previous year. He was following me up Fifth Avenue while I, in turn, was stalking yet another quarry. I recognized him: he wore a blue bow tie with white polka dots. In no mood for literary encounters, I gave him a scowl and he abandoned the chase just north of Rockefeller Center. I don't recall how my own pursuit ended. We walked a lot in the golden age.

"I believe we also went to Florence that season and were entertained by that marvelous old aesthete Berenson." No, that was someone else. "And then one afternoon Gore took me to the Convent of the Blue Nuns to meet the great philosopher and essayist, by then an octogenarian and semi-invalid, Santayana." I had to drag Tennessee to meet Santayana. Neither had heard of the other. But Tennessee did stare at the old man with great interest. Afterward, the Bird remarked, "Did you notice how he said 'in the days when I had secretaries, *young men*?'"

In the *Memoirs* Tennessee tells us a great deal about his sex life, which is one way of saying nothing about oneself. Details of this body and that body tend to blur on the page as they do in life. Tennessee did not get around to his first homosexual affair until he was well into his twenties, by which time he had achieved several mature as well as sexually meaningful and life-enhancing heterosexual relationships. Except he wasn't really all that enhanced by these "mature" relationships. Lust for the male set his nerves to jangling. Why was he such a late-developer? Well, this was close to half a century ago, and Tennessee was the product of that Southern puritan environment where all sex was sin and unnatural sex was peculiarly horrible.

I think that the marked difference between my attitude toward sex and that of Tennessee made each of us somewhat startling to the other. I never had the slightest guilt or anxiety about what I always took to be a normal human appetite. He was—and is—guilt-ridden, and although he tells us that he believes in no afterlife, he is still too much the puritan not to believe in sin. At some deep level Tennessee truly believes that the homosexualist is wrong and that the heterosexualist is right. Given this all-pervading sense of guilt, he is drawn in both life and work to the idea of expiation, of death.

Tennessee tells of his affair with a dancer named Kip. But Kip left him; got married; died young. Then Tennessee was drawn to a pseudonymous lover in New Orleans; that affair ended in drink and violence. For a number of years Tennessee lived with an Italo-American, Frank Merlo. Eventually they fell out. They were reunited when Frank was dying of cancer. Frank's last days were sufficiently horrifying to satisfy any puritan's uneasy conscience while, simultaneously, justifying the romantic's extreme vision of the world: "I shall but love thee better after death."

The other line running through Tennessee's emotional life is what I call the Monster Women. Surrogate mothers one might say if Tennessee's own mother, Miss Edwina, were not so implacably in this world, even as I write these lines. Currently convinced that the blacks signal to one another during the long St. Louis nights by clanging the lids of the trash cans, Miss Edwina is every inch the Amanda of *The Glass Menagerie*. In fact, so powerful is Tennessee's creation that in the presence of Miss Edwina one does not listen to her but only to what he has made of her.

"I had forty gentlemen callers that day," she says complacently. We are having dinner in the restaurant of the Robert Clay Hotel in Miami. Delicately she holds a fork with a shrimp on it. Fork and shrimp proceed slowly to her mouth while Tennessee and I stare, hypnotized not only by the constant flow of conversation but by the never-eaten shrimp for just as she is about to take the first bite, yet another anecdote wells up from deep inside her . . . ah, *solipsistic* brain and the fork returns to the plate, the shrimp untouched. "Tom, remember when that little dog took the hat with the plume and ran all 'round the yard . . . ?" This is also from *The Glass Menagerie*. Tennessee nervously clears his throat. Again the shrimp slowly rises to the wide straight mouth which resembles nothing so much as the opening to a miniature letter box—one designed for engraved invitations only. But once again the shrimp does not arrive. "Tom, do you remember . . . ?"

Tennessee clears his throat again. *"Mother, eat your shrimp."*

"Why," counters Miss Edwina, "do you keep making that funny sound in your throat?"

"Because, Mother, when you destroy someone's life you must expect certain nervous disabilities."

Yet Tennessee went on adding even more grotesque ladies than Miss Edwina to his life. I could never take any of them from Carson McCullers to Jane Bowles to Anna Magnani. Yes, yes, yes, they were superb talents all. Part of the artistic heritage of the twentieth century. I concede their talent, their glory, their charm—for Tennessee but not for me. Carson spoke only of her work. Of its greatness. The lugubrious Southern sing-song voice never stopped: "Did ya see muh lovely play? Did ya lahk muh lovely play? Am Ah gonna win the Pew-litzuh prahzz?" Jane ("the finest writer of fiction we have in the States") Bowles was more original. She thought and talked a good deal about food and made powerful scenes in restaurants. The best that one could say of Magnani was that she liked dogs. When Marlon Brando agreed to act with her in the film of Tennessee's *Orpheus Descending*, he warned, "When I do a scene with her, I'm going to carry a rock in each hand."

I don't know what Tennessee gets from the Monster Women, but if they give him solace nothing else matters. Certainly he has a huge appetite for the grotesque not only in art but in life. In fact, he is dogged by the grotesque. Once, in the airport at Miami, we were stopped by a plump middle-aged man who had known Tennessee whom he called Tom from the old days in St. Louis. The man seemed perfectly ordinary. He talked to Tennessee about friends they had in common. Then I noticed that the man was carrying a large string bag containing two roast turkeys and a half-dozen loaves of bread. "What," I asked, "is that?" The man gave us a knowing wink. "Well, I got me two roast turkeys in there. And also these loaves of bread *because you know about the food in Miami.*" Then he was gone. It would seem that the true artist need never search for a subject; the subject always knows where to find him.

It is curious how friends actually regard one another—or think they do—when memoir-time rolls around, and the boneyard beckons. A figure of some consequence in our far-off golden age was the composer-novelist Paul Bowles. From time to time over the years, Tennessee has bestowed a number of Walter Winchellish Orchids on Paul as well as on Jane (I fear that a lifetime on Broadway has somewhat corrupted the Bird's everyday speech and prose although nothing, happily, can affect the authenticity of those voices in his head). Certainly Bowles was an early hero of Tennessee's.

But now let us see what Bowles makes of Tennessee in *his* memoir *Without Stopping*. "One morning when we were getting ready to leave for the beach" (this was Acapulco, 1940), "someone arrived at the door and asked to see me. It was a round-faced, sun-burned young man in a big floppy sombrero and a striped sailor sweater, who said his name was Tennessee Williams, that he was a playwright, and that Lawrence Langner of the Theatre Guild had told him to look me up. I asked him to come in and installed him in a hammock, explaining that we had to hurry to the beach with friends. I brought him books and magazines and rum and coke, and told him to ask the servants for sandwiches if he got hungry. Then we left. Seven hours later we got back to the house and found our visitor lying contentedly in the hammock, reading. We saw him again each day until he left."

Paul Bowles used to quote Virgil Thomson's advice to a young music critic: Never intrude your personal opinions when you write music criticism. "The words that you use to describe what you've heard will be the criticism." Bowles on Tennessee demonstrates a mastery of the unsaid. Needless to say, Tennessee read what Bowles had written about him. Now watch the Bird as he strikes . . .

"It was there in Acapulco that summer that I first met Jane and Paul Bowles. They were staying at a pension in town and Paul was, as ever, upset about the diet and his stomach. The one evening that we spent together that summer was given over almost entirely to the question of what he could eat in Acapulco that he could digest, and poor little Janie kept saying, 'Oh, Bubbles, if you'd just stick to cornflakes and fresh fruit!' and so on and so on. None of her suggestions relieved his dyspeptic humor.

"I thought them a very odd and charming couple." I think I give Tennessee that round, on points. But Bowles's prose still remains the perfect model for judgment by indirection even though, like Tennessee, he occasionally gets the facts wrong. Bowles writes: "Gore had just played a practical joke on Tennessee and Truman Capote which he recounted to me in dialect, as it were. He had called Tennessee on the telephone and, being a stupendous mimic, had made himself into Truman for the occasion. Then, complete with a snigger, he induced Tennessee to make uncomplimentary remarks about Gore's writing."

This is a curious variation on the actual story. A number of times I would ring Tennessee, using Capote's voice. The game was to see how long it would take him to figure out that it was not Capote. One day I rang and spoke to what I thought was Tennessee. But it was Frank Merlo, newly installed in the flat. I had not got beyond my imitable whine, "This is *Tru*man," when Frank began to attack Tennessee. I broke the connection. Frank never knew whether or not I had repeated his complaints to Tennessee. I did not. But years later I did tell Bowles the story.

Back to 1948: "In those days Truman was about the best companion you could want," writes Tennessee. "He had not turned bitchy. Well, he had not turned *maliciously* bitchy. But he was full of fantasies and mischief." That summer Capote arrived in Paris where Tennessee and I were staying at the Hôtel de l'Université ("A raffish hotel but it suited Gore and me perfectly as there was no objection to young callers"), and Capote would keep us entranced with mischievous fantasies about the great. Apparently, the very sight of him was enough to cause lifelong heterosexual men to tumble out of unsuspected closets. When Capote refused to surrender his virtue to the drunken Errol Flynn, "Errol threw *all* my suitcases out of the window of the Beverly Wilshire Hotel!" I should note here that the young Capote was no less attractive in his person then than he is today.

When Tennessee and I would exchange glances during these stories, Capote would redouble his efforts. Did we know that Albert Camus was in love with him? Yes, Camus! Madly in love. Recently Capote's biographer told me that the Capote-Camus connection might well prove to be a key chapter. No doubt it will also provide a startling footnote to the life story of Camus, a man known until now as a womanizer. Then Capote showed us a gold and amethyst ring. "From André Gide," he sighed. Happily, I was able to check that one out. A few days later I called on Gide in the company of my English publisher. "How," I asked in my best Phillips Exeter French, "did you find Truman Capote?" "Who?" Gide asked. I suspect that it was then, in the fabulous summer of '48, that the nonfiction novel was born.

To return again to 1948, I have a bit more to report on that season.

"Frankie and I had been out late one evening and when we returned to the apartment the transom on the front door was open and from within came the voice of Truman Capote, shrill with agitation. . . . In the apartment were Truman, Gore Vidal, and a female policeman. . . . It seemed that Truman and Gore, still on friendly terms at this point, had got a bit drunk together and had climbed in through the transom of the apartment to wait for me and Frankie."

Before this story petrifies into literary history, let me amend the record. Tennessee, an actress, and I came back to Tennessee's flat to find Capote and a friend in the clutches of the law. They had indeed been caught entering the flat. But by the time we arrived, Capote had matters well under control. Plainclotheswoman and plainclothesman were listening bug-eyed to Capote, who was telling them *every*thing about the private lives of Mr. and Mrs. Charles Chaplin.

Tennessee's asides on the various personages who have come his way are often amusing, sometimes revelatory. He describes a hilarious dinner with the Russian performer Yevtushenko, who saw fit to lecture Tennessee on commercialism, sexual perversion, and the responsibilities of art while swilling expensive wine. Tennessee admired Dylan Thomas until he actually met him and received "this put-down: 'How does it feel to make all that Hollywood money?' " There was also the snub from Sartre. Tennessee gave a party at the Hôtel de l'Université, hoping that Sartre would come. Instead the Master sat a few blocks away at a café, and for several hours he made a point of *not* coming to the party despite the pleas of various emissaries.

Tennessee omits to mention a splendid lunch given us at the Grand Véfour by Jean Cocteau, who wanted the French rights to *A Streetcar Named Desire* for Jean Marais to act in. I came along as translator. Marais looked beautiful but sleepy. Cocteau was characteristically brilliant. He spoke no English but since he could manage an occasional "the" sound as well as the final "g," he often gave the impression that he was speaking English. Tennessee knew no French. He also had no clear idea just who Cocteau was, while Cocteau knew nothing about Tennessee except

that he had written a popular American play with a splendid part in it for
his lover Marais. Between Tennessee's solemn analyses of the play and
Cocteau's rhetoric about theater (the long arms flailed like semaphores
denoting some dangerous last junction), no one made any sense at all except Marais who broke his long silence to ask, apropos the character
Stanley Kowalski, "Will I have to use a Polish accent?"

Although Marais and Cocteau broke up soon afterward, Cocteau did
the play without Marais. Cocteau's adaptation was, apparently, a gorgeous mess. Naked black youths writhed through beaded curtains while
Arletty, miscast as Blanche, struck attitudes among peacock feathers.

The situation of a practicing playwright in the United States is not a
happy one, to understate the matter. Broadway is more and more an
abandoned parcel of real estate. Except for a native farce or two and a
handful of "serious" plays imported from the British Isles, Broadway is
noted chiefly for large and usually bad musicals. During the theater season of 1947–48 there were 43 straight plays running on Broadway. In
1974–75 there were 18, mostly imported. Adventurous plays are now
done off-Broadway and sometimes off-off . . . where our memoirist ended
up as a performer in *Small Craft Warnings*.

Unique among writers, the American playwright must depend upon
the praise of journalists who seldom know very much about anything save
the prejudices of their employers. With the collapse of a half-dozen newspapers in the last third of a century, the success of a play now depends
almost entirely upon the good will of the critic for *The New York Times*.
The current reviewer is an amiable and enthusiastic Englishman who
knows a good deal about ballet but not so much about the social and political nuances of his adopted land. Yet at sixty-four Tennessee Williams
is still trying to curry favor with the press. Of *Small Craft Warnings*,
"Clive Barnes" (in *The New York Times*) "was cautiously respectful. With
the exception of Leonard Harris, I disregard TV reviews. I suppose they
were generally negative."

Then Tennessee has second thoughts. And a new paragraph: "To say
that I disregard TV reviews is hardly the total truth. How could I disregard any review which determines the life or death of a production?"
How indeed? Yet after thirty years of meaningless praise and equally
meaningless abuse, it is no wonder that Tennessee is a bit batty. On

those rare occasions when Tennessee's literary peers have got around to looking at his work, the result has been depressing: witness, Mary McCarthy's piece "A Streetcar Named Success."

There have been complaints that these *Memoirs* tell us too much about Tennessee's sex life and too little about his art. Personally, I find the candor about his sex life interesting if not illuminating. At the worst, it will feed that homophobia which is too much a part of the national psyche. Yet perhaps it is better to write this sort of thing oneself rather than leave it to others to invent.

Recently that venerable vendor of book-chat Alfred Kazin wrote, "Vidal gets more literary mileage out of his sex life than anyone since Oscar Wilde and Jean Cocteau." This struck me as breathtakingly wrong. First, neither Wilde nor Cocteau ever exploited his sex life for "mileage." Each was reticent in public. Eventually the law revealed the private life of the first, while friends (and an ambiguous sort of unsigned memoir) revealed the life of the second. The book-chat writer does mention the admittedly too many interviews I've lately given to magazines like *Playboy* where sex is always a Solemn and Sacred subject and where I, too, am Solemn but never personal. As evidence of my seeking mileage he quotes the rather lame " 'In youth I never missed a trick . . . I tried everything . . . I could no more go to bed with somebody whose work I admired than I could . . . well, make love to a mirror. Fame in others switches off desire.' " Not, I would say, the most prurient of giveaway lines. Except in *Two Sisters*, a memoir done with mirrors, I have not used myself as a subject for private analysis on the ground that since we live in a time where the personality of the writer is everything and what he writes is nothing, only a fool would aid the enemy by helping to trivialize life, work.

A columnist reports that Tennessee was obliged to cut his *Memoirs* in half because of the "filth." I hope that we are given that other half one day; and I doubt that there will be much "filth," only indiscretions which ought to be interesting. After all, Tennessee has known or come across a great many of our time's movers and shakers. I say "come across" because for a long period he was . . . well, inattentive. Sometimes the stupefying combination of Nembutal and vodka (now abandoned) addled him. I was present when Edna Ferber (yes, Edna Ferber) came over to our table at a restaurant and introduced herself. With considerable charm, she told

Tennessee how much she admired him. He listened to her with eyes that had narrowed to what Miss Ferber would have described as "mere slits." As she walked away, the Bird hissed, "Why is that woman attacking me?"

Tennessee is the sort of writer who does not develop; he simply continues. By the time he was an adolescent he had his themes. Constantly he plays and replays the same small but brilliant set of cards. I am not aware that any new information (or feeling?) has got through to him in the twenty-eight years since our Roman spring. In consequence, we have drifted apart. "Gore no longer receives me," said the Bird to one of his innumerable interviewers; and he put this down to my allegedly glamorous social life. But the reason for the drifting apart is nothing more than difference of temperament. I am a compulsive learner of new things while the Bird's occasional and sporadic responses to the world outside the proscenium arch have not been fortunate. "Castro was, after all, a gentleman," he announced after an amiable meeting with the dictator. Tell that to the proscribed fags of Cuba.

Tennessee's much publicized conversion to Roman Catholicism took place during the time of his great confusion. Shortly after the Bird was received into the arms of Mother Church, a Jesuit priest rang him up and asked if he would like an audience with the Pope? a meeting with the head of the Jesuit order? Oh yes. Yes! Tennessee was delighted. The next morning the priest arrived to take Tennessee to the Vatican where, presumably, the Pope was waiting on tenderhooks to examine the Church's latest haul. Unfortunately, Tennessee had forgotten all about the audience. He would have to beg off, he said; he was just not up to the Pope that day. The priest was stunned. The Pope's reaction has not been recorded.

The Jesuits, however, are made of tougher material. The secretary of the Black Pope rang to say that since a cocktail party had been arranged, Mr. Williams was going to be there, or else. The Bird was present. Almost immediately, he began to ham it up about God. Now if there is anything a Jesuit likes less than chat of God, it is having to listen to the religious enthusiasm of a layman. Trying to deflect Tennessee from what was fast turning into a Billy Graham exhortation about God and goodness, one of the Jesuits asked, "How do you start to write a play, Mr. Williams?" The Bird barely paused in his glorious ascent. "I start," he said sharply, "with a sentence." He then told the assembled members of the Society of Jesus that ever since becoming a Roman Catholic, he had felt a divine presence constantly with him. The Jesuits shifted uneasily at this. Like the old trouper he is, the Bird then paused abruptly in midflight in order to see just what effect he was having. After a moment of embarrassed silence, one of the Jesuits asked, timidly, "Is this presence a *warm* presence?"

"There is," said the Bird firmly, "no temperature."

But despite the "conversion," Tennessee now writes, "I am unable to believe that there is anything but permanent oblivion after death. . . . For me, what is there but to feel beneath me the steadily rising current of mortality and to summon from my blood whatever courage is native to it, and once there was a great deal." As he ends the *Memoirs*, he thinks back upon Hart Crane, whose legend has always haunted him. But though a romantic, Tennessee is no Crane. For one thing, it is too late to choose an abrupt death at sea. For another, art is too beguiling and difficult: "life is made up of moment-to-moment occurrences in the nerves and the perceptions, and try as you may, you can't commit them to the actualities of your own history."

But Tennessee continues to try. Now he has invited the world to take a close look at him, more or less as he is (the lighting of course has been carefully arranged, and he is not one to confuse an Entrance with an Exit). The result should be gratifying. The Glorious Bird is not only recognized but applauded in the streets. When he came to sign copies of the *Memoirs* in a large Manhattan bookstore, nearly a thousand copies were sold and the store had to be shut because of overcrowding. The resemblance to the latter days of Judy Garland would be disquieting were it not for the happy fact that since Tennessee cannot now die young he will probably not die at all (his grandfather lived for almost a century). In any case, artists who continue to find exhilarating the puzzles art proposes never grow bored and so have no need of death.

As for life? Well, that is a hard matter. But it was always a hard matter for those of us born with a sense of the transiency of these borrowed atoms that make up our corporeal being.

"I need," Tennessee writes with sudden poignancy, "somebody to laugh with." Well, don't we all, Bird? Anyway, be happy that your art has proved to be one of those stones that really did make it to Henge, enabling future magicians to gauge from its crafty placement not only the dour winter solstice of our last days but the summer solstice, too—the golden dream, the mimosa, the total freedom, and all that lovely time unspent now spent.

The New York Review of Books
February 5, 1976

EDMUND WILSON:

THIS CRITIC AND THIS GIN

AND THESE SHOES

On February 2, 1821, gin-drinker Lord Byron wrote in his Ravenna Journal: "I have been considering what can be the reason why I always wake at a certain hour in the morning, and always in very bad spirits—I may say, in actual despair and despondency, in all respects—even of that which pleased me overnight. . . . In England, five years ago, I had the same kind of hypochondria, but accompanied with so violent a thirst that I have drank as many as fifteen bottles of soda-water in one night, after going to bed, and been still thirsty. . . . What is it?—liver?"

In Edmund Wilson's journal, published as *Upstate*, he wrote, in 1955: "One evening (August 13, Saturday) I drank a whole bottle of champagne and what was left of a bottle of old Grand-Dad and started on a bottle of red wine—I was eating Limburger cheese and gingersnaps. This began about five in the afternoon—I fell asleep in my chair, but woke up when Beverly came, thinking it was the next morning. I decided to skip supper; and felt queasy for the next twenty-four hours." The sixty-year-old Wilson does not ask, what is it? as Byron did. Wilson knows. "This kind of life," he writes, rather demurely, "in the long run, does, however, get rather unhealthy."

About the time that Wilson was munching on those gingersnaps and Limburger cheese, washed down with fiery waters, I received a letter from Upton Sinclair (whom I had never met), asking me about something. Then, obsessively, from left field, as it were, Sinclair denounced John Barleycorn. In the course of a long life, practically every writer Sinclair had known had died of drink, starting with his friend Jack London. Needless to say, this was not the sort of unsolicited letter that one likes to read while starting on one's fifteenth bottle of soda water, or to be precise and up-to-date, Coca-Cola, Georgia's sole gift to a nation whose first century was recently described in a book titled *The Alcoholic Republic* . . . of letters, I remember adding to myself when I first saw the book.

In this century, it would be safe to say that a significant percent of American writers are to a greater or lesser degree alcoholics and why this should be the case I leave to the medicine men. Alcoholism ended the careers of Hemingway, Fitzgerald, and Faulkner, to name three fashionable novelists of our mid-century. Out of charity toward the descendants and keepers of the still flickering flames of once glorious literary figures, I shall name no other names. Heavy drinking stopped Hemingway from writing anything of value in his later years; killed Fitzgerald at forty-four; turned the William Faulkner of *As I Lay Dying* into a fable.

Meanwhile, the contemporary of these three blasted stars, Edmund Wilson, outlived and outworked them all; he also outdrank them. Well into his seventies, Wilson would totter into the Princeton Club and order a half-dozen martinis, to be prepared not sequentially but simultaneously—six shining glasses in a bright row, down which Wilson would work, all the while talking and thinking at a rapid pace. To the end of a long life, he kept on making the only thing he thought worth making: sense, a quality almost entirely lacking in American literature where stupidity—if sufficiently sincere and authentic—is deeply revered, and easily achieved. Although this *was* a rather unhealthy life in the long run, Wilson had a very long run indeed. But then, he was perfect proof of the proposition that the more the mind is used and fed the less apt it is to devour itself. When he died, at seventy-seven, he was busy stuffing his head with irregular Hungarian verbs. Plainly, he had a brain to match his liver.

Edmund Wilson was the last of a leisurely educated generation who were not obliged, if they were intellectually minded, to join the hicks and hacks of Academe. Wilson supported himself almost entirely by literary journalism, something not possible today if only because, for all practical purposes, literary journalism of the sort that he practiced no longer exists. Instead, book-chat is now dominated either by academic bureaucrats, crudely pursuing bureaucratic careers, or by journalists whose "leprous jealousy" (Flaubert's pretty phrase) has made mephitic the air of our alcoholic literary republic. But then, Flaubert thought that "critics write criticism because they are unable to be artists, just as a man unfit to bear arms becomes a police spy." Wilson would have challenged this romantic notion. Certainly, he would have made the point that to write essays is as much an aspect of the literary artist's temperament as the ability to evoke an alien sensibility on a page while sweating to avoid a double genitive. In any case, Wilson himself wrote stories, plays, novels. He knew how such things were made even if he was not entirely a master of any of these forms.

Of what, then, was Edmund Wilson a master? That is a question in need of an answer, or answers; and there are clues in the book at hand, *The Thirties: From Notebooks and Diaries of the Period*. At the time of Wilson's death, eight years ago, he was editing the notebooks that dealt with the Twenties. He had already finished *Upstate*, a chronicle of his works and days from the early Fifties to 1970. *Upstate* is a highly satisfactory Wilsonian book, filled with sharp personal details, long scholarly asides on those things or people or notions (like New York religions) that had caught his fancy. Although he had planned to rework his earlier records, he soon realized that he might not live long enough to complete them. He then designated, in his will, that Professor Leon Edel edit the remains, with the injunction that the text be published the way he wrote it, except for straightening out "misspellings and faulty punctuations" (but not, apparently, faulty grammar: Wilson often "feels badly"—it *is* liver). With *The Thirties*, Professor Edel had his work cut out for him because, he writes, "It is clear from the condition of the typescript that [Wilson] intended to do much more work on this book." That is understatement.

At the beginning of the Thirties, Wilson completed *Axel's Castle*; at the end, he had finished *To the Finland Station*. He wrote for *The New Republic*, supported, briefly, the American Communist party, visited the Soviet Union, Detroit, Appalachia, Scottsboro, and tried a season of teaching at the University of Chicago. The decade, in a sense, was the making of him as critic and triple thinker. Emotionally, it was shattering: in 1930 he married Margaret Canby; in 1932 she died. He also conducted a wide range of affairs, many on the raunchy side.

Professor Edel rather flinches at Wilson's "record of his own copulations" in general and the notes about his marriage in particular (so unlike the home life of our own dear Master): "some readers may be startled by this intimate candid record of a marriage." But Professor Edel is quick to remind us that this is all part of "the notebooks of a chronicler, a way of tidying the mind for his craft of criticism. . . . He tries, rather, to be a camera, for this is what he finds most comfortable." Well, yes and no.

In 1930 Edmund Wilson was thirty-five. He was a member of the minor Eastern gentry, a Princeton graduate, a World War I overseas noncombatant. In the Twenties, he had lived the life of the roaring boy but unlike the other lads that light-footed it over the greensward, he never stopped reading and writing and thinking. Thanks, in large part, to the Christers who had managed to prohibit the legal sale of spirits, alcohol was as much a curse to that generation as Gin Lane had been to the poor of eighteenth-century London. I suspect that a great deal of the grimness of this volume is a result of hangover and its concomitant despairs. At the same time, it is the record of an astonishing constitution: Wilson would write while he was drinking—something I should not have thought possible for anyone, even his doomed friend Scott Fitzgerald.

From thirty-five to forty-five men go from relative youth to middle age. The transit is often rocky. As a man's life settles into a rut, in mindless rut the man is apt to go. Certainly, this was true of Wilson, as readers of *Memoirs of Hecate County* might have suspected and as readers of *The Thirties* will now know for certain. During the so-called "ignoble" decade, despite constant drinking, Wilson was sexually very active. He enjoyed trade in the form of the Slavic Anna, a working-class woman whose proletarian ways fascinated him. He had sex with a number of those women who used to hang about writers, as well as with ladies at the edge of the great world. He bedded no Oriane but he knew at least one Guermantes *before* her translation to the aristocracy.

Although Wilson's bedmates are sometimes masked by initials, he enjoys writing detailed descriptions of what Professor Edel calls his "copulations." These descriptions are mechanistic, to say the least. Since they are not connected with character, they are about as erotic as a *Popular Mechanics* blueprint of the sort that is said to appeal to the growing boy. I am not sure just why Wilson felt that he should write so much about cock and cunt except that in those days it was a very daring thing to do, as Henry Miller had discovered when his books were burned and as Wilson was to discover when his own novel, *Memoirs of Hecate County*, was banned.

In literature, sexual revelation is a matter of tact and occasion. Whether or not such candor is of interest to a reader depends a good deal on the revealer's attitude. James Boswell is enchanting to read on sex because he is by self, as well as by sex, enchanted and possessed. The author of *My Secret Life* (if for real) is engaging because he is only interested in getting laid as often as possible in as many different ways and combinations. We also don't know what he looks like—an important aid to masturbation. Frank Harris (not for real) has the exuberance of a natural liar and so moves the reader toward fiction.

The list now starts to get short. The recently published (in English) letters of Flaubert are interesting because he has interesting things to say about what he sees and does in the brothels and baths of North Africa. Also, tactfully, mercifully, he never tells us what he feels or Feels. The sex that Flaubert has with women and men, with boys and girls, is fascinating to read about (even though we know exactly how *he* looks). This is due, partly, to the fact that his experiences are, literally, exotic as well as erotic and, partly, to that famous tone of voice. Today one is never quite certain why memoirists are so eager to tell us what they do in bed. Unless the autobiographer has a case to be argued, I suspect that future readers will skip those sexual details that our writers have so generously shared with us in order to get to the gossip and the jokes.

In Wilson's notebooks, he liked to describe sex in the same way that he liked "doing" landscapes. "It is certainly very hard," he concedes, "to write about sex in English without making it unattractive. *Come* is a horrible word to apply to something ecstatic." Finally, he did neither sex scenes nor landscapes very well. But in sexual matters, he has no real case to make, unlike, let us say, the committed homosexualist who thinks, incorrectly, that candor will so rend the veil that light will be shed upon what the society considers an abominable act and in a blaze of clarity and charity all will be forgiven. This is naïve, as Wilson himself demonstrates in these pages. He was very much an American of his time and class and the notebooks are filled with innumerable references to "fairies" that range from derisive to nervous; yet Wilson also admits to occasional homosexual reveries which he thought "were a way of living in the grip of the vise, getting away into a different world where those values that pressed me did not function."

Nevertheless, it is disquieting to find Wilson, in the Thirties (having admired Proust and Gide), quite unable to accept the fact that a fairy could be a major artist. In *Axel's Castle*, he has great trouble admitting, or not admitting, the sexual source of Proust's jealousy.

On the other hand, he made a curious and admirable exception in the case of Thornton Wilder.

During the Twenties and Thirties, Wilder was one of the most celebrated and successful American novelists. He was also one of the few first-rate writers the United States has produced. Fortunately for Wilder's early reputation, he was able to keep his private life relatively secret. As a result, he was very much a hero in book-chat land. In *The Twenties* Wilson describes a meeting with Wilder. He was startled to find Wilder "a person of such positive and even peppery opinions." Wilson had not read any of Wilder's novels because he thought that "they must be rather on the fragile and precious side" (what else can a fairy write?). As it turned out, each had been reading the new installment of Proust's novel and Wilson was delighted to find that Wilder thought Saint Loup's homosexuality unjustified. Over the years, Wilson was to review Wilder seriously and well. When Wilder was the victim of a celebrated Marxist attack, Wilson came to Wilder's defense—not to mention literature's. But the word was out and Thornton Wilder's reputation never recovered; to this day, he is a literary nonperson. Nevertheless, it is to Wilson's credit that he was able to overcome his horror of fairydom in order to do justice to a remarkable contemporary.

Of a certain Victorian Englishman it was said that no lady's shoe, unescorted, was safe in his company. It could be said of Edmund Wilson that, like Cecil B. DeMille, "he never met a woman's foot he didn't like." Is there any reader of Wilson's novel *I Thought of Daisy* who does not recall Wilson's description of a girl's feet as being like "moist cream cheeses"? But Wilson's podophilia did not stop there: he could have made a fortune in women's footwear. From *The Thirties*: ". . . shoes, blue with silver straps, that arched her insteps very high . . . ," "Katy's little green socks and untied gray moccasins . . . ," "young Scotch girl M.P. [with] large feet bulging out of black shoes . . . ," ". . . silver open-work shoes that disclosed her reddened toenails, such a combination as only she could wear. . . ." In *The Thirties*, I counted twenty-four references to shoes and feet; each, let me quickly say, belonging to a woman. When it came to shoes, Wilson was sternly heterosexual—not for him the stud's boot or the little lad's Ked. But, to be absolutely precise, there is one very odd reference. Wilson is struck by the number of Chicago men who wear spats. Reverie: "Excuse me, sir. But a hook is loose on your left spat. As chance would have it, I have with me a spats-hook. If you'll allow me, sir. . . ." Whenever Wilson strikes the Florsheim note, he is in rut.

As a lover, Wilson is proud of his "large pink prong." (Surely, Anaïs Nin said it was "short and puce"—or was that Henry Miller's thumb?) In action, "My penis went in and out so beautifully sensitively, caressing (me) each time so sweet-smoothly (silkily). . . ." Yet he refers, clinically, to his "all too fat and debauched face" not to mention belly. He was a stubby little man who drank a lot. But his sexual energy matched his intellectual energy; so much for Freud's theory of sublimation.

The section called "The Death of Margaret" is fascinating, and quite unlike anything else he was ever to write. He started scribbling in a notebook aboard an airliner in 1932, en route to California where his wife of two years had just died of a fall. A compulsive writer, Wilson felt, instinctively, that by a close running description of what he saw from the plane window and in the air terminals he could get control of the fact of death and loss, or at least neutralize the shock in the act of re-creation. He writes a good many impressionistic pages of the trip before he gets to Margaret. Some very odd items: "—touching fellow passenger's thigh, moving over to keep away from it, did he move, too?—shutting eyes and homosexual fantasies, losing in vivid reality from Provincetown, gray, abstract, unreal sexual stimulus—also thought about coming back with Jean Gorman on train as situation that promises possibilities; but couldn't stomach it—young man too big, not my type—" Then impressions of his time together with Margaret: "I felt for the first time how

she'd given me all my self-confidence, the courage that I hadn't had before to say what I thought. . . ."

In Santa Barbara, he stays with her family. "At Mrs. Waterman's
house [Margaret's mother], when I began to cry, she said, I've never broken down. . . ." "Second night: homosexual wet dream, figures still rather
dim, a boy. Third night: nightmare—the trolls were in the dark part of the
cellar. . . ." Finally, the inevitable epitaph: "After she was dead, I loved
her." That is the story of every life—and death. For the next decade, Wilson dreams of Margaret and writes down the dreams. In these dreams he
usually knows that she is dead but, somehow, they can overcome this ob-
stacle. They don't; even in dreams. Eurydice always stays put: It is the
blight man was born for.

During the Thirties, Wilson's interests were more political than literary. The Depression, the New Deal, the Soviet experiment absorbed him.
Wilson is at his most attractive and, I should think, characteristic when
he describes going to Russia. He wanted to think well of Communism,
and, to a point, he was enthralled by the "classless" society and by the
way that one man, Lenin, "has stamped his thought and his language on
a whole people." This is not the treason but the very nature of the true
clerk: the word as absolute can be motor to behavior and to governance.
Gradually, Wilson is disillusioned about Stalin and the state he was
making.

But what is fascinating to read today is not Wilson's account of what
he saw and did but the way that he goes about taking on a subject, a language, a world. This is what sets him apart from all other American critics. He has to get to the root of things. He will learn Hebrew to unravel
the Dead Sea scrolls. Read a thousand windy texts to figure out the Civil
War. Learn Russian to get past the barrier of Constance Garnett's prose.
He was the perfect autodidact. He wanted to know it all. Or, as he wrote,
after he had a nervous breakdown in the Thirties, "I usually know exactly
what I want to do, and it has only been when I could not make up my
mind that I have really gone to pieces."

Early in *The Thirties*, Wilson is a fellow traveler of the American Communists' *faute de mieux*. He can see no other way out of the Depression
than an overthrow of the form of capitalism that had caused it. Before
the election of 1932, he wrote: "Hoover stands frankly for the interests

of the class who live on profits as against the wage-earning classes. Franklin Roosevelt, though he speaks as a Democrat in the name of the small businessmen and farmers and is likely to be elected by them in the expectation that he can do something for them, can hardly be imagined effecting any very drastic changes in the system which has allowed him to get into office. Whatever amiable gestures he may make, he will be largely controlled by the profit-squeezing class just as Hoover is." This is prescient. Apropos the fireside chats: "Roosevelt's unsatisfactory way of emphasizing his sentences, fairyish, or as if there weren't real conviction behind him—in spite of his clearness and neatness—but regular radio announcers, I noticed later, did the same thing. (The remoteness of the speaker from his audience.)" It is a pity that Wilson, who was on the fringes of the New Deal, never got to know the president. "Roosevelt is reported to have answered when someone had said to him that he would either be the best president the country had ever had or the most hated: No—that he would either be the most popular or the last."

Wilson often traveled to Washington in the Thirties and he had a sense of the place (derived from Henry Adams?) that makes him sound like one of us cliff-dwellers: "Washington is really a hollow shell which holds the liberalism of the New Deal as easily as the crooks and thugs of the Harding Administration—no trouble to clean it out every night and put something else in the past Administration's place."

Wilson goes to see one Martha Blair—"a rather appealing mouth and slim arms, though pale thyroid eyes: pink flowered print dress, with sleeves that gave a glimpse of her upper arms . . . she complained of the small town character of Washington—if you said you had another engagement, people asked you what it was—when she had said she was going to Virginia for the weekend they had asked her where in Virginia." It is odd to see this old formidable "socialite" of my childhood (she was then in her early thirties) as viewed from a totally different angle. Martha Blair kept company in those days with Arthur Krock of *The New York Times*. They were known as Martha'n'Artha. Wilson thinks they were married in 1934. I don't. At about that time, I remember there was a great row between my mother and her husband over whether or not the unmarried couple Martha and Arthur could stay overnight at our house in Virginia— where she was so often headed. My mother won that round. They were often at Merrywood, and Arthur Krock was the first Jew that I ever met. Anti-Semitism was in full boisterous American flower in the Thirties, and Wilson's record of conversations and attitudes haunt a survivor in much the same way that the background of a Thirties movie will reverse time, making it possible to see again a *People's Drug* store (golden lettering), straw hats, squared-off cars, and the actual light that encompassed one as a child, the very same light that all those who are now dead saw then.

Wilson notes, rather perfunctorily, friends and contemporaries. Scott Fitzgerald makes his usual appearances, and in his usual state. Once again we get the Hemingway-Wilson-Fitzgerald evening. "When Scott was lying in the corner on the floor, Hemingway said, Scott thinks that his penis is too small. (John Bishop had told me this and said that Scott was in the habit of making this assertion to anybody he met—to the lady who sat next to him at dinner and who might be meeting him for the first time.) I explained to him, Hemingway continued, that it only seemed to him small because he looked at it from above. You have to look at it in the mirror. (I did not understand this.)" I have never understood what Hemingway meant either. For one thing, Fitzgerald had obviously studied his diminutive part in a mirror. Even so, he would still be looking down at it unless, like a boy that I went to school with, he could so bend himself as to have an eye to eye, as it were, exchange with the Great American (Male) Obsession.

"Scott Fitzgerald at this time [1934] had the habit of insulting people, and then saying, if the victim came back at him: 'Can't take it, huh?' (I learned years later from Morley Callaghan that this was a habit of Hemingway's, from whom Scott had undoubtedly acquired it.)" There is altogether too little about Wilson's friend Dawn Powell, one of the wittiest of our novelists, and the most resolutely overlooked. But then American society, literary or lay, tends to be humorless. What other culture could have produced someone like Hemingway and *not* seen the joke?

Wilson's glimpses of people are always to the point. But they are brief. He is far more interested in writing descriptions of landscapes. I cannot think where the terrible habit began. Since Fitzgerald did the same thing in his notebooks, I suppose someone at Princeton (Professor Gauss? Project for a scholar-squirrel) must have told them that a writer must constantly describe things as a form of finger-exercise. The result is not unlike those watercolors Victorian girls were encouraged to turn out. Just as Wilson is about to tell us something quite interesting about e. e. cummings, he feels that he must devote a page or two to the deeply boring waterfront at Provincetown. A backdrop with no action in front of it is to no point at all.

There were trolls in the cellar of Wilson's psyche, and they tended to come upstairs "When I was suffering from the bad nerves of a hangover. . . ." There is also an echo of Mrs. Dalloway's vastation in the following passage: "Getting out of an elevator in some office building—I must have been nervously exhausted—I saw a man in a darkened hall— he was in his shirt sleeves with open neck, had evidently been working around the building—his eyes were wide open, and there seemed to be no expression on his face: he looked, not like an ape, but like some kind of primitive man—and his staring face, as I stared at him, appalled me: humanity was still an animal, still glaring out of its dark caves, not yet having mastered the world, not even comprehending what he saw. I was frightened—at him, at us all. *The horrible look of the human race.*"

As a critic, Wilson was not always at his best when it came to the design or pattern of a text—what used to be called aesthetics. He liked data, language. He did not have much sympathy for the New Critics with their emphasis on text *qua* text. After all, nothing human exists in limbo; nothing human is without connection. Wilson's particular genius lay in his ability to make rather more connections than any other critic of his time. As Diderot said of Voltaire: "He knows a great deal and our young poets are ignorant. The work of Voltaire is full of things; their works are empty."

But Wilson was quite aware that "things" in themselves are not enough. Professor Edel quotes from Wilson's Princeton lecture: "no matter how thoroughly and searchingly we may have scrutinized works of literature from the historical and biographical point of view . . . we must be able to tell the good from the bad, the first-rate from the second-rate. We shall not otherwise write literary criticism at all."

We do not, of course, write literary criticism at all now. Academe has won the battle in which Wilson fought so fiercely on the other side. Ambitious English teachers now invent systems that have nothing to do with literature or life but everything to do with those games that must be played in order for them to rise in the academic bureaucracy. Their works are empty indeed. But then, their works are not meant to be full. They are to be taught, not read. The long dialogue has broken down. Fortunately, as Flaubert pointed out, the worst thing about the present is the future. One day there will be no . . . But I have been asked not to give the game away. Meanwhile, I shall drop a single hint: Only construct!

The New York Review of Books
September 25, 1980

WILLIAM DEAN HOWELLS

1

On May 1, 1886, American workers in general and Chicago's workers in particular decided that the eight-hour workday was an idea whose time had come. Workers demonstrated, and a number of factories were struck. Management responded in kind. At McCormick Reaper strikers. were replaced by "scabs." On May 3, when the scabs left the factory at the end of a long traditional workday, they were mobbed by the strikers. Chicago's police promptly opened fire and America's gilded age looked to be cracking open.

The next night, in Haymarket Square, the anarchists held a meeting presided over by the mayor of Chicago. A thousand workers listened to many thousands of highly incendiary words. But all was orderly until His Honor went home; then the police "dispersed" the meeting with that tact which has ever marked Hog City's law-enforcement officers. At one point, someone (never identified) threw a bomb; a number of policemen and workers were killed or wounded. Subsequently, there were numerous arrests and in-depth grillings.

Finally, more or less at random, eight men were indicted for "conspiracy to murder." There was no hard evidence of any kind. One man was not even in town that day while another was home playing cards. By and large, the great conservative Republic felt no compassion for anarchists, even the ones who had taken up the revolutionary game of bridge; worse, an eight-hour workday would drive a stake through the economy's heart.

On August 20, a prejudiced judge and jury found seven of the eight men guilty of murder in the first degree; the eighth man (who had not been in town that night) got fifteen years in the slammer because he had a big mouth. The anarchists' counsel, Judge Roger A. Pryor, then appealed the verdict to the Supreme Court.

During the short hot summer of 1886, the case was much discussed. The peculiar arbitrariness of condemning to death men whom no one had seen commit a crime but who had been heard, at one time or another, to use "incendiary and seditious language" was duly noted in bookish circles. Yet no intellectual of the slightest national importance spoke up. Of America's famous men of letters, Mark Twain maintained his habitual silence on any issue where he might, even for an instant, lose the love of the folks. Henry James was in London, somewhat shaken by the recent failure of not only *The Bostonians* but *The Princess Casamassima*. The sad young man of *The Princess Casamassima* is an anarchist, who has had, like James himself that year, "more news of life than he knew what to do with." Although Henry Adams's education was being conducted that summer in Japan, he had made, the previous year, an interesting comment on the American political system—or lack of one:

> *Where no real principle divides us . . . some queer mechanical balance holds the two parties even, so that changes of great numbers of voters leave no trace in the sum total. I suspect the law will someday be formulated that in democratic societies, parties tend to an equilibrium.*

As the original entropy man, Adams had to explain, somehow, the election of the Democrat Grover Cleveland in 1884, after a quarter-century of Republican abolitionist virtue and exuberant greed.

Of the Republic's major literary and intellectual figures (the division was not so clearly drawn then between town, as it were, and gown), only one took a public stand. At forty-nine, William Dean Howells was the author of that year's charming "realistic" novel, *Indian Summer*; he was also easily the busiest and smoothest of America's men of letters. Years before, he had come out of Ohio to conquer the world of literature; and had succeeded. He had been the first outlander to be editor of the *Atlantic Monthly*. In the year of the Haymarket Square riot, he had shifted the literary capital of the country from Boston to New York when he took over *Harper's Monthly*, for which he wrote a column called "The Editor's Study"; and a thousand other things as well. That summer Howells had been reading Tolstoi. In fact, Tolstoi was making a socialist out of him; and Howells was appalled by Chicago's judge, jury, and press. He was also turning out his column, a hasty affair by his own best standards but positively lapidary by ours.

In the September 1886 issue of *Harper's*, Howells, who had done so much to bring Turgenev and Tolstoi to the attention of American readers, decided to do the same for Dostoevsky, whose *Crime and Punishment* was then available only in a French translation. Since Howells had left school at fifteen, he had been able to become very learned indeed. He had taught himself Latin and Greek; learned Spanish, German, Italian, and French. He read many books in many languages, and he knew many things. He also wrote many books; and many of those books are of the first rank. He was different from us. Look at Dean run! Look at Dean read! Look-say what Dean writes!

While the Haymarket Square riots were causing Howells to question the basis of the American "democracy," he was describing a Russian writer who had been arrested for what he had written and sent off to Siberia where he was taken out to be shot but not shot—the kind of fun still to be found to this very day south of our borders where the dominoes roam. As Howells proceeded most shrewdly to explain Dostoevsky to American readers, he rather absently dynamited his own reputation for the next century. Although he admired Dostoevsky's art, he could find little similarity between the officially happy, shadowless United States and the dark Byzantine cruelties of czarist Russia:

> It is one of the reflections suggested by Dostoevsky's book that whoever struck a note so profoundly tragic in American fiction would do a false and

mistaken thing. . . . Whatever their deserts, very few American novelists
have been led out to be shot, or finally expelled to the rigors of a winter at
Duluth. . . . We invite our novelists, therefore, to concern themselves with
the more smiling aspects of life, which are the more American, and to seek
the universal in the individual rather than the social interests. It is worth
while even at the risk of being called commonplace, to be true to our well-
to-do actualities.

This was meant to be a plea for realism. But it sounded like an invitation
to ignore the sort of thing that was happening in Chicago. Ironists are often inadvertent victims of their own irony.

On November 2, 1887, the Supreme Court denied the anarchists' appeal. On November 4, Howells canvassed his literary peers. What to do?
The dedicated abolitionist of thirty years earlier, George William Curtis,
whose lecture *Political Infidelity* was a touchstone of political virtue, and
the noble John Greenleaf Whittier agreed that something must be done;
but they were damned if they were going to do it. So the belletrist who
had just enjoined the nation's scribblers to address themselves to the
smiling aspects of a near-perfect land hurled his own grenade at the
courts.

In an open letter to the *New York Tribune* (published with deep re-
luctance by the ineffable Whitelaw Reid) Howells addressed all right-
thinking persons to join with him in petitioning the governor of Illinois to
commute the sentences. No respectable American man of letters had
taken on the American system since Thomas Paine, who was neither
American nor respectable. Of the Supreme Court, Howells wrote, it
"simply affirmed the legality of the forms under which the Chicago court
proceeded; it did not affirm the propriety of trying for murder men fairly
indictable for conspiracy alone . . ." The men had been originally con-
victed of "constructive conspiracy to commit murder," a star-chamberish
offense, based on their fiery language, and never proved to be relevant to
the actual events in Haymarket Square. In any case, he made the point
that the Supreme Court

by no means approved the principle of punishing them because of their frantic opinions, for a crime which they were not shown to have committed. The justice or injustice of their sentence was not before the highest tribunal of our law, and unhappily could not be got there. That question must remain for history, which judges the judgment of courts, to deal with; and I, for one, cannot doubt what the decision of history will be.

Howells said that the remaining few days before the men were executed should be used to persuade the governor to show mercy. In the course of the next week the national press attacked Howells, which is what the American system has a national press for.

On November 11, four of the men, wearing what looked like surgical gowns, were hanged. Of the others, one had committed suicide and two had had their sentences commuted. On November 12, Howells, undaunted by the national hysteria now directed as much against him as against the enemies of property, wrote another public letter:

It seems of course almost a pity to mix a note of regret with the hymn of thanksgiving for blood growing up from thousands of newspapers all over the land this morning; but I reflect that though I write amidst this joyful noise, my letter cannot reach the public before Monday at the earliest, and cannot therefore be regarded as an indecent interruption of the Te Deum.

By that time journalism will not have ceased, but history will have at least begun. All over the world where civilized men can think and feel, they are even now asking themselves, For what, really, did those four men die so bravely? Why did one other die so miserably? Next week the journalistic theory that they died so because they were desperate murderers will have grown even more insufficient than it is now for the minds and hearts of dispassionate inquirers, and history will make the answer to which she must adhere for all time, They died in the prime of the first Republic the world has ever known, for their opinions' sake *[original emphasis].*

Howells then proceeds to make the case against the state's attorney general and the judge and the shrieking press. It is a devastating attack: "I have wished to deal with facts. One of these is that we had a political execution in Chicago yesterday. The sooner we realize this, the better for us." As polemic, Howells's letter is more devastating and eloquent than Emile Zola's *J'accuse*; as a defense of the right to express unpopular opinions, it is the equal of what we mistakenly take to be the thrust of Milton's *Areopagitica*.

Unfortunately, the letter was not published in the year 1887. Eventually, the manuscript was found in an envelope addressed to Whitelaw Reid. The piece had been revised three times. It is possible that a copy had been sent to Reid who had not published it; it is possible that Howells had had second thoughts about the possibilities of libel actions from judge and state's attorney general; it is possible that he was scared off by the general outcry against him. After all, he had not only a great career to worry about but an ill wife and a dying daughter. Whatever the reason, Howells let his great moment slip by. Even so, the letter-not-sent reveals a powerful mind affronted by "one of those spasms of paroxysmal righteousness to which our Anglo-Saxon race is peculiarly subject . . ." He also grimly notes that this "trial by passion, by terror, by prejudice, by hate, by newspaper" had ended with a result that has won "the approval of the entire nation."

I suspect that the cautious lifetime careerist advised the Tolstoian socialist to cool it. Howells was in enough trouble already. After all, he was the most successful magazine editor in the country; he was a best-selling novelist. He could not afford to lose a public made up mostly of ladies. So he was heard no more on the subject. But at least he, alone of the country's writers, had asked, publicly, on November 4, 1887, that justice be done.

Howells, a master of irony, would no doubt have found ironic in the extreme his subsequent reputation as a synonym for middle-brow pusillanimity. After all, it was he who was the spiritual father of Dreiser (whom he did nothing for, curiously enough) and of Stephen Crane and Harold Frederic and Frank Norris, for whom he did a very great deal. He managed to be the friend and confidant of both Henry James and Mark Twain, quite a trick. He himself wrote a half-dozen of the Republic's best novels. He was learned, witty, and generous.

Howells lived far too long. Shortly before his death at the age of eighty-four, he wrote his old friend Henry James: "I am comparatively a dead cult with my statues cut down and the grass growing over me in the pale moonlight." By then he had been dismissed by the likes of Sinclair Lewis as a dully beaming happy writer. But then Lewis knew as little of the American literary near-past as today's writers know, say, of Lewis. If Lewis had read Howells at all, he would have detected in the work of this American realist a darkness sufficiently sable for even the most lost-and-found of literary generations or, as Howells wrote James two years after the Haymarket Square riots: "After fifty years of optimistic content with 'civilization' and its ability to come out all right in the end, I now abhor it, and feel that it is coming out all wrong in the end unless it bases itself on a real equality." What that last phrase means is anyone's guess. He is a spiritual rather than a practical socialist. It is interesting that the letter was written in the same year that Edward Bellamy's *Looking Backward: 2000–1887* was published. The ideas of Robert Owen that Howells had absorbed from his father (later a Swedenborgian like Henry James, Sr.) were now commingled with the theories of Henry George, the tracts of William Morris, and, always, Tolstoi. Howells thought that there must be a path through the political jungle of a republic that had just hanged four men for their opinions; he never found it. But as a novelist he was making a path for himself and for others, and he called it realism.

2

On Thanksgiving Day 1858, the twenty-one-year-old Howells was received at the court of the nineteen-year-old first lady of Ohio, Kate Chase, a handsome ambitious motherless girl who acted as hostess to her father the governor, Salmon P. Chase, a handsome ambitious wifeless man who was, in Abraham Lincoln's thoughtful phrase, "on the subject of the Presidency, a little insane."

Howells had grown up in Ohio; his father was an itinerant newspaper editor and publisher. He himself was a trained printer as well as an ambitious but not insane poet. Under the influence of Heine, he wrote a number of poems; one was published in the *Atlantic Monthly*. He was big in Cleveland. Howells and Kate got on well; she teased him for his social awkwardness; he charmed her as he charmed almost everyone. Although he wrote about the doings of the Ohio legislature for the Cincinnati *Gazette*, he preferred the company of cultivated ladies to that of politicians. A passionate autodidact, he tended to prefer the company of books to people. But through Kate he met future presidents and was served at table by his first butler.

In a sense the Chase connection was the making of Howells. When Lincoln won the Republican presidential nomination in 1860, Howells was chosen, somewhat improbably, to write a campaign biography of the candidate. Characteristically, Howells sent a friend to Springfield to chat with the subject of his book; he himself never met Lincoln. He then cobbled together a book that Lincoln did not think too bad. One suspects that he did not think it too good, either. Shortly before the president was shot, he withdrew the book for the second time from the Library of Congress: nice that he did not have a copy of it on the coffee table in the Blue Room, but then Lincoln was so unlike, in so many ways, our own recent sovereigns.

Once Lincoln was president, Chase became secretary of the treasury. Chase proposed that the campaign biographer be rewarded with a consulate. But nothing happened until Howells himself went to Washington where he found an ally in Lincoln's very young and highly literary second secretary, John Hay, who, with the first secretary, John Nicolay, finally got Howells the consulate at Venice.

It is odd to think that a writer as curiously American as Howells should have been shaped by the Most Serene Republic at a bad moment in that ancient polity's history—the Austrian occupation—rather than by the United States at the most dramatic moment in that polity's history: the Civil War. Odd, also, that Howells managed, like the other two major writers of his generation, to stay out of the war. Neither Mark Twain nor Henry James rushed to the colors.

Since Howells had practically no official work to do, he learned Italian and perfected his German and French. He turned out poems that did not get printed in the *Atlantic*. "Not one of the MSS you have sent us," wrote the editor, "swims our seas." So Howells went off the deep end, into prose. He wrote Venetian sketches of great charm; he was always to be a good—even original—travel writer. Where the previous generation of Irving and Hawthorne had tended to love far too dearly a ruined castle wall, Howells gave the reader not only the accustomed romantic wall but the laundry drying on it, too. The Boston *Advertiser* published him.

Then came the turning point, as Howells termed it, in his life. He had acquired a charming if garrulous wife, who talked even more than Mark Twain's wife, or as Twain put it, when Elinor Howells entered a room "dialogue ceased and monologue inherited its assets and continued the business at the old stand." Howells wrote a serious study of the Italian theater called "Recent Italian Comedy," which he sent to the *North American Review*, the most prestigious of American papers, coedited by his friend James Russell Lowell and Charles Eliot Norton. At the time, Boston and Cambridge were in the throes of advanced Italophilia. Longfellow was translating Dante; and all the ladies spoke of Michelangelo. Lowell accepted the essay. Howells was now on his way, as a *serious* writer.

After nearly four years in Venice, which he did not much care for, Howells returned to New York. With a book of sketches called *Venetian Life* at the printers, he went job hunting. He was promptly hired by E. L. Godkin to help edit *The Nation*. Not long after, he was hired by the *Atlantic Monthly* as assistant to the editor; then from 1871 to 1881 he was editor in chief. In Boston, Howells was now at the heart of an American literary establishment which had no way of knowing that what looked to be eternal noon was actually Indian summer—for New England.

Just before Howells had gone to Venice, he had made the rounds of New England's literary personages. He had met Holmes and Hawthorne whom he had liked; and Emerson whom he had not. Now, at the *Atlantic*, every distinguished writer came his editorial way; and soon he himself would be one of them. But what sort of writer was he to be? Poetry was plainly not his métier. Journalism was always easy for him, but he was ambitious. That left the novel, an art form which was not yet entirely "right." The American product of the 1860s was even less "aesthetic" than the English and neither was up to the French, who were, alas, sexually vicious, or to the Russians, who were still largely untranslated except for the Paris-based Turgenev. At this interesting moment, Howells had one advantage denied his contemporaries, always excepting Henry James. He could read—and he had read—the new Europeans in the original. He went to school to Zola and Flaubert. Realism was in the European air, but how much reality could Americans endure? Out of the tension between the adventurousness of Flaubert and the edgy reticence of Hawthorne came the novels of William Dean Howells.

From Heine, Howells had learned the power of the plain style. Mark Twain had also learned the same lesson—from life. Whereas the previous generation of Melville and Hawthorne had inclined to elevated, even "poetic" prose, Twain and Howells and James the First were relatively straightforward in their prose and quotidian in their effects—no fauns with pointed ears need apply. In fact, when Howells first met Hawthorne, he shyly pointed to a copy of *The Blithedale Romance* and told the great man that that was his own favorite of the master's works. Hawthorne appeared pleased; and said, "The Germans like it, too."

But realism, for Howells, had its limits. He had grown up in a happy if somewhat uncertain environment: His father was constantly changing jobs, houses, religions. For a writer, Howells himself was more than usually a dedicated hypochondriac whose adolescence was shadowed by the certainty that he had contracted rabies which would surface in time to kill him at sixteen. Like most serious hypochondriacs, he enjoyed full rude health until he was eighty. But there were nervous collapses. Also, early in life, Howells had developed a deep aversion to sexual irregularity, which meant any form of sexuality outside marriage. When his mother befriended a knocked-up seamstress, the twelve-year-old Howells refused to pass her so much as the salt at table.

In Venice he could not get over the fact that there could be no social intercourse of any kind with unmarried girls (unlike the fun to be had with The American Girl, soon to be celebrated not only by Henry James but by Howells himself), while every married woman seemed bent on flinging even the purest of young bachelors into the sack. Doubtless, he kept himself chaste until marriage. But he railed a good deal against European decadence, to the amusement of the instinctively more worldly, if perhaps less operative Henry ("Oh, my aching back!") James, who used to tease him about the latest descriptions of whorehouses to be found in French fiction. Nevertheless, for a writer who was to remain an influence well into the twentieth century, an aversion to irregular sexuality was not apt to endear him to a later generation which, once it could put sex into the novel, proceeded to leave out almost everything else. Where the late-nineteenth-century realistic novel might be said to deal with social climbing, the twentieth-century novel has dealt with sexual climbing, an activity rather easier to do than to write about.

The Library of America now brings us four of Howells's novels written between 1875 and 1886. Before the publications of these four novels, Howells had already published his first novel, *Their Wedding Journey* (1871); his second novel, *A Chance Acquaintance* (1873); as well as sketches of Italy, people, and yet another personage. Elinor Mead Howells was a cousin of President Rutherford (known to all good Democrats as Rather-fraud) B. Hayes. So the campaign biographer of Lincoln, duly and dutifully and dully, wrote a book called *Sketch of the Life and Character of Rutherford B. Hayes* (1876). Thanks to Cousin Hayes, Howells was now able to reward those who had helped him. James Russell Lowell was sent to London as American ambassador.

Of the books written before *A Foregone Conclusion* (the first of the four now reissued), the ever-polite but never fraudulent Turgenev wrote Howells in 1874:

> *Accept my best thanks for the gracious gift of your delightful book* Their Wedding Journey, *which I have read with the same pleasure experienced before in reading* A Chance Acquaintance *and* Venetian Life. *Your literary physiognomy is a most sympathetic one; it is natural, simple and clear—and in the same time—it is full of unobtrusive poetry and fine humor. Then—I feel the peculiar American stamp on it—and that is not one of the least causes of my relishing so much your works.*

This was written in English. In a sense, Turgenev is responding to Howells's championing of his own work (Howells had reviewed *Lisa* and *Rudin*) but he is also responding to a sympathetic confrere, a young writer whom he has influenced though not so much as has "the peculiar American stamp." Unfortunately, Turgenev never lived to read the later books. It would be interesting to see what he might have made of *A Modern Instance*, a book as dark and, at times, as melodramatic as a novel by Zola whose *L'Assommoir* Turgenev disliked.

A Foregone Conclusion (1875) has, as protagonist, the—what else?— American consul at Venice. The consul is a painter (young writers almost always make their protagonists artists who practice the one art that they themselves know nothing about: It's the light, you see, in Cimabue). The consul attracts a young priest, Don Ippolito, who wants to emigrate to America and become an inventor. It is no accident that practically the first building in Washington to be completed in imperial marble splendor was the Patent Office. Don Ippolito is a sort of Italian Major Hoople. The inventions don't really work but he keeps on because "Heaven only knows what kind of inventor's Utopia our poor, patent-ridden country appeared to him in those dreams of his, and I can but dimly figure it to myself." Here the auctorial "I" masquerades as the "I" of the consul, Ferris, who is otherwise presented in the objective third person. Howells has not entirely learned Turgenev's lesson: stay out of the narrative. Let the characters move the narration and the reader. Howells's native American garrulousness—and tendentiousness—occasionally breaks in.

Enter, inexorably, middle-aged American lady and daughter—Mrs. Vervain and Florida. This was four years before Howells's friend sicked *Daisy Miller* on to a ravished world. But then The American Girl was to be a Howells theme, just as it was to be James's and, later, and in a much tougher way, Mrs. Wharton's. As every writer then knew, the readers of novels were mostly women, and they liked to read about the vicissitudes of young women, preferably ladies. But while James would eventually transmute his American girls into something that Euripides himself might find homely (e.g., Maggie Verver), Howells tends, gently, to mock. Incidentally, I do not believe that it has ever before been noted that the portrait of Florida is uncannily like Kate Chase.

It is a foregone conclusion that American girl and American mother ("the most extraordinary combination of perfect fool and perfect lady I ever saw") will miss the point to Don Ippolito and Venice and Europe, and that he will miss the point to them. Don Ippolito falls in love with Florida. The Americans are horrified. How can a priest sworn to celibacy . . . ? Since they are Protestants, the enormity of his fall from Roman Catholic grace is all the greater. Although Don Ippolito is perfectly happy to give up the Church, they will not let him. Mother and daughter flee. As for Ferris, he has misunderstood not only Don Ippolito but Florida's response to him. Don Ippolito dies—with the comment to Ferris, "You would never see me as I was."

The consul goes home to the States and joins the army. Like so many other characters in the works of those writers who managed to stay out of the Civil War, Ferris has a splendid war: "Ferris's regiment was sent to a part of the southwest where he saw a good deal of fighting and fever and ague" (probably a lot easier than trying to get a job at the *Atlantic*). "At the end of two years, spent alternately in the field and the hospital, he was riding out near the camp one morning in unusual spirits, when two men in butternut fired at him: one had the mortification to miss him; the bullet of the other struck him in the arm. There was talk of amputation at first . . ." Pre-dictaphone and word processor, it was every writer's nightmare that he lose his writing arm. But, worse, Ferris is a painter: *he can never crosshatch again*. Broke, at a loose end, he shows an old picture at an exhibition. Florida sees the picture. They are reunited. Mrs. Vervain is dead. Florida is rich. Ferris is poor. What is to be done?

It is here that the avant-garde realism of Howells shoves forward the whole art of the popular American novel: "It was fortunate for Ferris, since he could not work, that she had money; in exalted moments he had thought this a barrier to their marriage; yet he could not recall anyone who had refused the hand of a beautiful girl because of the accident of her wealth, and in the end, he silenced his scruples." This is highly satisfying.

Then Howells, perhaps a bit nervous at just how far he has gone in the direction of realism, tosses a bone of marzipan to the lady-reader: "It might be said that in many other ways he was not her equal; but one ought to reflect how very few men are worthy of their wives in any sense."

Sighs of relief from many a hammock and boudoir! How well he knows the human heart.

Howells smiles at the end; but the smile is aslant, while the point to the tragedy (not Ferris's for he had none, but that of Don Ippolito) is that, during the subsequent years of Ferris's marriage, Don Ippolito "has at last ceased to be even the memory of a man with a passionate love and a mortal sorrow. Perhaps this final effect in the mind of him who has realized the happiness of which the poor priest vainly dreamed is not the least tragic phase of the tragedy of Don Ippolito."

This coda is unexpectedly harsh—and not at all smiling. A priest ought not to fall in love. It is a foregone conclusion that if you violate the rules governing sexuality, society will get you, as Mrs. Wharton would demonstrate so much more subtly in *The Age of Innocence*; and Henry James would subtly deny since he knew, in a way that Howells did not, that the forbidden cake could be both safely eaten and kept. It is an odd irony that the donnée on which James based *The Ambassadors* was a remark that the fifty-seven-year-old Howells made to a friend in Paris: No matter what, one ought to have one's life; that it was too late for him, personally, but for someone young . . . "Don't, at any rate, make *my* mistake," Howells said. "Live!"

Kenneth S. Lynn has put the case, persuasively to my mind, that the "happy endings" of so many of Howells's novels are deliberately "hollow or ironic. After all, it was Howells who had fashioned the, to Edith Wharton, "lapidary phrase": Americans want tragedies with happy endings. There are times when Howells's conclusion—let's end with a marriage and live happily ever after—carry more formidable weight than the sometimes too-lacquered tragic codas of James: "We shall never be again as we were." The fact is that people are almost always exactly as they were and they will be so again and again, given half a chance.

At forty-four, the highly experienced man of letters began his most ambitious novel, *A Modern Instance*. Although the story starts in a New England village, the drama is acted out in the Boston of Howells's professional life, and the very unusual protagonist is a newspaperman on the make who charms everyone and hoodwinks a few; he also puts on too much weight, steals another man's story, and makes suffer the innocent young village heiress whom he marries. In a sense, Howells is sending himself up; or some dark side of himself. Although Bartley Hubbard is nowhere in Howells's class as a writer, much less standard-bearer for Western civilization, he is a man who gets what he wants through personal charm, hard work, and the ability to write recklessly and scandalously for newspapers in a way that the young William Randolph Hearst would capitalize on at century's end, thus making possible today's antipodean "popular" press, currently best exemplified by London's giggly newspapers.

Unlike Howells, or the Howells that we think we know, Bartley is sexually active; he is not about to make the Howells-Strether mistake. He *lives* until he is murdered by a man whom he may have libeled in a western newspaper. It would have been more convincing if an angry husband had been responsible for doing him in, but there were conventions that Howells felt obliged to observe, as his detractors, among them Leslie Fiedler, like to remind us. Mr. Fiedler writes in *Love and Death in the American Novel* (1975):

> *Only in* A Modern Instance, *written in 1882 [sic: 1881], does Howells deal for once with a radically unhappy marriage; and here he adapts the genteel-sentimental pattern which had substituted the bad husband (his Bartley Hubbard has "no more moral nature than a baseball") for the Seducer, the long-suffering wife for the Persecuted Maiden or fallen woman.*

Mr. Fiedler, of course, is—or was in 1960—deeply into "the reality of dream and nightmare, fantasy and fear," and for him Howells is "the author of flawlessly polite, high-minded, well-written studies of untragic, essentially eventless life in New England—the antiseptic upper-middlebrow romance. Yet his forty books [sic: he means novels, of which Howells wrote thirty-five; there are close to one hundred books], in which there are no seductions and only rare moments of violence, are too restrictedly 'realistic', too . . . ," *et cetera.*

Mr. Fiedler gets himself a bit off the hook by putting those quotes around the word realistic. After all, Howells had developed an aesthetic of the novel: and if he preferred to shoot Bartley offstage, why not? The classic tragedians did the same. He also inclined to Turgenev's view that the real drama is in the usual. Obviously, this is not the way of the romantic writer but it is a no less valid way of apprehending reality than that of Melville or Faulkner, two writers Howells would have called "romancers," about as much a term of compliment with him as "too unrestrictedly 'realistic'" is to Mr. Fiedler. Without rehashing the tired Redskin versus Paleface debate of the 1940s, it should be noted that there is something wrong with a critical bias that insists upon, above all else, "dream and nightmare, fantasy and fear" but then when faced with the genuine article in, say, the books of William Burroughs or James Purdy or Paul Bowles starts to back off, nervously, lighting candles to The Family and all the other life-enhancing if unsmiling aspects of American life that do *not* cause AIDS or social unrest.

Whatever our romantic critics may say, Bartley Hubbard is an archetypal American figure, caught for the first time by Howells: the amiable, easygoing bastard, who thinks nothing of taking what belongs to another. Certainly Mark Twain experienced the shock of recognition when he read the book: "You didn't intend Bartley for me but he *is* me just the same . . ." James, more literary, thought the character derived from Tito, in the one (to me) close-to-bad novel of George Eliot, *Romola*. In later years Howells said that he himself was the model. Who was what makes no difference. There is only one Bartley Hubbard, and he appears for the first time in the pages of a remarkable novel that opened the way to Dreiser and to all those other realists who were to see the United States plain. The fact that there are no overt sexual scenes in Howells ("no palpitating divans," as he put it) does not mean that sexual passion is not a powerful motor to many of the situations, as in life. On the other hand, the fact that there are other motors—ambition, greed, love of power—simply extends the author's range and makes him more interesting to read than most writers.

In this novel, Howells is interesting on the rise of journalism as a "serious" occupation. "There had not yet begun to be that talk of journalism as a profession which has since prevailed with our collegians . . ." There is also a crucial drunk scene in which Bartley blots his copybook with Boston; not to mention with his wife. It is curious how often Howells shows a protagonist who gets disastrously drunk and starts then to fall. Mark Twain had a dark suspicion that Howells always had *him* in mind when he wrote these scenes. But for Mr. Fiedler, "drunkenness is used as a chief symbol for the husband's betrayal of the wife." Arguably, it would have been better (and certainly more manly) if Bartley had cornholed the Irish maid in full view of wife and child, but would a scene so powerful, even *existential*, add in any way to the delicate moral balances that Howells is trying to make?

After all, Howells is illuminating a new character in American fiction, if not life, who, as "he wrote more than ever in the paper . . . discovered in himself that dual life, of which every one who sins or sorrows is sooner or later aware: that strange separation of the intellectual activity from the suffering of the soul, by which the mind toils on in a sort of ironical indifference to the pangs that wring the heart; the realization that in some ways his brain can get on perfectly well without his conscience." This is worthy of the author of *Sentimental Education*; it is also the kind of insight about post-Christian man that Flaubert so often adverted to, indirectly, in his own novels and head-on in his letters.

The Rise of Silas Lapham (1885) begins with Bartley Hubbard brought back to life. It is, obviously, some years earlier than the end of *A Modern Instance*. Bartley is interviewing a self-made man called Silas Lapham who has made a fortune out of paint. Lapham is the familiar diamond in the rough, New England Jonathan style. He has two pretty daughters, a sensible wife, a comfortable house; and a growing fortune, faced with all the usual hazards. Howells makes the paint business quite as interesting as Balzac made paper making. This is not entirely a full-hearted compliment to either; nevertheless, each is a novelist fascinated by the way the real world works; and each makes it interesting to read about.

In a sense, Silas Lapham's rise is not unlike that of William Dean

Howells: from a small town to Boston back street to Beacon Street on the Back Bay. But en route to the great address there are many lesser houses and Howells is at his best when he goes house hunting—and building. In fact, one suspects that, like Edith Wharton later, he would have made a splendid architect and interior decorator. In a fine comic scene, a tactful architect (plainly the author himself) guides Lapham to Good Taste. " 'Of course,' resumed the architect, 'I know there has been a great craze for black walnut. But it's an ugly wood . . .' " All over the United States there must have been feminine gasps as stricken eyes were raised from the page to focus on the middle distance where quantities of once-beauteous black shone dully by gaslight; but worse was to come: " '. . . and for a drawing room there is really nothing like white paint. We should want to introduce a little gold here and there. Perhaps we might run a painted frieze round under the cornice—garlands of roses on a gold ground; it would tell wonderfully in a white room.' " From that moment on, no more was black walnut seen again in the parlors of the Republic, while the sale of white paint soared; gold, too.

The rise of Lapham's house on Beacon Hill is, in a sense, the plot of the book, as well as the obvious symbol of worldly success. Howells makes us see and feel and smell the house as it slowly takes shape. Simultaneously, a young man called Tom Corey wants to work for Lapham. Since Corey belongs to the old patriciate, Lapham finds it hard to believe Corey is serious. But the young man is sincere; he really likes the old man. He must also work to live. There are romantic exchanges between him and the two daughters; there is an amiable mix-up. Finally, Tom says that it is Penelope not her sister whom he wants to marry. Mr. and Mrs. Lapham are bemused. In the world of the Coreys they are a proto–Maggie and Jiggs couple.

Corey takes Lapham to a grand dinner party where the old man gets drunk and chats rather too much. It is the same scene, in a sense, as Bartley's fall in the earlier novel, but where Bartley could not have minded less the impression he made, Lapham is deeply humiliated; and the fall begins. He loses his money; the new house burns down; by then, the house is an even more poignant character than Lapham, and the reader mourns the white-and-gold drawing room gone to ash. But there is a happy enough ending. Maggie and Jiggs return to the Vermont village

of their origin (which they should never have left?) while Corey marries
Penelope.

> *It would be easy to point out traits in Penelope's character which finally rec-*
> *onciled all her husband's family and endeared her to them. These things*
> *continually happen in novels; and the Coreys, as they had always promised*
> *themselves to do, made the best, and not the worst, of Tom's marriage. . . .*
> *But the differences remained uneffaced, if not uneffaceable, between the*
> *Coreys and Tom Corey's wife.*

The young couple move from Boston. Then Howells shifts from the specific to the general:

> *It is certain that our manners and customs go for more in life than our qual-*
> *ities. The price that we pay for civilization is the fine yet impassable differ-*
> *entiation of these. Perhaps we pay too much; but it will not be possible to*
> *persuade those who have the difference in their favor that this is so. They*
> *may be right; and at any rate the blank misgiving, the recurring sense of dis-*
> *appointment to which the young people's departure left the Coreys is to be*
> *considered. That was the end of their son and brother for them; they felt*
> *that; and they were not mean or unamiable people.*

This strikes me as a subtle and wise reading of the world—no, not *a*
world but *the* world; and quite the equal of James or Hardy.

Whether or not this sort of careful social reading is still of interest to
the few people who read novels voluntarily is not really relevant. But then
today's "serious" novel, when it is not reinventing itself as an artifact of
words and signs, seldom deals with the world at all. One is no longer
shown a businessman making money or his wife climbing up or down the
social ladder. As most of our novelists now teach school, they tend to tell
us what it is like to be a schoolteacher, and since schoolteachers have
been taught to teach others to write only about what they know, they tell
us what they know about, too, which is next to nothing about the way the
rest of the population of the Republic lives.

In a sense, if they are realists, they are acting in good faith. If you
don't know something about the paint business you had better not

choose a protagonist who manufactures paint. Today, if the son of an Ohio newspaper editor would like to be a novelist, he would not quit school at fifteen to become a printer, and then learn six languages and do his best to read all the great literary figures of the present as well as of the past so that he could introduce, say, Barthes or Gadda to the American public while writing his own novels based on a close scrutiny of as many classes of society as he can get to know. Rather, he would graduate from high school; go on to a university and take a creative writing course; get an M.A. for having submitted a novel (about the son of an Ohio editor who grew up in a small town *and found out about sex* and wants to be a writer and so goes to a university where he submits, etc.).

Then, if he is truly serious about a truly serious literary career, he will become a teacher. With luck, he will obtain tenure. In the summers and on sabbatical, he will write novels that others like himself will want to teach just as he, obligingly, teaches their novels. He will visit other campuses as a lecturer and he will talk about his books and about those books written by other teachers to an audience made up of ambitious young people who intend to write novels to be taught by one another to the rising generation and so on and on. What tends to be left out of these works is the world. World gone, no voluntary readers. No voluntary readers, no literature—only creative writing courses and English studies, activities marginal (to put it tactfully) to civilization.

3

Civilization was very much on Howells's mind when he came to write *Indian Summer* (1886). He deals, once more, with Americans in Italy. But this time there are no Don Ippolitos. The principals are all Americans in Florence. A middle-aged man, Theodore Colville, meets, again, Mrs. Bowen, a lady who once did not marry him when he wanted to marry her. She married a congressman. She has a young daughter, Effie. She is a widow.

Colville started life as an architect, a suitable occupation for a Howells character; then he shifted to newspaper publishing, an equally suitable profession. In Des Vaches, Indiana, he published, successfully, the *Democrat-Republican* newspaper. Although he lost a race for Congress, he has received from former political opponents "fulsome" praise. Like most American writers Howells never learned the meaning of the word *fulsome*. Colville then sold his newspaper and went to Europe because "he wanted to get away, to get far away, and with the abrupt and total change in his humor he reverted to a period in his life when journalism and politics and the ambition of Congress were things undreamed of." He had been young in Italy, with a Ruskinian interest in architecture; he had loved and been rejected by Evelina—now the widow Bowen. He looks at Florence: "It is a city superficially so well known that it affects one somewhat like a collection of views of itself: they are from the most striking points, of course, but one has examined them before, and is disposed to be critical of them." The same goes for people one has known when young.

Mrs. Bowen has a beautiful young friend named Imogene. Colville decides that he is in love with Imogene, and they drift toward marriage. There are numerous misunderstandings. Finally, it is Mrs. Bowen not Imogene who is in love with Colville. The drama of the three of them (a shadowy young clergyman named Morton is an undelineated fourth) is rendered beautifully. There are many unanticipated turns to what could easily have been a simpleminded romantic novella.

When Colville is confronted with the thought of his own great age (forty-one), he is told by a very old American expatriate:

> At forty, one has still a great part of youth before him—perhaps the richest and sweetest part. By that time the turmoil of ideas and sensations is over; we see clearly and feel consciously. We are in a sort of quiet in which we peacefully enjoy. We have enlarged our perspective sufficiently to perceive things in their true proportion and relation; we are no longer tormented with the lurking fear of death, which darkens and imbitters our earlier years; we have got into the habit of life; we have often been ailing and we have not died . . .

Finally, "we are put into the world to be of it." Thus, Howells strikes the Tolstoian note. Yes, he is also smiling. But even as *Indian Summer* was being published, its author was attacking the state of Illinois for the murder of four workmen. He also sends himself up in the pages of his own

novel. A Mrs. Amsden finds Colville and Imogene and Effie together after an emotional storm. Mrs. Amsden remarks that they form an interesting, even dramatic group:

> *"Oh, call us a passage from a modern novel," suggested Colville, "if you're*
> *in a romantic mood. One of Mr. James's."*
>
> *"Don't you think we ought to be rather more of the great world for that?*
> *I hardly feel up to Mr. James. I should have said Howells. Only nothing hap-*
> *pens in that case."*

For this beguiling modesty Howells no doubt dug even deeper the
grave for his reputation. How can an American novelist who is ironic
about himself ever be great? In a nation that has developed to a high art
advertising, the creator who refuses to advertise himself is immediately
suspected of having no product worth selling. Actually, Howells is fascinated with the interior drama of his characters, and quite a lot happens—to the reader as well as to the characters who are, finally, suitably
paired: Imogene and Mr. Morton, Colville and Mrs. Bowen.

The Library of America has served William Dean Howells well. Although the spiritual father of the library, Edmund Wilson, did not want
this project ever to fall into the hands of the Modern Language Association, all four of the novels in the present volume bear the proud emblem
of that association. One can only assume that there are now fewer scholars outside Academe's groves than within. I found no misprints; but there
are eccentricities.

In *A Modern Instance* (p. 474) we read of "the presidential canvas of
the summer"; then (p. 485) we read "But the political canvass . . ." Now
a tent is made of canvas and an election is a canvass of votes. It is true
that the secondary spelling of "canvass" is "canvas" and so allowable;
nevertheless, it is disturbing to find the same word spelled two ways
within eleven pages. On page 3 the variant spelling "ancles" is used for
"ankles." On page 747 Howells writes "party-colored statues" when,
surely, "parti-colored" was nineteenth-century common usage as opposed
to the Chaucerian English "party." Of course, as the editors tell us, "In
nineteenth-century writings, for example, a word might be spelled in

more than one way, even in the same work, and such variations might be carried into print."

Anyway, none of this is serious. There are no disfiguring footnotes. The notes at the back are for the most part helpful translations of foreign phrases in the text. The chronology of Howells's life is faultless but, perhaps, skimpy. For those who are obliged for career reasons to read Howells, this is a useful book. For those who are still able to read novels for pleasure, this is a marvelous book.

For some years I have been haunted by a story of Howells and that most civilized of all our presidents, James A. Garfield. In the early 1870s Howells and his father paid a call on Garfield. As they sat on Garfield's veranda, young Howells began to talk about poetry and about the poets that he had met in Boston and New York. Suddenly, Garfield told him to stop. Then Garfield went to the edge of the veranda and shouted to his Ohio neighbors. "Come over here! He's telling about Holmes, and Longfellow, and Lowell, and Whittier!" So the neighbors gathered around in the dusk; then Garfield said to Howells, "Now go on."

Today we take it for granted that no living president will ever have heard the name of any living poet. This is not, necessarily, an unbearable loss. But it is unbearable to have lost those Ohio neighbors who actually read books of poetry and wanted to know about the poets.

For thirty years book-chat writers have accused me of having written that the novel is dead. I wrote no such thing but book-chat writers have the same difficulty extracting meaning from writing as presidents do. What I wrote was, "After some three hundred years the novel in English has lost the general reader (or rather the general reader has lost the novel), and I propose that he will not again recover his old enthusiasm." Since 1956, the audience for the serious (or whatever this year's adjective is) novel has continued to shrink. Arguably, the readers that are left are for the most part involuntary ones, obliged by the schools to read novels that they often have little taste for. The fact that a novelist like Howells—or even Bellow—is probably no longer accessible to much of anyone would be bearable if one felt that the sense of alternative worlds

or visions or—all right, Leslie—nightmares, fantasies, fears could be obtained in some other way. But movies are no substitute while television
is, literally, narcotizing: The human eye was not designed to stare at a
light for any length of time. Popular prose fictions are still marketed with
TV and movie tie-ins, but even the writers or word-processors of these
books find it harder and harder to write simply enough for people who
don't really know how to read.

Obviously, there is a great deal wrong with our educational system, as
President Reagan recently, and rather gratuitously, noted. After all, an educated electorate would not have elected him president. It is generally
agreed that things started to go wrong with the schools after the First
World War. The past was taught less and less, and Latin and Greek
ceased to be compulsory. Languages were either not taught or taught
so badly that they might just as well not have been taught at all, while
American history books grew more and more mendacious, as Frances
FitzGerald so nicely described (*America Revised*, 1979), and even basic
geography is now a nonsubject. Yet the average "educated" American has
been made to believe that, somehow, the United States must lead the
world even though hardly anyone has any information at all about those
countries we are meant to lead. Worse, we have very little information
about our own country and its past. That is why it is not really possible
to compare a writer like Howells with any living American writer because
Howells thought that it was a good thing to know as much as possible
about his own country as well as other countries while our writers today,
in common with the presidents and paint manufacturers, live in a present without past among signs whose meanings are uninterpretable.

Edmund Wilson's practical response was to come up with the idea of
making readily available the better part of American literature; hence, the
Library of America. It is a step in the right direction. But will this library
attract voluntary readers? Ultimately—and paradoxically—that will depend on the schools.

Since no one quite knows what a university ought to do, perhaps *that*
should be the subject of our educational system. What variety of things
should *all* educated people know? What is it that we don't know that we

need to know? Naturally, there is a certain risk in holding up a mirror to the system itself (something the realistic novelist always used to do) because one is apt to see, glaring back, the face of Caliban or, worse, plain glass reflecting glass. But something must now be done because Herzen's terrible truth is absolutely true: "The end of each generation is itself."

The New York Review of Books
October 27, 1983

DAWN POWELL:

THE AMERICAN WRITER

1

Once upon a time, New York City was as delightful a place to live in as to visit. There were many amenities, as they say in brochures. One was something called Broadway, where dozens of plays opened each season, and thousands of people came to see them in an area which today resembles downtown Calcutta without, alas, that subcontinental city's deltine charm and intellectual rigor.

One evening back there in once upon a time (February 7, 1957, to be exact) my first play opened at the Booth Theatre. Traditionally, the playwright was invisible to the audience: One hid out in a nearby bar, listening to the sweet nasalities of Pat Boone's rendering of "Love Letters in the Sand" from a glowing jukebox. But when the curtain fell on this particular night, I went into the crowded lobby to collect someone. Overcoat collar high about my face, I moved invisibly through the crowd, or so I thought. Suddenly a voice boomed-tolled across the lobby. "*Gore!*" I stopped; everyone stopped. From the cloakroom a small round figure, rather like a Civil War cannon ball, hurtled toward me and collided. As I looked down into that familiar round face with its snub nose and shining bloodshot eyes, I heard, the entire crowded lobby heard: "*How could you do this?* How could you *sell out* like this? To *Broadway*! To *Commercialism*! How could you give up *The Novel*? Give up the *security*? The security of knowing that every two years there will be—like clockwork—*that five-hundred-dollar advance!*" Thirty years later, the voice still echoes in my mind, and I think fondly of its owner, our best comic novelist. "The field," I can hear Dawn Powell snarl, "is not exactly overcrowded."

On the night that *Visit to a Small Planet* opened, Dawn Powell was fifty-nine years old. She had published fourteen novels, evenly divided between accounts of her native Midwest (and how the hell to get out of there and make it to New York) and the highly comic New York novels, centered on Greenwich Village, where she lived most of her adult life. Some twenty-three years earlier, the Theatre Guild had produced Powell's comedy *Jig Saw* (one of *her* many unsuccessful attempts to sell out to commercialism), but there was third-act trouble and, despite Spring Byington and Ernest Truex, the play closed after forty-nine performances.

For decades Dawn Powell was always just on the verge of ceasing to be a cult and becoming a major religion. But despite the work of such dedicated cultists as Edmund Wilson and Matthew Josephson, John Dos Passos and Ernest Hemingway, Dawn Powell never became the popular writer that she ought to have been. In those days, with a bit of luck, a good writer eventually attracted voluntary readers and became popular. Today, of course, "popular" means bad writing that is widely read while good writing is that which is taught to involuntary readers. Powell failed on both counts. She needs no interpretation and in her lifetime she should have been as widely read as, say, Hemingway or the early Fitzgerald or the mid O'Hara or even the late, far too late, Katherine Anne Porter. But Powell was that unthinkable monster, a witty woman who felt no obligation to make a single, much less a final, down payment on Love or The Family; she saw life with a bright Petronian neutrality, and every host at life's feast was a potential Trimalchio to be sent up.

In the few interviews that Powell gave, she often mentions as her favorite novel, surprisingly for an American, much less for a woman of her time and place, the *Satyricon*. This sort of thing was not acceptable then any more than it is now. Descriptions of warm, mature, heterosexual love were—and are—woman's writerly task, and the truly serious writers really, heartbreakingly, flunk the course while the pop ones pass with bright honors.

Although Powell received very little serious critical attention (to the extent that there has ever been much in our heavily moralizing culture), when she did get reviewed by a really serious person like Diana Trilling (*The Nation*, May 29, 1948), *la* Trilling warns us that the book at hand is no good because of "the discrepancy between the power of mind revealed on every page of her novel [*The Locusts Have No King*] and the insignificance of the human beings upon which she directs her excellent intelligence." Trilling does acknowledge the formidable intelligence but because Powell does not deal with morally complex people (full professors at Columbia in mid journey?), "the novel as a whole . . . fails to sustain the excitement promised by its best moments."

Apparently, a novel to be serious must be about very serious—even solemn—people rendered in a very solemn—even serious—manner. Wit? What is that? But then we all know that power of mind and intelligence count for as little in the American novel as they do in American life. Fortunately neither appears with sufficient regularity to distress our solemn middle-class middlebrows as they trudge ever onward to some Scarsdale of the mind, where the red light blinks and blinks at pier's end and the fields of the republic rush forward ever faster like a rug rolling up.

Powell herself occasionally betrays bewilderment at the misreading of her work. She is aware, of course, that the American novel is a middlebrow middle-class affair and that the reader/writer must be as one in pompous self-regard. "There is so great a premium on dullness," she wrote sadly (Robert Van Gelder, *Writers and Writing*, New York: Scribner's, 1946), "that it seems stupid to pass it up." She also remarks that

> *it is considered jolly and good-humored to point out the oddities of the poor or of the rich. The frailties of millionaires or garbage collectors can be made to seem amusing to persons who are not millionaires or garbage collectors. Their ways of speech, their personal habits, the peculiarities of their thinking are considered fair game. I go outside the rules with my stuff because I can't help believing that the middle class is funny, too.*

Well, she was warned by four decades of book-chatterers.

My favorite was the considered judgment of one Frederic Morton (*The New York Times*, September 12, 1954):

> *But what appears most fundamentally lacking is the sense of outrage which serves as an engine to even the most sophisticated [sic] satirist. Miss Powell does not possess the pure indignation that moves Evelyn Waugh to his absurdities and forced Orwell into his haunting contortions. Her verbal equipment is probably unsurpassed among writers of her genre—but she views the antics of humanity with too surgical a calm.*

It should be noted that Mr. Morton was the author of the powerful, purely indignant, and phenomenally compassionate novel, *Asphalt and Desire*. In general, Powell's books usually excited this sort of commentary. (Waugh *indignant*? Orwell hauntingly *contorted*?) The fact is that Americans have never been able to deal with wit. Wit gives away the scam. Wit blows the cool of those who are forever expressing a sense of hoked-up outrage. Wit, deployed by a woman with surgical calm, is a brutal assault upon nature—that is, Man. Attis, take arms!

Finally, as the shadows lengthened across the greensward, Edmund Wilson got around to his old friend in *The New Yorker* (November 17, 1962). One reason, he tells us, why Powell has so little appeal to those Americans who read novels is that "she does nothing to stimulate feminine day-dreams [sexist times!]. The woman reader can find no comfort in identifying herself with Miss Powell's heroines. The women who appear in her stories are likely to be as sordid and absurd as the men." This sexual parity was—is—unusual. But now, closer to century's end than 1962, Powell's sordid, absurd ladies seem like so many Mmes. de Staël compared to our latter-day viragos.

Wilson also noted Powell's originality: "Love is not Miss Powell's theme. Her real theme is the provincial in New York who has come on from the Middle West and acclimatized himself (or herself) to the city and made himself a permanent place there, without ever, however, losing his fascinated sense of an alien and anarchic society." This is very much to the (very badly written) point. Wilson finds her novels "among the most amusing being written, and in this respect quite on a level with

those of Anthony Powell, Evelyn Waugh, and Muriel Spark." Wilson's review was of her last book, *The Golden Spur*; three years later she was
dead of breast cancer. "Thanks a lot, Bunny," one can hear her mutter as
this belated floral wreath came flying through her transom.

Summer. Sunday afternoon. Circa 1950. Dawn Powell's duplex living
room at 35 East Ninth Street. The hostess presides over an elliptical
aquarium filled with gin: a popular drink of the period known as the martini. In attendance, Coby—just Coby to me for years, her *cavaliere ser-
vente*; he is neatly turned out in a blue blazer, rosy faced, sleek silver hair
combed straight back. Coby can talk with charm on any subject. The fact
that he might be Dawn's lover has never crossed my mind. They are so
old. A handsome, young poet lies on the floor, literally at the feet of e. e.
cummings and his wife, Marion, who ignore him. Dawn casts an occasional maternal eye in the boy's direction; but the eye is more that of the
mother of a cat or a dog, apt to make a nuisance. Conversation flows. Gin
flows. Marion Cummings is beautiful; so indeed is her husband, his eyes
a faded denim blue. Coby is in great form. Though often his own subject,
he records not boring triumphs but improbable disasters. He is always
broke, and a once distinguished wardrobe is now in the hands of those
gay receivers, his landladies. This afternoon, at home, Dawn is demure;
thoughtful. 'Why,' she suddenly asks, eyes on the long body beside the
coffee table, "do they never have floors of their own to sleep on?"

Cummings explains that as the poet lives in Philadelphia he is too far
from his own floor to sleep on it. Not long after, the young poet and I paid
a call on the Cummingses. We were greeted at the door by an edgy Marion. "I'm afraid you can't come in." Behind her an unearthly high scream
sounded. "Dylan Thomas just died," she explained. "Is that Mr. Cummings screaming?" asked the poet politely, as the keening began on an
even higher note. "No," said Marion. "That is not Mr. Cummings. That
is Mrs. Thomas."

But for the moment, in my memory, the poet is forever asleep on the
floor while on a balcony high up in the second story of Dawn's living
room, a gray blurred figure appears and stares down at us. "Who," I ask,
"is that?"

Dawn gently, lovingly, stirs the martinis, squints her eyes, says, "My husband, I think. It is Joe, isn't it, Coby?" She turns to Coby, who beams and waves at the gray man, who withdraws. "Of course it is," says Coby. "Looking very fit." I realize, at last, that this is a *ménage à trois* in Greenwich Village. My martini runs over.

2

To date the only study of Dawn Powell is a doctoral dissertation by Judith Faye Pett (University of Iowa, 1981). Miss Pett has gathered together a great deal of biographical material for which one is grateful. I am happy to know, at last, that the amiable Coby's proper name was Coburn Gilman, and I am sad to learn that he survived Dawn by only two years. The husband on the balcony was Joseph Gousha, or Goushé, whom she married November 20, 1920. He was musical; she literary, with a talent for the theater. A son was born retarded. Over the years, a fortune was spent on schools and nurses. To earn the fortune, Powell did every sort of writing, from interviews in the press to stories for ladies' magazines to plays that tended not to be produced to a cycle of novels about the Midwest, followed by a cycle of New York novels, where she came into her own, dragging our drab literature screaming behind her. As doyenne of the Village, she held court in the grill of the Lafayette Hotel—for elegiasts the Lafayette was off Washington Square, at University Place and Ninth Street.

Powell also runs like a thread of purest brass through Edmund Wilson's *The Thirties*: "It was closing time in the Lafayette Grill, and Coby Gilman was being swept out from under the table. Niles Spencer had been stuttering for five minutes, and Dawn Powell gave him a crack on the jaw and said, '*Nuts* is the word you're groping for.' " Also, "[Peggy Bacon] told me about Joe Gousha's attacking her one night at a party and trying to tear her clothes off. . . . I suggested that Joe had perhaps simply thought that this was the thing to do in Dawn's set. She said, 'Yes: he thought it was a social obligation.' " Powell also "said that Dotsy's husband was very much excited because the Prince of Wales was wearing a zipper fly, a big thing in the advertising business." A footnote to this text says that "Dawn Powell (1897–1965)" and Wilson carried on a corre-

spondence in which she was Mrs. Humphry Ward and he "a seedy literary man named Wigmore." Later, there is a very muddled passage in
which, for reasons not quite clear, James Thurber tells Dawn Powell that
she does not *deserve* to be in the men's room. That may well be what it
was all about.

I have now read all of Powell's novels and one of the plays.* Miss Pett
provides bits and pieces from correspondence and diaries, and fragments
of book-chat. Like most writers, Powell wrote of what she knew. Therefore, certain themes recur, while the geography does not vary from that
of her actual life. As a child, she and two sisters were shunted about from
one midwestern farm or small town to another by a father who was a
salesman on the road (her mother died when she was six). The maternal
grandmother made a great impression on her and predisposed her toward boardinghouse life (as a subject not a residence). Indomitable old
women, full of rage and good jokes, occur in both novel cycles. At twelve,
Powell's father remarried, and Dawn and sisters went to live on the stepmother's farm. "My stepmother, one day, burned up all the stories I was
writing, a form of discipline I could not endure. With thirty cents earned
by picking berries I ran away, ending up in the home of a kind aunt in
Shelby, Ohio." After graduation from the local high school, she worked
her way through Lake Erie College for Women in Painesville, Ohio. I
once gave a commencement address there and was struck by how red-
brick New England Victorian the buildings were. I also found out all that
I could about their famous alumna. I collected some good stories to tell
her. But by the time I got back to New York she was dead.

Powell set out to be a playwright. One play ended up as a movie while

---

*I have omitted an interesting short novel because it is not part of the New York cycle.
Powell made one trip to Europe after the war. Although Paris was no match for the Village, Powell, ever thrifty, uses the city as a background for a young man and woman
trapped in *A Cage for Lovers* (published the year that Dawn roared at me in the Booth
Theatre). The girl is a secretary-companion to a monster-lady, and the young man her
chauffeur. The writing is austere; there are few characters; the old lady, Lesley Patterson,
keeper of the cage, is truly dreadful in her loving kindness. In a rather nice if perhaps too
neat ending, they cage *her* through her need to dominate. Thus, the weak sometimes
prevail.

another, *Big Night*, was done by the Group Theatre in 1933. But it was the First World War not the theater that got Powell out of Ohio and to New York in 1918, as a member of the Red Cross: The war ended before her uniform arrived. Powell wrote publicity. Married. Wrote advertising copy (at the time Goushé or Gousha was an account executive with an advertising agency). Failure in the theater and need for money at home led her to novel writing and the total security of that five-hundred-dollar advance each of us relied on for so many years. Powell's first novel, *Whither*, was published in 1925. In 1928 Powell published *She Walks in Beauty*, which she always maintained, mysteriously, was really her first novel. For one thing, the Ohio heroine of *Whither* is already in New York City, like Powell herself, working as a syndicated writer who must turn out thirty thousand words a week in order to live (in Powell's case to pay for her child's treatments). In a sense, this New York novel was premature; with her second book, Powell turns back to her origins in the Western Reserve, where New Englanders had re-created New England in Ohio; and the tone is dour Yankee, with a most un-Yankeeish wit.

The Ohio cycle begins with *She Walks in Beauty*, which is dedicated to her husband, Joe. The story is set in Powell's youth before the First World War. The book was written in 1927. Popular writers of the day: Thornton Wilder had published *The Bridge of San Luis Rey* in the same year as Powell's first but really second novel. Louis Bromfield received the Pulitzer Prize for *Early Autumn* (a favorite Bromfield phrase, "candy pink and poison green," occasionally surfaces in Powell) while Cather's *Death Comes for the Archbishop* was also published in 1927. The year 1925, of course, had been the most remarkable in our literary history. After commemorating life in the Midwest, Sinclair Lewis brought his hero Arrowsmith to New York City, a pattern Powell was to appropriate in her Ohio cycle. Also in that miraculous year alongside, as it were, *Whither*: Theodore Dreiser's *An American Tragedy*, Dos Passos's *Manhattan Transfer*, Fitzgerald's *The Great Gatsby*. It is interesting that Dreiser, Lewis, Hemingway, Fitzgerald, Dos Passos, and the popular Bromfield were all, like Powell, midwesterners with a dream of some other great good place, preferably Paris but Long Island Sound and social climbing would do.

Powell briskly shows us the town of Birchfield. Dorrie is the dreamy, plain, bright sister (always two contrasting sisters in these early novels); she stands in for Powell. Linda is the vain, chilly one. Aunt Jule keeps a boardinghouse. The Powell old lady makes her debut: "She pinned her muslin gown at the throat, dropped her teeth with a cheerful little click in the glass of water on the table, and turned out the gas." The "cheerful" launches us on the Powell style. The story is negligible: Who's going to make it out of the sticks first. In the boardinghouse there is an old man who reads Greek; his son has already made it to the big city, where he is writing a trilogy. Powell doesn't quite see the fun of this yet. But Dorrie falls for the young man, Dorrie "with that absurd infantile tilt to her nose" (Dawn to a T). Also Dorrie's tact is very like her creator's. A theatrical couple of a certain age are at the boardinghouse. The actress, Laura, tries on a hat. " 'It will look wonderful on Linda,' Dorrie vouchsafed pleasantly. 'It's too young for you, Aunt Laura.' " The adverb "pleasantly" helps make the joke, a point of contention between no-adverbs Graham Greene and myself. I look to the adverb for surprise. Greene thinks that the verb should do all the work.

Dorrie observes her fellow townspeople—nicely? "He had been such a shy little boy. But the shyness had settled into surliness, and the dreaminess was sheer stupidity. Phil Lancer was growing up to be a good Birchfield citizen." Points of view shift wildly in Powell's early books. We are in Linda's mind, as she is about to allow a yokel to marry her. "Later on, Linda thought, after they were married, she could tell him she didn't like to be kissed." The book ends with Dorrie still dreaming that the trilogist will come and take her off to New York.

In 1929 came *The Bride's House*. One suspects that Powell's own wit was the result of being obliged for so long to sing for her supper in so many strange surroundings: "Lotta's children arrived, . . . three gray, horrid-looking little creatures and their names were Lois and Vera and Custer . . . 'We've come to stay!' they shouted. . . . 'We've come to stay on the farm with Uncle Stephen and Aunt Cecily. Aren't you glad?' " No one is, alas. But these children are well-armored egotists. " 'She tells lies,' Lois hissed in George's ear. 'I'm the pretty one and she's the bright one. She told the conductor we lived in the White House. She's a very bad girl and mother

and I can't do a thing with her. . . . Everything she says is a lie, Cousin Sophie, except when it hurts your feelings then it's true.'" A child after absolutely no one's heart.

Unfortunately, Powell loses interest in the children; instead we are
told the story of Sophie's love for two men. The grandmother character
makes a dutiful appearance, and the Powell stock company go rather mechanically through their paces. Powell wants to say something original
about love but cannot get the focus right: "A woman needed two lovers,
she finally decides, one to comfort her for the torment the other caused
her." This is to be a recurring theme throughout Powell's work and, presumably, life: Coby versus Joe? or was it Coby *and* Joe?

Dance Night (1930) is the grittiest, most proletarian of the novels. There
are no artists or would-be artists in Lamptown. Instead there is a railroad
junction, a factory, the Bon Ton Hat Shop, where the protagonists, a
mother and son, live close to Bill Delaney's Saloon and Billiard Parlor.
Like the country, the town has undergone the glorious 1920s boom; now
the Depression has begun to hit. Powell charts the fortunes of the
mother-milliner, Elsinore Abbott, and her adolescent son, Morry. Elsinore's husband is a traveling salesman; he affects jealousy of his wife,
who has made a go of her shop but given up on her life.

Morry gets caught up in the local real estate boom. He also gets involved with a waif, Jen, from an orphanage, who has been adopted by the
saloon-keeper as a sort of indentured slave. Jen dreams of liberating her
younger sister, Lil, from the home where their mother had deposited
them. Jen is not much of an optimist: "People last such a little while with
me. There's no way to keep them, I guess, that's why I've got to go back
for Lil because I know how terrible it is to be left always—never see people again." It took Powell a long time to work all this out of her system.
Happily, farce intrudes. A young swain in a romantic moment "slid his
hand along her arm biceps and pressed a knuckle in her arm-pit. 'That's
the vein to tap when you embalm people,' he said, for he was going to be
an undertaker."

The highest work for a Lamptown girl is telephone operator, then
waitress, then factory hand. Powell has a Balzacian precision about these

things; and she remembers to put the price tag on everything. Money is always a character in her novels, as it was in Balzac's. In fact, Powell makes several references to Balzac in her early books as well as to his Eugénie Grandet.

Morry grows up and his mother hardly notices him: "She had moved over for Morry as you would move over for someone on a street car, certain that the intimacy was only for a few minutes, but now it was eighteen years and she thought, why Morry was hers, hers more than anything else in the world was." This revelation shatters no earth for her or for him; and one can see how distressing such realism must have been—as it still is—for American worshipers of the family. Love, too.

Morry gets involved with a builder who indulges him in his dreams to create handsome houses for a public that only wants small lookalike boxes jammed together. Meanwhile, he loves Jen's sister, Lil, while Jen loves him: a usual state of affairs. The only bit of drama, indeed melodrama, is the return of Morry's father; there is a drunken fight between father and son, then a row between father and Elsinore, whom he accuses, wrongly, of philandering. Finally, "wearing down her barriers," she reaches for a pistol: "This was one way to shut out words. . . . She raised the gun, closed her eyes and fired." Although everyone knows that she killed her husband the town chooses to believe it was suicide, and life goes on. So does Morry who now realizes that he must go away: "There'd be no place that trains went that he wouldn't go."

In 1932, Powell published *The Tenth Moon*. This is a somewhat Catheresque novel composed with a fuguelike series of short themes (the influence of her ex-music-critic husband?). Connie Benjamin is a village Bovary, married to a cobbler, with two daughters; she once dreamed of being a singer. Connie lives now without friends or indeed a life of any kind in a family that has not the art of communication with one another. Connie daydreams through life while her daughters fret ("They went to bed at ten but whispered until twelve, remembering through all their confidences to tell each other nothing for they were sisters"). The husband works in amiable silence. Finally, Connie decides to have a social life. She invites to supper her daughter's English teacher; she also invites the music teacher, Blaine Decker, an exquisite bachelor, as adrift as Connie in dreams of a career in music that might have been.

Powell now introduces one of her major themes: the failed artist who with luck, might have been—what? In dreams, these characters are always on stage; in life, they are always in the audience. But Blaine has actually been to Paris with his friend, a glamorous one-shot novelist, Starr Donnell (Glenway Wescott?). Blaine and Connie complement and compliment each other. Connie realizes that she has been "utterly, completely, hideously unhappy" for fifteen years of marriage. Yet each pretends there are compensations to village life and poverty. " 'Isn't it better, I've often thought,' she said, 'for me to be here keeping up with my interests in music, keeping my ideals, than to have failed as an opera singer and been trapped into cheap musical comedy work?' " To hear them tell it, they are as one in the contentment of failure.

But Blaine still hears his mother's voice from offstage, a Powellesque killer: "I sometimes wonder, Blaine, if I didn't emphasize the artistic too much in your childhood, encouraging you and perhaps forcing you beyond your real capacity in music. It was only because you did so poorly in school, dear. . . ." Powell always knows just how much salt a wound requires.

Although the dreamers "talked of music until the careers they once planned were the careers they actually had but given up for the simple joys of living," knowing "success would have destroyed us," Connie goes too far. First, she tries indeed to sing and, for an instant, captures whatever it was she thought that she had and promptly hemorrhages—tuberculosis. Second, she confides to Blaine that she lost a career, home, virginity to Tony the Daredevil, a circus acrobat, who abandoned her in Atlantic City, where the kindly cobbler met and married her. He needed a wife; she could not go home. Blaine is made furious by the truth.

Then daughter Helen runs off with a boy, and the dying Connie pursues her. She finds that Helen has not only managed to get herself a job with a theatrical stock company but she is about to drop the boy; and Connie "knew almost for a certainty that Helen would climb the heights she herself had only glimpsed." Connie goes home to die, and Powell shifts to the dying woman's point of view:

When Dr. Arnold's face flashed on the mirror she thought, "This must be the way one dies. People collect on a mirror like dust and something rushes through your mind emptying all the drawers and shelves to see if you're leaving anything behind." . . . What a pity, she thought, no one will ever know these are my last thoughts—that Dr. Arnold's mouth was so small.

At the end Connie is spared nothing, including the knowledge that her husband never believed that she came of a good family and studied music and only fell once from grace with an acrobat. Blaine goes off to Paris as a tour guide.

With *The Story of a Country Boy* (1934) she ends the Ohio cycle. This is the most invented of the novels. There is no pretty sister, no would-be artist, no flight from village to city. Instead Powell tells the story of a conventional young man, a country boy, who becomes a great success in business; then he fails and goes home to the country, no wiser than before. Ironically, Powell was doing the exact reverse in her own life, putting down deep lifelong roots in that village called Greenwich, far from her own origins. In a sense, this book is a good-bye to all that.

Again, one gets the boom and bust of the Twenties and early Thirties. Chris Bennett is the all-American boy who makes good. He is entirely self-confident and sublimely unaware of any limitations. Yet, in due course he fails, largely because he lacks imagination. There is a good deal of Warren Harding, Ohio's favorite son, in his makeup. He is more striking in appearance than reality. Also, Powell was becoming more and more fascinated by the element of chance in life, as demonstrated by Harding's incredible election (those were simple times) to the presidency. "Chris could not remember ever being unsure of himself except in little details of social life where his defects were a source of pride rather than chagrin." He also wonders "if pure luck had brought him his success." He is right to wonder: It has. When he finally looks down from the heights he falls. No fatal flaw—just vertigo.

A splendid new character has joined the stock company, a former U.S. senator who sees in Chris the sort of handsome mediocrity that,

properly exploited, could be presidential. John J. Habbiman's drunken soliloquies are glorious:

> *"Tell them I died for Graustark," said the Senator in a faraway voice. He*
> *sombrely cracked peanuts and ate them, casting the shells lightly aside with*
> *infinite grace. "What wondrous life is this I lead. Ripe apples drop about my*
> *head."*

Powell also developed an essayistic technique to frame her scenes. A
chapter will begin with a diversion:

> *In the utter stillness before dawn a rat carpentered the rafters, a nest of field*
> *mice seduced by unknown applause into coloratura ambitions, squeaked*
> *and squealed with amateur intensity. . . . Here, at daybreak, a host of black-*
> *birds were now meeting to decide upon a sun, and also to blackball from*
> *membership in the committee a red-winged blackbird.*

Unfortunately, her main character is too schematic to interest her or the
reader. In any case, except for one final experiment, she has got Ohio out
of her system; she has also begun to write more carefully, and the essays
make nice point counterpoint to the theatricality of her scene writing.

The theater is indeed the place for her first New York invention, *Jig
Saw* (1934), a comedy. The gags are generally very good but the plotting
is a bit frantic. Claire is a charming lady, whose eighteen-year-old daughter, Julie, comes to stay with her in a Manhattan flat. Claire has a lover;
and a best woman friend to make the sharper jokes. Julie "is a very well
brought up young lady—easy to see she has not been exposed to home
life." Again it takes two to make a mate: "It takes two women to make
your marriage a success." To which Claire's lover, Del, responds, "Have it
your way—then Claire and I have made a success of my marriage to Margaret."

A young man, Nathan, enters the story. Both mother and daughter
want him. Julie proves to be more ruthless than Claire. Julie moves in on
Nathan and announces their coming marriage to the press. He is appalled; he prefers her mother. But Julie is steel: "I can make something
of you, Nate. Something marvelous." When he tries to talk her out of

marriage, she declares, "I expect to go through life making sacrifices for you, dear, giving up my career for you." When he points out that she has never had a career, she rises to even greater heights: "I know. That's what makes it all the more of a sacrifice. I've never had a career. I never will have. Because I love you so much." Nate is trapped. Claire wonders if she should now marry Del, but he advises against it: "You're the triangular type. . . ." With a bit of the sort of luck that so fascinated Powell by its absence in most lives, she might have had a successful commercial career in the theater. But that luck never came her way in life, as opposed to imagination. Finally, Powell's bad luck on Broadway was to be our literature's gain.

3

The New York cycle begins with *Turn, Magic Wheel* (1936), dedicated to Dwight Fiske, a sub-Coward nightclub performer for whom Powell wrote special material. Powell now writes about a writer, always an edgy business. Dennis Orphen is a male surrogate for Powell herself. He is involved with two women, of course. He is also on the scene for good: He reappears in almost all her books, and it is he who writes finis to *The Golden Spur*, some twenty years later, as the Lafayette Hotel is being torn down and he realizes that his world has gone for good. But in 1936 Dennis is eager, on the make, fascinated by others: "his urgent need to know what they were knowing, see, hear, feel what they were sensing, for a brief moment to *be* them." He is consumed by a curiosity about others which time has a pleasant way of entirely sating.

Corinne is the profane love, a married woman; Effie is the sacred love, the abandoned wife of a famous writer called Andrew Callingham, Hemingway's first appearance in Powell's work. Effie is a keeper of the flame; she pretends that Andrew will come back: "Why must she be noble, frail shoulders squared to defeat, gaily confessing that life was difficult but that was the way things were?" Dennis publishes a *roman à clef*, whose key unlocks the Callingham/Hemingway story, and he worries that Effie may feel herself betrayed because Dennis completely dispels her illusion that the great man will return to her. As Dennis makes his New York rounds, the Brevoort Café, Longchamps, Luchow's, he encounters

Okie, the ubiquitous man about town who will reappear in the New York novels, a part of their Balzacian detail. Okie edits an entertainment guide magazine, writes a column, knows everyone, and brings everyone together. A party is going on at all hours in different parts of the town, and Powell's characters are always on the move, and the lines of their extramarital affairs cross and recross. The essays now grow thoughtful and there are inner soliloquies:

> *Walter missed Bee now but sometimes he thought it was more fun talking to Corinne about how he loved Bee than really being with Bee, for Bee never seemed to want to be alone with him, she was always asking everyone else to join them. In fact the affair from her point of view was just loads of fun and that was all. She never cried or talked about divorce or any of the normal things, she just had a fine time as if it wasn't serious at all.*

Powell is much concerned with how people probably ought to behave but somehow never do. The drinking is copious: "Corinne went into the ladies room and made up again. It was always fun making up after a few Pernods because they made your face freeze so it was like painting a statue." Of course, "Walter was as mad as could be, watching the cunning little figure in the leopard coat and green beret patter out of the room." Whenever "cunning" or "gaily" or "tinkling" is used, Powell is stalking dinner, with the precision of a saber-toothed tiger. She also notes those "long patient talks, the patient civilized talks that, if one knew it, are the end of love."

There are amusing incidents rather than a plot of the sort that popular novels required in those days: Effie is hurt by Orphen's portrayal of her marriage in his book; Corinne vacillates between husband and lover; the current Mrs. Callingham goes into the hospital to die of cancer. There are publishers who live in awe of book reviewers with names like Gannett, Hansen, Paterson. One young publisher "was so brilliant that he could tell in advance that in the years 1934–35 and –36 a book would be called exquisitely well-written if it began: 'The boxcar swung out of the yards. Pip rolled over in the straw. He scratched himself where the straw itched him.' " Finally, the book's real protagonist is the city:

In the quiet of three o'clock the Forties looked dingy, deserted, incredibly nineteenth century with the dim lamps in dreary doorways; in these midnight hours the streets were possessed by their ancient parasites, low tumbledown frame rooming houses with cheap little shops, though by day such remnants of another decade retreated obscurely between flamboyant hotels.

That city is now well and truly gone.

"Fleetingly, Effie thought of a new system of obituaries in which the lives recorded were criticized, mistaken steps pointed out, structure condemned, better paths suggested." This is the essence of Dawn Powell: The fantastic flight from the mundane that can then lead to a thousand conversational variations, and the best of her prose is like the best conversation where no *escalier* is ever wit's receptacle. As a result, she is at her best with The Party; but then most novels of this epoch were assembled around The Party, where the characters proceed to interact and the unsayable gets said. Powell has a continuing hostess who is a variation on Peggy Guggenheim, collecting artists for gallery and bed. There is also a minor hostess, interested only in celebrities and meaningful conversation. She quizzes Dennis: " 'Now let's talk,' she commanded playfully [Powell's adverbs are often anesthetic preparatory for surgery]. 'We've never really had a nice talk, have we, Dennis? Tell me how you came to write? I suppose you had to make money so you just started writing, didn't you?' " Callingham himself comes to The Party. Powell's affection for the real Hemingway did not entirely obscure his defects, particularly as viewed by an ex-wife, Effie, who discovers to her relief "there was no Andy left, he had been wiped out by Callingham the Success as so many men before him had been wiped out by the thing they represented." Effie frees herself from him and settles back into contented triangularity with Dennis and Corinne. Cake had; ingested, too.

In 1938, with *The Happy Island*, the Powell novel grows more crowded and The Party is bigger and wilder. This time the rustic who arrives in the city is not a young woman but a young man. Powell is often more at home with crude masculine protagonists, suspecting, perhaps, that her kind of tough realism might cause resentment among those who think of women as the fair sex.

A would-be playwright, Jeff Abbott (related to Morry?), arrives on the bus from Silver City; a manager has accepted his play with the ominous telegram, CASTING COMPLETE THIRD ACT NEEDS REWRITING [like that of *Jig Saw*] COME IMMEDIATELY. Jeff has two friends in the city. One is Prudence Bly, a successful nightclub singer; the other is Dol, a gentleman party giver and fancier of young men. At the book's end, Dol gives great offense by dying, seated in a chair, at his own party. How like him! the guests mutter.

Prudence is the most carefully examined of Powell's women. She is successful; she drinks too much; she is seldom involved with fewer than two men. But it is the relationships between women that make Powell's novels so funny and original. Jean Nelson, a beautiful dummy, is Prudence's best friend; each needs the other to dislike. At the novel's beginning, Jean has acquired Prudence's lover Steve. The two girls meet for a serious drunken chat over lunch. "You aren't jealous of me, are you, Prudence?" "*Jealous?* Jealous? Good God, Jean, you must think this is the Middle Ages!" Prudence then broods to herself:

> *Why do I lunch with women anyway? . . . We always end up sniveling over men and life and we always tell something that makes us afraid of each other for weeks to come. . . . Women take too much out of you, they drink too much and too earnestly. They drink the way they used to do china painting, and crewel work and wood burning.*

In the restaurant things grow blurred: " 'You're so good to everyone,' sighed Jean. 'You really are.' Nothing could have enraged Prudence more or been more untrue." Finally, Jean goes: "Prudence looked meditatively after Jean as she wove her way earnestly through tables and knees. The girl did look like a goddess but the trouble was she walked like one, too, as if her legs had been too long wound in a flag."

Prudence's forebears include, yet again, the eccentric grandmother. This one is rich, and "Prudence was always glad her grandmother had been neither kind nor affectionate." The escape from Silver City had been easy. The grandmother was indifferent to everyone, including "her surly young Swedish chauffeur." A great traveler, Mrs. Bly "always wanted to buy one dinner with two plates, as if he were a Pekinese, and, more alarming still, to take one room in the hotels where they stayed. . . . After all, she explained, she always slept with her clothes on so there was nothing indecent in it." In addition, Mrs. Bly is a sincere liar, who believes that she was on the *Titanic* when it was sunk; and was courted by the czar.

Jeff Abbott and Prudence meet. They have an affair. Jeff is sublimely humorless, which intrigues Prudence. He is also a man of destiny, doomed to greatness in the theater. " 'I never yet found anything to laugh at in this world,' said Jeff. 'You never heard of a great man with a sense of humor, did you? Humor's an anesthetic, that's all, laughing gas while your guts are jerked out.' " Since they are not made for each other, marriage is a real possibility. Prudence is growing unsure of herself:

> *She could not find the place where the little girl from Ohio, the ambitious, industrious little village girl, merged into the* Evening Journal *Prudence Bly,* The Town and Country *Bly. There were queer moments between personalities, moments such as the hermit crab must have scuttling from one stolen shell to the next one. . . . Prudence Bly was not so much a person as a conspiracy.*

Then Powell, in a quick scuttle, briefly inhabits her own shell:

> *Prudence slew with a neat epithet, crippled with a true word, then, seeing the devastation about her and her enemies growing, grew frightened of revenge, backed desperately, and eventually found the white flag of Sentimentality as her salvation. For every ruinous* mot *she had a tear for motherhood.*

The failure of Jeff's powerful play does not disturb him, and Prudence is somewhat awed since worldly success is the only thing that makes the island happy. But "he belongs to the baffling group of confident writers who need no applause. For them a success is not a surprise but cause for wonder that it is less than international. . . . A failure proves that a man is too good for his times." When he says he wants to buy a farm in the Midwest and settle down and write, Prudence is

astonished. When he does exactly that, she goes with him. Integrity at
last. No more glamour. No more happy island. Only fields, a man, a
woman. In no time at all, she is climbing the walls and heading back to
New York where she belongs. Since Jean has let go of Steve, he receives
her amiably (but then hardly anyone has noticed her departure). The
book ends with: "Prudence's looks, [Steve] reflected with some surprise,
were quite gone. She really looked as hard as nails, but then so did most
women eventually." That excellent worldly novelist Thackeray never
made it to so high a ground.

Angels on Toast (1940); war has begun to darken the skyline. But the
turning wheel's magic is undiminished for Ebie, a commercial artist,
whose mother is in the great line of Powell eccentrics. Ebie lives with another working woman, Honey, who "was a virgin (at least you couldn't
prove she wasn't), and was as proud as punch of it. You would have
thought that it was something that had been in the family for generations." But Ebie and Honey need each other to talk at, and in a tavern

> *where O. Henry used to go . . . they'd sit in the dark smoked-wood booth*
> *drinking old-fashioneds and telling each other things they certainly wished*
> *later they had never told and bragging about their families, sometimes mak-*
> *ing them hot-stuff socially back home, the next time making them roman-*
> *tically on the wrong side of the tracks. The family must have been on wheels*
> *back in the Middle West, whizzing back and forth across tracks at a mere*
> *word from the New York daughters.*

Brooding over the novel is the downtown Hotel Ellery. For seventeen dollars a week Ebie's mother, Mrs. Vane, lives in contented genteel squalor.

> BAR *and* GRILL: *it was the tavern entrance to a somewhat medieval look-*
> *ing hotel, whose time-and-soot-blackened façade was frittered with fire-*
> *escapes, . . . its dark oak-wainscotting rising high to meet grimy black walls,*
> *its ship windows covered with heavy pumpkin chintz. . . . Once in you were*
> *in for no mere moment. . . . The elderly lady residents of the hotel were*

without too much obvious haste taking their places in the grill-room, nod-
ding and smiling to the waitresses, carrying their knitting and a slender
volume of some English bard, anything to prop against their first
Manhattan . . . as they sipped their drinks and dipped into literature. It was
sip and dip, sip and dip until cocktail time was proclaimed by the arrival of
the little cocktail sausage wagon.

In its remoteness, this world before television could just as easily be that
of *St. Ronan's Well*.

It is also satisfying that in these New York novels the city that was
plays so pervasive a role. This sort of hotel, meticulously described,
evokes lost time in a way that the novel's bumptious contemporary, early
talking movies, don't.

Another curious thing about these small, venerable, respectable hotels, there
seemed no appeal here to the average newcomer. BAR *and* GRILL, *for in-*
stance, appealed to seemingly genteel widows and spinsters of small in-
comes. . . . Then there were those tired flashes-in-the-pan, the one-shot
celebrities, and, on the other hand, there was a gay younger group whose
loyalty to the BAR *and* GRILL *was based on the cheapness of its martinis. Over*
their simple dollar lunches (four martinis and a sandwich) this livelier set
snickered at the older residents.

Ebie wants to take her mother away from all this so that they can live together in Connecticut. Mrs. Vane would rather die. She prefers to lecture the bar on poetry. There is also a plot: two men in business, with
wives. One has an affair with Ebie. There is a boom in real estate; then
a bust. By now, Powell has mastered her own method. The essay-
beginnings to chapters work smartly:

In the dead of night wives talked to their husbands, in the dark they talked
and talked while the clock on the bureau ticked sleep away, and the last
street cars clanged off on distant streets to remoter suburbs, where in new
houses bursting with mortgages and the latest conveniences, wives talked in
the dark, and talked and talked.

The prose is now less easygoing; and there is a conscious tightening of the language although, to the end, Powell thought one thing was different *than* another while always proving not her mettle but metal.

Powell is generally happiest in the BAR and GRILL or at the Lafayette or Brevoort. But in *A Time to Be Born* (1942) she takes a sudden social leap, and lands atop the town's social Rockies. Class is the most difficult subject for American writers to deal with as it is the most difficult for the English to avoid. There are many reasons. First, since the Depression, the owners of the Great Republic prefer not to be known to the public at large. Celebrities, of the sort that delight Powell, fill the newspapers while the great personages are seldom, if ever, mentioned; they are also rarely to be seen in those places where public and celebrities go to mingle. "Where," I asked the oldest of my waiter-acquaintances at the Plaza (we've known each other forty years), "have the nobles gone?" He looked sad. "I'm told they have their own islands now. Things"—he was vague—"like that."

As I read my way through Powell I noted how few names she actually does drop. There is a single reference to the late Helen Astor, which comes as a mild shock. Otherwise the references are no more arcane than Rockefeller equals money (but then John D. had hired the first press agent). In a sense, midwesterners were the least class-conscious of Americans during the first half of the twentieth century and those who came from the small towns (Hemingway, Dreiser, Powell herself) ignore those drawing rooms where Henry James was at home amongst pure essences, whose source of wealth is never known but whose knowledge of what others know is all that matters. Powell, agreeably, knows exactly how much money everyone makes (not enough) and what everything costs (too much). As for value, she does her best with love, but suspects the times are permanently inflationary for that overhyped commodity. Powell never gets to Newport, Rhode Island, in her books but she manages Cape Cod nicely. She inclines to the boozy meritocracy of theater and publishing and the art world both commercial and whatever it is that Fifty-seventh Street was and is.

But in *A Time to Be Born*, she takes on the highest level of the meri-

tocracy (the almost-nobles) in the form of a powerful publisher and his
high-powered wife, based, rather casually, on Mr. and Mrs. Henry Luce.
At last Powell wil have a fling at those seriously important people Diana
Trilling felt that she was not up to writing about. But since one person is
pretty much like another, all are as one in art, which alone makes the difference. Humble Ebie is neither more nor less meaningful than famous
Amanda. It's what's made of them in art. Powell does have a good deal of
fun with Julian and Amanda Evans, and the self-important grandeur of
their lives. But Powell has no real interest in power or, more to this particular point, in those whose lives are devoted to power over others. Powell is with the victims. The result is that the marginal characters work
rather better than the principals. One never quite believes that Julian
owns and operates sixteen newspapers. One does believe Vicki Haven,
who comes from the same Ohio town as Amanda, authoress of a *Forever
Amber* best-seller that has been written for her by the best pen-persons
and scholar-squirrels that Julian's money can buy. Ken Saunders, a reasonably failed hack, gets Powell's full attention: he is a friend of Dennis
Orphen, who makes an obligatory appearance or two as does the great
novelist, Andrew Callingham, still hugely at large.

Powell sets *A Time* (magazine?) *to Be Born* in that time *not* to be born,
the rising war in the West:

> *This was a time when the true signs of war were the lavish plumage of the
> women; Fifth Avenue dress shops and the finer restaurants were filled with
> these vanguards of war. Look at the jewels, the rare pelts, the gaudy birds on
> elaborate hair-dress and know that war was here; already the women had in-
> herited the earth. The ominous smell of gunpowder was matched by a rising
> cloud of Schiaparelli's Shocking. The women were once more armed, and
> their happy voices sang of destruction to come. . . . This was a time when
> the artists, the intellectuals, sat in cafés and in country homes and accused
> each other over their brandies or their California vintages of traitorous ten-
> dencies. This was a time for them to band together in mutual antagonism,
> a time to bury the professional hatchet, if possible in each other. . . . On
> Fifth Avenue and Fifty-fifth Street hundreds waited for a man on a hotel
> window ledge to jump; hundreds waited with craning necks and thirsty
> faces as if this single person's final gesture would solve the riddle of the*

world. Civilization stood on a ledge, and in the tension of waiting it was a
relief to have one little man jump.

I know of no one else who has got so well the essence of that first war-
year before we all went away to the best years of no one's life.

Again the lines of love and power cross and recross as they do in novels
and often, too, in life. Since Julian publishes newspapers and magazines
and now propaganda for England, much of it written in his wife's name,
there is a Sarrautesque suspicion of language in Powell's reflections. A
publisher remarks, "A fact changes into a lie the instant it hits print." But
he does not stop there. "It's not print, it's the word," he declares. "The
Spoken Word, too. The lie forms as soon as the breath of thought hits air.
You hear your own words and say—'That's not what I mean. . . .'" Powell
is drawing close to the mystery of literature, life's quirky—quarkish—
reflection.

Amanda's power world does not convince quite as much as the Village life of Vicki and Ken and Dennis Orphen. Earlier readers will be
happy to know that cute Corinne "had considered leaving her husband
for Dennis Orphen for two or three years, and during her delay" the husband had divorced her "with Corinne still confused by this turn of
events. . . . She wanted a little more time to consider marrying Dennis."
When in doubt, do nothing, is the Powellesque strategy for life. Ken goes
back and forth between Amanda and Vicki. For a time Amanda is all-
conquering:

She knew exactly what she wanted from life, which was, in a word, every-
thing. She had a genuine distaste for sexual intimacy . . . but there were so
many things to be gained by trading on sex and she thought so little of the
process that she itched to use it as currency once again.

This time with the great writer-hunter Callingham. As it is, ironically, she
gets knocked up by Ken and falls out with Julian. But she is never not
practical: On the subject of writing, she believes that "the tragedy of the
Attic poets, Keats, Shelley, Burns was not that they died young but that

they were obliged by poverty to do all their own writing." Amanda's descendants are still very much with us: sweet lassies still saddened at the thought of those too poor to hire someone who will burn with a bright clear flame, as he writes their books for them.

It is plain that Powell was never entirely pleased with the Ohio cycle. She had a tendency to tell the same story over and over again, trying out new angles, new points of view, even—very occasionally—new characters. Finally, in mid-war, she made one last attempt to get Ohio (and herself) right. *My Home Is Far Away* (1944) is lapidary—at least compared to the loose early works. New York has polished her style; the essays glitter convincingly. The rural family is called Willard. A Civil War veteran for a grandfather; missing the odd eye, limb. Two sisters again: Lena the pretty one, Marcia the bright one. Powell again holds up the mirror to her past: "The uncanniness of [Marcia's] memory was not an endearing trait; invariably guests drew respectfully away from the little freak and warmed all the more to the pretty unaffected normalcy of little Lena." The book begins when father, mother, daughters leave a contented home. Suddenly, there is a nightmare vision: A man in a balloon floats across a starry sky. Home is now forever faraway.

Too clever by more than half and too much obliged throughout a peripatetic childhood to sing for a supper prepared by tone-deaf strangers, Powell hammered on the comic mask and wore it to the end. But when the dying mother has a horrendous vision of the man in the balloon, the mask blinks—for the last time.

Aunt Lois has a boardinghouse. The girls work. The old ladies are more than ever devastating. " 'A grandmother doesn't like children any more than a mother does,' she declared. 'Sometimes she's just too old to get out of tending them, that's all, but I'm not.' " Lena goes first. Then Marcia leaves town, as Powell left town, and catches that train "which will go everywhere on earth that is not home." On a foggy pane of glass, she writes, with her finger, *Marcia Willard*. Dawn Powell.

4

After the war, Powell returned to the New York cycle for good. She published a book of short stories, *Sunday, Monday and Always* (1952). There are occasional ill-omened visits back home but no longer does she describe the escape; she has escaped for good. There are some nice comic moments. Edna, a successful actress, comes home to find her rustic family absorbed in radio soap operas. Although she is quite willing to describe her exciting life, the family outmaneuvers her. " 'Well, Edna,' cackled Aunt Meg, hugging her. 'I declare I wouldn't have known you. Well, you can't live that life and not have it show, they tell me.' " The "they tell me" is masterful. Powell's ear for the cadences of real-life talk only improved with time.

The final New York novels, *The Locusts Have No King* (1948), *The Wicked Pavilion* (1954), and *The Golden Spur* (1962), demonstrate Powell's ultimate mastery of subject, art, self. Where the last two are near-perfect in execution, *The Locusts Have No King* ("yet they, all of them go forth by bands": Proverbs) shares some of the helter-skelterness of the early books. It is as if before Powell enters her almost-benign Prospero phase, she wants to cut loose once more at The Party.

This time the literary scene of the Forties gets it. The protagonist, Frederick Olliver, is a young man of integrity (a five-hundred-dollar-advance man) and literary distinction and not much will. He has been having an affair with Lyle, part of a married team of writers: Lyle is all taste and charm. But Frederick Olliver meets Dodo in a bar. Dodo is deeply, unrepentantly vulgar and self-absorbed. She says, "Pooh on you," and talks baby talk, always a sign for Powell of Lilithian evil. They meet in one of Powell's best bars downtown, off Rubberleg Square, as she calls it. The habitués all know one another in that context and, often, no other: parallel lives that are contiguous only in the confines of a cozy bar.

Frederick takes Dodo to a publisher's party (our friend Dennis is there) and Dodo manages to appall. Lyle is hurt. Everyone is slightly fraudulent. A publisher who respects Frederick's integrity offers him the editorship of *Haw*, a low publication which of course Frederick makes a success of. Lyle writes her husband's plays. There is a literary man who talks constantly of Jane Austen, whom he may not have read, and teaches at the League for Cultural Foundations (a.k.a. The New School), where "classes bulged with middle-aged students anxious to get an idea of what it would be like to have an idea." But under the usual bright mendacities of happy island life, certain relationships work themselves out. The most Powellesque is between two commercial artists, Caroline and Lorna:

> *Ever since their marriages had exploded Caroline and Lorna had been in each other's confidence, sharing a bottle of an evening in Lorna's studio or Caroline's penthouse. In fact they had been telling each other everything for so many years over their cups that they'd never heard a word each other had said.*

In an ecstasy of female bonding, they discuss their lost husbands:

> *They told each other of their years of fidelity—and each lamented the curse of being a one-man woman. Men always took advantage of their virtue and Caroline agreed with Lorna that, honestly, if it could be done over again, she'd sleep with every man who came along instead of wasting loyalty on one undeserving male. After a few drinks, Caroline finally said she had slept with maybe forty or fifty men but only because she was so desperately unhappy. Lorna said she didn't blame anyone in Caroline's domestic situation for doing just that, and many times wished she had not been such a loyal sap about George, but except for a few vacation trips and sometimes being betrayed by alcohol she had really never—well, anyway, she didn't blame anyone.*

Revelations bombard deaf ears. "Frequently they lost interest in dinner once they had descended below the bottle's label and then a remarkable inspiration would come to open a second bottle and repeat the revelations they had been repeating for years to glazed eyes and deaf ears." Finally, "Both ladies talked in confidence of their frustrations in the quest for love, but the truth was they had gotten all they wanted of the commodity and had no intention of making sacrifice of comfort for a few Cupid feathers." Powell was a marvelous sharp antidote for the deep-warm-sincere love novels of that period. Today she is, at the least, a bright counterpoint to our lost-and-found literary ladies.

Powell deals again with the, always to her, mysterious element of luck in people's careers. When one thinks of her own bad luck, the puzzlement has a certain poignancy. But she can be very funny indeed about the admiration that mediocrity evokes on that happy island where it has never been possible to be too phony. Yet when Frederick, free of his bondage to Dodo, returns to Lyle, the note is elegiac: "In a world of destruction one must hold fast to whatever fragments of love are left, for sometimes a mosaic can be more beautiful than an unbroken pattern." We all tended to write this sort of thing immediately after Hiroshima, *mon assassin*.

The Wicked Pavilion (1954) is the Café Julien is the Lafayette Hotel of real life. The title is from *The Creevey Papers*, and refers to the Prince Regent's Brighton Pavilion, where the glamorous and louche wait upon a mad royal. Dennis Orphen opens and closes the book in his by now familiarly mysterious way. He takes no real part in the plot. He is simply still there, watching the not-so-magic wheel turn as the happy island grows sad. For him, as for Powell, the café is central to his life. Here he writes; sees friends; observes the vanity fair. Powell has now become masterful in her setting of scenes. The essays—preludes, overtures—are both witty and sadly wise. She has also got the number to Eisenhower's American, as she brings together in this penultimate rout all sorts of earlier figures, now grown old: Okie is still a knowing man about town and author of the definitive works on the painter Marius; Andy Callingham is still a world-famous novelist, serene in his uncontagious self-love; and the Peggy Guggenheim figure is back again as Cynthia, an art gallery owner and party giver. One plot is young love: Rick and Ellenora who met at the Café Julien in wartime and never got enough of it or of each other or of the happy island.

A secondary plot gives considerable pleasure even though Powell lifted it from a movie of the day called *Holy Matrimony* (1943) with Monty Woolley and Gracie Fields, from Arnold Bennett's novel *Buried Alive*. The plot that Powell took is an old one: A painter, bored with life or whatever, decides to play dead. The value of his pictures promptly goes so high that he is tempted to keep on painting after "death." Naturally, sooner or later, he will give himself away: Marius paints a building that had not been built before his "death." But only two old painter friends have noticed this, and they keep his secret for the excellent reason that one of them is busy turning out "Marius" pictures, too. Marius continues happily as a sacred presence, enjoying in death the success that he never had in life: "Being dead has spoiled me," he observes. It should be noted that the painting for this novel's cover was done by Powell's old friend, Reginald Marsh.

A new variation on the Powell young woman is Jerry: clean-cut, straight-forward, and on the make. But her peculiar wholesomeness does not inspire men to give her presents; yet "the simple truth was that with her increasingly expensive tastes she really could not afford to work. . . . As for settling for the safety of marriage, that seemed the final defeat, synonymous in Jerry's mind with asking for the last rites." An aristocratic lady, Elsie, tries unsuccessfully to launch her. Elsie's brother, Wharton, and sister-in-law, Nita, are fine comic emblems of respectable marriage. In fact, Wharton is one of Powell's truly great and original monsters, quite able to hold his own with Pecksniff:

> *Wharton had such a terrific reputation for efficiency that many friends swore that the reason his nose changed colors before your very eyes was because of an elaborate Rimbaud color code, indicating varied reactions to his surroundings. . . . Ah, what a stroke of genius it had been for him to have found Nita! How happy he had been on his honeymoon and for years afterward basking in the safety of Nita's childish innocence where his intellectual shortcomings, sexual coldness and caprices—indeed his basic ignorance—would not be discovered. . . . He was well aware that many men of his quixotic moods preferred young boys, but he dreaded to expose his inexperience to one of his own sex, and after certain cautious experiments realized that his anemic lusts were canceled by his overpowering fear of gossip. . . . Against the flattering background of Nita's delectable purity, he blossomed forth as the all-round He-man, the Husband who knows everything. . . . He soon taught her that snuggling, hand-holding, and similar affectionate demonstrations were kittenish and vulgar. He had read*

somewhere, however, that breathing into a woman's ear or scratching her at
the nape of the neck drove her into complete ecstasy. . . . In due course Nita
bore him four daughters, a sort of door prize for each time he attended.

The Party is given by Cynthia now, and it rather resembles Proust's
last roundup: "There are people here who have been dead twenty years,"
someone observes, including "the bore that walks like a man." There is a
sense of closing time; people settle for what they can get. "We get sick of
our clinging vines, he thought, but the day comes when we suspect that
the vines are all that hold our rotting branches together." Dennis Orphen
at the end records in his journal the last moments of the wicked pavilion
as it falls to the wrecker's ball:

It must be that the Julien was all that these people really liked about each
other for now when they chance across each other in the street they look
through each other, unrecognizing, or cross the street quickly with the vague
feeling that here was someone identified with unhappy memories—as if the
other was responsible for the fall of the Julien.

What had been a stage for more than half a century to a world is gone
and "those who had been bound by it fell apart like straws when the bal-
ing cord is cut and remembered each other's name and face as part of a
dream that would never come back."

In 1962, Powell published her last and, perhaps, most appealing novel,
The Golden Spur. Again, the protagonist is male. In this case a young
man from Silver City, Ohio (again), called Jonathan Jaimison. He has
come to the city to find his father. Apparently twenty-six years earlier his
mother, Connie, had had a brief fling with a famous man in the Village;
pregnant, she came home and married a Mr. Jaimison. The book opens
with a vigorous description of Wanamaker's department store being torn
down. Powell is now rather exuberant about the physical destruction of
her city (she wrote this last book in her mid-sixties, when time was doing the same to her). There is no longer a Dennis Orphen on the scene;
presumably, he lies buried beneath whatever glass-and-cement horror re-

placed the Lafayette. But there are still a few watering holes from the Twenties, and one of them is The Golden Spur, where Connie mingled with the bohemians.

Jonathan stays at the Hotel De Long, which sounds like the Vanderbilt, a star of many of Powell's narratives. Jonathan, armed with Connie's cryptic diary, has a number of names that might be helpful. One is that of Claire van Orphen (related to Dennis?), a moderately successful writer, for whom Connie did some typing. Claire now lives embalmed in past time. She vaguely recalls Connie, who had been recommended to her by the one love of her life, Major Wedburn, whose funeral occurs the day Jonathan arrives at the De Long. Claire gives Jonathan possible leads; meanwhile, his presence has rejuvenated her. She proposes to her twin sister, Bea, that they live together and gets a firm no. The old nostalgia burned down long ago for the worldly Bea. On the other hand, Claire's career is revived, with the help of a professionally failed writer who gets "eight bucks for fifteen hundred words of new criticism in a little magazine or forty for six hundred words of old criticism in the Sunday book section." He studies all of Claire's ladies' magazine short stories of yesteryear; he then reverses the moral angle:

> "In the old days the career girl who supported the family was the heroine and the idle wife was the baddie," Claire said gleefully. "And now it's the other way round. In the soap operas, the career girl is the baddie, the wife is the goodie because she's better for business. . . . Well, you were right. CBS has bought the two [stories] you fixed, and Hollywood is interested."

Powell herself was writing television plays in the age of Eisenhower and no doubt had made this astonishing discovery on her own.

Jonathan is promptly picked up by two girls at The Golden Spur; he moves in with them. Since he is more domestic than they, he works around the house. He is occasionally put to work in bed until he decides that he doesn't want to keep on being "a diaphragm-tester." Among his possible fathers is Alvine Harshawe alias Andrew Callingham alias Ernest Hemingway. Alvine is lonely; "You lost one set of friends with each marriage, another when it dissolved, gaining smaller and smaller batches each time you traded in a wife." Alvine has no clear memory of Connie but toys with the idea of having a grown son, as does a famous painter named Hugow. Another candidate is a distinguished lawyer, George Terrence, whose actress daughter, unknown to him, is having an affair with Jonathan. Terrence is very much school of the awful Wharton of *The Wicked Pavilion*, only Terrence has made the mistake of picking up a young actor in the King Cole Bar of the St. Regis Hotel; the actor is now blithely blackmailing him in a series of letters worthy of his contemporary *Pal Joey*. Terrence welcomes the idea of a son but Jonathan shies away: He does not want his affair with the daughter to be incestuous.

Finally, Cassie, the Peggy Guggenheim character, makes her appearance, and The Party assembles for the last time. There are nice period touches: girls from Bennington are everywhere. While Cassie herself "was forty-three—well, all right, forty-eight, if you're going to count every lost weekend—and Hugow's betrayal had happened at birthday time, when she was frightened enough by the half-century mark reaching out for her before she'd even begun to have her proper quota of love." Cassie takes a fancy to Jonathan and hires him to work at her gallery. He has now figured out not only his paternity but his maternity and, best of all, himself. The father was Major Wedburn, who was, of course, exactly like the bore that his mother, Connie, married. The foster father appears on the scene, and there is recognition of this if not resolution. As for Connie, she had slept with everyone who asked her because "she wanted to be whatever anybody expected her to be, because she never knew what she was herself." Jonathan concludes, "That's the way I am." At an art gallery, he says, "I have a career of other people's talents."

   The quest is over. Identity fixed. The Party over, Jonathan joins Hugow in his cab. "He was very glad that Hugow had turned back downtown, perhaps to the Spur, where they could begin all over." On that blithe note Powell's life and lifework end; and the wheel stops; the magic's gone—except for the novels of Dawn Powell, all of them long since out of print just as her name has been erased from that perpetually foggy pane, "American Literature."

The New York Review of Books
November 5, 1987

MONTAIGNE

"In every work of genius," wrote Emerson, "we recognize our own rejected thoughts; they come back to us with a certain alienated majesty."
After four centuries, Montaigne's curious genius still has that effect on
his readers and, time and again, one finds in his self-portrait one's own
most brilliant *aperçus* (the ones that somehow we forgot to write down
and so forgot) restored to us in his essays—attempts—to assay—value—
himself in his own time as well as, if he was on the subject, all time, if
there is such a thing.

For thirty years I have kept Donald M. Frame's translation of *The
Complete Works of Montaigne* at, if not bedside, hand. There are numerous interlocking Olympic circles on the maroon binding where glasses
were set after I had written some no longer decipherable commentary in
the margin or, simply, "How true!" I never actually read all of *The Complete Works*, but I did read here and there, and I reread favorite essays
rather more than I ever tried to read the famous "Apology for Raymond
Sebond," who needed, I used to think, neither apology nor indeed memorial. But the generation of the twenty-first century is now in place, and to
celebrate its entry into the greenhouse there is a new translation of *The
Complete Essays of Montaigne* by M. A. Screech who, years ago, so ably—
even sternly—led me through Rabelais.

It has taken me one month to read every one of the 1,269 pages.

(Montaigne, III 8: "I have just read through at one go Tacitus's *History* [something which rarely happens to me, it is twenty years since I spent one full hour at a time on a book]. . . .") I enjoyed comparing Screech with Frame. Where Frame is sonorous and euphemistic, Screech is sharp and up-to-date, as readers of his *Montaigne and Melancholy* (1983) might suspect. Although my nature inclines me to enrol Montaigne in the relativist school of Lucretius and the Epicureans, thus making him proto-Englightenment, Screech firmly nails Montaigne within the Roman Catholic Church of his day, beleaguered as it was by the Reformation, which took the form of civil war in France between Catholics and Protestants, an ideological, that is pointless, war of the crude sort that has entertained us for so much of our own science-ridden century.

Michel Eyquem was born in 1533 at his father's estate, Montaigne, east of Bordeaux. A family of fish and wine merchants, the Eyquems were minimally ennobled by the acquisition of Montaigne, which gave them their "de." The mother's family were Spanish Jewish, presumably long since converted. When schism came, Michel, his parents, two brothers, and a sister remained Catholic, while one brother and two sisters became Protestant. By the 1560s, there was an out-and-out civil war that continued to Michel's death in 1592. The Montaigne family remained on amiable terms not only with the Catholic court at Paris but with that Protestant sovereign of nearby Navarre who so proverbially celebrated a Mass in order to become King Henry IV of France.

Montaigne's education was odd but useful. As his tutor spoke no French, Latin became his first language, spoken and written, until he was six. Then he went on to spend seven years at a Latin school, where he was immersed in the Roman classics; but little Greek. He also learned the agreed-upon French of the day, as well as Gascon dialect. He was more or less trained to be a soldier, a lawyer, an estate manager, and what used to be called a "gentleman," a category that no longer exists in our specialized time. As such, Montaigne naturally hated lying, and it was his essay on the subject that first drew me to him years ago. "Lying is an accursed vice. It is only our words which bind us together and make us human. If we realized the horror and weight of lying, we would see that it is more worthy of the stake than other crimes. . . . Once let the tongue acquire the habit of lying and it is astonishing how impossible it is to make it give it up" (I 8). As one who has been obliged to spend a lifetime in diverse liar-worlds (worlds where the liar is often most honored when he is known to be lying and getting away with it), I find Montaigne consoling.

Montaigne's father became Mayor of Bordeaux, while his son spent thirteen years in the city's legal council. It was during this period that he met a fellow public servant, Étienne de La Boëtie. Each was to become the other's other self. "If you press me to say why I loved him, I feel that it can only be expressed by replying 'Because it was him: because it was me.' . . . We were seeking each other before we set eyes on each other . . ." (I 28). Their relationship was an intense dialogue on every possible subject. De La Boëtie inclined to stoicism. He had written against tyranny. He died young.

Montaigne's letter to his father on de La Boëtie's last days is rather like that of Ammianus Marcellinus on the death of the Emperor Julian, something of a hero to Montaigne if not to the Holy Office. (Letter to father: "He gave up the ghost at about three o'clock on the Wednesday morning, August 18th, 1563, after living 32 years, nine months, and 17 days. . . .")

Certainly, we are all in poor de La Boëtie's debt for dying, because Montaigne was never to find another soulmate and so, in due course, after marriage, children, the inheritance of the estate, "In the year of Christ 1571, at the age of thirty-eight, on the last day of February, his birthday, Michel de Montaigne, long weary of the servitude of the court and of public employment . . .", retired to Montaigne, where he then began to make attempts at understanding everything, which meant, principally, the unknowable (so Socrates thought) self. In the absence of a friend to talk to or an Atticus to write to, Montaigne started writing to himself about himself and about what he had been reading which became himself. He made many attempts to try—essayer—to find his form. "If I had somebody to write to I would readily have chosen it as the means of publishing my chatter. . . . Unless I deceive myself my achievement then would have been greater" (I 40). At first, he wrote short memoranda— how to invest a city, or what one is to make of a certain line of Seneca.

Later, he settled for the long essay that could be read in an hour. He did a lot of free-associating, as "all subjects are linked to each other" (III 5). Essentially, he wrote as a man of action, involved in the world both locally and nationally. He was personally esteemed by Catherine de Medici, Henry III, Marguerite de Valois, and Henry of Navarre, who twice visited him at Montaigne and would, as King of France, have made him a counsellor had the essayist not made one final attempt to understand death—life by dying.

The greatest action of this man of action was to withdraw to his library in order to read and think and write notes to himself that eventually became books for the world:

> At home I slip off to my library (it is on the third storey of a tower); it is easy
> for me to oversee my household from there. I am above my gateway and have
> a view of my garden, my chicken-run, my backyard and most parts of my
> house. There I can turn over the leaves of this book or that, a bit at a time
> without order or design. Sometimes my mind wanders off, at others I walk
> to and fro, noting down and dictating these whims of mine. . . . My library
> is round in shape, squared off only for the needs of my table and chair: as it
> curves round, it offers me at a glance every one of my books ranged on five
> shelves all the way along. It has three splendid and unhampered views and
> a circle of free space sixteen yards in diameter (III 3).

Montaigne seems to have read every Latin author extant; he was also much intrigued with contemporary stories of the Americas and other exotic places where cannibals and realms of gold coexisted. Much of his writing starts with a quotation that sets him to ruminating on his own, buttressed by more quotations, making a sort of palimpsest. If nothing else, he was a superb arranger of other men's flowers. He was particularly drawn to biographical anecdote, and it was lucky for him that not long after he settled in his tower room, Bishop Jacques Amyot published a French translation of Plutarch, who quickly became Montaigne's most useful source and touchstone. In fact, one wonders what the essays would have been like without Plutarch. Would Montaigne have found so attractive those human titans, Alexander and Caesar? Or those paradigms of human virtue, Epaminondas and Cato the Younger?

Among the thousand books on the five shelves, Montaigne returns most often to Lucretius and Seneca. He reveres Homer, but he is happiest with those two worldly writers who appeal to his own worldliness. The first because of his sense of the diversity—even relativity—of things, the second as a wise counsellor, not only in the conduct of a life at home but at a dangerous court. He turns often to Cicero, but he is vaguely disapproving of the vanity of that politician, ever avid, especially in retirement, for glory. Cicero "said he wanted to use his withdrawal and his repose from affairs of state to gain life ever-lasting through his writings" (I 39). Then Montaigne, slyly, quotes Persius: "Does *knowing* mean nothing to you, unless somebody else knows that you know it?"

I thought of a chat with Robert Lowell at my Hudson river house forty years ago. Somehow, we had got on to the subject of Julius Caesar's character. I mentioned Cicero's letter to Atticus on how unnerving it was to have Caesar as a house guest. "But," said Lowell, "remember how pleased Cicero was when Caesar praised his consulship." Of course, each of us wanted the other to know that *he* had read the letter and that, if nothing else, we held, in common, a small part of the classical heritage—so etiolated! so testeronish! so Eurocentric!—that Montaigne had spent his life in communion with. I wonder what a poet and a novelist would have in common to talk about nowadays. After all, a shared knowledge of old books was probably the largest part of the "loving friendship" between Étienne and Montaigne. Today they would share—what? Robert Altman's films?

Montaigne disliked pedants. He notes that in his local dialect they are called *Lettreferits*—word-struck. He himself is after other game than words or "words about words": "scribbling seems to be one of the symptoms of an age of excess" (III 9). "We work merely to fill the memory, leaving the understanding and the sense of right and wrong. . . . Off I go, rummaging about in books for sayings which please me—not so as to store them up (for I have no storehouses) but so as to carry them back to the book, where they are no more mine than they were in their original place. We only know, I believe, what we know now: 'knowing' no more consists in what we once knew than in what we shall know in the future" (I 24). He frets about his poor memory. "I am so outstanding a forgetter that, along with all the rest, I forget even my own works and writings.

People are constantly quoting me to me without my realising it" (II 17). This is a bit swank. But writers often forget what they have written, since the act of writing is a letting go of a piece of one's mind, and so an erasure. Montaigne's first two volumes of essays were published in 1580: he was forty-seven. Eight years later, he revised the first two volumes and published a third. From the beginning, he was accepted as a classic in the Roman sense, or as a writer *utile-doux*, as the French styled the great works.

Montaigne was much concerned with his body and believed Sebond's proposition that man is a marriage between soul and body. He hated doctors, a family tradition to which he not only adhered but attributed the long lives in the male line (he himself was dead at sixty, rather younger than father and grandfather). He feared kidney stones, which tortured his father and, finally, himself. To cure "the stone," he visited spas everywhere and took the baths: "I reckon that bathing in general is salubrious and I believe that our health has suffered . . . since we lost the habit. . . . we are all the worst for having our limbs encrusted and our pores blocked up with filth" (II 37). Of himself, "my build is a little below the average. This defect is not only ugly but unbecoming, especially in those who hold commands . . ." (II 17), but "my build is tough and thick-set, my face is not fat but full, my complexion is between the jovial and the melancholic. . . . Skill and agility I have never had . . . except at running (at which I was among the average)."

He records without despair or even pride that he has almost no gifts for music, dancing, tennis, wrestling, and none at all for swimming, fencing, vaulting, and jumping.

My hand is so clumsy that I cannot even read my own writing, so that I prefer to write things over again rather than to give myself the trouble of disentangling my scribbles. . . . That apart, I am quite a good scholar! I can never fold up a letter neatly, never sharpen a pen, never carve passably at table, nor put harness on horse, nor bear a hawk properly nor release it, nor address hounds, birds or horses. My bodily endowments are, in brief, in close harmony with my soul's. There is no agility, merely a full firm vigour, but I can stick things out.

Like his father, he wore mostly black and white. "Whether riding or walking I have always been used to burdening my hand with a cane or stick, even affecting an air of elegance by leaning on it with a distinguished look on my face" (II 25).

He deplored the codpieces of the previous generation, which drew attention to and exaggerated the unmentionables. He had had sex at so early an age that he could not recall just when. Like Abraham Lincoln, he contracted syphilis ("a couple of light anticipatory doses") (III 3). For this vileness, American universities would erase him from the canon, if they could, since no great man has ever had syphilis or engaged in same-sexuality. On Greek love, Montaigne understood exactly what Achilles and Patroclus were up to in the sack and he found their activities "rightly abhorrent to our manners" on the novel ground that what was not equal in body-mind could not be love, much less "perfect love." The man chose not another man but a boy for his looks. It was Montaigne's view that true love, sexual or not, meant the congruence of two men as equals. This was the highest form of human relationship. He does note that "male and female are cast in the same mould: save for education and custom the difference between them is not great" (III 6). Theoretically, if a woman was educated as a man and met her male equal, this could be the "perfect love": but he gives no examples. Odd, since Plutarch had filled him in on Aspasia and Pericles. But then he did not place Pericles very high; thought him a tricky orator. Of course, he had not read Thucydides.

On "Some Lines of Virgil," he has a good time with sex, as both necessity and madness. "The genital activities of mankind are so natural, so necessary and so right: what have they done to make us never dare to mention them without embarrassment . . . ? We are not afraid to utter the words 'kill,' 'thief,' or 'betray' " (III 5). Yet "The whole movement of the world tends and leads towards copulation. It is a substance infused through everything; it is the centre—towards which all things turn." He comments on the uncontrollability—and unreliability—of the male member. "Every man knows . . . that he has a part of his body which often stirs, erects, and lies down again without his leave. Now such passive movements which only touch our outside cannot be called ours" (II 6). (Screech thinks that Montaigne never read Augustine's *Confessions*.)

Montaigne notes priapic cults in other lands and times. Finally, all in all, he favors arranged marriages: "A good marriage (if there be such a thing) rejects the company and conditions of Cupid; it strives to reproduce those of loving friendship" (III 5). Incidentally, nowhere does Montaigne mention his wife. There is one reference to his daughter Léonor, and a mysterious panegyric to a sort of adopted daughter that, Screech thinks, may have been written by herself in a posthumous edition, which gives rise to the agreeable notion that there may have been some sort of Ibsen plot unfolding in old Périgord. Rousseau thought that Montaigne ought to have told us a lot more about his private life, but then Rousseau was no gentleman.

On politics, Montaigne was deeply but not dully conservative. That is, he did not, figuratively or literally, believe in witches:

> *I abhor novelty, no matter what visage it presents, and am right to do so, for I have seen some of its disastrous effects. That novelty (the wars of religion) which has for so many years beset us is not solely responsible, but one can say with every likelihood that it has incidentally caused and given birth to them all. . . . Those who shake the State are easily the first to be engulfed in its destruction. The fruits of dissension are not gathered by the one who began it: he stirs and troubles the water for other men to fish in (I 23).*

A nice presage of France's revolution two centuries later, though not particularly applicable to the American adventure that actually turned the whole world upside down. But in the midst of a civil war over religion, the absolutist must appear more than usually monstrous: "There is a great deal of self-love and arrogance in judging so highly of your opinions that you are obliged to disturb the public peace in order to establish them" (I 23). Plainly, he was not the sort of conservative who would have admired that radical British prime minister who, for a decade, so strenuously disturbed the death-like peace of those sunnily arid North Sea islands.

Montaigne was very much school of the-devil-we-know: "Not as a matter of opinion but of truth, the best and most excellent polity for each nation is the one under which it has been sustained. Its form and its essential advantages depend upon custom. It is easy for us to be displeased

with its present condition; I nevertheless hold that to yearn for an oligarchy in a democracy or for another form of government in a monarchy
is wrong and insane" (III 9). He regarded any fundamental change as "the
cure of illness by death. . . . My own contemporaries here in France
could tell you a thing or two about that!"

Since I want Montaigne on my side in the great task of reworking my
own country's broken-down political system, I must invoke him—like
Scripture—in another context. "The most desirable laws are those which
are fewest, simplest and most general. I think moreover that it would be
better to have none at all than to have them in the profusion as we do
now. . . . When King Ferdinand sent colonies of immigrants to the Indies
he made the wise stipulation that no one should be included who had
studied jurisprudence, lest law suits should pullulate in the New World"
(III 13), causing endless faction and altercation. Since *our* New World is
entirely paralyzed by lawyers hired by pullulating polluters of politics as
well as of environment and put in place to undo many thousands of laws
made by other lawyers, I cannot think Montaigne would be so cruel as
not to want us to rid ourselves of such a government, but I suppose he
would echo mockingly his young contemporary Shakespeare's final solution for lawyers, while suggesting that it might do us Americans a world
of good if each took a course or two in torts and malfeasances since, from
the beginning, we were intended to be a lawyerly republic and must not
change.

Common sense is a phrase, if not a quality, much revered in the
bright islands of the North Sea. Montaigne is often accused of possessing this rare quality, but what most strikes me in his meanderings is the
*un*commonness of his sense. He turns a subject round and round and
suddenly sees something that others had not noticed. He is also inclined
to humor, usually of the dead-pan sort: "Herodotus tells us of a certain
district of Libya where men lie with women indiscriminately, but where,
once a child can toddle, it recognizes its own father out of the crowd, natural instinct guiding its first footsteps. There are frequent mistakes, I believe . . ." (II 8).

Of literary style, he wrote: "I want things to dominate, so filling the
thoughts of the hearer that he does not even remember the words. I like
the kind of speech which is simple and natural, the same on paper as on

the lip; speech which is rich in matter, sinewy, brief and short" (I 26). As for "the French authors of our time. They are bold enough and proud enough not to follow the common road; but their want of invention and their power of selection destroy them. All we can see is some wretched affectation of novelty, cold and absurd fictions which instead of elevating their subject batter it down" (III 5). He delighted in Boccaccio, Rabelais, and the *Basia* of Johannes Secundus. Of poets, he put Virgil highest, especially the *Georgics*; then Lucretius, Catullus, and Horace. He finds Aesop interestingly complex. "Seneca is full of pithy phrases and sallies; Plutarch is full of matter. Seneca inflames you and stirs you: Plutarch is more satisfying and repays you more. Plutarch leads us: Seneca drives us" (II 10). He seems to be looking ahead at our own scribbling time when he writes, "There are so many ways of taking anything, that it is hard for a clever mind *not* to find in almost any subject something or other which appears to serve his point, directly or indirectly. That explains why an opaque, ambiguous style has been so long in vogue" (II 12).

From 1581 to 1585, Montaigne served as Mayor of Bordeaux: "People say that my period of office passed without trace or mark. Good!" In 1582, the Pope dealt him a grievous blow by replacing the Julian calendar with the Gregorian, which lopped eleven days off everyone's life. "Since I cannot stand novelty even when corrective. I am constrained to be a bit of a heretic in this case" (III 10). He enjoyed his fame as a writer but noted "that in my own climate of Gascony they find it funny to see me in print; I am valued the more, the farther from home knowledge of me has spread . . ." (III 2). In the Frame translation, there is a "How true" in the margin next to what could be the mark of a tear, if it did not still smell of whisky. In a variation on Aesop, he notes, "A hundred times a day when we go mocking our neighbour we are really mocking ourselves; we abominate in others those faults which are most manifestly our own, and with a miraculous lack of shame and perspicacity, are astonished by them" (III 8). Perhaps this universal failing is why "I study myself more than any other subject. That is my metaphysics; that is my physics" (III 13).

In a comment on Montaigne's most celebrated essay, "On the Education of Children," Sainte-Beuve remarked that "he goes too far, like a child of Aristippus who forgets Adam's fall." He is "*simply* Nature . . . Nature in all its Grace-less completeness." The clarity—charity, too—with which he saw his world has made him seem a precursor of the age of Enlightenment, even that of Wordsworth. But Screech does not allow us so easily to appropriate him to our secular ends, and Montaigne's Epicurean stoicism is more than balanced by his non-questioning—indeed defense—of the traditional faith. For him, his translation of the *Theologia Naturalis* of Raymond Sebond was to be regarded as a prophylactic against the dread Luther.

Incidentally, Screech's own translation is as little ambiguous as possible; it is also demotic. Where Frame writes "ruminating," Screech writes "chewing over," "frenzied" becomes "raging mad," "loose-boweled" becomes "squittering," a word that I was obliged to look up—"to void thin excrement." We are all in Screech's debt for giving us back a word so entirely useful that no critic's portmanteau should ever again be without it. On the other hand, Frame's "this bundle of so many disparate pieces is being composed" becomes the perhaps less happy phrase "all the various pieces of this faggot are being bundled together . . ."

"The writer's function is not without arduous duties. By definition, he cannot serve those who make history; he must serve those who are subject to it." Montaigne would not have agreed with Albert Camus. In a sense, Montaigne is writing for the rulers (Henry IV was particularly taken by his essay "On High Rank as a Disadvantage"). Educate the rulers, and they will not torment their subjects. But Montaigne's political interests are aside from his main point, the exploration of self. Once he had lost Étienne, he was all he had; so he wrote a book about himself. "I am most ignorant about myself. I marvel at the assurance and confidence everyone has about himself, whereas there is virtually nothing that I *know* I know. . . . I think that I am an ordinary sort of man, except in considering myself to be one. . . . That I find my own work pardonable is not so much for itself or its true worth as from a comparison with others' writings which are worse—things which I can see people taking seriously" (II 17).

Vanity of any sort amuses him. Even the great Julius Caesar is ticked off: "Observe how Caesar spreads himself when he tells us about his ingenuity in building bridges and siege-machines; in comparison, he is quite cramped when he talks of his professional soldiering, his valour or the way he conducts his wars. His exploits are sufficient proof that he was an outstanding general: he wants to be known as something else rather different: a good engineer" (I 17).

Montaigne begins his essays (first thought of as *rhapsodies*—confused medleys) with a pro forma bow to Cicero–Plato: "Cicero says that philosophizing is nothing other than getting ready to die. That is because study and contemplation draw our souls somewhat outside ourselves keeping them occupied away from the body, a state which both resembles death and which forms a kind of apprenticeship for it; or perhaps it is because all the wisdom and argument in the world eventually come down to one conclusion which is to teach us not to be afraid of dying" (I 20). In this way "all the labour of reason must be to make us live well."

Montaigne's reigning humor may have been melancholic, but he is hardly morbid in his musings on that good life which leads to a good death. He is a true stoic, despite occasional obeisance to the Holy Spirit, a post-Platonic novelty now running down. He is even a bit sardonic: "Everybody goes out as though he had just come in. Moreover, however decrepit a man may be, he thinks he still has another twenty years." But "I have adopted the practice of always having death not only in my mind but on my lips. There is nothing I inquire about more readily than how men have died: what did they say? How did they look?" Like me, when he read a biography, he first skipped to the end to see how its subject died. As his book—and life—proceed, he is more than ever aware of the diversity within the unity of things and the inability to know very much of what came before us because, "Great heroes lived before Agamemnon. Many there were: yet none is lamented, being swept away unknown into the long night."

After the arrival of kidney stones, Montaigne occasionally strikes a bleak note: "I am on the way out: I would readily leave to one who comes later whatever wisdom I have learnt about dealing with the world. . . . At the finish of every task the ending makes itself known. My world is over: my mould has been emptied; I belong entirely to the past" (III 10). But before self-pity could spread her great fluffy wings, he then makes a joke about being cruelly robbed of eleven days of life by the Pope's new calendar. Meanwhile, "Time and custom condition us to anything strange: nevertheless, the more I haunt myself and know myself the more my misshapenness amazes me and the less I understand myself" (III 11). Finally, "We confuse life with worries about death, and death with worries about life. One torments us; the other terrifies us" (III 12). Yet,

> *If we have not known how to live, it is not right to teach us how to die, making the form of the end incongruous with the whole. If we have known how to live steadfastly and calmly we shall know how to die the same way. . . . death is indeed the ending of life, but not therefore its end: it puts an end to it, it is its ultimate point: but it is not its objective. Life must be its own objective, its own purpose. . . . Numbered among its other duties included under the general and principal heading,* How to Live, *there is the subsection,* How to Die.

Thus, Montaigne firmly reverses the Cicero–Plato notion that "to philosophize is to learn how to die" and enjoins us to meditate not on unknowable, irrelevant death but on life which can be known, at least in part. Sixteen years of observing himself and reading and rereading the thousand books in the round library had convinced him not only that life was all there is but that "Each man bears the entire form of man's estate" (III 2). At the end, Montaigne had met himself at last; and everyone else, too. On September 13, 1592, he died in bed while listening to Mass. What one would give to know what he said, how he looked, just before he, too, entered the long night.

Meanwhile, Screech now replaces Frame at my bedside. Anglophones of the next century will be deeply in his debt. Despite his insistence on the Catholicism of Montaigne, the good Screech does note that Montaigne uses the word Fortune—in the sense of fate—350 times. That is satisfying.

The Times Literary Supplement
June 26, 1992

RABBIT'S OWN BURROW

A decade ago, thanks to the success of America's chain bookstores with their outlets in a thousand glittering malls, most "serious" fiction was replaced by mass-baked sugary dough—I mean books—whose huge physical presence in the shops is known, aptly to the trade, as "dumps": outward and visible sign of Gresham's Law at dogged work. In spite of this, the fact that John Updike's latest novel, *In the Beauty of the Lilies*, briefly made it to the bottom of the *New York Times* best-seller list is remarkable. As it is a rare week when any "serious" novel is listed, one is usually so grateful that there are still those who want to read an even halfway good novelist, one ought never to discourage those readers whom he attracts. Also, what is the point of attacking writers in a period where—save for prize-mad pockets of old London—they are of so little consequence?

In observance of this law of a dying species, I have hardly mentioned, much less reviewed, Updike in the past, and he has observed the same continence with regard to me. But, lately, as I turn the pages of *The New Yorker*, where his poems, short stories, and book reviews have been appearing for so many years, I note an occasional dig at me. Apparently, I do not sufficiently love the good, the nice America, is the burden of his *épingles*. In sere and yellow leaf, Updike is now in superpatriot mood and on the attack. For instance, apropos the movie star Lana Turner (whom, to his credit, he appreciates): "Fifty years ago we were still a nation of

builders and dreamers, now whittlers and belittlers set the cultural tone."
O vile Whittlers! O unGodly Belittlers! Of whom, apparently, I am one.

Although I've never taken Updike seriously as a writer, I now find him
the unexpectedly relevant laureate of the way we would like to live now,
if we have the money, the credentials, and the sort of faith in our country and its big God that passes all understanding. Finally, according to the
mainline American press, Updike has now got it all together, and no less
an authority than *The New Yorker*'s George Steiner (so different from Europe's one) assures us that Updike now stands alongside Hawthorne and
Nabokov, when, surely, he means John P. Marquand and John O'Hara.

Prior to immersion in next year's Pulitzer Prize novel, I read Updike's
memoir, *Self-Consciousness* (1989), written in the writer's fifty-seventh
year. Self-consciousness is a good theme, if meant ironically. After all,
save to self, we are, none of us, worth much fussing about, run-of-
the-mill poor, bare forked animals—or was it radishes?—that we are. Anyway, I hoped that he would make some self-mocking play on his own
self-consciousness as opposed to Socrates' examined life. Hope quickly
extinguished. There is no examination of the self, as opposed to an unremitting self-consciousness that tells us why he was—is—different—
but not too much different—from others and what made him the way he
is—always *is*, as he doesn't much change in his own story, a small-town
Philoctetes whose wound turns out to be an unpretty skin condition
called psoriasis. "Yet what was my creativity, my relentless need to produce but a parody of my skin's embarrassing overproduction?"

John Updike's father was of Dutch-American stock; his mother
German. He was born in 1932, in modest circumstances at Shillington,
Pennsylvania. The mother was a would-be writer, constantly typing away
and sending out stories that returned to her like so many boomerangs.
The son would soon outdo the mother, *his* stories returning home in the
pages of *The New Yorker*.

The Shillington that he describes is a sunny place, despite the Depression of the 1930s and some labor strikes; more than once, Updike
edgily refers to the election by the nearby city of Reading of a *socialist*
mayor. Happily, for his school of Biedermeier novels, the world outside
himself seems never to have caught his proper interest until the dread
1960s, when "bright young men who are born with silver spoons in their

mouth . . . were selling this nation out." But that was long after he was a "plain child, ungainly youth. Lacking brothers and sisters, [he] was shy and clumsy in the give and take . . . of human exchange." Of contemporaries who did not care for school, "I could not understand how anybody could rebel against a system so clearly benign." But then he is always true to his "docile good child nature."

Yet under all this blandness and acceptance of authority in any form, there is a growing puzzlement. "Social position in America is not easy to be precise about," he notes; then, warily, he tries to place his high-school teacher father: "My family sold asparagus and pansies for odd money, embarrassing me." But unlike a Fitzgerald or an O'Hara (most Irish Catholic writers in America are born with perfect radar on how to make it all the way to the blue light at landing's end—or pass out at the bar in the attempt), Updike seems to have missed whatever gentry there may have been in the neighborhood. All he knows is that his mother says that we are much "nicer" than a lot of other people, which is important if not very useful, as his father is a definite nonsuccess, and so Updike concludes that:

> *Life breeds punchers and counterpunchers, venturers like my father and ambushers like me: the venturer risks rebuff and defeat; the ambusher . . . risks fading away to nothing. . . . All those years in Shillington, I had waited to be admired, waited patiently . . . burrowing in New York magazines and English mystery novels for the secret passageway out, the path of avoidance and vindication. I hid a certain determined defiance. . . . I would "show" them, I would avenge all the slights and abasements visited upon my father—the miserly salary, the subtle tyranny of his overlords at the high school, the disrespect of his students, the laughter in the movie house at the name of Updike.*

Not exactly Richard III. Rather the inner rebellion of a shy, ambitious, small creature—a rabbit?—preparing to abandon its nice safe burrow for a world elsewhere, for a place across the water in nearby sinful Manhattan.

Shillington was to remain central to Updike's intense consciousness of self. In footnotes to his memoir, he solemnly quotes from his own work to show just how he has used the "real" life of his small town in fiction. Over and over again he writes of the Lutheran Grace Church, the elementary school, the post office, of youthful revels at Stephens' Luncheonette. Not since Sinclair Lewis has a naturalistic writer been so merciless to his reader as Updike. Endlessly, he describes shops and their contents, newspaper advertisements, streets that go here, there, and everywhere except into the—this—reader's mind. Places and people seem to interest him only when reduced, as cooks say, to receipts not dishes. Certainly all the words he uses are there on the page, but what they stand for is not. Only he himself is recorded with careful attention, as he notes his aim of "impersonal egoism," and "always with some natural hesitation and distaste" when it comes to memoir-writing; yet he soldiers on, and we learn that only after the family moved from Shillington does he masturbate—and so a lifelong adhesion to heterosexuality begins, at least in the mind. With *jouissance*, he comes into his kingdom, love in hand.

As a fellow *New Yorker* writer, S. J. Perelman, puts it in a letter to Ogden Nash in 1965, "J. Updike . . . read extracts from three works of his to the assembled scholars, which I didn't personally hear as I was overtaken by the characteristic nausea that attacks me when this youth performs on the printed pages. But Cheever brought me tidings that all dealt with masturbation, a favorite theme of Updike's." Of course, Perelman was a bit of a grouch; and who could have foretold that in three years' time this onanistic "youth" would write *Couples*, a celebration of marriage and its saucy twin, adultery, the only important subjects of middlebrow fiction, saving God Himself and His America? It should be noted that Christianity seems always to have been a fact for Updike, starting with the Grace Lutheran and other churches of Shillington; later, as an outward and visible sign of niceness and of belongingness, he remains a churchgoer when he moves up the social scale to Ipswich, Massachusetts, where he achieves that dream of perfect normality which is not only American and Christian but—when in the company of other upwardly mobile couples—ever so slightly bohemian.

———

Although Updike seems never to have had any major psychic or physical wound, he has endured all sorts of minor afflictions. In the chapter "At war with my skin," he tells us in great detail of the skin condition that sun and later medicine would clear up; for a long time, however, he was martyr to it as well as a slave to his mirror, all the while fretting about what "normal" people would make of him. As it proved, they don't seem to have paid much attention to an affliction that, finally, "had to do with self love, with finding myself acceptable . . . the price high but not impossibly so; I must pay for being me." The price for preserving me certainly proved to be well worth it when, in 1955, he was rejected for military conscription, even though the empire was still bogged down in Korea and our forces were increased that year from 800,000 to three million—less Updike, who, although "it pains me to write these pages," confesses that he was "far from keen to devote two years to the national defense." He was later to experience considerable anguish when, almost alone among serious writers, he would support the Vietnam War on the ground that who am I "to second-guess a president?" One suspects that he envies the clear-skinned lads who so reluctantly fought for the land *he* so deeply loves.

"I had a stammer that came and went." But he is ever game: "As with my psoriasis, the affliction is perhaps not entirely unfortunate." Better than to be born with a silver spoon in one's mouth is to be born at the heart of a gray cloud with a silver lining. The stammer does "make me think twice about going onstage and appearing in classrooms and at conferences," but "Being obliging by nature and anxious for approval, I would never say no if I weren't afraid of stuttering. Also, as I judge from my own reactions, people who talk too easily and comfortably . . . arouse distrust in some atavistic, pre-speech part of ourselves; we turn off." Take that, Chrysostom Chatterbox! Characteristically, he is prompt to place a soothing Band-Aid on his own wound: he quotes Carlyle, who observes of Henry James: "a stammering man is never a worthless man." Whatever that means. (Also, *pace* Carlyle, the Master did not stammer; he filibustered elaborately, cunningly, with pauses so carefully calculated that if one dared try to fill one, he would launch a boa-constrictor of a sentence at the poor mesmerized, oh, dear, rabbit! of an auditor.) Finally, Updike confesses to unease with certain groups that your average distinguished author must address. He is afraid of New York audiences especially: "They are too smart and left wing for me. . . ." This seems to mean politically minded Jews, so unlike the *nice* Southern college audiences with whom he is most at home.

Dental problems occupy many fascinating pages. But then I am a sucker for illness and debilities and even the most homely of exurban *memento mori*. Finally, relatively late in life, he develops asthma! This splendid coda (to date) of the Updike physical apparatus is something of a master stroke, and, as I once coughed along with Hans Castorp and his circle, I now find myself wheezing along with Updike; but then I, too, am mildly asthmatic.

The psychic Updike is dealt with warily. The seemingly effortless transition from the Shillington world to Harvard and then to the *New Yorker* staff is handled with Beylesque brevity. He notes, but does not demonstrate, the influence on him of such Christian conservative writers as G. K. Chesterton and C. S. Lewis and Jacques Maritain, while the names Karl Barth and Kierkegaard are often treated as one word, Barthegaard. He tells us that, as a novelist, "my models were the styles of Proust and Henry Green—dialogue and meditation as I read them (one in translation)." Which one? We shall never know. But for those of us who reveled in the French translations of Green, I can see how attractive those long irregular subjunctive-laden "tender explorations" must have been for Updike, too. Although every other American novelist of the past half-century seems to regard Proust as his "model," one finds no trace of Proust in Updike's long lists of consumer goods on sale in shops as well as of human characteristics that start with external features, followed by internal "meditations" on the true character of the Character.

Despite all of Updike's book-reviewing, one gets the sense that books have not meant much to him, young or old; but then he was originally attracted to the graphic arts (he attended the Ruskin School at Oxford), and the minor technical mysteries of lettering nibs and scratchboard. . . . "And my subsequent career carries coarse traces of its un-ideal origins in popular, mechanically propagated culture." This is endearing; also, interesting—"I was a cultural bumpkin in love not with writing, but with print." And, like everyone else of the time, with the movies, as he will demonstrate in his latest novel.

Easily, it would appear, he became an all-round writer for *The New Yorker* "of the William Shawn era (1951–87) . . . a club of sorts, from within which the large rest of literary America . . . could be politely disdained. . . . While I can now almost glimpse something a bit too trusting in the serene sense of artistic well-being, of virtual invulnerability, that being published in *The New Yorker* gave me for over thirty years. . . ." During much of this time, he seemed unaware that the interesting, indeed major, writers of the period did not belong to his club, either because they were too disturbing for the mild Shawn or because they could not endure the radical editing and rewriting that the quintessential middlebrow magazine imposed on its writers. "I shook with anger," Perelman wrote in 1957, "at their august editorial decisions, their fussy little changes and pipsqueak variations on my copy." Nabokov, published at Edmund Wilson's insistence, needed all of Wilson's help in fighting off editorial attempts to make his prose conform to the proto–Ralph Lauren house impersonation of those who fit, socially, in the roomy top-drawer-but-one. Unlike that original writer, Nabokov, Updike, ever "the good child," throve under strict supervision and thought himself on Parnassus, a harmless, even beguiling misunderstanding so long as the real world never confronted him, which, of course, it did.

The Vietnam war jolted Updike into the nearest he has yet come to self-examination as opposed to self-consciousness. "I was a liberal," he notes at some point. That is, he didn't like Nixon when he was at Harvard, and he voted for Kennedy. But now he strikes the Pecksniffian note as he invokes class distinctions. Of liberals at Harvard, "they, Unitarian or Episcopalian or Jewish, support Roosevelt and Truman and Stevenson out of enlightenment, *de haut en bas*, whereas in my heart of hearts, I however, veneered with an education and button-down shirts, was *de bas*. They, secure in the upper-middle class, were Democrats out of human sympathy and humanitarian largesse, because this was the party that helped the poor. Our family had simply *been* poor, and voted Democrat out of crude self-interest." He is now moving into McCarthy, Wallace, Buchanan country. Resentment, for Updike a slow-blooming plant, is starting to put forth lurid flowers, suitable for funeral wreaths to be laid upon his carefully acquired affluent niceness as well as upon the sort of company that it had earned him, which, almost to a man, stood against the war that he accepts and even, for a time, favors. Suddenly he starts scrabbling in search of peasant roots to show that he is really *dans le vrai*—unlike those supercilious silver-spoon-choked snobs who dare "second-guess" presidents.

"Was I conservative? I hadn't thought so, but I did come from what I could begin to see" (after a third of a century?) "was a conservative part of the country. . . . The Germans of Berks County didn't move on, like the typical Scots-Irish frontier-seeking Americans. They stayed put, farming the same valleys and being buried in the same graveyards. . . ." Presumably, this stay-put mindset ought to have made him isolationist and antiwar when it came to military adventures in far-off places where other Americans, whom he knew little of, fought Asians, whom he knew nothing of. But, startlingly, he chooses to interpret the passivity of his ancestral tribes as the reason for his own unquestioning acceptance of authority: if the president wants you to go fight the Viet Cong in order to contain the Viet Cong's mortal enemy, China, you must not question, much less second-guess him: You will go fight when and where he tells you to, unless you are lucky enough to be kept safe at home by psoriasis. For the first time, the apolitical, ahistorical Updike was faced with what pop writers call an Identity Crisis.

"By my mid-thirties, through diligence and daring" (if one did not know better, one might think the second adjective ironic), "I had arrived at a lifestyle we might call genteel bohemian—nice big house (broad floorboards, big fireplaces). . . . We smoked pot, wore dashikis and love beads, and frugged ourselves into a lather while the Beatles and Janis Joplin sang away on the hi-fi set. I was happy enough to lick the sugar of the counterculture; it was the pill of antiwar, anti-administration, anti-'imperialist' protest that I found oddly bitter." He notes that the frugging technocrats *et al.* of his acquaintance simply sloughed off the war as an "administration blunder." But writers, artists, even the very voices to whose sound Updike frugged, began very early to object to the war, while "I whose stock in trade as an American author included an intuition into the mass consciousness and an identification with our national fortunes—thought it sad that our patriotic myth of invincible virtue was crashing, and shocking that so many Americans were gleeful at the crash." This is worthy of Nixon at his unctuous best; yet to give that canny old villain his due, Nixon wouldn't have believed a word he was saying. Incidentally, who was "gleeful" at so much mindless carnage? And what honest citizen would *not* be grateful that a "myth" of any kind, no matter how "patriotic," be dispelled?

When intellectuals, for want of any other word, were asked to contribute their views to a book called *Authors Take Sides on Vietnam*, Updike admitted that he was "uncomfortable" about our military adventure, but wondered "how much of the discomfort has to do with its high cost, in lives and money, and how much with its moral legitimacy." This is wondrously callous. Of course, television had not yet shown us too many lives, much less money, being lost on prime time, but Updike weighs them as nothing in the balance when compared to the moral decision made by our elected leaders, who must know best—otherwise they would not be our elected leaders. Loyal to authority, he favors intervention "if it does some good," because "the crying need is for genuine elections whereby the South Vietnamese can express their will. If their will is for Communism, we should pick up our chips and leave." But the American government had stopped the Vietnamese from holding such elections a decade earlier, because, as President Eisenhower noted in his memoirs, North and South Vietnam would have voted for the Communist Ho Chi Minh and "we could not allow that." Updike's ignorance—innocence, to be kind—is not very reassuring, even when he echoes Auden on how "it is foolish to canvass writers upon political issues." Our views, as he says, "have no more authority than those of any reasonably well-educated citizen." Certainly, the views of a writer who knew nothing of the political situation in Vietnam weren't worth very much, but, as an American writer identified with our national fortunes, Updike does acknowledge that writers are supposed to be attuned to the human as well as to the moral aspects of engaging in war, particularly one so far from our shores, so remote from our interests. As Updike's wife at the time told him, "It's their place." But by then it was too late. Mild Rabbit had metamorphosed into March Hare.

Letter to *The New York Times*: "I discover myself named . . . as the lone American writer 'unequivocally for' the United States intervention in Vietnam." He notes that he is not alone. Apparently James Michener, "an old Asia hand," and Marianne Moore, an old baseball hand, thought that the Commies should be stopped by us anywhere and everywhere . . . or, in Updike's case, by *them*, the Americans obliged to fight. He finds such opponents as Jules Pfeiffer and Norman Mailer "frivolous." Mailer had written, "The truth is maybe we need a war. It may be the last of the tonics. From Lydia Pinkham to Vietnam in sixty years, or bust." Mailer was being Swiftian. But Updike is constitutionally unable to respond to satire, irony, wit, rhetorical devices that tend to be offensive to that authority which he himself means to obey.

Updike takes offense at a "cheerful thought by James Purdy: 'Vietnam is atrocious for the dead and maimed innocent, but it's probably sadder to be a live American with only the Madison Avenue Glibbers for a homeland and a God.' " Rabbit will go to his final burrow without ever realizing the accuracy of Purdy's take on the society in which Updike was to spend his life trying to find a nice place for himself among his fellow Glibbers.

For a certain kind of quotidian novelist, there is nothing wrong in leaving out history or politics. But there is something creepy about Updike's overreaction to those of us who tried to stop a war that was destroying (the dead to one side) a political and economic system that had done so well by so many rabbits. Updike is for the president, any president, right or wrong, because at such a time "it was a plain citizen's duty to hold his breath and hope for the best." For thirteen years? Then, with unexpected passion, he sides with what he takes to be the majority of Americans against those members of the upper class whom he once emulated and now turns upon: "Cambridge professors and Manhattan lawyers and their guitar-strumming children thought they could run the country and the world better than this lugubrious bohunk from Texas (Johnson). These privileged members of a privileged nation . . . full of aesthetic disdain for their own defenders." At some point, unclear to me, the Viet

Cong must have bombed San Diego. "At a White House dinner in June of 1965, I saw what seemed to me a touching sight: Johnson and Dean Rusk . . . giving each other a brief hug in passing—two broad-backed Southern boys, trying to hold the fort."

After the thrill of watching those whom Unser Gott had placed over us, Updike turns manic ("My face would become hot, my voice high and tense and wildly stuttery"). He grieves for "the American soldiers, derided and mocked at home. . . ." This is purest Johnson. Whenever LBJ was attacked for having put the troops in Vietnam for no clear reason, he would charge those who questioned presidential mischief with disloyalty—even treason—against our brave boys, when, of course, it was he and Eisenhower and Kennedy and Ford and Nixon who supported the sacrifice of our brave boys in a war that none of these presidents could ever, with straight face, explain; a war whose longtime executor, Robert McNamara, now tells us that he himself never did figure out. But in the presence of Authority, Updike is like a bobby-soxer at New York's Paramount Theater when the young Frank Sinatra was on view. Out of control, he writes, "Under the banner of a peace-movement . . . war was being waged by a privileged few upon the administration and the American majority that had elected it." The reverse was true. Finally Wall Street marched against the war, and Nixon surrendered, weightier matters, like impeachment, on his mind.

"Reading a little now, I realize how little I knew, for all my emotional involvement, about the war itself, a war after all like other wars. . . ." But it was not like other wars. No matter, the March Hare has turned his attention to other legitimacies, such as God. "Western culture from Boethius to Proust had transpired under the Christian enchantment." What an odd pairing! Plainly, Updike doesn't know much about Boethius. It is true that after his execution by the Emperor Theodoric in A.D. 525, he was taken over by the Christian establishment (Latin team) as a patristic authority, even though, in his last work, *The Consolation of Philosophy* (a "golden volume," according to Gibbon), he is mostly Platonist except when he obeys the injunction "follow God" in imitation not of the tripartite Christian wonder but of Pythagoras. As for the half-Jew Proust, so emotionally and artistically involved in the Dreyfus case, Christianity in action could hardly have been "enchanting." But Updike, in theological mood, is serenely absolutist: "Among the repulsions of atheism for me has been its drastic uninterestingness as an intellectual position." This is very interesting.

At times, reading Updike's political and cultural musings, one has the sense that there is no received opinion that our good rabbit does not hold with passion. "The fights for women's rights and gay rights emerged enmeshed with the Vietnam protest and have outlived it. Though unconsciously resisting the androgyny, which swiftly became—as all trends in a consumer society become—a mere fashion, I must have felt challenged." As American women have been trying to achieve political and economic parity with men for two centuries, how can these activities be considered "mere fashion" or a new consumer trend? For Updike, fags and dykes are comical figures who like their own sex and so cannot be taken seriously when they apply for the same legal rights under the Constitution that fun-loving, wife-swapping exurbanites enjoy. Reality proved too much for him. "I found the country so distressing in its civil fury" that he, along with current wife and Flopsy, Mopsy, and Cottontail, fled to London "for the school year of 1968–69." The year, one should note, of the three "decadent" best-sellers, *Portnoy's Complaint, Myra Breckinridge,* and his own *Couples.*

Today, Rabbit seems at relative peace. He addresses a letter to his grandchildren full of family lore. Along the way, he has acquired an African son-in-law. He is full of Shillington self-effacing gracefulness on what—if any—race problem there might still be in the grand old United States, converted during the Reagan years—golden years for bunnies— to a City on a Hill where he can now take his ease and enjoy the solace of Religion, pondering "the self [which] is the focus of anxiety; attention to others, self-forgetfulness and living like [sic] the lilies are urged."

Between *Self-Consciousness* (1989) and the current *In the Beauty of the Lilies,* Updike has published three novels, a book of short stories, and one of critical pieces. He is, as Dawn Powell once said of herself, "fixed in facility," as are most writers-for-life; a dying breed, I suspect, as, maw ajar, universal Internet swallows all. Meanwhile, Updike has written his

Big Book, the story of four generations of American life, starting in 1910 and ending more or less today in—and on—television, as practically everything does in what the bemused Marx thought might be our "exceptional" republic.

Before the outbreak of the Civil War, John Brown, a yeoman from Connecticut, destined to be forever connected with Osawatomie, Kansas, set himself up as a unilateral abolitionist of slavery in a state torn between pro- and antislavery factions. Updike probably first encountered him, as I did, in the film *Santa Fe Trail* (1940), where he was made gloriously incarnate by Raymond Massey. With a band of zealots, Brown occupied the federal arsenal at Harpers Ferry, Virginia. The nation suddenly was afire. Inevitably, Brown was defeated and hanged by the state of Virginia, thus making him a martyr for the North, while a song, "John Brown's Body," was set to a rousing old English folk tune. The poet Julia Ward Howe, listening to troops sing the demotic words to "John Brown's Body," in a Delphic fever of inspiration, wrote her own words for what would later be known as "The Battle Hymn of the Republic," one of the few stirring pieces of national music to give the "Marseillaise" a run for its Euro-francs.

Updike has chosen for his title one of the least mawkish, if not entirely coherent, quatrains from Howe's lyrics. "In the beauty of the lilies Christ was born across the sea / With a glory in his bosom that transfigures you and me / As he died to make men holy, let us die to make men free / While God is marching on." Precisely why God has chosen this moment to go marching—on to where?—is a secret as one with the source of the sacred river Alph. But, no matter, this is rousing stuff. It is patriotic; it favors the freedom of black slaves at the South; it is botanically incorrect— no lilies at Bethlehem in December, as opposed to all those iconographic lilies during April's immaculate conception. But the text fits Updike's evening mood; it also provides him with an uplifting sonorous title, though a more apt title could have been found in the quatrain that begins, "I have seen Him in the watch-fires of an hundred circling camps; / They have builded Him an altar in the evening dews and damps." Updike has well and truly builded us a novel that might well and truly be called "The Evening Dews and Damps." He has also written easily the most intensely political American novel of the last quarter-century.

The story begins in the grounds of a baronial estate in Paterson, New Jersey. Shillington territory. But this is not your usual Rabbit story. On the lawn, D. W. Griffith is making a film with Mary Pickford. We hear little more about this film, but the modern note has been struck. Now we must defer satisfaction, as Updike gives us a list of things, visible and invisible, in the immediate neighborhood—like New York City only fifteen miles to the east of Paterson "lying sullenly snared within the lowland loop of the Passaic River." One wonders what editor Shawn might have made of that "sullenly." Surely, there must have been a house ukase against the pathetic fallacy. But Updike has always liked to signal with his adverbs as he conforms with his adjectives. Besides, he is now off the *New Yorker* page and on to his very own page.

The first section is titled "Clarence." The Reverend Clarence Arthur Wilmot of the Fourth Presbyterian Church, whose address we are given as well as the church's dimensions, physically and spiritually, along with those of Clarence himself, "a tall narrow-chested man of forty-three," etc., etc., who has, at this moment, suddenly, almost idly, lost his faith. A promising beginning which might have been more effective without the weeds of description that precede it. Even so, there *it* is, on the third page—the Problem. In order to refute a lapsing parishioner, Clarence has been reading the atheist Robert Ingersoll's *Some Mistakes of Moses*, and, in the process, in a flash of utter darkness, he comes to the conclusion that Ingersoll was "quite right." Shaken, Clarence makes his way home through a forest of description and into his house with its "leaded rectangles of stained glass the color of milky candies and the foot of the dark walnut staircase that, in two turnings punctuated by rectangular newel posts whose point had been truncated . . ." We are spared nothing, rectangular or otherwise.

Clarence ponders free will versus predestination, the sort of thing that at a church school like St. Albans, to the south of Paterson in Washington, D.C., most boys had pretty much wrapped up before the onset of puberty—or Grace, whichever took place first. We meet wife and mother, Stella, supervising the cook in the kitchen. Tonight there will be supper for some important Presbyterians. Money for the church will be discussed. Clarence listens to kitchen chatter: "The eavesdropping clergyman, numbed by his sudden atheism . . ." Then we're off to a description of lots and lots of things in the house including a Tiffany-glass chandelier, with scalloped edges. Updike never quite knows what to do with his lists of random objects or physical human characteristics. In this, he resembles a more graceful James Michener, whose huge books are simply compendia of thousands of little facts collected by researchers and deposited helter-skelter in his long "novels."

Updike also provides us with reading lists of those books that encourage and discourage Christian faith. Clarence is suffering from a mini-vastation, somewhat diluted by Updike's sudden introduction of "real people" into the book, or at least of real names culled from contemporary newspapers. There is Mary Pickford at the start. Then a son of Theodore Roosevelt gets married. We are given the list of ushers, dazzling society names of the day. Updike will keep on doing this for the entire sixty-year period covered by his narrative. But a technique that worked so well for John Dos Passos in *USA* simply stops dead what story Updike has to tell.

Updike, unlike his alleged literary models, Henry Green and Proust, describes to no purpose. In fact, Green, as I recall, describes hardly anything, relying on a superlative ear for a wide variety of speech patterns, while Updike's characters all speak in the same tone of voice, their dialogue a means to get them from one plot point to the next. As one trudges through these descriptions, one wishes that Updike had learned less from his true models, Marquand and O'Hara, and more from the middle James, who, as a lord of the pertinent and the relevant, knew that nothing need be described or, indeed, *told* unless it suggests, while never naming, the presence in the deep of monsters, as the author, off-page, turns ever tighter the screw.

Although in *The Spoils of Poynton* mother and son fight over the contents of a great house, we are never told just *what* is being fought over. James leaves the details to the reader's imagination. But such continence has never been the way of the commercial American writer, no matter how elevated his theme or resourceful his art. For Updike, Poynton is a Sotheby's catalogue.

James only needed to describe—was it one crucifix?—to represent a house full of rare furniture and objects worth killing for. The naturalistic Dos Passos used movielike cuts and intercuts of headlines to act as useful counterpoint to a narrative that takes place in public, as opposed to strictly private, time. Since most people get the news of their day through press and television, why not use or at least mimic these sources? The naturalistic Updike seems to think that just about any item will do in the way of color, and, in a sense, he is right; one has only to consider the huge popularity of Michener's myriad-fact novels with an unsophisticated reading public that likes to think that valuable time is not being wasted on a made-up story, that the reader is really getting the inside dope on, let's say, Detroit and the auto business or, in Updike's case, on the United States' second most profitable export after aerospace—showbiz and Hollywood. But whereas a few million small facts are the object of the Michenerian enterprise, Updike is more conventionally ambitious. He wants to dramatize the forces that have driven the United States ever leftward, even further away from the marching, lily-born God, away from family values and obedience to Authority, away from *The New Yorker*'s benign fact-checkers and sentence-polishers, so sadly absent now when he really needs them.

After James's disasters in the theater, he famously returned to prose with a new sharp intensity. He had learned that nothing is to be noted unless it is absolutely essential to the dramatic revelation of even the vaguest figure in the carpet. As far as I know, Updike has never submitted himself to the strict discipline of relevance one learns from theater. And yet, parenthetically, his one attempt at a play, *Buchanan Dying* (1974), though probably unstageable as written, is a superb work of mimesis, the last thoughts of the enigmatic president from Pennsylvania whose cautious inertness helped bring on the Civil War and imperial Lincoln. The effect is startling and unique, unlike . . .

"Dialogue and meditation" is how Updike, inaccurately, describes the manner of his early "model," Henry Green. Updike himself writes long, long descriptions interspersed with brief snatches of dialogue. In theory . . . no, no theory! . . . *ideally*, both description and dialogue should forward narrative, as in most pop writing. Realistic storytellers in English oscillate between the *démeublement* of Raymond Carver and the richly detailed settings, physical and psychic, of James Purdy. For a true master of effects, either way works. But if, like Updike, one means to go into the wholesale furniture business, one had better be prepared to furnish, in appropriate manner, great Poynton itself. I realize that in a world where democracy is on the rise everywhere except in American politics, one style can never be better than another, 'cause my feelings are just as deep as yours and how can you criticize my voice, my style which is Me? To which some of us old meanies must respond, well, dear, if you choose to send your letter to the world then here's the answer, assuming the letter was not returned to sender for lack of correct address or sufficient postage.

Years ago, in unkind mood, Norman Mailer referred to Updike's writing as the sort of prose that those who know nothing about writing think good. Today, theory, written preferably in near-English academese, absorbs the specialist, and prose style is irrelevant. Even so, what is one to make of this sentence: "The hoarse receding note drew his consciousness . . . to a fine point, and while that point hung in his skull starlike he fell asleep upon the adamant bosom of the depleted universe"? Might Updike not have allowed one blind noun to slip free of its seeing-eye adjective?

Plot, four generations of the Wilmot family. After Clarence's loss of faith, he sells encyclopedias, perseveres in his failure, as did Updike's own father, each to be avenged by a descendant; though not by Clarence's son, Teddy, who occupies the next chunk of time—and novel-space. Now we go into the Updike time machine. "And then it was a new decade; and drinking was illegal all across the nation, and Attorney General A. Mitchell Palmer accused the IWW of causing the railroad strikes. . . . Mary Pickford and Douglas Fairbanks were married in a Hollywood dream come true, and Europe twisted and turned with coups and riots and little wars" (which ones?), "and the Democrats at their convention put up James Cox and another Roosevelt, and Bill Tilden . . . and . . . and . . . and . . ."

Teddy doesn't know what to do with his life. He is passive and not very bright. He works in a bottle-top factory; studies accounting. Mean-

while, he struggles for light beneath his author's thick blankets of research, intended to give us the sense of a world and a time in which
Teddy himself has neither place nor perceptible interest: "And now the
sordidness of illusions was leaking out of Hollywood itself. . . . Fatty Ar-
buckle, unsolved mystery of director William Desmond Taylor . . ." But
there is some point to all this news from outside, because, in the next
slice of the Wilmot saga, Teddy's daughter, Esther or Essie, will become
a Movie Star and avenge—"ambush," as Updike did—a world that paid
no attention to his father, her grandfather. When Teddy goes to work in
Addison's Drug Store (Stephenson's back in Shillington), we are given
page after page of what is sold in the store. Then Teddy marries a crip-
pled girl with a strong character. Teddy gives up being a soda jerk and becomes a career postman. He endures a happy marriage, until his wife, as
fictional characters tend to do, falls through one of the interstices in Updike's web of Passing Parade notes on world events: "Jews and Arabs
fought in Jerusalem; Chinese and Russians battled along the Manchurian
border." Social notes from all over. Teddy smokes Old Golds.

Part Three. We shift from Teddy to Essie/Alma. I found myself curious that Updike did not choose to shift from third to first person in his
studies of four generations. Since all his character writing is in essentially
the same tone of voice, he might have dramatized—well, differenti-
ated—his four protagonists by giving each a distinctive voice. But he remains in the lazy third person: Now she thinks this . . . now she does
that . . . now Japan invades Manchuria.

In Essie's section, the Shillington/Basingstoke movie house is central,
and Essie, now a beauty, is thrilled by what she sees on the screen, ideal
life writ large in celluloid. Ambitious, for a dull Wilmot, she enters a
beauty contest, where she meets a photographer from New York. "There
was something mystical in the way the camera lapped up her inner states
through the thin skin of her face. She had known as a child she was the
center of the universe and now proof was accumulating, click by click."
She becomes a model. An actress. A star, as Alma De Mott.

But for Updike, Essie is early blighted. Even before Hollywood and
stardom she is taken in by liberals—Commies, too. Plainly, sinister os-

mosis was taking place at the movie house in her hometown. The liberal image of America the Bad was like some insidious virus contained in the celluloid, bacteria which, under the optimum condition of hot light projected through its alien nesting ground on to the screen, bred discontent in those not sufficiently vaccinated against Doubt by benign school and good church. So ravaged was Essie by Red films like *Now, Voyager* ("Why ask for the moon when we have the stars?") that she actually objected to the loyalty oaths inflicted on so many Americans by President Truman's administration, oaths that the self-conscious Updike cannot, like his father, find objectionable. When Essie's little brother, Danny, says, "I hate Communists," she says, "What do you know about anything? Who do you think beat Hitler's armies?" And so the green twig was bent by the product of MGM and the Brothers Warner.

Before Essie leaves New York for Hollywood, Updike helpfully tells us the names "of the big Hollywood movies at the end of the Forties." He also lists the foreign films that ravished Essie. Curiously, he forgets to rate the Italian neorealists for Leftist content. In New York, Essie is taken up by a queer cousin, Patrick. He is worldly, knows his Manhattan: like all homosexuals, he is "sensitive" but "frustrating . . . and not just sexually; some inner deflection kept him on the sidelines of life, studying painting but not wanting to paint himself, and even sneering at those that did try"; but then "the arts, especially minor arts like window dressing, were dominated by them." Patrick manages her career for a time: "A comforting accreditation . . . to have a poof bring her in."

Before Alma makes it to the silver screen, she serves time in live television. Updike tells us all about what it was like; but then there is a firm in New York that will do intensive research on any subject a writer might want—from the Golden Age of Television, say, to the flora and fauna of Brazil. I am certain that Updike, the artist, would never resort to so brazen a crib; even so, many of his small piled-up facts are so rotelike in their detail and his use of them so completely haywire that—well, *vichyssoise qui mal y pense*.

"Alma would play opposite, within the next few years, both Gary Cooper and . . . Clark Gable." Boldly, Updike tells us a lot of personal things about Cooper and Gable which he could only have got from fan magazines or showbiz biographies. Updike is now frugging wildly into

Collins Sisters territory. But where the Bel-Air Brontës are well advanced in the art and arts of popular fiction and write *romans à clef* with phallic keys, Updike, ever original, disposes with the keys. Confidently, he tells us about "Coop's" aches and pains, about Clark's career anxieties and sex. Updike has now made it to the heart of the heart of pop fiction: "there was in Gable a loneliness too big for Alma to fill. Where Cooper was a sublime accident (he reached over, while the wind rushed past and the sun beat sparkling dents in the Pacific below, and cupped his hand around her skull) . . . Gable had never been anything but an aspiring actor. . . . He had been so long a star he had forgotten to find mortal satisfactions." Why ask for the butterscotch when we can have the fudge?

For a beautiful heroine like Alma, sex is *de rigueur*, but though she fucks like a minx, the sexagenarian Updike has lost some of his old brio. Alma marries a nobody with a body; he never makes it in the business but makes a baby. Meanwhile, she grows more and more un-American. Proud to be a Hollywood liberal, she is prone to quarrel with her kid brother, Danny, now a CIA honcho. "Well, Danny darling, the movies have never pretended to be anything except entertainment. But what you're doing pretends to be a great deal more."

"It pretends to be history," he said quickly. "It *is* history. Cast of billions. The future of the globe is at stake. I kid you not." Nice touch, this last. Television slang of the 1950s.

Alma De Mott rises and falls and rises again. She is clearly based— research to one side—on Yvonne de Carlo's performance as an up-down-up movie star of a certain age in Sondheim's musical comedy *Follies*, whose signature song was "I'm Still Here."

Time now to shift to Alma's son, Clark, named for . . . you guessed it. In the family tradition, he is a born Shillington loser. He is, of course, conscious of being a celebrity as a star's son. But the connection does him no particular good. He also has a stepfather called Rex. When he asks Alma why she married Rex, she "told him calmly, Because he is all cock."

Clark is in rebellion against the Communism of his mother and her friends—pinks if not reds—and, worse, unabashed enemies of the United States in the long, long, war against the Satanic Ho Chi Minh. "Mom, too, wanted North Vietnam to win, which seemed strange to Clark, since America has been pretty good to her." As irony, this might have been telling, but irony is an arrow that the Good Fiction Fairy withheld from the Updike quiver. Consequently, this *non sequitur* can only make perfect sense to a writer who believes that no matter how misguided, tyrannous, and barbarous the rulers of one's own country have become, they *must* be obeyed; and if one has actually made money and achieved a nice place in the country that they have hijacked then one must be doubly obedient, grateful, too. Under Hitler, many good Germans, we are told, felt the same way.

There is nothing, sad to say, surprising in Updike's ignorance of history and politics and of people unlike himself; in this, he is a standard American and so a typical citizen of what Vice-President Agnew once called the greatest nation in the country. But Updike has literary ambitions as well as most of the skills of a popular writer, except, finally, the essential one without which nothing can ever come together to any useful end as literature, empathy. He is forever stuck in a psychic Shillington–Ipswich–New York world where everything outside his familiar round is unreal. Because of this lack of imagination, he can't really do much even with the characters that he does have some feeling for because they exist in social, not to mention historic, contexts that he lacks the sympathy—to use the simplest word—to make real.

Many of Updike's descriptions of Hollywood—the place—are nicely observed. Plainly, he himself *looked* at the Three B's—Beverly Hills, Bel-Air, Brentwood—"the palm trees, the pink low houses, the Spanishness, the endlessness . . . the winding palm-lined streets of Beverly Hills, where there was no living person in sight but Japanese and Mexican gardeners wheeling dead palm fronds out from behind hedges of oleander and fuchsias." "The wealth here was gentle wealth, humorous wealth even; these fortunes derived from art and illusion and personal beauty and not, as back home, from cruel old riverside mills manufacturing some ugly and stupid necessity like Trojans or bottlecaps." The "humorous" is an inspired adjective, proving there is a lot to be said for firsthand observation. But then, alas, he must tell us about *how* films were made in the 1950s and what the makers were like, including Columbia's Harry Cohn, a much-written-about monster. Once inside the celluloid kitchen, Updike falls far, far behind the Bel-Air Brontës at their cuisine-art.

Alma is still here, as the song goes, while the son, Clark, works at a Colorado ski resort, owned by his great-uncle. Clark has gone through the usual schools and done the usual drugs and had the usual run-of-the-mill sex available to a movie star's child. Now he must *find* himself—if there is a self to find—in a partially pristine Colorado rapidly being undone by ski resorts and the greenhouse effect.

Except for Alma, who knew from the beginning that she was unique in her beauty and sweet self-love, none of Updike's protagonists has any idea of what to do with himself during the seventy years or so that he must mark time in this vale of tears before translation to sunbeam-hood in Jesus' sky-condo. Happily, if tragically, true meaning comes to Clark in Colorado.

Updike, nothing if not up-to-date, re-creates the celebrated slaughter at Waco, Texas, where the charismatic David Koresh and many of his worshipers were wiped out in their compound by federal agents. In Updike's fiction, a similar messiah and his worshipers withdraw to Colorado in order to live in Christian fellowship until the final trump, due any day now. An attractive girl leads Clark to the Lower Branch Temple and to Jesse, a Vietnam veteran who is now a "high-ranch messiah." As a novelist, Updike often relies on the wearisome trick of someone asking a new character to tell us about himself. Within the rustic temple, skeptical Clark and primitive Scripture-soaked Jesse tell us about themselves. Clark: "Yeah, well. What was I going to say? Something. I don't want to bore you." Jesse: "You will never find Jesse bored. Never, by a recital of the truth. Weary, yes, and sore-laden with the sorrows of mankind, but never bored." A good thing, too, considering the level of the dialogue. Jesse fulminates with biblical quotes from the likes of Ezekiel, while Clark wimps on and on about the emptiness of gilded life in the Three B's.

The actual events at Waco revealed, terribly, what a paranoid federal apparatus, forever alert to any infraction of its stern prohibitions, was capable of when challenged head-on by nonconformists. How, I wondered, will Updike, a born reactionary, deal with the state's conception of itself as ultimate arbiter of everything, no matter how absurd? Even "the good child" must be appalled by the slaughter of Jesse and his fellow believers by a mindless authority.

Since we shall witness all this through Clark's eyes, Updike has made him even more passive than his usual protagonists. Too much acid in the Vipers Lounge? Clark does have a scene with Uncle Danny, who explains the real world to him in terms that the editorial page of *The Wall Street Journal* might think twice about publishing. Danny: "Vietnam was a hard call. . . . But somebody always has to fight." (In the case of Vietnam, somebody proved to be poor white and black males.) "You and I walk down the street safe, if we do, because a cop around the corner has a gun. The kids today say the state is organized violence and they're right. But it matters who's doing the organizing . . . Joe Stalin . . . or our bumbling American pols. I'll take the pols every time." Thus, straw villain undoes straw hero, neither, of course, relevant to the issue, but Updike–Danny (true empathy may have been achieved at last) is now in full swing: "The kids today . . . grow long hair . . . smoke pot and shit on poor Tricky Dicky" only because of "the willingness of somebody else to do their fighting for them. What you can't protect gets taken away. . . ." Hobbesian world out there. Danny does admit that we got nothing out of Vietnam, not even "thanks"—one wonders from whom he thinks gratitude ought to come. But, no matter. Danny hates Communism. Hates Ho Chi Minh. Hates those "Hollywood fatcats and bleeding hearts" who oppose the many wars. Even so, "I try to be dispassionate about it. But I love this crazy, wasteful, self-hating country in spite of myself." It would seem that Updike–Danny has not got the point. The people of the country don't hate the country, only what has been done to it by those who profit from hot and cold wars and, in the process, bring to civilian governance a murderous military mentality, witness Waco.

How does Clark take all this? "To Clark, Uncle Danny seemed a treasure, a man from space who was somehow his own. . . ." Clark has not known many employees of the CIA, for whom this sort of bombast is the order of the day. That order flows not only through the pages of *The Wall Street Journal* but throughout most of the press, where Hume's Opinion is shaped by the disinformation of a hundred wealthy tax-exempt American foundations such as Olin, Smith-Richardson, Bradley, Scaife and Pew, not to mention all the Christian coalitions grinding out a worldview of Us against Them, the Us an ever-smaller group of propertied Americans and the Them the rest of the world.

Clark would now be ripe for neo-conhood, but for the fact that he was never a con or anything at all until he drifted into Jesse's orbit, already set on a collision course with the U.S. government, which allows no group the pleasure of defiance even in the name of the One in whose Image we were fashioned. Jesse has been stockpiling weapons for "The Day of Reckoning." Lovingly, Updike lists the arsenal. Clark suddenly realizes that here, at last, is the perfect orgasm, something well worth dying for. "The gun was surprising: provocative like a woman, both lighter and heavier than he would have thought." The ultimate love story of a boy and his gun, "ready to become a magic wand." Disappointingly, at the end, Updike is too patriotic or too timid to allow federal law-enforcement officers to destroy the temple along with the men, women, and children that Jesse has attracted to him. Colorado State Troopers do Caesar's work, unlike Waco, where Caesar himself did the deed.

At the end, Clark turns on Jesse and betrays him. In order to save the children from the Conflagration, Clark "shot the false prophet twice." Although Clark himself perishes, he dies a hero, who saved as many lives as he could from the false prophet whom he had, for no coherent reason, briefly served. Finally, world television validates Clark's life and end. Who could ask for anything more?

Stendhal's view that politics in a work of art is like a pistol shot at a concert is true, but what is one to do in the case of a political work that deals almost exclusively with true patriot versus nonpatriot who dares criticize the common patria? I quoted at length from Updike's *Self-Consciousness* in order to establish what human material this inhuman novel is based on. I have also tried to exercise empathy, tried to feel, as President Clinton likes to say, the author's pain. Actually, to find reactionary writing similar to Updike's, one must turn back to John Dos Passos's *Midcentury*, or to John Steinbeck's *The Winter of Our Discontent*. But Updike, unlike his predecessor Johns, has taken to heart every far-out far-right piety currently being fed us.

Also, despite what Updike must have thought of as a great leap up the social ladder from Shillington obscurity to "Eliotic" Harvard and then on to a glossy magazine, he has now, Antaeus-like, started to touch base with that immutable Dutch-German earth on which his ladder stood. Recent American wars and defeats have so demoralized our good child that he has now come to hate that Enlightenment which was all that, as a polity, we ever had. He is symptomatic, then, of a falling back, of a loss of nerve; indeed, a loss of honor. He invokes phantom political majorities, righteous masses. Time to turn to Herzen on the subject: "The masses are indifferent to individual freedom, liberty of speech; the masses love authority. They are still blinded by the arrogant glitter of power, they are offended by those who stand alone . . . they want a social government to rule for their benefit, and not against it. But to govern themselves doesn't enter their heads."

Updike's work is more and more representative of that polarizing within a state where Authority grows ever more brutal and malign while its hired hands in the media grow ever more excited as the holy war of the few against the many heats up. In this most delicate of times, Updike has "builded" his own small, crude altar in order to propitiate—or to invoke?—"the fateful lightning of His terrible swift sword."

The Times Literary Supplement
April 26, 1996

Part Two

READING

THE

WORLD

PASSAGE TO EGYPT

"Are you German, sir?" A small, dark youth stepped from behind a palm tree into the full light of the setting sun which turned scarlet the white shirt and albino red the black eyes. He had been watching me watch the sun set across the Nile, now blood-red and still except for sailboats tacking in a hot, slow breeze. I told him that I was American but was used to being mistaken for a German: in this year of the mid-century, Germans are everywhere, and to Arab eyes we all look alike. He showed only a moment's disappointment.

"I have many German friends," he said. "Two German friends. *West* German friends. Perhaps you know them?" He pulled a notebook out of his pocket and read off two names. Then, not waiting for an answer, all in a rush, he told me that he was a teacher of Arabic grammar, that he was going to Germany, *West* Germany (he emphasized the *West* significantly), to write a book. What sort of book? A book about West Germany. The theme? He responded with some irritation: "A Book About West Germany." That was what the book would be about. He was a poet. His name was Ahmed. "Welcome," he said, "welcome!" His crooked face broke into a smile. "Welcome to Luxor!" He invited me to his house for mint tea.

As we turned from the bank of the Nile, a long, haunting cry sounded across the water. I had heard this same exotic cry for several evenings, and I was certain that it must be of ancient origin, a hymn perhaps to Ikhnaton's falling sun. I asked Ahmed what this lovely aria meant. He listened a moment and then said, "It's this man on the other side who says: will the ferryboat please pick him up?" So much for magic.

Ahmed led the way through narrow streets to the primary school where he taught. It was a handsome modern building, much like its counterparts in Scarsdale or Darien. He took me inside. "You must see what the children make themselves. Their beautiful arts." On the entrance-hall table their beautiful arts were exhibited: clay figures, carved wood, needlework, all surrounding a foot-long enlargement in clay of the bilharzia, a parasite which is carried by snails in the irrigation ditches; once it invades the human bloodstream, lungs and liver are attacked and the victim wastes away; some ninety percent of the fellahin suffer from bilharzia. "Beautiful?" he asked. "Beautiful," I said.

On the wall hung the exhibit's masterpiece, a larger than life-size portrait of Nasser, painted in colors recalling Lazarus on the fourth day. A somewhat more talented drawing next to it showed students marching with banners in a street. I asked Ahmed to translate the words on the banners. "Our heads for Nasser," he said with satisfaction. I asked him if Nasser was popular with the young. He looked at me as though I had questioned the next day's sunrise. Of course Nasser was loved. Had I ever been in Egypt before? Yes, during the winter of 1948, in the time of the bad fat King. Had things improved? I told him honestly that they had indeed. Cairo had changed from a nineteenth-century French provincial capital surrounded by a casbah to a glittering modern city, only partially surrounded by a casbah. He asked me what I was doing in Egypt, and I told him I was a tourist, not mentioning that I had an appointment to interview Nasser the following week for an American magazine.

Ahmed's house is a large one, four stories high; here he lives with some twenty members of his family. The parlor is a square room with a high ceiling from which hangs a single unshaded light bulb. Two broken beds serve as sofas. I sat on one of the beds while Ahmed, somewhat nervously, ordered mint tea from a sister who never emerged from the dark hall. Then I learned that his father was also a teacher, and that an uncle worked in Nasser's office; obviously a prosperous family by Luxor standards.

I was offered the ceremonial cigarette. I refused; he lit up. He was sorry his father was not there to meet me. But then again, puffing his cigarette, he was glad, for it is disrespectful to smoke in front of one's father. Only recently the father had come unexpectedly into the parlor. "I was smoking a cigarette and when he came in, oh! I bit it hard, like this, and have to swallow it down! Oh, I was sick!" We chuckled at his memory.

When the mint tea arrived (passed to us on a tray from the dark hall, only bare arms visible), Ahmed suggested we sit outside where it was cool. Moonlight blazed through a wooden trellis covered with blossoming wisteria. We sat on stiff wooden chairs. He switched on a light momentarily to show me a photograph of the girl he was to marry. She was pretty and plump and could easily have been the editor of the yearbook in any American high school. He turned off the light. "We modern now. No more arranged marriages. Love is everything. Love is why we marry. Love is all." He repeated this several times, with a sharp intake of breath after each statement. It was very contagious, and I soon found myself doing it. Then he said, "Welcome," and I said, "Thank you."

Ahmed apologized for the unseasonable heat. This was the hottest spring in years, as I had discovered that day in the Valley of the Kings where the temperature had been over a hundred and the blaze of sun on white limestone blinding. "After June, Luxor is *impossible!*" he said proudly. "We all go who can go. If I stay too long, I turn dark as a black in the sun." Interestingly enough, there is racial discrimination in Egypt. "The blacks" are second-class citizens: laborers, servants, minor government functionaries. They are the lowest level of Egyptian society in every way except one: there are no Negro beggars. That is an Arab monopoly. Almsgivers are blessed by the Koran, if not by Nasser, who has tried to discourage the vast, well-organized hordes of beggars.

"To begin with, I had naturally a very light complexion," said Ahmed, making a careful point, "like the rest of my family, but one day when I was small the nurse upset boiling milk on me and ever since that day I have been somewhat dark." I commiserated briefly. Then I tried a new tack. I asked him about his military service. Had he been called up yet? A new decree proposed universal military service, and I thought a discussion of it might get us onto politics. He said that he had not been called up because of a *very interesting story*. My heart sank, but I leaned forward

with an air of sympathetic interest. Suddenly, I realized I was imperson-
ating someone. But who? Then when he began to talk and I to respond
with small nods and intakes of breath, I realized that it was E. M. Forster.
I was the Forster of *A Passage to India* and this was Dr. Aziz. Now that I
had the range, my fingers imperceptibly lengthened into Forsterian
claws; my eyes developed an uncharacteristic twinkle; my upper lip
sprouted a ragged gray moustache, while all else turned to tweed.

"When the British attacked us at Suez, I and these boys from our
school, we took guns and together we marched from Alexandria to Suez
to help our country. We march for many days and nights in the desert.
We have no food, no water. Then we find we are lost and we don't know
where we are. Several die. Finally, half dead, we go back to Alexandria
and we march in the street to the place where Nasser is. We ask to see
him, to cheer him, half dead all of us. But they don't let us see him. Finally, my uncle hears I am there and he and Nasser come out and, ah,
Nasser congratulates us, we are heroes! Then I collapse and am unconscious one month. That is why I have *not* to do military service." I was
impressed and said so, especially at their getting lost in the desert, which
contributed to my developing theory that the Arabs are disaster-prone:
they *would* get lost, or else arrive days late for the wrong battle.

Ahmed told me another story of military service, involving friends.
"Each year in the army they have these . . . these . . ." We searched
jointly—hopelessly—for the right word until E. M. Forster came up with
"maneuvers," which was correct. I could feel my eyes twinkling in the
moonlight.

"So these friends of mine are in this maneuvers with guns in the
desert and they have orders: *shoot to kill*. Now one of them was Ibrahim,
my friend. Ibrahim goes to this outpost in the dark. They make him stop
and ask him for the password and he . . ." Sharp intake of breath. "He has
forgotten the password. So they say, 'He must be the enemy.' " I asked if
this took place in wartime. "No, no, *maneuvers*. My friend Ibrahim say,
'Look, I forget. I *did* know but now I forget the password but you know
me, anyway, you know it's Ibrahim.' And he's right. They do know it was
Ibrahim. They recognize his voice but since he cannot say the password
they shot him."

I let E. M. Forster slip to the floor. "Shot him? Dead?"

"Dead," said my host with melancholy satisfaction. "Oh, they were very sorry because they knew it was Ibrahim, but, you see, *he did not know the password*, and while he was dying in the tent they took him to, he said it was all right. They were right to kill him."

I found this story hard to interpret. Did Ahmed approve or disapprove of what was done? He was inscrutable. There was silence. Then he said, "Welcome," and I said, "Thank you." And we drank more mint tea in the moonlight.

I tried again to get the subject around to politics. But beyond high praise for everything Nasser has done, he would volunteer nothing. He did point to certain tangible results of the new regime. For one thing, Luxor was now a center of education. There were many new schools. All the children were being educated. In fact he had something interesting to show me. He turned on the lamp and opened a large scrapbook conveniently at hand. It contained photographs of boys and girls, with a scholastic history for each. Money had to be raised to educate them further. It *could* be done. Each teacher was obliged to solicit funds. "Look what my West German friends have given," he said, indicating amounts and names. Thus I was had, in a good cause. I paid and walked back to the hotel.

On the way back, I took a shortcut down a residential street. I had walked no more than a few feet when an old man came rushing after me. "Bad street!" he kept repeating. I agreed politely, but continued on my way. After all, the street was well lit. There were few people abroad. A shout from an upstairs window indicated that I should halt. I looked up. The man in the window indicated I was to wait until he came downstairs. I did. He was suspicious. He was from the police. *Why* was I in that street? I said that I was taking a walk. This made no sense to him. He pointed toward my hotel, which was in a slightly different direction. That was where I was supposed to go. I said yes, but I wanted to continue in *this* street, I liked to walk. He frowned. Since arrest was imminent, I turned back. At the hotel I asked the concierge why what appeared to be a main street should be forbidden to foreigners. "Oh, 'they' might be rude," he said vaguely. "You know. . . ." I did not know.

In the diner on the train south to Aswan I had breakfast with a young government official from the Sudan. He was on his way home to

Khartoum. He had a fine smile and blue-black skin. On each cheek there were three deep scars, the ritual mark of his tribe—which I recognized, for I had seen his face only the day before on the wall of the Temple of Luxor. Amenhotep III had captured one of his ancestors in Nubia; five thousand years ago the ritual scars were the same as they are now. In matters of religion Africans are profound conservatives. But otherwise he was a man of our time and world. He was dressed in the latest French fashion. He had been for two years on an economic mission in France. He spoke English, learned at the British school in Khartoum.

We breakfasted on musty-tasting dwarfish eggs as dust filtered slowly in through closed windows, covering table, plates, eggs with a film of grit. A fan stirred the dusty air. Parched, I drank three Coca-Colas—the national drink—and sweated. The heat outside was already 110 degrees, and rising. For a while we watched the depressing countryside and spoke very little. At some points the irrigated land was less than a mile wide on our side of the river: a thin ribbon of dusty green ending abruptly in a blaze of desert where nothing at all grew, a world of gray sand as far as the eye could see. Villages of dried-mud houses were built at the desert's edge so as not to use up precious land. The fellahin in their ragged clothes moved slowly about their tasks, quite unaware of the extent of their slow but continual decline. In the fifth century B.C., Herodotus was able to write: "As things are at present these people get their harvest with less labor than anyone else in the world; they have no need to work with plow or hoe, or to use any other of the ordinary methods of cultivating their land; they merely wait for the river of its own accord to flood the fields." But all that has changed. Nearly thirty million people now live in a country whose agriculture cannot support half that number.

"I used to think," said the Sudanese at last, "that Egypt was a fine place, much better than the Sudan. A big country. Rich. But now I know how lucky we are. There is no one at home poor like this." He pointed to several ragged men in a field. Two lay listlessly in the sun. The others worked slowly in the field, narcotized by the heat; the diet of the fellahin is bread and stewed tea and not much of that. I asked him what he thought of Nasser's attacks on his government (recently there had been a disagreement over Nile water rights and Nasser had attacked the Sudanese president with characteristic fury). "Oh, we just laugh at him. We just laugh at him," he repeated as though to convince himself. I asked him why Nasser was continuously on the offensive not only against the West but against the rest of the Arab world. He shrugged. "To impress his own people, I suppose. We don't like it, of course. But perhaps it makes him feel big. Makes them . . ." He pointed to a group of villagers drawing water from a canal. "Makes them forget."

Aswan is the busiest and most optimistic of Egypt's cities. On its outskirts a brand-new chemical factory employs several thousand people. There is a sense of urgency in the city's life, for it is here that all of Egypt's hopes are concentrated: the High Dam is being built. When the dam—the world's largest—is completed in 1970, vast tracts of desert will be made arable and electrical power will be supplied cheaply for the whole country. It should be recalled that the United States had originally agreed to finance a part of the dam, but in 1956 John Foster Dulles withdrew our support and the Soviet obligingly filled the vacuum. Not only are the Russians now financing the dam, but their engineers are building it.

The government had arranged that I be shown around by one of the Egyptian engineers, a cautious, amiable man who spoke not only English but Russian. "I like the Russians very much," he announced firmly as we got into his car. He would show me everything, he said. Nothing to hide.

It was sundown as we approached the barren hills where a huge channel is being cut contiguous to the Nile. Ten thousand men work three eight-hour shifts. Most of the heavy work is done in the cool of the night. Off to the left of the road I noticed a fenced-in compound containing a number of small, modern apartment houses. "The Russians," said my guide. It was a pleasant scene: women chatted in doorways while through uncurtained windows one could see modern kitchens where dinners were cooking. A large sign forbade the taking of photographs.

"How many Russians are there in Aswan?" I asked. He looked at me bewildered. "What you say?" He took refuge in pidgin English. I repeated the question very slowly and distinctly. He looked puzzled. He lost all his English until I made it impossible for him not to understand me.

"You mean how many Russians altogether? Or how many Russian

engineers?" he countered, playing for time. "After all, there are wives and children, and sometimes visitors and . . ." I told him carefully and slowly that I would like to know, first, how many Russians altogether; then I would like to know how many of those were engineers. Of course he had thought that what I wanted to know was the actual number of technicians, and in what categories. After all, there were civil engineers, electrical engineers, and so on, but none of *that* was secret. "We have no secrets! Everything open! Anything you want to know we tell you!" He beamed expansively and parked the car in front of a small circular building. Not until I got out did I realize he had not answered the question.

We now stood on a low hill with a long view of the digging. It was a startling sight. Beneath us was the vast channel already cut from the rock. The sun was gone by now, and the channel—more like a crater— was lit by hundreds of electric lights strung on poles. A perpetual haze of dust obscured the view. Russian diesel trucks roared up and down the sides of the crater, adding to the shrill chatter of drills in stone. Behind us a whole town of new buildings had been somewhat casually assembled: machine shops, technical schools, a hospital. In the desert beyond these buildings, a thousand low black tents were pitched, each with its own campfire. Here the workers lived in stern, nomadic contrast to the modern world they were making.

We entered the circular building which contained a large detailed model of the completed dam. On the walls, diagrams, maps, photographs demonstrated the work's progress and dramatized the fertile Egypt-to-be. I met more Egyptian engineers.

We studied the models and I tried unsuccessfully to sound knowledgeable about turbines. I asked how the workers were recruited. Were they local? How quickly could people who had never used machinery be trained? I was told that the fellahin were surprisingly adaptable. They were trained in schools on the spot. Most of the workers are recruited locally. "But the main thing," said my guide, "is that they know how important all this is. And they do."

I had been told that the dam was some forty weeks behind in its current schedule. But not being an expert in these matters, I could not tell from looking at what I was shown if things were going well or badly, behind or on schedule. The most I could gather was that the engineers were genuinely enthusiastic about their work. Morale is high. And I am ready to testify that they have dug a fine big hole.

We drove to the center of the channel, a good mile from the exhibition hall and at least a hundred yards below the surface of the desert. The air in the crater is almost unbreathable: part dust, part exhaust. A constant haze dims the lights on their poles. The noise is continual and deafening. Hundreds of drills in long, chattering rows break the sandstone floor of the crater, while Russian steam shovels tear at the cliff. I noticed that all the Russian machines looked improvised. No two steam shovels were alike.

We made our way to the entrance of a tunnel cut into a sandstone hill. This was a shortcut to the place where the first turbines were to be set up. At the entrance of the tunnel we were stopped by the only Russian I was to see: a gray, middle-aged man with a tired face. After a long discussion, he gave permission for me to enter the tunnel. "With every Egyptian engineer," said my guide, "there is also a Russian engineer." It was obvious who was in charge.

The tunnel was brightly lit; the noise of drilling was stunningly amplified by stone walls. I was surprised to see occasional puddles of water on the tunnel floor. I daydreamed: The diggers had struck underground springs. That meant there was water in the desert, deep down, and if there was water deep down, all of Egypt's problems were solved. Obviously no one else had figured out the true meaning of the puddles. I turned to my guide. We shouted at one another and I learned that the puddles were caused not by springs but by seepage from the nearby Nile. The nightmare of the dam builders is that the Nile's water might begin to seep at too great a rate through the sandy walls of the crater, wrecking not only the project but possibly diverting the river's course as well.

Finally, lungs protesting, I said that I had seen enough. This time two engineers drove me back to the hotel, where we drank a ceremonial beer together and I complimented them not only on their enthusiasm but on their courage. At the earliest, the dam will be completed in 1970, which means that these men are dedicating their professional lives to a single project. "But we do this, as Nasser says, for the good of our people," said my original guide solemnly. The other engineer was equally solemn: "No, for the good of all humanity." Taking advantage of this suddenly warm mood, I asked again how many Russians were working on the dam. I got two blank looks this time. "What you say?" And I was no wiser when they left.

The next day in Aswan I was able to obtain an unofficial view of what is really going on. There is a good deal of friction between Egyptians and Russians. Much of it is due to the language barrier. The Russians speak only Russian, the Egyptians speak English or French, sometimes both, but few have learned Russian. The professional interpreters are hopeless because, though they can cope with ordinary conversation, they do not know the technical terms of either language. "We use sign language mostly," said one technician glumly. "Everything is too slow."

Another problem is machinery. It is well known that the Soviet has always had a somewhat mystical attitude toward that sine qua non of the machine age: the interchangeable part. It seems to go against the Slavic grain to standardize. Consequently, when a machine breaks down (usually in six months' time) it must be replaced entirely. Efforts to "cannibalize," as the mechanics put it, are futile since a part from one drill will not fit another drill. As a result, Swedish drills are now being imported, at considerable cost.

Humanly, the Russians are praised for their ability to survive without complaint the terrible heat. "But," said one Egyptian, "heat is bad for their babies. They turn all red and get sick so they have to send them home." The Russians keep almost entirely to themselves. One of the livelier engineers was the most critical: "They don't go out; they don't dance; they don't do nothing. Just eat and drink!" He shook his head disapprovingly, for the Egyptian with any money is a happy fellow who wants to have a good time in whatever is the going way: alcohol has lately caught on, despite the Prophet's injunction, while the smoking of hashish and kif has gone into decline, the result of stringent new laws against their sale and use. Also the emancipation of women is progressing nicely and women are to be seen in public places. Dancing is popular. In fact, the twist was the rage of Cairo's nightclubs until Nasser banned it.

Sooner or later every Egyptian connected with the High Dam denounces John Foster Dulles. He is the principal demon in the Egyptian hell, largely because the engineers still wish the Americans would come in on the dam—speaking only as technicians, they add quickly, reminding one that they are, after all, Western-trained and used to Western machinery and procedures. Also they find Western life sympathetic. But what's done is done . . . and we would look sadly at one another . . . such is Allah's will. The Soviet is committed to the dam to the end. I suspect that they wish they were out of it: spending four hundred million dollars to build the largest dam in the world in the midst of a desert is a venture more apt than not to leave all participants exhausted and disenchanted with one another. And there, but for the grace of John Foster Dulles, go we.

At my hotel in Cairo I found a message from the president's office. My appointment was canceled, but His Excellency would see me in the next few days. I telephoned the appointments secretary. When? They would let me know. I was to stand by. Meanwhile, there were many people in and out of the Cabinet I could see. Name anyone. I picked Mohammed Hassanein Heikal. He is editor of Cairo's chief newspaper, *Al Ahram*. He is supposed to have written *The Philosophy of the Revolution*, Nasser's *Mein Kampf* (a rather touching work reminiscent more of Pirandello than of Hitler). Heikal is the president's alter ego. An appointment was made for late that afternoon.

I had a drink in a nearby hotel bar with an English journalist who had been some years in Egypt. He is a short, red-faced man who speaks Arabic; he demonstrates the usual love-hate for Nasser which one soon gets used to. "He's a dictator, but then they all are. They have to be. He's personally honest, which few of them are. But the main thing is he's the first man ever to try to do anything for the people here. *The first*. Ever! And it's not just demagoguery. He means it. But the problems! He's inherited the old bureaucracy, the most corrupt in the world. On top of that there aren't enough trained people to run the country, much less all the new business he confiscated last year. The foreigners who used to manage things are gone. Alexandria's a ghost town. Even so, in spite of everything, he's made these people proud to be Egyptians." I said that I thought nationalistic pride, of de Gaulle's *la gloire* sort, too luxurious an emotion in a dangerous world.

"That's not the point. This isn't manifest-destiny stuff. It's that these people really believed they were inferior to everybody else. They thought they really were scum . . . wogs. For centuries. Well, Nasser's changed all that. He's shown them they're like anybody else. We said Egyptians could never run the Suez Canal. Remember? Well, they run it a lot better than we ever did." I asked him about Arab imperialism. Nasser has proposed himself as leader of the Arab world, a new Saladin. Through his radio and through the thousands of Cairo-trained schoolteachers sent out to the various Arab countries, Nasser has tried to incite the people to overthrow their "reactionary" governments and to unite with him in some vague but potent hegemony.

The Englishman laughed. "The joke of course is the Egyptians aren't Arab at all. The Arabs conquered Egypt and stayed. But so have a lot of other races. Nasser himself is only part Arab. The Copts have no Arab blood, while everyone else is a mixture. The Egyptians used to be contemptuous of the Arabs. In fact, their word for Arab means a nomad, a wild man, a . . ." "Hick?" I supplied, and he nodded. "Now everyone's trying to claim pure Arab descent."

We spoke of the more ruthless side of Nasser's reign. Egypt is a police state. Arrests are often indiscriminate. Currently, a journalist is in jail for having provided an American newspaper with the information—accurate—that Nasser is a diabetic. There is nothing resembling representative government. The middle class is in a state of panic.

I asked him about Nasser personally. What sort of a man was he? I got the familiar estimate: great personal charm, most reasonable in conversation, entirely lacking in personal vanity and ostentation . . . he still lives at Heliopolis in the house he owned as a colonel. He tends to be nervous with foreigners, especially with the British and the French. They put him on the defensive. He is a devoted family man, a puritan who was profoundly shocked during his first Cairo meeting with Indonesia's President Sukarno, who gaily asked, "Now, where are the girls?" He worries about gaining weight. He admires Tito because he "showed me how to get help from both sides—without joining either." Nasser in his passion for Egypt has also declared, "I will treat with the devil himself if I have to for my country." But he is wary of foreign commitments. He has said: "An alliance between a big and a small power is an alliance between the wolf and the sheep, and it is bound to end with the wolf devouring the sheep." His relations with the Soviet are correct but not warm. He has imprisoned every Egyptian Communist he can find. He took advantage of a Soviet offer to give technical training to Egyptian students, but when he discovered that their first six months in Moscow were devoted to learning Marxist theory, he withdrew the students and rerouted them to the West. He is thought to be genuinely religious. He is obsessed, as well he might be, by the thought of sudden death.

"He's at the Barrage right now. That's his place downriver. You may as well know you're going to have a hard time seeing him." He looked about to make sure that the ubiquitous barman—a government informer—was out of earshot. Then he whispered: "Nasser was shot at yesterday." I contained my surprise and the Englishman played this dramatic scene with admirable offhandedness. "Complete censorship, of course. It won't hit the papers. He wasn't hurt, but his bodyguard was killed. So he's holed up at the Barrage for the rest of this week." Who shot at him? The Englishman shrugged. Saudi Arabia, Yemen, Syria, Iraq, Israel—any number of governments would like Nasser dead.

I sat in the anteroom of the editor of *Al Ahram*. His secretary went on with her work. I glanced at her desk (I can read upside down if the type is sufficiently large) and noted a copy of the American magazine *Daedalus*. Seeing my interest, she gave it to me. It featured an article on birth control. Heikal himself had made many marginal notes. "A problem, isn't it?" I said. She nodded. "A problem."

I was shown into the editor's office. Heikal is a short, lean man, handsome in the way that certain actors of the Thirties who played suave villains with pencil moustaches were handsome. He smokes cigars. He gives an impression of great energy. He shook my hand; then he darted back to his desk where he was correcting proofs of an editorial. Would I mind? He always liked to go over them at the last minute. He made marginal notes. He puffed cigar smoke. He is an actor, I decided, giving a performance: Malraux without genius. He has the half-challenging, half-placating manner of those men who are close to a prince.

I waited patiently for quite a few minutes. Finally, he slapped his pencil down with a flourish. He was mine. I asked him how many printer's errors he had found. "Eight," he said precisely, "but mostly I like to change at the last minute." I mentioned *Daedalus* and birth control. "A problem," he said. They were doing their best, of course, but it would take twenty years to educate the people. It was a formidable task.

I then made the error of referring to *The Philosophy of the Revolution* as his book. "My book? *My* book? It is Nasser's book." I said that I had thought it was at least a joint effort. "You've been reading Robert St. John's *The Boss*," which indeed I had. "Well, that is not the only mistake in that book," he said drily. I remarked that it was neither shameful nor unusual for politicians to be helped in their literary work. Even President Kennedy had once been accused of having used a ghost to write an entire book. "Yes," said Heikal knowledgeably, "but Sorensen works for Kennedy. I don't work for Nasser. He is my friend. My leader. But I don't work for him." He discussed American politics for a moment; he was the only Egyptian politician or editor I met who knew much about American affairs. I mentioned the recent letter Kennedy had written to Nasser, a personal letter whose contents were more or less known to everyone. Nasser had been sufficiently moved to answer Kennedy personally, not going through the usual Foreign Office machinery. This exchange had been much discussed in Cairo. It was believed that a new era had begun; that the two young presidents would understand one another. But the crux to the renewed dialogue was unchanged: What about Israel? Was there a solution to the Arab-Israel conflict?

"None," said Heikal firmly, ending all debate. "How can there be?" Before I could stop him, he was off in full tirade. I was reminded of 1948, of the seven hundred thousand Arabs driven from their Palestinian homes, of the predatoriness of Israeli foreign policy, and how it is written on the wall of the Knesset that there would one day be a Jewish empire from the Mediterranean to the Euphrates. He spoke of Jewish ingratitude. "The Arabs are the only people *never* to persecute Jews," he said with some accuracy. "English, French, Germans, Spanish, at one time or another every country in Europe persecuted them, but never we. During the last war, we were friends to them. Then they do this! They dispossess Arabs from their homes. They move into a land which isn't theirs. The Jews," he said, with a note of triumph, "are not a race, they're a religion." There is nothing quite so chilling as to hear a familiar phrase in a new context. I relished it. "They are *Europeans*," he said grimly, coming to the point, "setting themselves up in *our* world. No, there is no solution!" But then he became reasonable. "The real fault of course is our weakness, and their strength. Our policy now is to build up Egypt. Perhaps when we are stronger economically there will be less to fear from the Israelis." This seems to be current Egyptian policy.

We discussed Nasser's "Arab socialism." Heikal was emphatic: it was not doctrinaire socialism. It was improvisational. Point-to-point navigation, as it were. I said that despite some of the methods used to expropriate businesses, there was no doubt that some kind of socialism was inevitable for Egypt and that Nasser had merely done the inevitable. But Heikal would not accept this small compliment. "Methods? Methods? You make us sound like Stalin, with your 'methods'!" I said I had not meant to compare Nasser to Stalin. He cut me off. "What we do is legal. Open. It is for the people. How can you accuse us of 'methods' . . ." This time I cut *him* off. With some irritation, I told him that I had no intention of repeating the various horror stories told me by those who had been ruined by his government, their businesses seized, their livelihoods ended. Even allowing for the natural exaggeration of victims, such methods were not apt to please those who were ruined by them. Nor was it only the large corporations which had been nationalized. Innumerable small businesses had also been taken over. An owner would come to work one morning to find an army officer sitting at his desk, directing what had been his business the day before.

Heikal was scornful. "So we take their money. So they are not happy. So what? At least they are still alive! That's something!" He felt this showed great restraint on the part of the government and perhaps he was right. I was reminded of Joseph Stalin's answer to Lady Astor when she asked him, "When are you going to stop killing people?" "The undesirable classes," said the tyrant, turning upon her his coldest eye, "never liquidate themselves."

Wanting to needle Heikal—an irresistible impulse—I said I didn't think that the endlessly vituperative style of Egypt's newspapers was very apt to win them any friends. Israel is the principal victim of these attacks, but any government which does not momentarily please Nasser will get the full treatment from the Arab press and radio.

Heikal took my question personally, as well he might. His voice slipped automatically into the singsong of rhetoric and denunciation. "We write this way because we feel this way. How can we help it? How can we be asked not to say what we feel so strongly? Take the British, *I*

hate the British. I can't help it. I saw them. I know them. Their contempt
for us. Their treachery. And over Suez they were not . . . kind." This was
an unexpected word. "You came into Suez with force." "They," I mur-
mured. "You tried to destroy us." "They," I said somewhat more loudly.
"All right," he said irritably, the tide of his rhetoric briefly stemmed. "*They*
wanted to destroy us. So how can we feel anything but hate for them?
Look what they did to the Arab world after 1918. They brought back the
kings, the sheiks, to keep us medieval. As if we were to occupy England
and restore the lords, break the country up into Saxon kingdoms. So how
can we express ourselves in any way except the way we do?" Like most
rhetorical questions, no answer was desired.

Actually, the fulminating style is inherent in the language (*vide* the
Old Testament). Semitic languages are curiously suited to the emotional
tirade, even when the speaker is not himself an emotional man. By nature Nasser is an unemotional speaker. As a rule he will bore his audiences for an hour or two, droning on sensibly about the state of the
nation. Then when he is in danger of losing them entirely, he allows the
language to do its natural work; he proposes that all Egypt's enemies
"choke in their rage" as well as other gaudy sentiments calculated to keep
his torpid audience awake. Yet to give Nasser his due he is, verbally, one
of the most continent of Arab leaders.

Heikal reverted to Israel. Did I realize that thirty-eight percent of
their budget went for the military as opposed to thirteen percent of
Egypt's budget? Having spent several days poring over the Egyptian
budget, I was surprised that anyone could have come up with any figure
for any department. The only ascertainable fact is that Egypt is flat broke.
But I accepted his figures. I did remark that it must be distressing for Israel—for any country—to be reminded daily that its neighbors, once they
awaken from their "deep slumber," will drive them into the sea. After all,
no one wants to be drowned. Heikal shook his head sadly: didn't I realize that the Israeli military expenditure was for offense, not defense? I
asked him point-blank: "Do you think Israel is planning an offensive war
against Egypt?" He shrugged. I then mentioned his own press's continual
reminder of Israel's financial dependence on the United States. This being true, did he really think that the United States would permit Israel
to embark on a military adventure? We had effectively stopped Israel,

France, and England at the time of Suez. Did he honestly believe that we would now allow Israel, by itself, to launch an attack on Egypt? He edged away. No, he did not think the United States would allow a unilateral action. "But," he added quickly, "you can't blame us for being on guard." Then again he reverted to what is the government's present line: we must strengthen Egypt, concentrate on home problems, create "Arab socialism," become a model for the rest of the Arab world.

As I left, I told him that if I saw Nasser at the end of the week I was perfectly willing to present to the American public Egypt's case against Israel, just as Egypt would like it presented. Partly out of a sense of mischief (we hear altogether too much of the other side) and partly out of a sense of justice, I thought that the Arab case *should* be given attention in the American press. As of now it has been disregarded. In fact, a few years ago the Egyptians, despairing of ever seeing their cause presented impartially in the usual "news" columns, tried to buy an advertisement in *The New York Times*. They were turned down. As a result, the Egyptians are somewhat cynical about our "free press." They are also quite aware that when Israel was being founded in 1948 and the Arabs protested to Harry Truman, he told them with characteristic bluntness: "I do not have hundreds of thousands of Arabs among my constituents." Heikal laughed when I told him that the Arab point of view might one day be given in the American national press. "Your press would never let you," he said with finality, as one journalist to another. "Don't even try."

Another week passed. More appointments were made with Nasser. Each was broken at the last minute, and I was advised to be patient. He would see me soon. But then the Syrian comedy began, disrupting Nasser's schedule. The President of Syria was removed by some army colonels in Damascus. A few days later the young captains in Aleppo tried to overthrow the older officers in Damascus who had overthrown the president. The young men in Aleppo declared that they were for Nasser; they wanted union again with Egypt. Was Nasser behind this plot? Some think yes. Some think no. I suspect no. As one of his closest advisers said, with what seemed candor: "We don't even know these boys in Aleppo. They're much younger than our group." It is protocol in the Middle East that only colonels may start revolutions. Generals are too old, captains too young. In any case, the colonels in Damascus triumphed

over the captains in Aleppo and then in a marvelous gesture of frustra-
tion the colonels restored the president they had overthrown in the first
place. There was no one else, apparently, available for the job. But by the
time this comedy had run its course I had fled Egypt, though just as I was
getting on the plane to Beirut there was yet another telephone message
from the president's office: "His Excellency will definitely see you tomorrow." But I was ready to go, shamefully demonstrating the difference between the amateur and the professional journalist. The professional
would have remained, as Hans Von Kaltenborn once remained six weeks,
to obtain an interview with Nasser. The amateur moves on.

"The Arabs are their own worst enemies," said a foreign diplomat in
Beirut. "They can't present anything to anyone without undermining
themselves. They are self-destructive. In fact, many of them actually believe that since this world is a mess, why bother to alter it when what
really matters is the Paradise to come." I was reminded of the Koran,
where it is written that "The life of the world is only play and idle talk
and pageantry."

The Arabs' religion contributes greatly to the difficulties they are ex-
periencing in the modern world. Americans tend to believe, in a vague,
soupy way, that all religion is A Good Thing. Richard Nixon was much
applauded when he said that a man's religion should never be a matter of
concern in politics, *unless of course he had no religion.* Nixon shook his
head gravely on that one. Yet some religions are more useful than others,
and some religions are downright dangerous to the human spirit and to
the building of a good society.

To understand the Arab world one must understand the Koran, a
work Goethe described as "A holy book which, however often we approach it, always disgusts us anew, but then attracts, and astonishes and
finally compels us to respect it." It is a remarkable work which I shall not
go into here except to note that its Five Pillars are: (1) the creed; (2) the
prayer; (3) the fast; (4) the pilgrimage to Mecca; (5) almsgiving. One unfortunate result of the last: the holiness which accrues to almsgivers has
fostered a demoralizing tradition of beggars. Also, in requesting aid of
other countries, the Arab nations are profoundly self-righteous and de-
manding, on the high moral ground that they are doing the giver a favor
by taking his money and making him more holy. The result has been that

until very recently American aid to Egypt was almost never acknowledged in the press or noted in any other way, except by complaints that the giver, if he weren't so selfish, ought to come through with ever more cash, making himself that much worthier in Allah's eyes. In any event, no quo for the quid is Arab policy, as both the Soviet and ourselves have discovered.

I found myself continually asking diplomats, journalists, and old Arab hands: Why should we give *any* aid to Egypt? What do we gain by it? What should we get from it? Answers were never very precise. Naturally, there was "the Soviet threat." If we don't help Egypt, the Russians will and the Middle East will come into "the Soviet sphere." For a number of reasons this is not likely to happen. Soviet policy in the Arab world has been even more unsuccessful than our own. In 1956, after jailing the local Communists (while accepting Soviet aid for the High Dam), Nasser said quite explicitly: "The Communists have lost faith in religion, which in their opinion is a myth. . . . Our final conclusion is that we shall never repudiate it in exchange for the Communist doctrine." The Muslim world and the Marxist world are an eternity apart. Paradise here and now on earth, as the result of hard work and self-sacrifice, is not a congenial doctrine to the Arab. Also, of some importance is the Egyptian's human response to the Russians: they find them austere, dogmatic, and rather alarming.

One is also reminded that whether Nasser chooses to be absorbed by the Soviet bloc or not, at a time of chaos the Soviets *might* move in and take the country by force. This drastic shift in the world balance of power is not easy to visualize. The Soviets, already overextended financially, are not apt to take on (any more than we are) the burden of governing a starving Egypt. But if they did, it is unlikely that they would then shut down the Suez Canal (England's old nightmare), since, after cotton, the canal is the main source of Egypt's revenue. I would suggest that the strategic value of Egypt to the West is very small, and it merely turns Nasser's head and feeds his sense of unreality for us to pretend that Egypt is of great consequence. Yet it is of *some* consequence, especially now.

The principal source of irritation between Nasser and the United States is Israel, a nation in which we have a large economic and emotional interest. But I got the impression from members of the Egyptian government that the continual tirades against Israel are largely for home consumption. Nations traditionally must have the Enemy to prod them into action. President Kennedy finds it difficult to get any large appropriation bill through our Congress unless he can first prove that it will contribute to the holy war against Communism. Once he has established that he is indeed striking a blow at the Enemy, he can get any money he needs, whether it is to explore the moon or to give assistance to the public schools. In the same way, Nasser needs the idea of Israel to goad his own people into the twentieth century.

Nasser once said to Miles Copeland, "If you want the cooperation of any Middle Eastern leader you must first understand his limitations—those limitations placed on him by the emotions and suspicions of the people he leads—and be reconciled to the fact that you can never ask him to go beyond those limitations. If you feel you *must* have him go beyond them, you must be prepared to help him lessen the limitations." A most rational statement of any politician's dilemma; and one which Dulles in his blithely righteous way ignored, causing Nasser to observe with some bitterness in 1956: "Dulles asked me to commit suicide." National leaders are always followers of public opinion. No matter how well-intentioned they might be privately, they are limited by those they govern. Paradoxically, this is truest of dictators.

Our current policy toward Nasser is sympathetic. It is hard to say to what extent he can or will respond, but it is evident that he is trying. His value to us is much greater now that he has, temporarily, given up hope of leading the Arab world, of becoming the new Saladin. He must make Egypt work first. He is perfectly—sadly—aware that Algeria and Morocco, two Arab nations potentially richer and politically more sophisticated than Egypt, may well provide new leadership for the Muslim world. His only remaining hope is to make "Arab socialism" a success. If it is, then the kings and the sheiks will eventually fall of their own corruption and incompetence, and Nasser's way will be the Arab's way.

What is our role? Since 1952 our assistance to Egypt has totaled $705,000,000. Over half this amount was given or lent in the last three years. So far the Egyptian government has been most scrupulous in its interest payments, etc. However, since July, 1961, when Nasser seized most of the nation's industries and businesses, he has opposed all private investment. The only assistance he will accept (the weak must be firm) is government-to-government, with no political strings. Again, why should we help him?

"Because," said an American economist, "any aid ties him to us, whether he likes it or not, whether he acknowledges it or not. If we help him build the new power plant in Cairo (with Westinghouse assistance), he will have to come to us in the future for parts and technicians. That's good business for us. That keeps *our* economy expanding." This, of course, is the standard rationale for America's foreign-aid program, and up to a point it is valid. Today's empires are held not with the sword but the dollar. It is the nature of the national organism to expand and proliferate. We truly believe that we never wanted a world empire simply because we don't suffer (since Teddy Roosevelt, at least) from a desire to see Old Glory waving over the parliaments of enslaved nations. But we do want to make a buck. We do want to maintain our standard of living. For good or ill, we have no other true national purpose. There is no passion in America for military glory, at least outside of Texas and Arizona. Our materialistic ethos is made quite plain in the phrase "the American way of life."

I submit that our lack of commitment to any great mystique of national destiny is the healthiest thing about us and the reason for our current success. We are simple materialists, not bent on setting fire to the earth as a matter of holy principle, unlike the True Believers with their fierce Either-Ors, their Red or Dead absolutes, when the truth is that the world need be neither, just comfortably pink and lively. Even aid to such a disagreeable and unreliable nation as Nasser's Egypt increases our sphere of influence, expands our markets, maintains our worldly empire. And we are an empire. Americans who would not have it so had best recall Pericles' admonition to those Athenians who wished to shirk imperial responsibilities. We may have been wrong to acquire an empire, Pericles said, but now that we possess one, it is not safe for us to let it go. Nor is it safe for the United States to opt out now. Luckily, our passion for trade and moneymaking and our relatively unromantic view of ourselves has made us surprisingly attractive to the rest of the world, especially to those countries whose rulers suffer from *folie de grandeur*.

Historians often look to the Roman Empire to find analogies with the United States. They flatter us. We live not under the Pax Americana, but the Pax Frigida. I should not look to Rome for comparison but rather to the Most Serene Venetian Republic, a pedestrian state devoted to wealth, comfort, trade, and keeping the peace, especially after inheriting the wreck of the Byzantine Empire, as we have inherited the wreck of the British Empire. Venice was not inspiring but it worked. Ultimately, our danger comes not from the idea of Communism, which (as an Archbishop of Canterbury remarked) is a "Christian heresy" whose materialistic aims (as opposed to means) vary little from our own; rather, it will come from the increasing wealth and skill of other Serene Republics which, taking advantage of our increasing moral and intellectual fatness, will try to seize our markets in the world. If we are to end, it will not be with a Bomb but a bigger Buck. Fortunately, under that sanctimoniousness so characteristic of the American selling something, our governors know that we are fighting not for "the free world" but to hold onto an economic empire not safe or pleasant to let go. The Arab world—or as a salesman would say, "territory"—is almost ours, and we must persevere in landing that account. It will be a big one some day.

Esquire
October 1963

PORNOGRAPHY

The man and the woman make love; attain climax; fall separate. Then she whispers, "I'll tell you who I was thinking of if you'll tell me who you were thinking of." Like most sex jokes, the origins of this pleasant exchange are obscure. But whatever the source, it seldom fails to evoke a certain awful recognition, since few lovers are willing to admit that in the sexual act to create or maintain excitement they may need some mental image as erotic supplement to the body in attendance. One perverse contemporary maintains that when he is with A he thinks of B and when he is with B he thinks of A; each attracts him only to the degree that he is able simultaneously to evoke the image of the other. Also, for those who find the classic positions of "mature" lovemaking unsatisfactory yet dare not distress the beloved with odd requests, sexual fantasy becomes inevitable and the shy lover soon finds himself imposing mentally all sorts of wild images upon his unsuspecting partner, who may also be relying on an inner theater of the mind to keep things going; in which case, those popular writers who deplore "our lack of communication today" may have a point. Ritual and magic also have their devotees. In one of Kingsley Amis's fictions, a man mentally conjugates Latin verbs in order to delay orgasm as he waits chivalrously for his partner's predictably slow response. While another considerate lover (nonfictional) can only reduce tempo by thinking of a large loaf of sliced white bread, manufactured by Bond.

Sexual fantasy is as old as civilization (as opposed to as old as the race), and one of its outward and visible signs is pornographic literature, an entirely middle-class phenomenon, since we are assured by many investigators (Kinsey, Pomeroy, et al.) that the lower orders seldom rely upon sexual fantasy for extra-stimulus. As soon as possible, the uneducated man goes for the real thing. Consequently he seldom masturbates, but when he does he thinks, we are told, of *nothing at all*. This may be the last meaningful class distinction in the West.

Nevertheless, the sex-in-the-head middle classes that D. H. Lawrence so despised are not the way they are because they want deliberately to be cerebral and anti-life; rather they are innocent victims of necessity and tribal law. For economic reasons they must delay marriage as long as possible. For tribal reasons they are taught that sex outside marriage is wrong. Consequently the man whose first contact with a woman occurs when he is twenty will have spent the sexually most vigorous period of his life masturbating. Not unnaturally, in order to make that solitary act meaningful, the theater of his mind early becomes a Dionysian festival, and should he be a resourceful dramatist he may find actual lovemaking disappointing when he finally gets to it, as Bernard Shaw did. One wonders whether Shaw would have been a dramatist at all if he had first made love to a girl at fourteen, as nature intended, instead of at twenty-nine, as class required. Here, incidentally, is a whole new line of literary-psychological inquiry suitable for the master's degree: "Characteristics of the Onanist as Dramatist." Late coupling and prolonged chastity certainly help explain much of the rich dottiness of those Victorians whose peculiar habits planted thick many a quiet churchyard with Rose La Touches.

Until recently, pornography was a small cottage industry among the grinding mills of literature. But now that sex has taken the place of most other games (how many young people today learn bridge?), creating and packaging pornography has become big business, and though the high courts of the American Empire cannot be said to be very happy about this state of affairs, they tend to agree that freedom of expression is as essential to our national life as freedom of meaningful political action is not. Also, despite our governors' paternalistic bias, there are signs that they are becoming less intolerant in sexual matters. This would be a good

thing if one did not suspect that they may regard sex as our bread and cir-
cuses, a means of keeping us off the political streets, in bed and out of
mischief. If this is so, we may yet observe the current president in his
mad search for consensus settling for the consensual.

Among the publishers of pornography ("merchants of smut," as they
say at the FBI), Maurice Girodias is uniquely eminent. For one thing, he
is a second-generation peddler of dirty books (or "d.b.'s," as they call
them on Eighth Avenue). In the 1930s his English father, Jack Kahane,
founded the Obelisk Press in Paris. Among Kahane's authors were Anaïs
Nin, Lawrence Durrell, Cyril Connolly, and of course Henry Miller, whose
books have been underground favorites for what seems like a century. Kahane died in 1939 and his son, Maurice Girodias (he took his mother's
name for reasons not given), continued Kahane's brave work. After the
war, Girodias sold Henry Miller in vast quantities to easily stimulated
GIs. He also revived *Fanny Hill*. He published books in French. He prospered. Then the terror began. Visionary dictatorships, whether of a single man or of the proletariat, tend to disapprove of irregular sex. Being
profoundly immoral in public matters, dictators compensate by insisting
upon what they think to be a rigorous morality in private affairs. General
de Gaulle's private morality appears to have been registered in his wife's
name. In 1946 Girodias was prosecuted for publishing Henry Miller. It
was France's first prosecution for obscenity since the trial of *Madame Bovary* in 1844. Happily, the world's writers rallied to Miller's defense, and
since men of letters are taken solemnly in France, the government
dropped its charges.

In a preface to the recently published *The Olympia Reader*, Girodias
discusses his business arrangements at length; and though none of us is
as candid about money as he is about sex, Girodias does admit that he
lost his firm not as a result of legal persecution but through incompetence, a revelation that gives him avant-garde status in the new pornography of money. Girodias next founded the Olympia Press, devoted to the
creation of pornography, both hard and soft core. His adventures as a
merchant of smut make a nice story. All sorts of writers, good and bad,
were set to work turning out books, often written to order. He would
think up a title (e.g., *With Open Mouth*) and advertise it; if there was sufficient response, he would then commission someone to write a book to

go with the title. Most of his writers used pseudonyms. Terry Southern and Mason Hoffenberg wrote *Candy* under the name of Maxwell Kenton. Christopher Logue wrote *Lust* under the name of Count Palmiro Vicarion, while Alex Trocchi, as Miss Frances Lengel, wrote *Helen and Desire*. Girodias also published Samuel Beckett's *Watt*, Vladimir Nabokov's *Lolita*, and J. P. Donleavy's *The Ginger Man*; perversely, the last three authors chose not to use pseudonyms.

Reading of these happy years, one recalls a similar situation just after the Second War when a number of New York writers were commissioned at so many cents a page to write pornographic stories for a United States Senator. The solon, as they say in smutland, never actually met the writers but through a go-between he guided their stories: a bit more flagellation here, a touch of necrophilia there. . . . The subsequent nervous breakdown of one of the Senator's pornographers, now a celebrated poet, was attributed to the strain of not knowing which of the ninety-six Senators he was writing for.[*]

In 1958 the Fourth French Republic banned twenty-five of Girodias's books, among them *Lolita*. Girodias promptly sued the Ministry of the Interior and, amazingly, won. Unfortunately, five months later, the General saw fit to resume the grandeur of France. De Gaulle was back; and so was Madame de Gaulle. The Minister of the Interior appealed the now defunct Fourth Republic's decision and was upheld. Since then, censorship has been the rule in France. One by one Girodias's books, regardless of merit, have been banned. Inevitably, André Malraux was appealed to and, inevitably, he responded with that elevated double-talk which has been a characteristic of what one suspects will be a short-lived Republic. Girodias is currently in the United States, where he expects to flourish. Ever since our Puritan republic became a gaudy empire, pornography has been a big business for the simple reason that when freedom of expression is joined with the freedom to make a lot of money, the dream of those whose bloody footprints made vivid the snows of Valley Forge is close to fulfillment and that happiness which our Constitution commands us to pursue at hand.

The Olympia Reader is a collection of passages from various books

---

[*]David Ignatius Walsh (Dem., Mass.).

published by Maurice Girodias since 1953. Reading it straight through is a curiously disjointed experience, like sitting through a program of movie trailers. As literature, most of the selections are junk, despite the presence of such celebrated contemporary figures as Nabokov, Genet, and Queneau; and of the illustrious dead, Sade and Beardsley.

Pornography is usually defined as that which is calculated to arouse sexual excitement. Since what arouses X repels Y, no two people are apt to respond in quite the same way to the same stimulus. One man's meat, as they say, is another man's poison, a fact now recognized by the American judiciary, which must rule with wearisome frequency on obscenity. With unexpected good sense, a judge recently observed that since the books currently before him all involved ladies in black leather with whips, they could not be said to corrupt the generality, since a taste for being beaten is hardly common and those who are aroused by such fantasies are already "corrupted" and therefore exempt from laws designed to protect the young and usual. By their nature, pornographies cannot be said to proselytize, since they are written for the already hooked. The worst that can be said of pornography is that it leads not to "antisocial" sexual acts but to the reading of more pornography. As for corruption, the only immediate victim is English prose. Mr. Girodias himself writes like his worst authors ("Terry being at the time in acute financial need . . .") while his moral judgments are most peculiar. With reverence, he describes his hero Sir Roger Casement (a "superlative pederast," whatever that is) as "politically confused, emotionally unbalanced, maudlin when depressed and absurdly naïve when in his best form; but he was exceptionally generous, he had extraordinary courage and a simple human wisdom which sprang from his natural goodness." Here, Mr. Girodias demonstrates a harmony with the age in which he lives. He may or may not have described Sir Roger accurately, but he has certainly drawn an accurate portrait of the Serious American Novelist, 1966.

Of the forty selections Mr. Girodias has seen fit to collect, at least half are meant to be literature in the most ambitious sense, and to the extent that they succeed, they disappoint; Beckett's *Watt*, Queneau's *Zazie*, Donleavy's *The Ginger Man* are incapable of summoning up so much as the ghost of a rose, to appropriate Sir Thomas Browne's handsome phrase. There is also a good deal of Henry Miller, whose reputation as a pornographer is largely undeserved. Though he writes a lot about sex, the only object he seems ever to describe is his own phallus. As a result, unless one lusts specifically for the flesh of Henry Miller, his works cannot be regarded as truly edifying. Yet at Miller's best he makes one irritably conscious of what it is like to be inside his skin, no mean feat . . . the pornographic style, incidentally, is contagious: the stately platitude, the arch paraphrase, the innocent line which starts suddenly to buck with unintended double meanings.

Like the perfect host or madam, Mr. Girodias has tried to provide something for everyone. Naturally there is a good deal of straightforward heterosexual goings-on. Mr. Girodias gives us several examples, usually involving the seduction of an adolescent male by an older woman. For female masochists (and male sadists) he gives us *Story of O*. For homosexual sadists (and masochists) *The Gaudy Image*. For negrophiles (and phobes) *Pinktoes*, whose eloquent author, Chester Himes, new to me, has a sense of humor which sinks his work like a stone. For anal eroticists who like science fiction there are passages from William Burroughs's *Naked Lunch* and *The Soft Machine*. For devotees of camp, new to the scene, the thirty-three-year-old *The Young and Evil* by Charles Henri Ford and Parker Tyler is a pioneer work and reads surprisingly well today. Parenthetically, it is interesting to note the role that clothes play in most of these works, camp, kinky, and straight. Obviously, if there is to be something for everyone, the thoughtful entrepreneur must occasionally provide an old sock or pair of panties for the fetishist to get, as it were, his teeth into. But even writers not aiming at the fetishist audience make much of the ritual taking off and putting on of clothes, and it is significant that the bodies thus revealed are seldom described as meticulously as the clothes are.

Even Jean Genet, always lyric and vague when celebrating cock, becomes unusually naturalistic and detailed when he describes clothes in an excerpt from *The Thieves' Journal*. Apparently when he was a boy in Spain a lover made him dress up as a girl. The experiment was a failure because "Taste is required . . . I was already refusing to have any. I forbade myself to. Of course I would have shown a great deal of it." Nevertheless, despite an inadequate clothes sense, he still tells us far more about the *travesti manqué* than he ever tells us about the body of Stilitano for whom he lusted.

In most pornography, physical descriptions tend to be sketchy. Hardcore pornographers seldom particularize. Inevitably, genitals are massive, but since we never get a good look at the bodies to which they are attached, the effect is so impersonal that one soon longs to read about those more modest yet entirely tangible archetypes, the girl and boy next door, two creatures far more apt to figure in the heated theater of the mind than the voluptuous grotesques of the pulp writer's imagination. Yet by abstracting character and by keeping his human creatures faceless and vague, the pornographer does force the reader to draw upon personal experience in order to fill in the details, thereby achieving one of the ends of all literary art, that of making the reader collaborator.

As usual, it is the Marquis de Sade (here represented by a section from *Justine*) who has the most to say about sex—or rather the use of others as objects for one's own pleasure, preferably at the expense of theirs. In true eighteenth-century fashion, he explains and explains and explains. There is no God, only Nature, which is heedless of the Good as well as of the Bad. Since Nature requires that the strong violate the weak and since it is demonstrably true that Nature made women weak and men strong, therefore . . . and so on. The Marquis's vision—of which so much has been made in this century—is nothing but a rather simpleminded Manicheism, presented with more passion than logic. Yet in his endless self-justification (un-Natural this: Nature never apologizes, never explains) Sade's tirades often strike the Marlovian note: "It is Nature that I wish to outrage. I should like to spoil her plans, to block her advance, to halt the course of the stars, to throw down the globes that float in space—to destroy everything that serves her, to protect everything that harms her, to cultivate everything that irritates her—in a word to insult all her works." But he stops considerably short of his mark. He not only refused to destroy one of her more diverting creations, himself, but he also opposed capital punishment. Even for a French *philosophe*, Sade is remarkably inconsistent, which is why one prefers his letters to his formal argument. Off duty he is more natural and less Natural. While in the Bastille he described himself as possessing an "extreme tendency in everything to lose control of myself, a disordered imagination in sexual matters such as has never been known in this world, an atheist to the point of fanaticism—in two words there I am, and so once again kill me or take me like that, because I shall never change." Latter-day diabolists have tried to make of his "disordered imagination in sexual matters" a religion and, as religions go, it is no more absurd than that of the crucified tripartite man-god. But though Nature is indeed nonhuman and we are without significance except to ourselves, to make of that same indifferent Nature an ally in behavior which is, simply, harmful to human society is to be singularly vicious.

Yet it is interesting to note that throughout all pornography, one theme recurs: the man or woman who manages to capture another human being for use as an unwilling sexual object. Obviously this is one of the commonest of masturbatory daydreams. Sade's originality was to try, deliberately, to make his fantasies real. But he was no Gilles de Rais. He lacked the organizational sense, and his actual adventures were probably closer to farce than to tragedy, more Charlie Chaplin trying to drown Martha Raye than Ilse Koch castrating her paramours at Buchenwald. Incidentally, it is typical of our period that the makers of the play *Marat/Sade* were much admired for having perversely reduced a splendid comic idea to mere tragedy.

Mr. Girodias's sampler should provide future sociologists with a fair idea of what sex was like at the dawn of the age of science. They will no doubt be as amused as most of us are depressed by the extent to which superstition has perverted human nature (not to mention thwarted Nature). Officially the tribal norm continues. The family is the central unit of society. Man's function is to impregnate woman in order to make children. Any sexual act that does not lead to the making of a child is untribal, which is to say antisocial. But though these assumptions are still held by the mass of human society in the West, the pornographers by what they write (as well as by what they omit to mention) show that in actual fact the old laws are not only broken (as always) but are being questioned in a new way.

Until this generation, even nonreligious enemies of irregular sexuality could sensibly argue that promiscuity was bad because it led to venereal disease and to the making of unwanted babies. In addition, sex was a dirty business since bodies stank and why should any truly fastidious person want to compound the filth of his own body's corruption with that of another? Now science has changed all that. Venereal disease has been contained. Babies need not be the result of the sexual act ("I feel so happy and safe now I take the pill"), while improved bathing facilities together with the American Mom's relentless circumcision of boys has made the average human body a temptingly hygienic contraption suitable for all sorts of experiment. To which the moralists can only respond: Rome born again! Sexual license and excessive bathing, as everyone knows, made the Romans effete and unable to stand up to the stalwart puritan savages from the German forests whose sacred mission was to destroy a world gone rotten. This simplistic view of history is a popular one, particularly among those who do not read history. Yet there *is* a basic point at issue and one that should be pondered.

Our tribal standards are an uneasy combination of Mosaic law and the warrior sense of caste that characterized those savage tribesmen who did indeed engulf the world of cities. The contempt for people in trade one still finds amongst the Wasp aristocracy, the sense of honor (furtive but'gnawing), the pride in family, the loyalty to class, and (though covert) the admiration for the military virtues and physical strength are all inherited not from our civilized predecessors who lived in the great cities but from their conquerors, the wandering tribesmen, who planted no grain, built no cities, conducted no trade, yet preyed successfully upon those who did these contemptible, unmanly things. Today of course we are all as mixed in values as in blood, but the unstated assumption that it is better to be physically strong than wise, violent than gentle, continent than sensual, landowner or coupon clipper than shopkeeper, lingers on as a memorial to those marauding tribes who broke into history at the start of the Bronze Age and whose values are with us still, as the Gallup Poll attested recently, when it revealed that the president's war in Vietnam is most popular in the South, the most "tribal" part of the United States. Yet the city is the glory of our race, and today in the West, though we are all city dwellers, we still accept as the true virtue the code of our wild conquerors, even though our actual lives do not conform to their laws, nor should they, nor should we feel guilty because they don't.

In ten thousand years we have learned how to lengthen human lives but we have found no way to delay human puberty. As a result, between the economics of the city and the taboos of the tribe we have created a monstrous sexual ethic. To mention the most notorious paradox: It is not economically convenient for the adolescent to marry; it is not tribally correct for him to have sex outside of marriage. Solutions to this man-made problem range from insistence upon total chastity to a vague permissiveness which, worriedly, allows some sexuality if those involved are "sincere" and "mature" and "loving." Until this generation, tribal moralists could argue with perfect conviction that there was only one correct sexual equation: man plus woman equals baby. All else was vice. But now that half the world lives with famine—and all the world by the year 2000, if Pope Paul's as yet unborn guests are allowed to attend (in his unhappy phrase) the "banquet of life"—the old equation has been changed to read: man plus woman equals baby equals famine. If the human race is to survive, population will have to be reduced drastically, if not by atomic war then by law, an unhappy prospect for civil liberties but better than starving. In any case, it is no longer possible to maintain that those sexual acts which do not create (or simulate the creation of) a child are unnatural; unless, to strike the eschatological note, it is indeed Nature's will that we perish through overpopulation, in which case reliable hands again clutch the keys of Peter.

Fortunately, the pornographers appear to be on the side of survival. They make nothing of virginity deflowered, an important theme for two thousand years; they make nothing of it for the simple reason we make little of it. Straightforward adultery no longer fascinates the pornographer; the scarlet letter has faded. Incest, mysteriously, seldom figures in current pornographies. This is odd. The tribal taboo remains as strong as ever, even though we now know that when members of the same family mate the result is seldom more cretinous or more sickly than its parents. The decline of incest as a marketable theme is probably due to today's inadequate middle-class housing. In large Victorian houses with many rooms and heavy doors, the occupants could be mysterious and exciting to one another in a way that those who live in rackety developments can never hope to be. Not even the lust of a Lord Byron could survive the fact of Levittown.

Homosexuality is now taken entirely for granted by pornographers because we take it for granted. But though there is considerable awareness nowadays of what people actually do, the ancient somewhat ambivalent hostility of the tribe persists; witness *Time* magazine's recent diagnosis of homosexuality as a "pernicious sickness" like influenza or opposing the war in Vietnam. Yet from the beginning, tribal attitudes have been confused on this subject. On the one hand, nothing must be allowed to deflect man the father from his procreative duty. On the other hand, man the warrior is more apt than not to perform homosexual acts. What was undesirable in peace was often a virtue in war, as the Spartans recognized, inventing the buddy system at the expense of the family unit. In general, it would seem that the more warlike the tribe, the more opportunistic the sexual response. "You know where you can find your sex," said that sly chieftain Frederick the Great to his officers, "—in the barracks." Of all the tribes, significantly, the Jews alone were consistently opposed not only to homosexuality but to any acknowledgment of the male as an erotic figure (cf. II Maccabees 4:7–15). But in the great world of pre-Christian cities, it never occurred to anyone that a homosexual act was less "natural" than a heterosexual one. It was simply a matter of taste. From Archilochus to Apuleius, this acceptance of the way people actually are is implicit in what the writers wrote. Suetonius records that of his twelve emperors, eleven went with equal ease from boys to girls and back again without Suetonius ever finding anything remarkable in their "polymorphous perverse" behavior. But all that, as Stanley Kauffmann would say, happened in a "different context."

Nevertheless, despite contexts, we are bisexual. Opportunity and habit incline us toward this or that sexual object. Since additional children are no longer needed, it is impossible to say that some acts are "right" and others "wrong." Certainly to maintain that a homosexual act in itself is antisocial or neurotic is dangerous nonsense, of the sort that the astonishing Dr. Edmund Bergler used to purvey when he claimed that he would "cure" homosexuals, as if this was somehow desirable, like changing Jewish noses or straightening Negro hair in order to make it possible for those who have been so altered to pass more easily through a world of white Christians with snub noses.

Happily, in a single generation, science has changed many old assumptions. Economics has changed others. A woman can now easily support herself, independent of a man. With the slamming of Nora's door, the family ceased to be the essential social unit. Also, the newly affluent middle class can now pursue other pleasures. In the film *The Collector*, a lower-class boy captures an educated girl and after alternately tormenting and boring her, he says balefully, "If more people had more time and money, there would be a lot more of this." This got an unintended laugh in the theater, but he is probably right. Sexual experiment is becoming more open. A placid Midwestern town was recently appalled to learn that its young married set was systematically swapping wives. In the cities, group sex is popular, particularly among the young. Yet despite the new freedoms that the pornographers reflect (sadly for them, since their craft must ultimately wither away), the world they show, though closer to human reality than that of the tribalists, reveals a new illness: the powerlessness that most people feel in an overpopulated and overorganized society.

The sado-masochist books that dominate this year's pornography are not the result of a new enthusiasm for the *vice anglais* so much as a symptom of helplessness in a society where most of the male's aggressive-creative drive is thwarted. The will to prevail is a powerful one, and if it is not fulfilled in work or in battle, it may find an outlet in sex. The man who wants to act out fantasies of tying up or being tied up is imposing upon his sex life a power drive which became socially undesirable once he got onto that escalator at IBM that will take him by predictable stages to early retirement and the medically prolonged boredom of sunset years. Solution of this problem will not be easy, to say the least.

Meanwhile, effort must be made to bring what we think about sex and what we say about sex and what we do about sex into some kind of realistic relationship. Indirectly, the pornographers do this. They recognize that the only sexual norm is that there is none. Therefore, in a civilized society law should not function at all in the area of sex except to protect people from being "interfered with" against their will.

Unfortunately, even the most enlightened of the American state codes (Illinois) still assumes that since adultery is a tribal sin it must be regarded as a civil crime. It is not, and neither is prostitution, that most useful of human institutions. Traditionally, liberals have opposed prostitution on the ground that no one ought to be forced to sell his body because of poverty. Yet in our Affluency, prostitution continues to flourish for the simple reason that it is needed. If most men and women were forced to rely upon physical charm to attract lovers, their sexual lives would be not only meager but in a youth-worshiping country like America painfully brief. Recognizing this state of affairs, a Swedish psychologist recently proposed state brothels for women as well as for men, in recognition of the sad biological fact that the middle-aged woman is at her sexual peak at a time when she is no longer able to compete successfully with younger women. As for the prostitutes themselves, they practice an art as legitimate as any other, somewhere between that of masseur and psychiatrist. The best are natural healers and, contrary to tribal superstition, they often enjoy their work. It is to the credit of today's pornographer that intentionally or not, he is the one who tells us most about the extraordinary variety of human sexual response. In his way he shows us as we are, rather like those Fun House mirrors which, even as they distort and mock the human figure, never cease to reflect the real thing.

The New York Review of Books
March 31, 1966

THE HOLY FAMILY

From the beginning of the Republic, Americans have enjoyed accusing the first magistrate of kingly ambition. Sometimes seriously but more often derisively, the president is denounced as a would-be king, subverting the Constitution for personal ends. From General Washington to the present incumbent, the wielder of power has usually been regarded with suspicion, a disagreeable but not unhealthy state of affairs for both governor and governed. Few presidents, however, have been accused of wanting to establish family dynasties, if only because most presidents have found it impossible to select a successor of any sort, much less promote a relative. Each of the Adamses and the Harrisons reigned at an interval of not less than a political generation from the other, while the two Roosevelts were close neither in blood nor in politics. But now something new is happening in the Republic, and as the Chinese say, we are living "in interesting times."

In 1960, with the election of the thirty-fifth president, the famous ambition of Joseph P. Kennedy seemed at last fulfilled. He himself had come a long way from obscurity to great wealth and prominence; now his eldest surviving son, according to primogeniture, had gone the full distance and become president. It was a triumph for the patriarch. It was also a splendid moment for at least half the nation. What doubts one may have had about the Kennedys were obscured by the charm and intelligence of John F. Kennedy. He appeared to be beautifully on to himself; he was also on to us; there is even evidence that he was on to the family, too. As a result, there were few intellectuals in 1960 who were not beguiled by the spectacle of a president who seemed always to be standing at a certain remove from himself, watching with amusement his own performance. He was an ironist in a profession where the prize usually goes to the apparent cornball. With such a man as chief of state, all things were possible. He would "get America moving again."

But then mysteriously the thing went wrong. Despite fine rhetoric and wise commentary, despite the glamor of his presence, we did not move, and if historians are correct when they tell us that presidents are "made" in their first eighteen months in office, then one can assume that the Kennedy administration would never have fulfilled our hopes, much less his own. Kennedy was of course ill-fated from the beginning. The Bay of Pigs used up much of his credit in the bank of public opinion, while his attempts at social legislation were resolutely blocked by a more than usually obstructive Congress. In foreign affairs he was overwhelmed by the masterful Khrushchev and not until the Cuban missile crisis did he achieve tactical parity with that sly gambler. His administration's one achievement was the test-ban treaty, an encouraging footnote to the cold war.

Yet today Kennedy dead has infinitely more force than Kennedy living. Though his administration was not a success, he himself has become an exemplar of political excellence. Part of this phenomenon is attributable to the race's need for heroes, even in deflationary times. But mostly the legend is the deliberate creation of the Kennedy family and its clients. Wanting to regain power, it is now necessary to show that once upon a time there was indeed a Camelot beside the Potomac, a golden age forever lost unless a second Kennedy should become the president. And so, to insure the restoration of that lovely time, the past must be transformed, dull facts transcended, and the dead hero extolled in films, through memorials, and in the pages of books.

The most notorious of the books has been William Manchester's *The Death of a President*. Hoping to stop Jim Bishop from writing one of his ghoulish *The Day They Shot* sagas, the Kennedys decided to "hire" Mr. Manchester to write their version of what happened at Dallas. Unfortunately, they have never understood that treason is the natural business of clerks. Mr. Manchester's use of Mrs. Kennedy's taped recollections did not please the family. The famous comedy of errors that ensued not only insured the book's success but also made current certain intimate details which the family preferred for the electorate not to know, such as the president's selection of Mrs. Kennedy's dress on that last day in order, as he put it, "to show up those cheap Texas broads," a remark not calculated to give pleasure to the clients of Neiman-Marcus. Also, the family's irrational dislike of President Johnson came through all too plainly, creating an unexpected amount of sympathy for that least sympathetic of magistrates. Aware of what was at stake, Mrs. Kennedy tried to alter a book which neither she nor her brothers-in-law had read. Not since Mary Todd Lincoln has a president's widow been so fiercely engaged with legend if not history.

But then, legend-making is necessary to the Kennedy future. As a result, most of the recent books about the late president are not so much political in approach as religious. There is the ritual beginning of the book which is the end: the death at Dallas. Then the witness goes back in time to the moment when he first met the Kennedys. He finds them strenuous but fun. Along with riotous good times, there is the constant question: How are we to elect Jack president? This sort of talk was in the open after 1956, but as long ago as 1943, according to *The Pleasure of His Company*, Paul B. Fay, Jr., made a bet that one day Jack would be JFK.

From the beginning the godhead shone for those who had the eyes to see. The witness then gives us his synoptic version of the making of the president. Once again we visit cold Wisconsin and dangerous West Virginia (can a young Catholic war hero defeat a Protestant accused of being a draft dodger in a poor mining state where primary votes are bought and sold?). From triumph to triumph the hero proceeds to the convention at Los Angeles, where the god is recognized. The only shadow upon that perfect day is cast, significantly, by Lyndon B. Johnson. Like Lucifer he challenged the god at the convention, and was struck down only to be raised again as son of morning. The deal to make Johnson vice-president still causes violent argument among the new theologians. Pierre Salinger in *With Kennedy* quotes JFK as observing glumly, "The whole story will never be known, and it's just as well that it won't be." Then the campaign itself. The great television debates (Quemoy and Matsu) in which Nixon's obvious lack of class, as classy Jack duly noted, did him in—barely. The narrowness of the electoral victory was swiftly erased by the splendor of the inaugural ("It all began in the cold": Arthur M. Schlesinger, Jr., *A Thousand Days*). From this point on, the thousand days unfold in familiar sequence and, though details differ from gospel to gospel, the story already possesses the quality of a passion play: disaster at Cuba One, triumph at Cuba Two; the eloquent speeches; the fine pageantry; and always the crowds and the glory, ending at Dallas.

With Lucifer now rampant upon the heights, the surviving Kennedys are again at work to regain the lost paradise, which means that books must be written not only about the new incarnation of the Kennedy godhead but the old. For it is the dead hero's magic that makes legitimate the family's pretensions. As an Osiris-Adonis-Christ figure, JFK is already the subject of a cult that may persist, through the machinery of publicity, long after all memory of his administration has been absorbed by the golden myth now being created in a thousand books to the single end of maintaining in power our extraordinary holy family.

The most recent batch of books about JFK, though hagiographies, at times cannot help but illuminate the three themes which dominate any telling of the sacred story: money, image-making, family. That is the trinity without which nothing. Mr. Salinger, the late president's press secretary, is necessarily concerned with the second theme, though he touches on the other two. Paul B. Fay, Jr. (a wartime buddy of JFK and under secretary of the Navy) is interesting on every count, and since he seems not to know what he is saying, his book is the least calculated and the most lifelike of the ones so far published. Other books at hand are Richard J. Whalen's *The Founding Father* (particularly good on money and family) and Evelyn Lincoln's *My Twelve Years with John F. Kennedy*, which in its simple way tells us a good deal about those who are drawn to the Kennedys.

While on the clerical staff of a Georgia congressman, Mrs. Lincoln decided in 1952 that she wanted to work for "someone in Congress who seemed to have what it takes to be President"; after a careful canvass, she picked the representative from the Massachusetts Eleventh District. Like the other witnesses under review, she never says *why* she wants to work for a future president; it is taken for granted that anyone would, an interesting commentary on all the witnesses from Schlesinger (whose *A Thousand Days* is the best political novel since *Coningsby*) to Theodore Sorensen's dour *Kennedy*. Needless to say, in all the books there is not only love and awe for the fallen hero who was, in most cases, the witness's single claim to public attention, but there are also a remarkable number of tributes to the holy family. From Jacqueline (Isis-Aphrodite-Madonna) to Bobby (Ares and perhaps Christ-to-be) the Kennedys appear at the very least as demigods, larger than life. Bobby's hard-working staff seldom complained, as Mr. Salinger put it, "because we all knew that Bob was working just a little harder than we were." For the same reason "we could accept without complaint [JFK's] bristling temper, his cold sarcasm, and his demands for always higher standards of excellence because we knew he was driving himself harder than he was driving us—despite great and persistent physical pain and personal tragedy." Mrs. Lincoln surprisingly finds the late president "humble"—doubtless since the popular wisdom requires all great men to be humble. She refers often to his "deep low voice" [*sic*], "his proud head held high, his eyes fixed firmly on the goals—sometimes seemingly impossible goals—he set for himself and all those around him." Mr. Schlesinger's moving threnody at the close of *his* gospel makes it plain that we will not see JFK's like again, at least not until the administration of Kennedy II.

Of the lot, only Mr. Fay seems not to be writing a book with an eye to holding office in the next Kennedy administration. He is garrulous and indiscreet (the Kennedys are still displeased with his memoirs even though thousands of words were cut from the manuscript on the narrow theological ground that since certain things he witnessed fail to enhance the image, they must be apocryphal). On the subject of the Kennedys and money, Mr. Fay tells a most revealing story. In December 1959, the family was assembled at Palm Beach; someone mentioned money, "causing Mr. [Joseph] Kennedy to plunge in, fire blazing from his eyes. 'I don't know what is going to happen to this family when I die,' Mr. Kennedy said. 'There is no one in the entire family, except Joan and Teddy, who is living within their means. No one appears to have the slightest concern for how much they spend.'" The tirade ended with a Kennedy sister running from the room in tears, her extravagance condemned in open

family session. Characteristically, Jack deflected the progenitor's wrath
with the comment that the only "solution is to have Dad work harder." A
story which contradicts, incidentally, Mr. Salinger's pious "Despite his
great wealth and his generosity in contributing all of his salaries as Congressman, Senator and President to charities, the President was not a
man to waste pennies."

But for all the founding father's grumbling, the children's attitude
toward money—like so much else—is pretty much what he wanted it to
be. It is now a familiar part of the sacred story of how Zeus made each of
the nine Olympians individually wealthy, creating trust funds which now
total some ten million dollars per god or goddess. Also at the disposal of
the celestials is the great fortune itself, estimated at a hundred, two hundred, three hundred, or whatever hundred millions of dollars, adminis-
tered from an office on Park Avenue, to which the Kennedys send their
bills, for we are told in *The Founding Father*, "the childhood habit of dependence persisted in adult life. As grown men and women the younger
Kennedys still look to their father's staff of accountants to keep track of
their expenditures and see to their personal finances." There are, of
course, obvious limitations to not understanding the role of money in the
lives of the majority. The late president was aware of this limitation and
he was forever asking his working friends how much money they made.
On occasion, he was at a disadvantage because he did not understand
the trader's mentality. He missed the point to Khrushchev at Vienna and
took offense at what, after all, was simply the boorishness of the market-
place. His father, an old hand in Hollywood, would have understood better the mogul's bluffing.

It will probably never be known how much money Joe Kennedy has
spent for the political promotion of his sons. At the moment, an estimated million dollars a year is being spent on Bobby's behalf, and this
sum can be matched year after year until 1972, and longer. Needless to
say, the sons are sensitive to the charge that their elections are bought.
As JFK said of his 1952 election to the Senate, "People say 'Kennedy
bought the election. Kennedy could never have been elected if his father
hadn't been a millionaire.' Well, it wasn't the Kennedy name and the Kennedy money that won that election. I beat Lodge because I hustled for
three years" (quoted in *The Founding Father*). But of course without the

Kennedy name and the Kennedy money, he would not even have been a contender. Not only was a vast amount of money spent for his election in the usual ways, but a great deal was spent in not so usual ways. For instance, according to Richard J. Whalen, right after the pro-Lodge Boston *Post* unexpectedly endorsed Jack Kennedy for the Senate, Joe Kennedy loaned the paper's publisher $500,000.

But the most expensive legitimate item in today's politics is the making of the image. Highly paid technicians are able to determine with alarming accuracy just what sort of characteristics the public desires at any given moment in a national figure, and with adroit handling a personable candidate can be made to seem whatever the times require. The Kennedys are not of course responsible for applying to politics the techniques of advertising (the two have always gone hand in hand), but of contemporary politicians (the Rockefellers excepted) the Kennedys alone possess the money to maintain one of the most remarkable self-publicizing machines in the history of advertising, a machine which for a time had the resources of the federal government at its disposal.

It is in describing the activities of a chief press officer at the White House that Mr. Salinger is most interesting. A talented image maker, he was responsible, among other things, for the televised press conferences in which the president was seen at his best, responding to simple questions with careful and often charming answers. That these press conferences were not very informative was hardly the fault of Mr. Salinger or the president. If it is true that the medium is the message and television is the coolest of all media and to be cool is desirable, then the televised thirty-fifth president was positively glacial in his effectiveness. He was a natural for this time and place, largely because of his obsession with the appearance of things. In fact, much of his political timidity was the result of a quite uncanny ability to sense how others would respond to what he said or did, and if he foresaw a negative response, he was apt to avoid action altogether. There were times, however, when his superb sense of occasion led him astray. In the course of a speech to the Cuban refugees in Miami, he was so overwhelmed by the drama of the situation that he practically launched on the spot a second invasion of that beleaguered island. Yet generally he was cool. He enjoyed the game of pleasing others, which is the actor's art.

He was also aware that vanity is perhaps the strongest of human emotions, particularly the closer one comes to the top of the slippery pole. Mrs. Kennedy once told me that the last thing Mrs. Eisenhower had done before leaving the White House was to hang a portrait of herself in the entrance hall. The first thing Mrs. Kennedy had done on moving in was to put the portrait in the basement, on aesthetic, not political grounds. Overhearing this, the president told an usher to restore the painting to its original place. "The Eisenhowers are coming to lunch tomorrow," he explained patiently to his wife, "and that's the first thing she'll look for." Mrs. Lincoln records that before the new Cabinet met, the president and Bobby were about to enter the Cabinet room when the president "said to his brother, 'Why don't you go through the other door?' The President waited until the Attorney General entered the Cabinet room from the hall door, and then he walked into the room from my office."

In its relaxed way Mr. Fay's book illuminates the actual man much better than the other books if only because he was a friend to the president, and not just an employee. He is particularly interesting on the early days when Jack could discuss openly the uses to which he was being put by his father's ambition. Early in 1945 the future president told Mr. Fay how much he envied Fay his postwar life in sunny California while "I'll be back here with Dad trying to parlay a lost PT boat and a bad back into a political advantage. I tell you, Dad is ready right now and can't understand why Johnny boy isn't 'all engines full ahead.' " Yet the exploitation of son by father had begun long before the war. In 1940 a thesis written by Jack at Harvard was published under the title *Why England Slept*, with a foreword by longtime, balding family friend Henry Luce. The book became a best-seller and (Richard J. Whalen tells us) as Joe wrote at the time in a letter to his son, "You would be surprised how a book that really makes the grade with high-class people stands you in good stead for years to come."

Joe was right of course and bookmaking is now an important part of the holy family's home industry. As Mrs. Lincoln observed, when JFK's collection of political sketches "won the Pulitzer prize for biography in 1957, the Senator's prominence as a scholar and statesman grew. As his book continued to be a best seller, he climbed higher up on public-opinion polls and moved into a leading position among presidential pos-

sibilities for 1960." Later Bobby would "write" a book about how he almost nailed Jimmy Hoffa; and so great was the impact of this work that
many people had the impression that Bobby had indeed put an end to the
career of that turbulent figure.

Most interesting of all the mythmaking was the creation of Jack the
war hero. John Hersey first described for *The New Yorker* how Jack's navy
boat was wrecked after colliding with a Japanese ship; in the course of a
long swim, the young skipper saved the life of a crewman, an admirable
thing to do. Later they were all rescued. Since the officer who survived
was Ambassador Kennedy's son, the story was deliberately told and retold
as an example of heroism unequaled in war's history. Through constant
repetition the simple facts of the story merged into a blurred impression
that somehow at some point a unique act of heroism had been committed by Jack Kennedy. The last telling of the story was a film starring Cliff
Robertson as JFK (the president had wanted Warren Beatty for the part,
but the producer thought Beatty's image was "too mixed up").

So the image was created early: the high-class book that made the
grade; the much-publicized heroism at war; the election to the House of
Representatives in 1946. From that point on, the publicity was constant
and though the congressman's record of service was unimpressive, he
himself was photogenic and appealing. Then came the Senate, the marriage, the illnesses, the second high-class book, and the rest is history.
But though it was Joe Kennedy who paid the bills and to a certain extent
managed the politics, the recipient of all this attention was meanwhile
developing into a shrewd psychologist. Mr. Fay quotes a letter written
him by the new senator in 1953. The tone is jocular (part of the charm
of Mr. Fay's book is that it captures as no one else has the preppish side
to JFK's character; he was droll, particularly about himself, in a splendid
W. C. Fields way): "I gave everything a good deal of thought. I am getting
married this fall. This means the end of a promising political career, as it
has been based up to now almost completely on the old sex appeal." After a few more sentences in this vein the groom-to-be comes straight to
the point. "Let me know the general reaction to this in the Bay area." He
did indeed want to know, like a romantic film star, what effect marriage
would have on his career. But then most of his life was governed, as
Mrs. Lincoln wrote of the year 1959, "by the public-opinion polls. We

were not unlike the people who check their horoscope each day before venturing out." And when they did venture out, it was always to create an illusion. As Mrs. Lincoln remarks in her guileless way: after Senator Kennedy returned to Washington from a four-week tour of Europe, "it was obvious that his stature as a Senator had grown, for he came back as an authority on the current situation in Poland."

It is not to denigrate the late president or the writers of his gospel that neither he nor they ever seemed at all concerned by the bland phoniness of so much of what he did and said. Of course politicians have been pretty much the same since the beginning of history, and part of the game is creating illusion. In fact, the late president himself shortly after Cuba Two summed up what might very well have been not only his political philosophy but that of the age in which we live. When asked whether or not the Soviet's placement of missiles in Cuba would have actually shifted the balance of world power, he indicated that he thought not. "But it would have politically changed the balance of power. It would have appeared to, and appearances contribute to reality."

From the beginning, the holy family has tried to make itself appear to be what it thinks people want rather than what the realities of any situation might require. Since Bobby is thought by some to be ruthless, he must therefore be photographed as often as possible with children, smiling and happy and athletic, in every way a boy's ideal man. Politically, he must *seem* to be at odds with the present administration without ever actually taking any important position that President Johnson does not already hold. Bobby's Vietnamese war dance was particularly illustrative of the technique. A step to the Left (let's talk to the Viet Cong), followed by two steps to the Right, simultaneously giving "the beards"—as he calls them—the sense that he is for peace in Vietnam while maintaining his brother's war policy. Characteristically, the world at large believes that if JFK were alive there would be no war in Vietnam. The mythmakers have obscured the fact that it was JFK who began our active participation in the war when, in 1961, he added to the six hundred American observers the first of a gradual buildup of American troops, which reached twenty thousand at the time of his assassination. And there is no evidence that he would not have persisted in that war, for, as he said to a friend shortly before he died, "I have to go all the way with this one." He could not suffer a second Cuba and hope to maintain the appearance of Defender of the Free World at the ballot box in 1964.

The authors of the latest Kennedy books are usually at their most interesting when they write about themselves. They are cautious, of course (except for the jaunty Mr. Fay), and most are thinking ahead to Kennedy II. Yet despite a hope of future preferment, Mr. Salinger's self-portrait is a most curious one. He veers between a coarse unawareness of what it was all about (he never, for instance, expresses an opinion of the war in Vietnam), and a solemn bogusness that is most putting off. Like an after-dinner speaker, he characterizes everyone ("Clark Clifford, the brilliant Washington lawyer"); he pays heavy tribute to his office staff; he praises Rusk and the State Department, remarking that "JFK had more effective liaison with the State Department than any President in history," which would have come as news to the late president. Firmly Mr. Salinger puts Arthur Schlesinger, Jr., in his place, saying that he himself never heard the president express a lack of confidence in Rusk. Mr. Salinger also remarks that though Schlesinger was "a strong friend" of the president (something Mr. Salinger, incidentally, was not), "JFK occasionally was impatient with their [Schlesinger's memoranda] length and frequency." Mrs. Lincoln also weighs in on the subject of the historian-in-residence. Apparently JFK's "relationship with Schlesinger was never that close. He admired Schlesinger's brilliant mind, his enormous store of information . . . but Schlesinger was never more than an ally and assistant."

It is a tribute to Kennedy's gift for compartmentalizing the people in his life that none knew to what extent he saw the others. Mr. Fay was an after-hours buddy. Mrs. Lincoln was the girl in the office. Mr. Salinger was a technician and not a part of the president's social or private or even, as Mr. Salinger himself admits, political life. Contrasting his role with that of James Hagerty, Mr. Salinger writes, "My only policy duties were in the information field. While Jim had a voice in deciding what the administration would do, I was responsible only for presenting that decision to the public in a way and at a time that would generate the best possible reception." His book is valuable only when he discusses the relations between press and government. And of course when he writes about himself. His 1964 campaign for the Senate is nicely told and it is good to know that he lost because he came out firmly for fair housing on the ground that "morally I had no choice—not after sweating out Birmingham and Oxford with John F. Kennedy." This is splendid but it might have made his present book more interesting had he told us something about that crucial period of sweating out. Although he devotes a chapter to telling how he did not take a fifty-mile hike, he never discusses Birmingham, Oxford, or the black revolution.

All in all, his book is pretty much what one might expect of a PR man. He papers over personalities with the reflexive and usually inaccurate phrase (Eisenhower and Kennedy "had deep respect for each other"; Mrs. Kennedy has "a keen understanding of the problems which beset mankind"). Yet for all his gift at creating images for others, Mr. Salinger seems not to have found his own. Uneasily he plays at being U.S. Senator, fat boy at court, thoughtful emissary to Khrushchev. Lately there has been a report in the press that he is contemplating writing a novel. If he does, Harold Robbins may be in the sort of danger that George Murphy never was. The evidence at hand shows that he has the gift. Describing his divorce from "Nancy, my wife of eight years," Mr. Salinger manages in a few lines to say everything. "An extremely artistic woman, she was determined to live a quieter life in which she could pursue her skills as a ceramicist. And we both knew that I could not be happy unless I was on the move. It was this difference in philosophies, not a lack of respect, that led to our decision to obtain a divorce. But a vacation in Palm Springs, as Frank Sinatra's guest, did much to revive my spirits."

Mr. Fay emerges as very much his own man, and it is apparent that he amused the president at a level which was more that of a playmate escorting the actress Angie Dickinson to the Inaugural than as serious companion to the prince. Unlike the other witnesses, Mr. Fay has no pretensions about himself. He tells how "the President then began showing us the new paintings on the wall. 'Those two are Renoirs and that's a Cézanne,' he told us. Knowing next to nothing about painters or paintings, I asked, 'Who are they?' The President's response was predictable, 'My God, if you ask a question like that, do it in a whisper or wait till we get outside. We're trying to give this administration a semblance of class.' " The president saw the joke; he also saw the image which must at all times be projected. Parenthetically, a majority of the recorded anecdotes about Kennedy involve keeping up appearances; he was compulsively given to emphasizing, often with great charm, the division between how things must be made to seem, as opposed to the way they are. This division is noticeable, even in the censored version of Mr. Manchester's *The Death of a President*. The author records that when Kennedy spoke at Houston's coliseum, Jack Valenti, crouched below the lectern, was able to observe the extraordinary tremor of the president's hands, and the artful way in which he managed to conceal them from the audience. This tension between the serene appearance and that taut reality add to the poignancy of the true legend, so unlike the Parson Weems version Mrs. Kennedy would like the world to accept.

Money, image, family: the three are extraordinarily intertwined. The origin of the Kennedy sense of family is the holy land of Ireland, priest-ridden, superstitious, clannish. While most of the West in the nineteenth century was industrialized and urbanized, Ireland remained a famine-ridden agrarian country, in thrall to politicians, homegrown and British, priest and lay. In 1848, the first Kennedy set up shop in Boston, where the Irish were exploited and patronized by the Wasps; not unnaturally, the Irish grew bitter and vengeful and finally asserted themselves at the ballot box. But the old resentment remained as late as Joe Kennedy's generation and with it flourished a powerful sense that the family is the only unit that could withstand the enemy, as long as each member remained loyal to the others, "regarding life as a joint venture between one generation and the next." In *The Fruitful Bough*, a privately printed cluster of tributes to the Elder Kennedy (collected by Edward M. Kennedy) we are told, in Bobby's words, that to Joe Kennedy "the most important thing . . . was the advancement of his children . . . except for his influence and encouragement, my brother Jack might not have run for the Senate in 1952." (So much for JFK's comment that it was his own "hustling" that got him Lodge's seat.)

The father is of course a far more interesting figure than any of his sons if only because his will to impose himself upon a society which he felt had snubbed him has been in the most extraordinary way fulfilled. He drove his sons to "win, win, win." But never at any point did he pause to ask himself or them just what it was they were supposed to win. He taught them to regard life as a game of Monopoly (a family favorite): you

put up as many hotels as you can on Ventnor Avenue and win. Consequently, some of the failure of his son's administration can be ascribed to
the family philosophy. All his life Jack Kennedy was driven by his father
and then by himself to be first in politics, which meant to be the president. But once that goal had been achieved, he had no future, no place
else to go. This absence of any sense of the whole emerged in the famous
exchange between him and James Reston, who asked the newly elected
president what his philosophy was, what vision did he have of the good
life. Mr. Reston got a blank stare for answer. Kennedy apologists are
quick to use this exchange as proof of their man's essentially pragmatic
nature ("pragmatic" was a favorite word of the era, even though its political meaning is opportunist). As they saw it: give the president a specific
problem and he will solve it through intelligence and expertise. A "philosophy" was simply of no use to a man of action. For a time, actual philosophers were charmed by the thought of an intelligent young empiricist
fashioning a New Frontier.

Not until the second year of his administration did it become plain
that Kennedy was not about to do much of anything. Since his concern
was so much with the appearance of things, he was at his worst when
confronted with those issues where a moral commitment might have in-
formed his political response not only with passion but with shrewdness.
Had he challenged the Congress in the Truman manner on such bills as
Medicare and Civil Rights, he might at least have inspired the country, if
not the Congress, to follow his lead. But he was reluctant to rock the
boat, and it is significant that he often quoted Hotspur on summoning
spirits from the deep: any man can summon, but will the spirits come?
JFK never found out; he would not take the chance. His excuse in private for his lack of force, particularly in dealing with the Congress, was
the narrow electoral victory of 1960. The second term, he declared,
would be the one in which all things might be accomplished. With a solid
majority behind him, he could work wonders. But knowing his character,
it is doubtful that the second term would have been much more useful
than the first. After all, he would have been constitutionally a lame duck
president, interested in holding the franchise for his brother. The family,
finally, was his only commitment and it colored all his deeds and judgment.

In 1960, after listening to him denounce Eleanor Roosevelt at some length, I asked him why he thought she was so much opposed to his candidacy. The answer was quick: "She hated my father and she can't stand it that his children turned out so much better than hers." I was startled at how little he understood Mrs. Roosevelt, who, to be fair, did not at all understand him, though at the end she was won by his personal charm. Yet it was significant that he could not take seriously any of her political objections to him (e.g., his attitude to McCarthyism); he merely assumed that she, like himself, was essentially concerned with family and, envying the father, would want to thwart the son. He was, finally, very much his father's son even though, as all the witnesses are at pains to remind us, he did not share that magnate's political philosophy—which goes without saying, since anyone who did could not be elected to anything except possibly the Chamber of Commerce. But the Founding Father's confidence in his own wisdom ("I know more about Europe than anybody else in this country," he said in 1940, "because I've been closer to it longer") and the assumption that he alone knew the absolute inside story about everything is a trait inherited by the sons, particularly Bobby, whose principal objection to the "talking liberals" is that they never know what's really going on, as he in his privileged place does but may not tell. The Kennedy children have always observed our world from the heights.

The distinguished jurist Francis Morrissey tells in *The Fruitful Bough* a most revealing story of life upon Olympus. "During the Lodge campaign, the Ambassador told [Jack and me] clearly that the campaign . . . would be the toughest fight he could think of, but there was no question that Lodge would be beaten, and if that should come to pass Jack would be nominated and elected President. . . . In that clear and commanding voice of his he said to Jack, 'I will work out the plans to elect you President. It will not be any more difficult for you to be elected President than it will be to win the Lodge fight . . . you will need to get about twenty key men in the country to get the nomination for it is these men who will control the convention. . . .' "

One of the most fascinating aspects of politician-watching is trying to determine to what extent any politician believes what he says. Most of course never do, regarding public statements as necessary noises to soothe the electorate or deflect the wrath of the passionate, who are forever mucking things up for the man who wants decently and normally to rise. Yet there are cases of politicians who have swayed themselves by their own speeches. Take a man of conservative disposition and force him to give liberal speeches for a few years in order to be elected and he will, often as not, come to believe himself. There is evidence that JFK often spellbound himself. Bobby is something else again. Andrew Kopkind in *The New Republic* once described Bobby's career as a series of "happenings": the McCarthy friend and fellow traveler of one year emerges as an intense New York liberal in another, and between these two happenings there is no thread at all to give a clue as to what the man actually thinks or who he really is. That consistency which liberals so furiously demanded of the hapless Nixon need not apply to any Kennedy.

After all, as the recent gospels point out, JFK himself was slow to become a liberal, to the extent he ever was (in our society no working politician can be radical). As JFK said to James MacGregor Burns, "Some people have their liberalism 'made' by the time they reach their late twenties. I didn't. I was caught in crosscurrents and eddies. It was only later that I got into the stream of things." His comment made liberalism sound rather like something run up by a tailor, a necessary garment which he regrets that he never had time in his youth to be fitted for. Elsewhere (in William Manchester's *Portrait of a President*) he explains those "currents and eddies." Of his somewhat reactionary career in the House of Representatives he said, "I'd just come out of my father's house at the time, and these were the things I knew." It is of course a truism that character is formed in one's father's house. Ideas may change but the attitude toward others does not. A father who teaches his sons that the only thing that matters is to be first, not second, not third, is obviously (should his example be followed) going to be rewarded with energetic sons. Yet it is hardly surprising that to date one cannot determine where the junior senator from New York stands on such a straightforward issue (morally if not politically) as the American adventure in Vietnam. Differing with the president as to which cities ought to be bombed in the North does not constitute an alternative policy. His sophisticated liberal admirers, however, do not seem in the least distressed by his lack of a position; instead they delight in the *uses* to which he has put the war in Vietnam in order to embarrass the usurper in the White House.

The cold-blooded jauntiness of the Kennedys in politics has a remarkable appeal for those who also want to rise and who find annoying—to the extent they are aware of it at all—the moral sense. Also, the success of the three Kennedy brothers nicely makes hash of the old American belief that by working hard and being good one will deserve (and if fortunate, receive) promotion. A mediocre representative, an absentee senator, through wealth and family connections, becomes the president while his youngest brother inherits the Senate seat. Now Bobby is about to become RFK because he is Bobby. It is as if the United States had suddenly reverted to the eighteenth century, when the politics of many states were family affairs. In those days, if one wanted a political career in New York one had best be born a Livingston, a Clinton, or a Schuyler; failing that, one must marry into the family, as Alexander Hamilton did, or go to work for them. In a way, the whole Kennedy episode is a fascinating throwback to an earlier phase of civilization. Because the Irish maintained the ancient village sense of the family longer than most places in the West and to the extent that the sons of Joe Kennedy reflect those values and prejudices, they are an anachronism in an urbanized nonfamily-minded society. Yet the fact that they are so plainly not of this time makes them fascinating, their family story is a glamorous continuing soap opera whose appeal few can resist, including the liberals, who, though they may suspect that the Kennedys are not with them at heart, believe that the two boys are educable. At this very moment beside the river Charles a thousand Aristotles dream of their young Alexanders, and the coming heady conquest of the earth.

Meanwhile, the source of the holy family's power is the legend of the dead brother, who did not much resemble the hero of the books under review. Yet the myth that JFK was a philosopher-king will continue as long as the Kennedys remain in politics. And much of the power they exert over the national imagination is a direct result of the ghastliness of what happened at Dallas. But though the world's grief and shock were genuine, they were not entirely for JFK himself. The death of a young leader necessarily strikes an atavistic chord. For thousands of years the man-god was sacrificed to ensure with blood the harvest, and there is always an element of ecstasy as well as awe in our collective grief. Also, Jack Kennedy was a television star, more seen by most people than their friends or relatives. His death in public was all the more stunning because he was not an abstraction called The President, but a man the people thought they knew. At the risk of *lèse-divinité*, however, the assassination of President Nixon at, let us say, Cambridge by what at first was thought to be a member of the ADA but later turned out to be a dotty Bircher would have occasioned quite as much national horror, mourning, and even hagiography. But in time the terrible deed would have been forgotten, for there are no Nixon heirs.

Beyond what one thinks of the Kennedys themselves, there remains the large question: What sort of men ought we to be governed by in the coming years? With the high cost of politics and image-making, it is plain that only the very wealthy or those allied with the very wealthy can afford the top prizes. And among the rich, only those who are able to please the people on television are Presidential. With the decline of the religions, the moral sense has become confused, to say the least, and intellectual or political commitments that go beyond the merely expedient are regarded with cheerful contempt not only by the great operators themselves but also by their admirers and, perhaps, by the electorate itself. Also, to be fair, politicians working within a system like ours can never be much more than what the system will allow. Hypocrisy and self-deception are the traditional characteristics of the middle class in any place and time, and the United States today is the paradigmatic middle-class society. Therefore we can hardly blame our political gamesmen for being, literally, representative. Any public man has every right to try and trick us, not only for his own good but, if he is honorable, for ours as well. However, if he himself is not aware of what he is doing or to what end he is playing the game, then to entrust him with the first magistracy of what may be the last empire on earth is to endanger us all. One does not necessarily demand of our leaders passion (Hitler supplied the age with quite enough for this century) or reforming zeal (Mao Tse-tung is incomparable), but one does insist that they possess a sense of community larger than simply personal power for its own sake, being first because it's fun. Finally, in an age of supercommunications, one must have a clear sense of the way things are, as opposed to the way they have been made to seem. Since the politics of the Kennedys are so often the work of publicists, it is necessary to keep trying to find out just who they are and what they really mean. If only because should *they* be confused as to the realities of Cuba, say, or Vietnam, then the world's end is at hand.

At one time in the United States, the popular wisdom maintained that there was no better work for a man to do than to set in motion some idea whose time had not yet arrived, even at the risk of becoming as unpopular as those politicians JFK so much admired in print and so little emulated in life. It may well be that it is now impossible for such men to rise to the top in our present system. If so, this is a tragedy. Meanwhile, in their unimaginative fierce way, the Kennedys continue to play successfully the game as they found it. They create illusions and call them facts, and between what they are said to be and what they are falls the shadow of all the useful words not spoken, of all the actual deeds not done. But if it is true that in a rough way nations deserve the leadership they get, then a frivolous and apathetic electorate combined with a vain and greedy intellectual establishment will most certainly restore to power the illusion-making Kennedys. Holy family and bedazzled nation, in their faults at least, are well matched. In any case, the age of the commune in which we have lived since the time of Jackson is drawing to a close and if historical analogies are at all relevant, the rise of the *signori* is about to begin, and we may soon find ourselves enjoying a strange new era in which all our lives and dreams are presided over by smiling, interchangeable, initialed gods.

Esquire
April 1967

HOMAGE TO DANIEL SHAYS

To govern is to choose how the revenue raised from taxes is spent. So far so good, or bad. But some people earn more money than others. Should they pay proportionately more money to the government than those who earn less? And if they do pay more money are they entitled to more services than those who pay less or those who pay nothing at all? And should those who pay nothing at all because they have nothing get anything? These matters are of irritable concern to our rulers, and of some poignancy to the rest.

Although the equality of each citizen before the law is the rock upon which the American Constitution rests, economic equality has never been an American ideal. In fact, it is the one unmentionable subject in our politics, as the senator from South Dakota recently discovered when he came up with a few quasi-egalitarian tax reforms. The furious and enduring terror of Communism in America is not entirely the work of those early cold warriors Truman and Acheson. A dislike of economic equality is something deep-grained in the American Protestant character. After all, given a rich empty continent for vigorous Europeans to exploit (the Indians were simply a disagreeable part of the emptiness, like chiggers), any man of gumption could make himself a good living. With extra hard work, any man could make himself a fortune, proving that he was a better man than the rest. Long before Darwin the American ethos was Darwinian.

The vision of the rich empty continent is still a part of the American unconscious in spite of the Great Crowding and its attendant miseries; and this lingering belief in the heaven any man can make for himself through hard work and clean living is a key to the majority's prevailing and apparently unalterable hatred of the poor, kept out of sight at home, out of mind abroad.

Yet there has been, from the beginning, a significant division in our ruling class. The early Thomas Jefferson had a dream: a society of honest yeomen, engaged in agricultural pursuits, without large cities, heavy industry, banks, military pretensions. The early (and the late) Alexander Hamilton wanted industry, banks, cities, and a military force capable of making itself felt in world politics. It is a nice irony that so many of today's laissez-faire conservatives think that they descend from Hamilton, the proponent of a strong federal government, and that so many liberals believe themselves to be the heirs of the early Jefferson, who wanted little more than a police force and a judiciary. Always practical, Jefferson knew that certain men would rise through their own good efforts while, sadly, others would fall. Government would do no more than observe this Darwinian spectacle benignly, and provide no succor.

In 1800 the Hamiltonian view was rejected by the people and their new President Thomas Jefferson. Four years later, the Hamiltonian view had prevailed and was endorsed by the reelected Jefferson. "We are all Hamiltonians now!" he might have exclaimed had he the grace of the thirty-seventh president, whose progress from moth to larva on so many issues gives delight. Between 1800 and 1805 Jefferson had seen to it that an empire *in posse* had become an empire *in esse*. The difference between Jefferson I and Jefferson II is reflected in the two inaugural addresses.

First Inaugural: "a wise and frugal government, which shall restrain men from injuring one another, which shall leave them otherwise free to regulate their own pursuit of industry and improvement, and shall not take from the mouth of labor the bread it has earned. This is the sum of good government. . . ." In other words, no taxes beyond a minimal levy in order to pay for a few judges, a postal service, small executive and legislative bodies.

Second Inaugural: Jefferson II was now discussing the uses to which taxes might be put (once the national debt was paid off, oh presidential chimera!), "*In time of peace*, to rivers, canals, roads, arts, manufactures, education, and other great objects within each State. *In time of war*—if injustice, *by ourselves*" (those italics, irresistibly, mine) "or others, must sometimes produce war. . . . War will be but a suspension of useful works. . . ." The idea of the rich empty continent best exploited by men unbugged by a central government had now been succeeded by the notion that government ought to pitch in and help with those roads and schools, but of course that's going to take money, so taxes must be raised to pay for these good things which benefit us all equally, don't they?

It is significant that nothing more elevated than greed changed the Dr. Jekyll of Jefferson I into the Mr. Hyde of Jefferson II. Like his less thoughtful countrymen, Jefferson could not resist a deal. Subverting the Constitution he had helped create, Jefferson bought Louisiana from Napoleon, acquiring its citizens without their consent; he then proceeded to govern them as if they had been conquered, all the while secretly—comically—maneuvering, by hook or by crook, to bag the Floridas. The author of the Declaration of Independence was quite able to forget the unalienable rights of anyone whose property he thought should be joined to our empire—a word which crops up frequently and unselfconsciously in his correspondence.

In the course of land-grabbing, Jefferson II managed to get himself into hot water with France, England, and Spain simultaneously, a fairly astonishing thing to do considering the state of politics in Napoleonic Europe. But then war is bound to result if you insist on liberating vast tracts of land from colonial nations as well as from home-grown Indians (they were equal to whites, Jefferson thought, in spite of their bad habits, but different from the hopeless black races which had started out white but then, in the unwholesome African climate, contracted a form of leprosy; enlightened optimists like Jefferson's friend the learned Dr. Rush were certain that advanced dermatology would one day restore to these dark peoples their lost prettiness). The result of this finagling was a series of panicky appropriations for the navy and the creation of the American military machine which in the last fiscal year cost us honest yeomen 75.8 billion dollars out of a total of 126 billion dollars paid in personal and corporate income taxes. Forever forgotten was the wisdom of Jefferson I: "Sound principles will not justify our taxing the industry of our fellow citizens to accumulate treasure for wars to happen we know not when, and which might not perhaps happen but from the temptation offered by that treasure."

It is a tribute to the Protestant passion for wanting always to appear to be doing good (particularly when one is robbing the till) that Americans have been constitutionally incapable (*double entendre* intended) of recognizing the truth about themselves or anyone else. Mixing his metaphors, celebrating the empire electric, appealing to the god Demos whose agent he thought himself to be, Jefferson II so clouded over our innate imperialism that we cannot to this day recognize the nature of American society, even as our bombs murder strangers (admittedly leprous) 8,000 miles away. Fortunately, the empire has taken such a shellacking in the last few years that critics (not yet loved) are being listened to at last, and it is now unlikely that even a yeomanry so constantly and deliberately misinformed from kindergarten days to wrap-up time in the Forest Lawn Slumber Room will ever allow another president the fun of destroying someone else's country in the name of Jefferson I self-determination. As the empire falls apart, things may yet come together again in a good—or at least more realistic—way.

To make sense of our situation a simple question must be asked. Why do we allow our governors to take so much of our money and spend it in ways that not only fail to benefit us but do great damage to others as we prosecute undeclared wars—which even our brainwashed majority has come to see are a bad proposition because of the cost of maintaining a vast military machine, not to mention a permanent draft of young men (an Un-American activity if there ever was one) in what is supposed to be peacetime? Whether he knows it or not, the middle-income American is taxed as though he were living in a socialist society. But for the money he gives the government he gets almost nothing back. He does pay for a lot of military hardware, and his congressman will point to all the jobs "defense" (that happy euphemism) contracts bring to his district, as if the same federal money could not create even more jobs doing things that need doing as well as benefiting directly the man who paid the taxes in the first place. Ultimate irony, the middle American still tends to believe that he is living in a Jefferson I society when, in fact, he has been for some decades in a Jefferson II world, allowing an imperial-minded elite to tax him in order to wage a holy war against something called Communism.

Fortunately, there are now signs that they don't make suckers like that any more. The taxpayers' revolt has begun. A dislike of all politicians is in the land. Word is out that the rich don't pay as much, proportionately, to maintain their empire as do the middle-income people. They hate Socialism and Communism and all the things good people are supposed to hate, but they are also beginning to wonder just why they have to give up so much of their income to fight those very same Commies Nixon likes to dine with in Peking and Moscow.

The fact is that our present governors are not very bright, and this may be our salvation. In 1968 they absent-mindedly gave us a president whose schizophrenic behavior and prose style ("This is *not* an invasion of Cambodia") is creepily apparent to even the most woolly-headed yeoman. Now three new books provide useful information about the small group who own the United States, how our economic and foreign policies are manipulated, how members of Congress are bought, how presidential candidates are selected and financed.

The mold that cast the mind of C. Wright Mills was not broken at his flesh's departure. Another such mind was promptly cast and labeled G. William Domhoff (those first initials and middle names are reminiscent of a generation of three-named Episcopalian clergymen). A Mills disciple, Domhoff has published *Who Rules America?* (1967) and *The Higher Circle* (1970). The subjects of those books are exactly what their titles suggest. Domhoff has now written another illuminating treatise called *Fat Cats and Democrats: The Role of the Big Rich in the Party of the Common Man.*

Domhoff's thesis is straightforward. The country is governed by a small elite which knows pretty much what it is up to and coordinates its various moves in foreign affairs and the economy. Most academics dispute this theory. They tend to be Jefferson I types who believe that the United States is a pluralist society filled with all sorts of dominations and powers constantly balancing and checking one another. To them, anyone who believes that an elite is really running the show is paranoid. But as

the late Delmore Schwartz once said with the weary lucidity of his own
rich madness, "Paranoids have real enemies, too." Admittedly, it is difficult at first to accept the proposition that the owners of the country also
rule it and that the electorate is nothing but a quadrennial chorus whose
function is to ratify with hosannahs one or the other of two presidential
candidates carefully picked for them by rulers who enjoy pretending
that ours is really government of, by, and for the you-know-who. In the
same manner, Tiberius always respectfully consulted a Senate to whose
irrelevant ranks his heir nicely added a racehorse.

Domhoff's style does not command admiration. His manner is dis-
concertingly gee whiz. He is given to easy liberal epithets like "Godfor-
saken Mississippi" yet forced to admit that except on the subject of race,
the proud folk down there are populist to the core, and populist is the
thing to be this year. But if one is not put off by the somewhat slap-dash
manner, Domhoff has seen and measured the tip of an iceberg which
most of the other passengers on the RMS *Titanic* have not noticed. He
also does his best to figure out what lies beneath the water.

Domhoff's method is to examine those committees and advisory
councils, federal and private, that do the actual work of making foreign
and economic policy (something like three-quarters of the federal budget
has to do with military and foreign aid expenditures—control the spending of that three-quarters and the U.S. is your thing). He then studies the
men who serve on these committees. Notes what schools they went to,
what banks they work for (most are lawyers or lawyer-bankers), what political contributions they make. He also records the overlapping that goes
on, or "linkage" as the American Metternich would say.

In 1968, for instance, 51 of 284 trustees and honorary trustees of the
Committee for Economic Development were also members of the Council on Foreign Relations, while 126 were members of the National Council of the Foreign Policy Association. Or as Domhoff puts it,

> *Policy formation is the province of a bipartisan power elite of corporate rich*
> *[Rockefeller, Mellon] and their career hirelings [Nixon, McNamara] who*
> *work through an interlocking and overlapping maze of foundations, univer-*
> *sities and institutes, discussion groups, associations and commissions. Polit-*

ical parties are only for finding interesting and genial people [usually ambi-tious middle-class lawyers] to ratify and implement these policies in such a way that the under classes feel themselves to be, somehow, a part of the gov-ernmental process. Politics is not exactly the heart of the action but it is nice work—if you can afford to campaign for it.

If Domhoff's thesis is even partly true (and at least one skeptic is per-suaded that it is) much of the malaise one detects among intelligent members of the Senate and House is understandable. It is not so much the removal of power from the Hill to the White House (a resourceful Congress can still break a president if they want, or at least bring him to heel); rather, it is the knowledge or suspicion that the legislative branch reflects not the electorate but the elite who pay for congressional cam-paigns and are duly paid off with agreeable tax laws and military procure-ment and foreign aid bills passed at the dark of the moon. There is a constant if gentle tugging of the reins—perhaps Caligula had the right idea about what a proper senator should be. "We don't seem to matter at all," said one East Coast senator to me some years ago. "And I don't know why. We're every bit as bright or brighter than the Borah–La Follette group. But we're just . . . well, nothing." Domhoff agrees and tells us why.

In *Fat Cats and Democrats*, Domhoff describes our rulers. Year in, year out, "About one percent of the population—a socially interacting upper class whose members go to prep schools, attend debutante balls, join ex-clusive clubs, ride to hounds and travel all over the world for business or pleasure—will continue to own 60 percent to 70 percent of all privately held corporate wealth and receive 24 percent of the national income." Domhoff tends to be a bit wide-eyed about the lifestyle of the nobles but, barring those riders to hounds, he seldom indulges in the sort of solemn generality recently dished up by a sociologist who discovered that most American banking is controlled by the Wasps (true) and that the Wasps at the top of the banking hierarchy have larger and fleshier ears than those farther down (true?).

Domhoff accepts the Ferdinand Lundberg formulation that there is only one political party in the United States and that is the Property Party, whose Republican wing tends to be rigid in maintaining the status quo and not given to any accommodation of the poor and the black. Although the Democratic wing shares most of the basic principles (that is to say, money) of the Republicans, its members are often shrewd enough to know that what is too rigid will shatter under stress. The Democrats have also understood for some time the nature of the American empire. While the Republicans indulge in Jefferson I rhetoric and unrealities, including isolationism, the Democrats have known all along that this is a Jefferson II world. As Dean Acheson put it in 1947, "You must look to foreign markets." As early as 1928 a distinguished member of the Republican wing of the Property Party saw its limitations. After all, Averell Harriman was involved in German zinc mines, Polish iron mines, and Soviet manganese. "I thought Republican isolationism was disastrous." And just before the 1929 crash, he switched.

But essentially the two wings of the Property Party are more alike than not. Witness the bipartisan foreign policy which the elite hammered out twenty-five years ago over the dead bodies of the Republican faithful. The Property Party has known from the beginning how and when to reconcile its two wings in order to survive. After all, according to Domhoff,

> *The American Constitution was carefully rigged by the noteholders, land speculators, rum runners, and slave holders who were the Founding Fathers, so that it would be next to impossible for upstart dirt farmers and indebted masses to challenge the various forms of private property held by these well read robber barons. Through this Constitution, the over-privileged attempted to rule certain topics out of order for proper political discussion. To bring these topics up in polite company was to invite snide invective, charges of personal instability, or financial ruin.*

In other words, don't start a political party in opposition to the Property Party. From Henry Wallace's Progressive Party, so viciously smeared by the liberal ADA, to today's sad attempt to field a People's Party, those who wish to promote economic equality should not be surprised to have their heads handed to them, particularly by a "free" press which refuses to recognize any alternative to the way things are.

Property is power, as those Massachusetts veterans of the revolution discovered when they joined Captain Daniel Shays in his resistance to the landed gentry's replacement of a loose confederation of states with a tax-levying central government. The veterans thought that they had been fighting a war for true independence. They did not want London to be replaced by New York. They did want an abolition of debts and a division of property. Their rebellion was promptly put down. But so shaken was the elite by the experience that their most important (and wealthiest) figure grimly emerged from private life with a letter to Harry Lee. "You talk of employing influence," wrote George Washington, "to appease the present tumults in Massachusetts. I know not where that influence is to be found, or if attainable, that it would be a proper remedy for the disorders. *Influence* is no *government*. Let us have one by which our lives, liberties and properties will be secured or let us know the worst at once." So was born the Property Party and with it the Constitution of the United States. We have known the "best" for nearly two hundred years. What would the "worst" have been like?

The rulers of the country are, according to Domhoff, 80 percent to 90 percent Republican. For the most part they are not isolationist. They know that money is to be made overseas either from peace or war, from the garrison state and its attendant machismo charms. Who then supports the Democratic wing? Labor is responsible for 20 percent to 25 percent of the party's financing. Racketeers from 10 percent to 15 percent—obviously certain areas like New York, Chicago, and Las Vegas interest these entrepreneurs more than, say, the Good Government League of Bangor, Maine. Around 15 percent is contributed by the "little man." The rest comes from the fat cats. Who are they? And why do they give money to the wrong wing of the Property Party?

Domhoff rather cold-bloodedly divides these perverse investors into two groups. Sentimental liberals—usually from rich families, reacting against Dad's Republicanism, and status seekers among new-money Jews and Catholics with some Texas oilmen thrown in. Yet the margin of action, like that of debate, is deliberately limited by the conservative as well as the reactionary wing of the Property Party. Or as Domhoff puts it, the elite Republicans "must accommodate the reactionaries just enough to keep them from forming an ultra-conservative party, just as it is the task of the wealthy moderate Democrats to assimilate or crush any sanguine liberals who try to stray through the left boundary of the sacred two-party system."

An uneasy alliance of Jewish bankers and Texas oilmen has financed most of the Democratic Party. Yet this Jewish-cowboy axis (Domhoff's phrase), powerful and rich though it is, represents only a small, moderately lunatic fringe to the sturdy fabric of the ruling class. They are the sports who give us Democratic presidential candidates guaranteed to speak of change and different deals while altering nothing. But then how could they change anything and still get the money to buy television spots?

Interestingly enough, Domhoff does not think that the Nixon Southern strategy has a chance of working at the congressional or local level. The South tends to be hawkish and racist—two chords the incumbent Property Party manager knows how to pluck. But the South is not about to support a party which is against federal spending. Nine Rehnquists would not be anywhere near enough to counterbalance the Southward flow of money from Treasury through the conduit of Southern Democratic Congressional leaders who have employed the seniority system to reverse that bad trip at the Appomattox Courthouse. They govern the House in tandem with machine Democrats from the North. Each takes in the other's washing. The Northerners get a few housing bills out of the Southerners, who in turn are granted military bases and agricultural subsidies. Both groups are devoted to keeping the Property Party prosperous and the money where it belongs, in the hands of the elite. Southern Democrats are not about to join with Nixon's true-blue Republicans in turning off federal aid.

At the congressional level, one can see how the elite works even more clearly than at the presidential level, where enthusiasm for attractive candidates often blinds even the sharpest critic (not to mention, very often, the candidate himself) to the charade being enacted by the Property Party. It is in the House and the Senate that the day-by-day dirty work is done, and Bella Abzug gives a splendid account (*Bella!*) of her two years in the House, trying to represent her constituents and her conscience, to the amusement of a genial body of corrupt politicians whose votes are all too often for sale to the highest bidder, usually in the form of cash in white envelopes, if Robert N. Winter-Berger's astonishing book *The Washington Pay-Off* is to be believed. With these two books, one ideological, the other muckraking, the bankruptcy of the House of Representatives has been duly filed.

Bella Abzug was elected from Lower Manhattan to end the war, gain equal rights for women and blacks, and generally be herself, serving the unpropertied. A bright lawyer as well as a formidable self-publicist, she immediately struck the fancy of the press (when they get her full range, she will be dropped—tense?). All in all, Abzug rather likes the floor managers of the Property Party. They are good fun and she always knows where she stands with them. "The men in the Club here are very charming to me," which they can afford to be since "they have all the power." They even "like to be entertained a bit. I don't mean in a ha-ha funny way, but in an interesting way." It is the liberals for whom she has real contempt. They have fallen for "the old crap, the anaesthesia of the liberals: If you want to get along, you've got to go along . . . very little men." They would rather fight one another for such posts as House Majority leader than unite to keep a reactionary from continuing in that job.

For five years (1964 to 1969) Mr. Winter-Berger was a Washington lobbyist, engaged in getting favors done for a wide range of people. Nathan Voloshen was his principal contact. This extraordinary man had known Representative John W. McCormack since 1945. In 1962, McCormack became Speaker of the House and Voloshen's "public relations" career soared. For use of the Speaker's opulent office in the Capitol, Voloshen paid McCormack $2,500 a month rent, a small amount considering the address. As clients came and went, the Speaker would assure them, "Nat can take care of that for you. Nat's my dear friend and I will do anything I can for him. Any friend of Nat's is a friend of mine." In one form or another, this speech is the ancient Washington formula to indicate that things will be done if you pay the price.

Eventually, Voloshen and company were nabbed by the embarrassingly honest Property Party maverick, U.S. Attorney Robert Morgenthau. Voloshen pleaded guilty. At the trial of one of Voloshen's henchmen,

McCormack pleaded ignorance which, according to the 1925 House Code of Ethics Act, made him innocent. Rather ludicrously, on the stand, McCor-

*mack said: "I am not an inquiring fellow." Actually, if ever a man always
knew precisely what was going on around him it was John McCormack.*

Mr. Winter-Berger also tells us that he was present in the Speaker's office when Lyndon Johnson sailed in and, thinking the Speaker was alone,
began a tirade with, "John, that son of a bitch is going to ruin me. If that
cocksucker talks, I'm gonna land in jail." Apparently the president did not
want his former Senate aide, Bobby Baker, to contest certain charges
brought against him. "I will give him a million dollars if he takes the rap,"
said Johnson.

It is no wonder that most newspapers and magazines have refused to
review this book and that many bookstores will not sell it. The fear is not
of libel. Something much more elemental is involved. If the corruption
and greed of the men the Property Party has placed in the Congress and
the White House become common knowledge, the whole rotten business could very well collapse and property itself would be endangered.
Had there actually been a two-party system in the United States, the incoming president would have taken advantage of such an extraordinary
scandal in the Democratic ranks. Instead, Nixon moved swiftly to remove
Robert Morgenthau from office. If there is one thing Nixon understands,
it is dominoes. Or as Mr. Winter-Berger puts it,

> *At the time, Voloshen said to me: "Mitchell is afraid that if any of the Con-
> gressmen are found guilty, the whole public image of the Congress would be
> destroyed." Voloshen also told me about the proviso which Attorney General
> Mitchell added to his offer to drop the case against Frenkil [Voloshen's pal]:
> House Speaker John McCormack would have to resign from Congress.
> Knowing how much McCormack loved his job and his life in the world
> of politics, I didn't think such a powerful man would go along. But in fact
> he did.*

Yet the personal enrichment of congressmen and their friends is small
potatoes compared to the way the great corporations use the government
and its money for their own ends. The recent ITT comedy was just one
example—and hardly investigated by the Property Party men in the Senate. The press also plays its supporting role. Mr. Winter-Berger notes that

the Bobby Baker scandal became big news with suspicious slowness. "Having been filed in the court records, information about the suit should have been available immediately to any newspaper reporter, but it took the Washington *Post* three days to find out about it and break the story." This was September 12, 1963. *The New York Times* did not think this news fit to print until October 5, and then buried it on page 19. Not until Bobby Baker resigned three days later, did he make the front page of the *Times*.

But then, as Domhoff has remarked, few substantive matters are considered fit for open discussion in our society. Every president is honest because he is our president and we are honest. An occasional congressman may fall from grace because there are always a few rotten apples in every barrel, but the majority are straightshooters. The Congress represents all the interests of the people, at least district by district and state by state. *The New York Times* will always call the shots if there is any funny business anywhere. Just as they will always support the best "liberal" candidate (Abzug has a nice horror story about how the *Times* killed a piece on her because it was too favorable). These threadbare myths sustain us. But for how much longer?

After the burning of Newark, the elite wondered, some more reluctantly than others, what might be next for burning if they did not appear to pay off the poor and/or black. To the amazement of the innocent, the Nixon administration came up with a family income plan for the poor which was favored (fathered?) by the Council for Economic Development. The council then set out to sell the plan to the Right Wing. Predictably, Ronald Reagan was opposed because of a "philosophical antipathy" which he thought reflected the prejudices of his constituency. A number of the council's leaders swiftly materialized in San Francisco and proceeded to instruct the public in the virtues of the plan. They stressed that not only businessmen but *experts* favored it. Even Democrats thought it sound. Gently chiding Reagan, they sold the program to California's media and public in a bipartisan way. The Property Party has no intention of actually putting this plan into effect, of course, but at least they now have something nice to talk about when the poor are restive. The fact that McGovern acts as if he might implement the plan has caused alarm.

Recently (June 18) one of the CED's members, Herbert Stein, now chairman of the President's Council of Economic Advisers, gave us the elite's latest view of McGovern's tax reforms. "All such plans count on the willingness of the non-poor to give money to the poor. There has to be such willingness because the non-poor greatly outnumber the poor and dominate the political process." Elegant sophistry. The not-so-poor do outnumber the poor but if the not-so-poor who are nicked heavily by taxes were to join with the poor they would outnumber the elite by 99 to 1. The politician who can forge that alliance will find himself, at best, the maker of a new society; at worst, in a hole at Arlington.

To maintain its grip on the nation, the Property Party must keep actual issues out of political debate. So far they have succeeded marvelously well. Faced with unemployment, Nixon will oppose abortion. Inflation? Marijuana is a halfway house to something worse. The bombing of North Vietnam? Well, pornographers are using the mailing lists of Cub Scouts. Persuading the people to vote against their own best interests has been the awesome genius of the American political elite from the beginning.

It will be interesting to see what happens to George McGovern. Appealing to the restive young, he came up with a number of tax reforms which threatened to alter the foundation of the Property Party. The result was a terrible squawking from the Alsops and the Restons. We were told that McGovern is the Goldwater of the left (a good joke since Goldwater represented the reactionary country club minority while McGovern would represent the not-so-poor to poor majority), but then any hack journalist knows that his ink-drugged readers will not stand for pot, abortion, amnesty. Now that McGovern is the candidate they have decided that he is, thank God, a pragmatist (i.e., a Property Party opportunist) and so will move where the votes are and where you can bet your sweet ass the Sulzbergers and Schiffs, the Luces and Grahams are.

With each passing day, McGovern will more and more come to resemble a Property Party candidate. This is fair enough, if not good enough. But what happens when he is elected? Then we will know—too late, I fear—to what extent he was simply exploiting the people's deep inchoate hatred of the Property Party in order to become that Party's loyal manager. This would be sad because 1972 could have been the year for a counterparty or for a transformation of the Democratic wing of the Property Party. But barring catastrophe (in the form of home-grown apple-pie fascism), the early response to McGovern (and Wallace, too) is the first indication we have had that there now exists a potential American majority willing to see its best interests served not through the restrictive Constitution of the elite but through the egalitarian vision of Daniel Shays and his road not taken—yet.

The New York Review of Books
August 10, 1972

PINK TRIANGLE AND
YELLOW STAR

A few years ago on a trip to Paris, I read an intriguing review in *Le Monde* of a book called *Comme un Frère, Comme un Amant*, a study of "Male Homosexuality in the American Novel and Theatre from Herman Melville to James Baldwin," the work of one Georges-Michel Sarotte, a Sorbonne graduate and a visiting professor at the University of Massachusetts. I read the book, found it interesting; met the author, found him interesting. He told me that he was looking forward to the publication of his book in the United States by Anchor Press/Doubleday. What sort of response did I think he would have? I was touched by so much innocent good faith. There will be no reaction, I said, because no one outside of the so-called gay press will review your book. He was shocked. Wasn't the book serious? scholarly? with an extensive bibliography? I agreed that it was all those things; unfortunately, scholarly studies having to do with fags do not get reviewed in the United States (this was before the breakthrough of Yale's John Boswell, whose ferociously learned *Christianity, Social Tolerance and Homosexuality* obliged even the "homophobic" *New York Times* to review it intelligently). If Sarotte had written about the agony and wonder of being female and/or Jewish and/or divorced, he would have been extensively reviewed. Even a study of black literature might have got attention (Sarotte is beige), although blacks are currently something of a nonsubject in these last days of empire.

I don't think that Professor Sarotte believed me. I have not seen him since. I also have never seen a review of his book or of Roger Austen's *Playing the Game* (a remarkably detailed account of American writing on homosexuality) or of *The Homosexual as Hero in Contemporary Fiction* by Stephen Adams, reviewed at much length in England and ignored here, or of a dozen other books that have been sent to me by writers who seem not to understand why an activity of more than casual interest to more than one-third of the male population of the United States warrants no serious discussion. That is to say, no serious *benign* discussion. All-out attacks on faggots are perennially fashionable in our better periodicals.

I am certain that the novel *Tricks* by Renaud Camus (recently translated for St. Martin's Press by Richard Howard, with a preface by Roland Barthes) will receive a perfunctory and hostile response out there in book-chat land. Yet in France, the book was treated as if it were actually literature, admittedly a somewhat moot activity nowadays. So I shall review *Tricks*. But first I think it worth bringing out in the open certain curious facts of our social and cultural life.

The American passion for categorizing has now managed to create two nonexistent categories—gay and straight. Either you are one or you are the other. But since everyone is a mixture of inclinations, the categories keep breaking down; and when they break down, the irrational takes over. You *have* to be one or the other. Although our mental therapists and writers for the better journals usually agree that those who prefer same-sex sex are not exactly criminals (in most of our states and under most circumstances they still are) or sinful or, officially, sick in the head, they must be, somehow, evil or inadequate or dangerous. The Roman Empire fell, didn't it? because of the fags?

Our therapists, journalists, and clergy are seldom very learned. They seem not to realize that most military societies on the rise tend to encourage same-sex activities for reasons that should be obvious to anyone who has not grown up ass-backward, as most Americans have. In the centuries of Rome's great military and political success, there was no differentiation between same-sexers and other-sexers; there was also a lot of crossing back and forth of the sort that those Americans who *do* enjoy inhabiting category-gay or category-straight find hard to deal with. Of the first twelve Roman emperors, only one was exclusively heterosexual.

Since these twelve men were pretty tough cookies, rigorously trained as warriors, perhaps our sexual categories and stereotypes are—can it really be?—false. It was not until the sixth century of the empire that same-sex sex was proscribed by church and state. By then, of course, the barbarians were within the gates and the glory had fled.

Today, American evangelical Christians are busy trying to impose on the population at large their superstitions about sex and the sexes and the creation of the world. Given enough turbulence in the land, these natural fascists can be counted on to assist some sort of authoritarian—but never, never totalitarian—political movement. Divines from Santa Clara to Falls Church are particularly fearful of what they describe as the gay liberation movement's attempt to gain "special rights and privileges" when all that the same-sexers want is to be included, which they are not by law and custom, within the framework of the Fourteenth Amendment. The divine in Santa Clara believes that same-sexers should be killed. The divine in Falls Church believes that they should be denied equal rights under the law. Meanwhile, the redneck divines have been joined by a group of New York Jewish publicists who belong to what they proudly call "the new class" (*né arrivistes*), and these lively hucksters have now managed to raise fag-baiting to a level undreamed of in Falls Church—or even in Moscow.

In a letter to a friend, George Orwell wrote, "It is impossible to mention Jews in print, either favorably or unfavorably, without getting into trouble." But there are times when trouble had better be got into before mere trouble turns into catastrophe. Jews, blacks, and homosexualists are despised by the Christian and Communist majorities of East and West. Also, as a result of the invention of Israel, Jews can now count on the hatred of the Islamic world. Since our own Christian majority looks to be getting ready for great adventures at home and abroad, I would suggest that the three despised minorities join forces in order not to be destroyed. This seems an obvious thing to do. Unfortunately, most Jews refuse to see any similarity between their special situation and that of the same-sexers. At one level, the Jews are perfectly correct. A racial or religious or tribal identity is a kind of fact. Although sexual preference is an even more powerful fact, it is not one that creates any particular social or cultural or religious bond between those so-minded. Although Jews would doubtless be Jews if there was no anti-Semitism, same-sexers would think little or nothing at all about their preference if society ignored it. So there *is* a difference between the two estates. But there is no difference in the degree of hatred felt by the Christian majority for Christ-killers and Sodomites. In the German concentration camps, Jews wore yellow stars while homosexualists wore pink triangles. I was present when Christopher Isherwood tried to make this point to a young Jewish movie producer. "After all," said Isherwood, "Hitler killed six hundred thousand homosexuals." The young man was not impressed. "But Hitler killed six *million* Jews," he said sternly. "What are you?" asked Isherwood. "In real estate?"

Like it or not, Jews and homosexualists are in the same fragile boat, and one would have to be pretty obtuse not to see the common danger. But obtuseness is the name of the game among New York's new class. Elsewhere, I have described the shrill fag-baiting of Joseph Epstein, Norman Podhoretz, Alfred Kazin, and the Hilton Kramer Hotel. *Harper's* magazine and *Commentary* usually publish these pieces, though other periodicals are not above printing the odd exposé of the latest homosexual conspiracy to turn the United States over to the Soviet Union or to structuralism or to Christian Dior. Although the new class's thoughts are never much in themselves, and they themselves are no more than spear carriers in the political and cultural life of the West, their prejudices and superstitions do register in a subliminal way, making mephitic the air of Manhattan if not of the Republic.

A case in point is that of Mrs. Norman Podhoretz, also known as Midge Decter (like Martha Ivers, *whisper* her name). In September of last year, Decter published a piece called "The Boys on the Beach" in her husband's magazine, *Commentary*. It is well worth examining in some detail because she has managed not only to come up with every known prejudice and superstition about same-sexers but also to make up some brand-new ones. For sheer vim and vigor, "The Boys on the Beach" outdoes its implicit model, *The Protocols of the Elders of Zion*.

Decter notes that when the "homosexual rights movement first burst upon the scene," she was "more than a little astonished." Like so many new-class persons, she writes a stilted sort of genteel-gentile prose not unlike—but not very like, either—*The New Yorker* house style of the

1940s and '50s. She also writes with the authority and easy confidence of someone who knows that she is very well known indeed to those few who know her.

Decter tells us that twenty years ago, she got to know a lot of pansies at a resort called Fire Island Pines, where she and a number of other new-class persons used to make it during the summers. She estimates that 40 percent of the summer people were heterosexual; the rest were not. Yet the "denizens, homosexual and heterosexual alike, were predominantly professionals and people in soft marginal business—lawyers, advertising executives, psychotherapists, actors, editors, writers, publishers, etc." Keep this in mind. Our authoress does not.

Decter goes on to tell us that she is now amazed at the recent changes in the boys on the beach. Why have they become so politically militant—and so ill groomed? "What indeed has happened to the homosexual community I used to know—they who only a few short years ago [as opposed to those manly 370-day years] were characterized by nothing so much as a sweet, vain, pouting, girlish attention to the youth and beauty of their bodies?" Decter wrestles with this problem. She tells us how, in the old days, she did her very best to come to terms with her own normal dislike for these half-men—and half-women, too: "There were also homosexual women at the Pines, but they were, or seemed to be, far fewer in number. Nor, except for a marked tendency to hang out in the company of large and ferocious dogs, were they instantly recognizable as the men were." Well, if I were a dyke and a pair of Podhoretzes came waddling toward me on the beach, copies of Leviticus and Freud in hand, I'd get in touch with the nearest Alsatian dealer pronto.

Decter was disturbed by "the slender, seamless, elegant and utterly chic" clothes of the fairies. She also found it "a constant source of wonder" that when the fairies took off their clothes, "the largest number of homosexuals had hairless bodies. Chests, backs, arms, even legs were smooth and silky. . . . We were never able to determine just why there should be so definite a connection between what is nowadays called their sexual preference [previously known to right-thinking Jews as an abomination against Jehovah] and their smooth feminine skin. Was it a matter of hormones?" Here Decter betrays her essential modesty and lack of experience. In the no doubt privileged environment of her Midwestern youth, she could not have seen very many gentile males without their clothes on. If she had, she would have discovered that gentile men tend to be less hairy than Jews except, of course, when they are not. Because the Jews killed our Lord, they are forever marked with hair on their shoulders—something that no gentile man has on *his* shoulders except for John Travolta and a handful of other Italian-Americans from the Englewood, New Jersey, area.

It is startling that Decter has not yet learned that there is no hormonal difference between men who like sex with other men and those who like sex with women. She notes, "There is also such a thing as characteristic homosexual speech . . . it is something of an accent redolent of small towns in the Midwest whence so many homosexuals seemed to have migrated to the big city." Here one detects the disdain of the self-made New Yorker for the rural or small-town American. "Midwest" is often a code word for the flyovers, for the millions who do not really matter. But she is right in the sense that when a group chooses to live and work together, they do tend to sound and look alike. No matter how crowded and noisy a room, one can always detect the new-class person's nasal whine.

Every now and then, Decter does wonder if, perhaps, she is generalizing and whether this will "no doubt in itself seem to many of the uninitiated a bigoted formulation." Well, Midge, it does. But the spirit is upon her, and she cannot stop because "one cannot even begin to get at the truth about homosexuals without this kind of generalization. They are a group so readily distinguishable." Except of course, when they are not. It is one thing for a group of queens, in "soft, marginal" jobs, to "cavort," as she puts it, in a summer place and be "easily distinguishable" to her cold eye just as Jewish members of the new class are equally noticeable to the cold gentile eye. But it is quite another thing for those men and women who prefer same-sex sex to other-sex sex yet do not choose to be identified—and so are not. To begin to get at the truth about homosexuals, one must realize that the majority of those millions of Americans who prefer same-sex sex to other-sex sex are obliged, sometimes willingly and happily but often not, to marry and have children and to conform to the guidelines set down by the heterosexual dictatorship.

Decter would know nothing of this because in her "soft, marginal" world, she is not meant to know. She does remark upon the fairies at the Pines who did have wives and children: "They were for the most part charming and amusing fathers, rather like favorite uncles. And their wives . . . drank." This dramatic ellipsis is most Decterian.

She ticks off Susan Sontag for omitting to mention in the course of an essay on camp "that camp is of the essence of homosexual style, invented by homosexuals, and serving the purpose of domination by ridicule." The word "domination" is a characteristic new-class touch. The powerless are always obsessed by power. Decter seems unaware that all despised minorities are quick to make rather good jokes about themselves before the hostile majority does. Certainly Jewish humor, from the Book of Job (a laff-riot) to pre-*auteur* Woody Allen, is based on this.

Decter next does the ritual attack on Edward Albee and Tennessee Williams for presenting "what could only have been homosexual relationships as the deeper truth about love in our time." This is about as true as the late Maria Callas's conviction that you could always tell a Jew because he had a hump at the back of his neck—something Callas herself had in dromedarian spades.

Decter makes much of what she assumes to be the fags' mockery of the heterosexual men at the Pines: "Homosexuality paints them [heterosexuals] with the color of sheer entrapment," while the fags' "smooth and elegant exteriors, unmussed by traffic with the detritus of modern family existence, constituted a kind of sniggering reproach to their striving and harried straight brothers." Although I have never visited the Pines, I am pretty sure that I know the "soft marginal" types, both hetero and homo, that hung out there in the 1960s. One of the most noticeable characteristics of the self-ghettoized same-sexer is his perfect indifference to the world of the other-sexers. Although Decter's blood was always at the boil when contemplating these unnatural and immature half-men, they were, I would suspect, serenely unaware of her and her new-class cronies, solemnly worshiping at the shrine of The Family.

To hear Decter tell it, fags had nothing to complain of then, and they have nothing to complain of now: "Just to name the professions and industries in which they had, and still have, a significant presence is to define the boundaries of a certain kind of privilege: theatre, music, letters, dance, design, architecture, the visual arts, fashion at every level—from head, as it were, to foot, and from inception to retail—advertising, jour-nalism, interior decoration, antique dealing, publishing . . . the list could go on." Yes. But these are all pretty "soft, marginal" occupations. And none is "dominated" by fags. Most male same-sexers are laborers, farm-ers, mechanics, small businessmen, schoolteachers, firemen, policemen, soldiers, sailors. Most female same-sexers are wives and mothers. In other words, they are like the rest of the population. But then it is hard for the new-class person to realize that Manhattan is not the world. Or as a somewhat alarmed Philip Rahv said to me after he had taken a drive across the United States, "My God! There are so many of them!" In the-ory, Rahv had always known that there were a couple of hundred million gentiles out there, but to see them, in the flesh, unnerved him. I told him that I was unnerved, too, particularly when they start showering in the Blood of the Lamb.

Decter does concede that homosexualists have probably not "estab-lished much of a presence in basic industry or government service or in such classic [new-classy?] professions as doctoring and lawyering but then for anyone acquainted with them as a group the thought suggests it-self that few of them have ever made much effort in these directions." Plainly, the silly billies are too busy dressing up and dancing the hully-gully to argue a case in court. Decter will be relieved to know that the percentage of same-sexers in the "classic" activities is almost as high, pro-portionately, as that of Jews. But a homosexualist in a key position at, let us say, the Department of Labor will be married and living under a good deal of strain because he could be fired if it is known that he likes to have sex with other men.

Decter knows that there have always been homosexual teachers, and she thinks that they should keep quiet about it. But if they keep quiet, they can be blackmailed or fired. Also, a point that would really distress her, a teacher known to be a same-sexer would be a splendid role model for those same-sexers that he—or she—is teaching. Decter would think this an unmitigated evil because men and women were created to breed; but, of course, it would be a perfect good because we have more babies than we know what to do with while we lack, notoriously, useful citizens at ease with themselves. That is what the row over the schools is all about.

Like most members of the new class, Decter accepts without question Freud's line (*Introductory Lectures on Psychoanalysis*) that "we actually describe a sexual activity as perverse if it has given up the aim of reproduction and pursues the attainment of pleasure as an aim independent of it." For Freud, perversion was any sexual activity involving "the abandonment of the reproductive function." Freud also deplored masturbation as a dangerous "primal affliction." So did Moses. But then it was Freud's curious task to try to create a rational, quasi-scientific basis for Mosaic law. The result has been not unlike the accomplishments of Freud's great contemporary, the ineffable and inexorable Mary Baker Eddy, whose First Church of Christ Scientist he was able to match with *his* First Temple of Moses Scientist.

Decter says that once faggots have "ensconced" themselves in certain professions or arts, "they themselves have engaged in a good deal of discriminatory practices against others. There are businesses and professions [which ones? She is congenitally short of data] in which it is less than easy for a straight, unless he makes the requisite gesture of propitiation to the homosexual in power, to get ahead." This, of course, was Hitler's original line about the Jews: they had taken over German medicine, teaching, law, journalism. Ruthlessly, they kept out gentiles; lecherously, they demanded sexual favors. "I simply want to reduce their numbers in these fields," Hitler told Prince Philip of Hesse. "I want them proportionate to their overall number in the population." This was the early solution; the final solution followed with equal logic.

In the 1950s, it was an article of faith in new-class circles that television had been taken over by the fags. Now I happen to have known most of the leading producers of that time and, of a dozen, the two who were interested in same-sex activities were both married to women who . . . did not drink. Neither man dared mix sex with business. Every now and then an actor would say that he had not got work because he had refused to put out for a faggot producer, but I doubt very much if there was ever any truth to what was to become a bright jack-o'-lantern in the McCarthy *Walpurgisnacht*.

When I was several thousand words into Decter's tirade, I suddenly realized that she does not know what homosexuality is. At some level she may have stumbled, by accident, on a truth that she would never have

been able to comprehend in a rational way. Although to have sexual relations with a member of one's own sex is a common and natural activity
(currently disapproved of by certain elements in this culture), there is no
such thing as a homosexualist any more than there is such a thing as a
heterosexualist. That is one of the reasons there has been so much difficulty with nomenclature. Despite John Boswell's attempts to give legitimacy to the word "gay," it is still a ridiculous word to use as a common
identification for Frederick the Great, Franklin Pangborn, and Eleanor
Roosevelt. What makes some people prefer same-sex sex derives from
whatever impulse or conditioning makes some people prefer other-sex
sex. This is so plain that it seems impossible that our Mosaic-Pauline-
Freudian society has not yet figured it out. But to ignore the absence of
evidence is the basis of true faith.

Decter seems to think that yesteryear's chic and silly boys on the
beach and today's socially militant fags are simply, to use her verb,
"adopting" what she calls, in her tastefully appointed English, a lifestyle.
On the other hand, "whatever disciplines it might entail, heterosexuality
is not something adopted but something accepted. Its woes—and they
have of course nowhere been more exaggerated than in those areas of the
culture consciously or unconsciously influenced by the propaganda of
homosexuals—are experienced as the woes of life."

"Propaganda"—another key word. "Power." "Propitiation." "Domination." What *does* the new class dream of?

Decter now moves in the big artillery. Not only are fags silly and a
nuisance but they are, in their unrelenting hatred of heterosexualists,
given to depicting them in their plays and films and books as a bunch of
klutzes, thereby causing truly good men and women to falter—even
question—that warm, mature heterosexuality that is so necessary to
keeping this country great while allowing new-class persons to make it
materially.

Decter is in full cry. Fags are really imitation women. Decter persists
in thinking that same-sexers are effeminate, swishy, girlish. It is true that
a small percentage of homosexualists are indeed effeminate, just as there
are effeminate heterosexualists. I don't know why this is so. No one
knows why. Except Decter. She believes that this sort "of female imitation pointed neither to sympathy with nor flattery of the female princi-

ple." Yet queens of the sort she is writing about tend to get on very well with women. But Decter can only cope with two stereotypes: the boys on the beach, mincing about, and the drab political radicals of gay liberation. The millions of ordinary masculine types are unknown to her because they are not identifiable by voice or walk and, most important, because they have nothing in common with one another except the desire to have same-sex relations. Or, put the other way around, since Lyndon Johnson and Bertrand Russell were both heterosexualists, what character traits did *they* have in common? I should think none at all. So it is with the invisible millions—now becoming less invisible—of same-sexers.

But Decter knows her Freud, and reality may not intrude: "The desire to escape from the sexual reminder of birth and death, with its threat of paternity—that is, the displacement of oneself by others—was the main underlying desire that sent those Fire Island homosexuals into the arms of other men. Had it been the opposite desire—that is, the positive attraction to the manly—at least half the boutiques, etc.," would have closed. Decter should take a stroll down San Francisco's Castro Street, where members of the present generation of fags look like off-duty policemen or construction workers. They have embraced the manly. But Freud has spoken. Fags are fags because they adored their mothers and hated their poor, hard-working daddies. It is amazing the credence still given this unproven, unprovable thesis.

Curiously enough, as I was writing these lines, expressing yet again the unacceptable obvious, I ran across Ralph Blumenthal's article in *The New York Times* (August 25), which used "unpublished letters and growing research into the hidden life of Sigmund Freud" to examine "Freud's reversal of his theory attributing neurosis in adults to sexual seduction in childhood." Despite the evidence given by his patients, Freud decided that their memories of molestation were "phantasies." He then appropriated from the high culture (a real act of hubris) Oedipus the King, and made him a complex. Freud was much criticized for this theory at the time—particularly by Sandor Ferenczi. Now, as we learn more about Freud (not to mention about the sexual habits of Victorian Vienna as

reported in police records), his theory is again under attack. Drs. Milton
Klein and David Tribich have written a paper titled "On Freud's Blind-
ness." They have studied his case histories and observed how he ignored
evidence, how "he looked to the child and only to the child, in uncover-
ing the causes of psychopathology." Dr. Karl Menninger wrote Dr. Klein
about these findings: "Why oh why couldn't Freud believe his own ears?"
Dr. Menninger then noted, "Seventy-five per cent of the girls we accept
at the Villages have been molested in childhood by an adult. And that's
today in Kansas! I don't think Vienna in 1900 was any less sophisticated."

In the same week as Blumenthal's report on the discrediting of the
Oedipus complex, researchers at the Kinsey Institute reported (*The Observer*, August 30) that after studying 979 homosexualists ("the largest
sample of homosexuals—black and white, male and female—ever questioned in an academic study") and 477 heterosexualists, they came to the
conclusion that family life has nothing to do with sexual preference. Apparently, "homosexuality is deep-rooted in childhood, may be biological
in origin, and simply shows in more and more important ways as a child
grows older. It is not a condition which therapy can reverse." Also, "homosexual feelings begin as much as three years before any sort of homosexual act, undermining theories that homosexuality is learned through
experience." There goes the teacher-as-seducer-and-perverter myth. Finally, "Psychoanalysts' theories about smothering mum and absent dad do
not stand investigation. Patients may tend to believe that they are true
because therapists subtly coach them in the appropriate memories of
their family life."

Some years ago, gay activists came to *Harper's*, where Decter was an editor, to demonstrate against an article by Joseph Epstein, who had announced, "If I had the power to do so, I would wish homosexuality off the
face of the earth." Well, that's what Hitler had the power to do in Germany, and did—or tried to do. The confrontation at *Harper's* now provides Decter with her theme. She tells us that one of the demonstrators
asked, "Are you aware of how many suicides you may be responsible for
in the homosexual community?" I suspect that she is leaving out the context of this somewhat left-field *cri de coeur*. After all, homosexualists have

more to fear from murder than suicide. I am sure that the actual conversation had to do with the sort of mischievous effect that Epstein's Hitlerian piece might have had on those fag-baiters who read it.

But Decter slyly zeroes in on the word "suicide." She then develops a most unusual thesis. Homosexualists hate themselves to such an extent that they wish to become extinct either through inviting murder or committing suicide. She notes that in a survey of San Francisco's homosexual men, half of them "claimed to have had sex with at least five hundred people." This "bespeaks the obliteration of all experience, if not, indeed, of oneself." Plainly Decter has a Mosaic paradigm forever in mind and any variation on it is abominable. Most men—homo or hetero—given the opportunity to have sex with 500 different people would do so, gladly; but most men are not going to be given the opportunity by a society that wants them safely married so that they will be docile workers and loyal consumers. It does not suit our rulers to have the proles tomcatting around the way that our rulers do. I can assure Decter that the thirty-fifth president went to bed with more than 500 women and that the well-known . . . but I must not give away the secrets of the old class or the newly-middle-class new class will go into shock.

Meanwhile, according to Decter, "many homosexuals are nowadays engaged in efforts at self-obliteration . . . there is the appalling rate of suicide among them." But the rate is not appreciably higher than that for the rest of the population. In any case, most who do commit—or contemplate—suicide do so because they cannot cope in a world where they are, to say the least, second-class citizens. But Decter is now entering uncharted country. She also has a point to make: "What is undeniable is the increasing longing among the homosexuals to do away with themselves— if not in the actual physical sense then at least spiritually—a longing whose chief emblem, among others, is the leather bars."

So Epstein will not be obliged to press that button in order to get rid of the fags. They will do it themselves. Decter ought to be pleased by this, but it is not in her nature to be pleased by anything that the same-sexers do. If they get married and have children and swear fealty to the family gods of the new class, their wives will . . . drink. If they live openly with one another, they have fled from woman and real life. If they pursue careers in the arts, heteros will have to be on guard against vicious covert assaults on heterosexual values. If they congregate in the fashion business the way that Jews do in psychiatry, they will employ only those heterosexuals who will put out for them.

Decter is appalled by the fag "takeover" of San Francisco. She tells us about the "ever deepening resentment of the San Francisco straight community at the homosexuals' defiant displays and power ['power'!] over this city," but five paragraphs later she contradicts herself: "Having to a very great extent overcome revulsion of common opinion, are they left with some kind of unappeased hunger that only their own feelings of hatefulness can now satisfy?"

There it is. *They are hateful.* They know it. That is why they want to eliminate themselves. "One thing is certain." Decter finds a lot of certainty around. "To become homosexual is a weighty act." She still has not got the point that one does not choose to have same-sex impulses; one simply has them, as everyone has, to a greater or lesser degree, other-sex impulses. To deny giving physical expression to those desires may be pleasing to Moses and Saint Paul and Freud, but these three rabbis are aberrant figures whose nomadic values are not those of the thousands of other tribes that live or have lived on the planet. Women's and gay liberation are simply small efforts to free men and women from this trio.

Decter writes, "Taking oneself out of the tides of ordinary mortal existence is not something one does from any longing to think oneself ordinary (but only following a different 'life-style')." I don't quite grasp this sentence. Let us move on to the next: "Gay Lib has been an effort to set the weight of that act at naught, to define homosexuality as nothing more than a casual option among options." Gay lib has done just the opposite. After all, people are what they are sexually not through "adoption" but because that is the way they are structured. Some people do shift about in the course of a life. Also, most of those with same-sex drives do indeed "adopt" the heterosexual lifestyle because they don't want to go to prison or to the madhouse or become unemployable. Obviously, there *is* an option but it is a hard one that ought not to be forced on any human being. After all, homosexuality is only important when made so by irrational opponents. In this, as in so much else, the Jewish situation is precisely the same.

Decter now gives us not a final solution so much as a final conclusion: "In accepting the movement's terms [hardly anyone has, by the way], heterosexuals have only raised to a nearly intolerable height the costs of the homosexuals' flight from normality." The flight, apparently, is deliberate, a matter of perverse choice, a misunderstanding of daddy, a passion for mummy, a fear of responsibility. Decter threads her clichés like Teclas on a string: "Faced with the accelerating round of drugs, S-M, and suicide, can either the movement or its heterosexual sympathizers imagine they have done anyone a kindness?"

Although the kindness of strangers is much sought after, gay liberation has not got much support from anyone. Natural allies like the Jews are often virulent in their attacks. Blacks in their ghettos, Chicanos in their barrios, and rednecks in their pulpits also have been influenced by the same tribal taboos. That Jews and blacks and Chicanos and rednecks all contribute to the ranks of the same-sexers only increases the madness. But the world of the Decters is a world of perfect illogic.

Herewith the burden of "The Boys on the Beach": since homosexualists choose to be the way they are out of idle hatefulness, it has been a mistake to allow them to come out of the closet to the extent that they have, but now that they are out (which most are not), they will have no choice but to face up to their essential hatefulness and abnormality and so be driven to kill themselves with promiscuity, drugs, S-M, and suicide. Not even the authors of *The Protocols of the Elders of Zion* ever suggested that the Jews, who were so hateful to them, were also hateful to themselves. So Decter has managed to go one step further than the *Protocols'* authors; she is indeed a virtuoso of hate, and thus do pogroms begin.

Tricks is the story of an author—Renaud Camus himself—who has twenty-five sexual encounters in the course of six months. Each of these encounters involves a pick-up. Extrapolating from Camus's sexual vigor at the age of 35, I would suspect that he has already passed the 500 mark and so is completely obliterated as a human being. If he is, he still writes very well indeed. He seems to be having a good time, and he shows no sign of wanting to kill himself, but then that may be a front he's keeping up. I am sure that Decter will be able to tell just how close he is to OD'ing.

From his photograph, Camus appears to have a lot of hair on his chest. I don't know about the shoulders, as they are covered, modestly, with a shirt. Perhaps he is Jewish. Roland Barthes wrote an introduction to *Tricks*. For a time, Barthes was much admired in American academe. But then, a few years ago, Barthes began to write about his same-sexual activities; he is now mentioned a bit less than he was in the days before he came out, as they say.

Barthes notes that Camus's book is a "text that belongs to literature." It is not pornographic. It is also not a Homosexual Novel in that there are no deep, anguished chats about homosexuality. In fact, the subject is never mentioned; it just is. Barthes remarks, "Homosexuality shocks less [well, he is—or was—French], but continues to be interesting; it is still at that stage of excitation where it provokes what might be called feats of discourse [see "The Boys on the Beach," no mean feat!]. Speaking of homosexuality permits those who aren't to show how open, liberal, and modern they are; and those who are to bear witness, to assume responsibility, to militate. Everyone gets busy, in different ways, whipping it up." You can say that again! And Barthes does. But with a nice variation. He makes the point that you are never allowed *not* to be categorized. But then, "say 'I am' and you will be socially saved." Hence the passion for the either/or.

Camus does not set out to give a panoramic view of homosexuality. He comments, in *his* preface, on the variety of homosexual expressions. Although there is no stigma attached to homosexuality in the French intellectual world where, presumably, there is no equivalent of the new class, the feeling among the lower classes is still intense, a memento of the now exhausted (in France) Roman Catholic Church's old dirty work ("I don't understand the French Catholics," said John Paul II). As a result, many "refuse to grant their tastes because they live in such circumstances, in such circles, that their desires are not only for themselves inadmissible but inconceivable, unspeakable."

It is hard to describe a book that is itself a description, and that is what *Tricks* is—a flat, matter-of-fact description of how the narrator meets the tricks, what each says to the other, where they go, how the rooms are furnished, and what the men do. One of the tricks is nuts; a number are very hairy—the narrator has a Decterian passion for the furry; there is a lot of anal and banal sex as well as oral and floral sex. *Frottage* flows. Most of the encounters take place in France, but there is one in Washington, D.C., with a black man. There is a good deal of comedy, in the Raymond Roussel manner.

Tricks will give ammunition to those new-class persons and redneck divines who find promiscuity every bit as abominable as same-sex relations. But that is the way men are when they are given freedom to go about their business unmolested. One current Arab ruler boasts of having ten sexual encounters a day, usually with different women. A diplomat who knows him says that he exaggerates, but not much. Of course, he is a Muslim.

The family, as we know it, is an economic, not a biological, unit. I realize that this is startling news in this culture and at a time when the economies of both East and West require that the nuclear family be, simply, God. But our ancestors did not live as we do. They lived in packs for hundreds of millennia before "history" began, a mere 5,000 years ago. Whatever social arrangements human society may come up with in the future, it will have to be acknowledged that those children who are needed should be rather more thoughtfully brought up than they are today and that those adults who do not care to be fathers or mothers should be let off the hook. This is beginning, slowly, to dawn. Hence, the rising hysteria in the land. Hence, the concerted effort to deny the human ordinariness of same-sexualists. A recent attempt to portray such a person sympathetically on television was abandoned when the Christers rose up in arms.

Although I would never suggest that Truman Capote's bright wit and sweet charm as a television performer would not have easily achieved for him his present stardom had he been a *hetero*sexualist, I do know that if he had not existed in his present form, another would have been run up on the old sewing machine because that sort of *persona* must be, for a whole nation, the stereotype of what a fag is. Should some macho film star like Clint Eastwood, say, decide to confess on television that he is really into same-sex sex, the cathode tube would blow a fuse. That could never be allowed. That is all wrong. That is how the Roman Empire fell.

There is not much *angst* in *Tricks*. No one commits suicide—but there is one sad story. A militant leftist friend of Camus's was a teacher in the south of France. He taught fourteen-year-old members of that old-est of all the classes, the exploited laborer. One of his pupils saw him in a fag bar and spread the word. The students began to torment what had been a favorite teacher. "These are little proles," he tells Camus, "and Mediterranean besides—which means they're obsessed by every possible macho myth, and by homosexuality as well. It's all they can think about." One of the boys, an Arab, followed him down the street, screaming "Fag-got!" "It was as if he had finally found someone onto whom he could pro-ject his resentment, someone he could hold in contempt with complete peace of mind."

This might explain the ferocity of the new class on the subject. They know that should the bad times return, the Jews will be singled out yet again. Meanwhile, like so many Max Naumanns (Naumann was a Ger-man Jew who embraced Nazism), the new class passionately supports our ruling class—from the Chase Manhattan Bank to the Pentagon to the Op-Ed page of *The Wall Street Journal*—while holding in fierce con-tempt faggots, blacks (see Norman Podhoretz's "My Negro Problem and Ours," *Commentary*, February 1963), and the poor (see Midge Decter's "Looting and Liberal Racism," *Commentary*, September 1977). Since these Neo-Naumannites are going to be in the same gas chambers as the blacks and the faggots, I would suggest a cease-fire and a common front against the common enemy, whose kindly voice is that of Ronald Reagan and whose less than kindly mind is elsewhere in the boardrooms of the Republic.

The Nation
November 14, 1981

THEODORE ROOSEVELT:

AN AMERICAN SISSY

In Washington, D.C., there is—or was—a place where Rock Creek crosses the main road and makes a ford which horses and, later, cars could cross if the creek was not in flood. Half a hundred years ago, I lived with my grandparents on a wooded hill not far from the ford. On summer days, my grandmother and I would walk down to the creek, careful to avoid the poison ivy that grew so luxuriously amid the crowded laurel. We would then walk beside the creek, looking out for crayfish and salamanders. When we came to the ford, I would ask her to tell me, yet again, what happened when the old President Roosevelt—not the current President Roosevelt—had come riding out of the woods on a huge horse just as two ladies on slow nags had begun a slow crossing of the ford.

"Well, suddenly, Mr. Roosevelt screamed at them, 'Out of my way!' " My grandmother imitated the president's harsh falsetto. "Stand to one side, women. *I am the President.*" What happened next? I'd ask, delighted. "Oh, they were both soaked to the skin by his horse's splashing all over them. But then, the very next year," she would say with some satisfaction, "*nice* Mr. Taft was the president." Plainly, there was a link in her mind between the Event at the Ford and the change in the presidency. Perhaps there was. In those stately pre-personal days you did not call ladies women.

The attic of the Rock Creek house was filled with thousands of books on undusted shelves while newspapers, clippings, copies of the *Congressional Record* were strewn about the floor. My grandmother was not a zealous housekeeper. There was never a time when rolled-up Persian rugs did not lie at the edge of the drawing room, like crocodiles dozing. In 1907, the last year but one of Theodore Roosevelt's administration, my grandfather came to the Senate. I don't think that they had much to do with each other. I found only one reference to TR—as he was always known—on the attic floor. In 1908, when Senator Gore nominated William Jennings Bryan for president, he made an alliterative aside, "I much prefer the strenuosity of Roosevelt to the sinuosity of Taft."

Years later I asked him why he had supported Bryan, a man who had never, in my grandfather's own words, "developed. He was too famous too young. He just stopped in his thirties." So why had he nominated Bryan for president? Well, at the time there were reasons: he was vague. Then, suddenly, the pale face grew mischievous and the thin, straight Roman mouth broke into a crooked grin. "After I nominated him at Denver, we rode back to the hotel in the same carriage and he turned to me and said, 'You know, I base my political success on just three things.' " The old man paused for dramatic effect. What were they? I asked. "I've completely forgotten," he said. "But I do remember wondering why he thought he was a success."

In 1936, Theodore Roosevelt's sinuous cousin Franklin brought an end to my grandfather's career in the Senate. But the old man stayed on in Rock Creek Park and lived to a Nestorian age, convinced that FDR, as he was always known, was our republic's Caesar while his wife, Eleanor, Theodore's niece, was a revolutionary. The old man despised the whole family except Theodore's daughter Alice Longworth.

Alice gave pleasure to three generations of our family. She was as witty—and as reactionary—as Senator Gore; she was also deeply resentful of her distant cousin Franklin's success while the canonization of her own first cousin Eleanor filled her with horror. "Isn't Eleanor no-ble," she would say, breaking the word into two syllables, each hummed reverently. "So very, *very* good!" Then she would imitate Eleanor's buck teeth which were not so very unlike her own quite prominent choppers. But Alice did have occasional, rare fits of fairness. She realized that what she felt for her cousins was "Simply envy. *We* were the President Roosevelt family. But then along came the Feather Duster," as she habitually referred to Franklin, "and we were forgotten." But she was exaggerating, as a number of new books attest, not to mention that once beautiful Dakota cliff defaced by the somber Gutzon Borglum with the faces of dead pols.

It is hard for Americans today to realize what a power the Roosevelts exerted not only in our politics but in the public's imagination. There had been nothing like them since the entirely different Adamses and there has been nothing like them since—the sad story of the Kennedys bears about as much resemblance to the Roosevelts as the admittedly entertaining and cautionary television series *Dallas* does to Shakespeare's chronicle plays.

From the moment in 1898 when TR raced up Kettle Hill (incorrectly known as San Juan) to April 12, 1945, when Franklin Roosevelt died, the Roosevelts were at the republic's center stage. Also, for nearly half that fifty-year period, a Roosevelt had been president. Then, as poignant coda, Eleanor Roosevelt, now quite alone, acted for seventeen years as conscience to a world very different from that of her uncle TR or even of FDR, her cousin-husband.

In the age of the condominium and fast foods, the family has declined not only as a fact but as a concept. Although there are, presumably, just as many Roosevelts alive today as there were a century ago, they are now like everyone else, scattered about, no longer tribal or even all of the same class. Americans can now change class almost as fast—downward, at least—as they shift from city to city or job to job. A century ago, a member of the patriciate was not allowed to drop out of his class no matter how little money he had. He might be allowed to retire from the world, like TR's alcoholic brother Elliott, in order to cultivate his vices, but even Elliott remained very much a part of the family until death—not his own kind—declassed him.

As a descendant of Theodore Roosevelt said to David McCullough, author of *Mornings on Horseback*, "No writer seems to have understood the degree to which [TR] was part of a clan." A clan that was on the rise, socially and financially, in nineteenth-century New York City. In three generations the Roosevelts had gone from hardware to plate glass to land development and banking (Chemical). By and large, the Roosevelts of that era were a solemn, hard-working, uninspired lot who, according to the *New York World*, had a tendency "to cling to the fixed and the venerable." Then, suddenly, out of this clan of solid burghers erupted the restless Theodore and his interesting siblings. How did this happen? *Cherchez la mère* is the usual key to the unexpected—for good or ill—in a family's history.

During Winston Churchill's last government, a minister found him in the Cabinet room, staring at a newspaper headline: one of his daughters had been arrested, yet again, for drunkenness. The minister said something consoling. Churchill grunted. The minister was then inspired to ask: "How is it possible that a Churchill could end up like this?" To which the old man replied: "Do you realize just *what* there was between the first Duke of Marlborough and *me*?" Plainly, a genetic disaster area had been altered, in Winston's case, by an American mother, Jennie Jerome, and in Theodore Roosevelt's case by a southern mother, named Mittie Bulloch, a beautiful, somewhat eccentric woman whom everyone delighted in even though she was not, to say the least, old New York. Rather, she was proudly southern and told her sons exciting stories of what their swashbuckling southern kin had done on land and sea. In later life, everyone agreed that Theodore was more Bulloch than Roosevelt just as his cousin Franklin was more Delano—or at least *Sara* Delano—than Roosevelt.

Mr. McCullough's book belongs to a new and welcome genre: the biographical sketch. Edmund Wilson in *Patriotic Gore* and Richard Hofstadter in *The American Political Tradition* were somewhat specialized practitioners of this art but, by and large, from Plutarch to Strachey, it has been more of a European than an American genre. Lately, American biography has fallen more and more into the hands not of writers but of academics. That some academics write very well indeed is, of course, perfectly true and, of course, perfectly rare. When it comes to any one of the glorious founders of our imperial republic, the ten-volume hagiography is now the rule. Under the direction of a tenured Capo, squads of graduate students spend years assembling every known fact, legend, statistic. The Capo then factors everything into the text, like sand into a cement mixer. The result is, literally, monumental, and unreadable. Even such minor figures as Ernest Hemingway and Sinclair Lewis have been accorded huge volumes in which every letter, telegram, drunken quarrel is memorialized at random. "Would *you* read this sort of book?" I asked Mark Schorer, holding up his thick life of Sinclair Lewis. He blinked, slightly startled by my bad manners. "Well," he said mildly, politely, "I must say I never really *liked* Lewis's work all that much."

Now, as bright footnotes to the academic texts, we are offered such books as Otto Friedrich's *Clover* and Jean Strouse's *Alice James*. These sketches seem to me to belong to literature in a way that Schorer's *Sinclair Lewis* or Dumas Malone's *Jefferson and His Time* do not—the first simply a journeyman compilation, the second a banal hagiography (with, admittedly, extremely valuable footnotes). In a sense, the reader of Malone et al. is obliged to make his own text out of the unshaped raw material while the reader of Strouse or Friedrich is given a finished work of literature that supplies the reader with an idiosyncratic view of the subject. To this genre *Mornings on Horseback* belongs: a sketch of Theodore Roosevelt's parents, brothers and sisters, wife, and self until the age of twenty-eight. Mr. McCullough has done a good swift job of sketching this family group.

Unfortunately, he follows in the wake not of the usual dull, ten-volume academic biography of the twenty-sixth president but of the first volume of Edmund Morris's *The Rise of Theodore Roosevelt*. This is bad luck for Mr. McCullough. Morris's work is not only splendid but covers the same period as Mr. McCullough, ending some years later with the death of McKinley. Where Mr. McCullough scores is in the portrait of the family, particularly during Theodore's youth. Fortunately, there can never be too much of a good thing. Since Morris's work has a different, longer rhythm, he does not examine at all closely those lesser lives which shaped—and explain, somewhat—the principal character.

Theodore Roosevelt, Senior, was a man of good works; unlike his wife Mittie. "She played no part in his good works, and those speculations on life in the hereafter or the status of one's soul, speculations that appear in Theodore's correspondence . . . are not to be found in what she wrote. She was not an agnostic exactly," writes McCullough, but at a time when the church was central to organized society she seems more than slightly indifferent or, as her own mother wrote, "If she was only a Christian, I think I could feel more satisfied."

Mittie's lack of religion was to have a lasting effect on her granddaughter Eleanor, the future Mrs. Franklin Delano Roosevelt. In 1870 Mittie placed her eldest child, Anna—known as Bamie—in Les Ruches, a girls' school at Fountainebleau. The school's creator was Mlle. Marie Souvestre, "a woman of singular poise and great culture, but also an outspoken agnostic . . . as brief as Bamie's time there would be, Mlle. Souvestre's influence would carry far." Indeed it did. In the next generation Bamie's niece Eleanor was also sent to school with Mlle. Souvestre, now removed to Allenwood in England. One of Mlle. Souvestre's teachers was Dorothy Bussy, a sister of Lytton Strachey and the pseudonymous as well as eponymous author of *Olivia* by Olivia, a story of *amitiés particulières* in a girls' school.

Bamie was not to marry until she was forty, while Eleanor's dislike of heterosexuality was lifelong ("*They* think of nothing else," she once said to me, grimly—and somewhat vaguely, for she never really said exactly who "they" were); it would seem that Mlle. Souvestre and her school deserve a proper study—before M. Roger Peyrefitte gets to it. Certainly, Eleanor had learned Mlle. Souvestre's lesson well: this world is the one that we must deal with and, if possible, improve. Eleanor had no patience with the other-worldly. Neither had her uncle TR. In a letter to Bamie, the future president says that he is marrying for a second time—the first wife had died. As a highly moral man, he is disgusted with himself. So much so that "were I sure there were a heaven my one prayer would be I might never go there, lest I should meet those I loved on earth who are dead."

A recurrent theme in this family chronicle is ill health. Bamie had a disfiguring curvature of the spine. Elliott had what sounds like epileptic fits. Then, at thirty-four, he was dead of alcoholism, in West 102nd Street, looked after by a mistress. Theodore, Junior's general physical fragility was made intolerable by asthma. Mr. McCullough has done a good deal of research into asthma, that most debilitating and frightening of nervous afflictions. "Asthma is repeatedly described as a 'suppressed cry for the mother'—a cry of rage as well as a cry for help." Asthmatics live in constant terror of the next attack, which will always seem to be—if indeed it is not—terminal.

Parenthetically, I ran into the Wise Hack not long ago—in the lobby of the Beverly Hills Hotel. Where else? He is now very old, very rich: he owns a lot of Encino. Although he will no longer watch a movie made after 1945, he still keeps an eye on "the product." He knows all the deals. "One funny thing," he said, wheezing from emphysema—not asthma. "You know, all these hotshot young directors they got now? Well, every last one of them is a fat sissy who likes guns. And every last one of them has those thick glasses and the asthma." But before I could get him to give me the essential data, as Mrs. Wharton used to say, he had been swept into the Polo Lounge by the former managing editor of *Liberty*.

I must say that I thought of the Wise Hack's gnomic words as I read Mr. McCullough's account of TR's asthma attacks, which usually took place on a Sunday "which in the Victorian era was still the Lord's day . . . the one day of the week when the head of the household was home from work. . . ." Sunday also involved getting dressed up and going to church, something TR did not like. On the other hand, he enjoyed everyone's attention once the attacks had ended. Eventually, father and son came under the spell of a Dr. Salter, who had written that "organs are made for action, not existence; they are made to *work*, not to be; and when they *work* well, they can *be* well." You must change your life, said Rilke's Apollo. And that is what the young TR did: he went to a gymnasium, became an outdoorsman, built up his fragile body. At Harvard he was five foot eight inches tall and weighed one hundred twenty-five pounds. In later life, he was no taller but he came to weigh more than two hundred pounds; he was definitely a butterball type, though a vigorous one. He also wore thick glasses; liked guns.

Unlike the sissies who now make violent movies celebrating those who kill others, Theodore was a sissy who did not know that he was one until he was able to do something about it. For one thing, none of the Roosevelt children was sent to school. They were tutored at home. The boys seemed not to have had a great deal to do with other boys outside their own tribe. When Theodore went to Harvard, he was on his own for the first time in his life. But even at Harvard, Mittie would not allow him to room with other boys. He had an apartment in a private house; and a manservant. At first, he was probably surprised to find that he was unpopular with the other students; but then he was not used to dealing with those he did not know. He was very much a prig. "I had a headache," he writes in his diary, aged eleven, "and Conie and Ellie made a tremendous noise playing at my expense and rather laughed when I remonstrated."

At Harvard, he was very conscious of who was and who was not a gentleman. "I stand 19th in the class. . . . Only one gentleman stands ahead of me." He did not smoke; he got drunk on only one occasion—when he joined the Porcellian Club; he remained "pure" sexually. He was a lively, energetic youth who spoke rapidly, biting off his words as if afraid there would not be enough breath for him to say what he wanted to say. Properly bespectacled and gunned since the age of thirteen, he shot and killed every bird and animal that he could; he was also a fair taxidermist. Toward the end of his Harvard career, he was accepted as what he was, a not unattractive New York noble who was also rich; his income was $8,000 a year, about $80,000 in today's money. In his last two years at Harvard "clothes and club dues . . . added up to $2,400, a sum the average American family could have lived on for six years."

In later years, Theodore was remembered by a classmate as "a joke . . . active and enthusiastic and that was all," while a girl of his generation said "he was not the sort to appeal at first." Harvard's President Eliot, who prided himself on knowing no one, remembered Theodore as "feeble" and rather shallow. According to Mr. McCullough, he made "no lasting male friendships" at Harvard, but then, like so many men of power, he had few attachments outside his own family. During the early part of his life he had only one friend—Henry Cabot (known as La-de-dah) Lodge, a Boston aristo-sissy much like himself.

The death of his father was a shattering experience; and the family grew even closer to one another than before. Then Theodore fell in love and added a new member to the clan. When TR met Alice Lee, she was seventeen and he was nineteen. "See that girl," he said to Mrs. Robert Bacon at a party. "I am going to marry her. She won't have me, but I am going to have *her*." Have her he did. "Alice," said Mrs. Bacon years later, "did not want to marry him, but she did." They were married October 27, 1880, on Theodore's twenty-second birthday. They lived happily ever after—for four years. Alice died of Bright's disease, shortly after giving birth to their daughter; a few hours earlier, in the same house, Mittie had died of typhoid fever. The double blow entirely changed Theodore's life. He went west to become a rancher, leaving little Alice with his sister Bamie. That same year Elliott also became a father when his wife, Anna Hall, gave birth to Eleanor.

In 1876, as General Grant's second administration fell apart in a storm of scandal and the winds of reform gathered force, New York State's great lord of corruption, Senator Roscoe Conkling, observed with characteristic sour wit: "When Dr. Johnson defined patriotism as the last refuge of a scoundrel, he ignored the enormous possibilities of the word reform." Since good Republicans like Theodore Roosevelt, Senior, could not endure what was happening to their party and country, they joined together to cleanse party, country.

As a member of the New York delegation to the Republican convention at Cincinnati, Theodore, Senior, helped deny both Conkling and James G. Blaine, another lord of corruption, the nomination for president. After a good deal of confusion the dim but blameless Rutherford B. Hayes was nominated. Although Hayes was not exactly *elected* president, he became the president as a result of the Republican Party's continued mastery of corruption at every level of the republic.

The new president then offered Theodore, Senior, the Collectorship of the Port of New York, a powerhouse of patronage and loot that had been for some years within Conkling's gift. And so it remained: thanks to Conkling's efforts in the Senate, Theodore, Senior, was denied the Collectorship. A week after this rejection, he wrote his son at Harvard to say that, all in all, he was relieved that he was not to be obliged to "purify our Customhouse." Nevertheless, he was glad that he had fought the good fight against the "machine politicians" who "think of nothing higher than their own interests. I fear for your future. We cannot stand so corrupt a government for any great length of time." This was the last letter from father to son. Two months later Theodore, Senior, was dead of cancer, at the age of forty-six.

Although TR worshiped his father, he does not seem to have been particularly interested in the politics of reform. During the Collectorship battle, he had wanted to be a naturalist; later he thought of writing, and began to compose what proved to be, or so one is told, a magisterial study

of the early years of the American navy, *The Naval War of 1812*. He also
attended Columbia Law School until 1881, when he got himself elected
to the New York State Assembly. He was twenty-three years old; as lively
and bumptious as ever.

Much had been made of what a startling and original and noble thing
it was for a rich young aristo to enter the sordid politics of New York
State. Actually, quite a number of young men of the ruling class were going into politics, often inspired by fathers who had felt, like Theodore,
Senior, that the republic could not survive so much corruption. In fact,
no less a grandee than the young William Waldorf Astor had been elected
to the Assembly (1877) while, right in the family, TR's Uncle Rob had
served in Congress, as a Democrat. There is no evidence that Theodore
went into politics with any other notion than to have an exciting time and
to rise to the top. He had no theory of government. He was, simply, loyal
to his class—or what he called, approvingly, "our kind." He found the
Tammany politicians repellent on physical and social as well as political
grounds.

To TR's credit, he made no effort at all to be one of the boys; quite
the contrary. He played the city dude to the hilt. In Albany, he arrived at
his first Republican caucus, according to an eyewitness, "as if he had
been ejected by a catapult. He had on an enormous great ulster . . . and
he pulled off his coat; he was dressed in full dress, he had been to dinner somewhere. . . ." Even then, his high-pitched voice and upper-class
accent proved to be a joy for imitators, just as his niece Eleanor's voice—
so very like his—was a staple of mimics for fifty years. To the press, he
was known, variously, as a "Jane-Dandy," "his Lordship," "Oscar Wilde,"
"the exquisite Mr. Roosevelt." He sailed above these epithets. He was in
a hurry to . . . do what?

Mr. McCullough quotes Henry James's description of a similar character in *The Bostonians* (published five years after Theodore's entry into
politics): "He was full of purpose to live . . . and with a high success; to
become great, in order not to be obscure, and powerful not to be useless." In politics, it is character rather than ideas that makes for success;
and the right sort of character combined with high energy can be fairly
irresistible. Although TR was the most literary of our post–Civil War
presidents, he had a mind that was more alert to fact than to theory. Like

his father, he was against corruption and machine politicians, and that was pretty much that—until he met Samuel Gompers, a rising young trade unionist. Gompers took the dude around the tenements of New York City; showed him how immigrants were forced to live, doing such sweated labor as making cigars for wealthy firms. TR had planned to oppose a bill that the Cigarmaker's Union had sponsored, outlawing the manufacture of cigars "at home." After all, TR was a laissez-faire man; he had already opposed a minimum wage of $2.00 a day for municipal workers. But the tour of the tenements so shocked the dude that he supported the Cigar Bill.

TR also began to understand just how the United States was governed. Predictably, he found the unsavory Jay Gould at the center of a web that involved not only financiers but judges and newspaper proprietors and, to his horror, people that he knew socially. He describes how a kindly friend of the family, someone whom he referred to as a "member of a prominent law firm," explained the facts of life to him. Since *everyone*, more or less openly, did business with the likes of Jay Gould, TR was advised to give up "the reform play" and settle down as a representative member of the city's ruling—as opposed to governing—class. This was the sort of advice that was guaranteed to set him furiously in motion. He had found, at last, the Horatio-at-the-bridge role that he had been looking for. He took on the powers that be; and he coined a famous phrase, "the wealthy criminal class." Needless to say, he got nowhere in this particular battle, but by the time he was twenty-six he had made a national name for himself, the object of the exercise. He had also proven yet again that he could take it, was no sissy, had what Mark Sullivan was to call "a trait of ruthless righteousness."

In 1884, TR was a delegate to the Republican convention where, once again, James G. Blaine was a candidate. Like his father before him, TR joined the reformers; and together they fought to eliminate Blaine; but this time the gorgeous old trickster finally got the nomination, only to lose the election to Grover Cleveland. But by the time Cleveland was elected, the young widower and ex-assemblyman was playing cowboy in the Dakota Badlands. Just before TR disappeared into the wilderness, he made what was to be the most important decision of his career. In 1884 the reform Republicans deserted Blaine much as the antiwar Democrats were to abandon Hubert Humphrey in 1968. But TR had already made up his mind that he was going to have a major political career and so, cold-bloodedly, he endorsed Blaine: "I have been called a reformer but I am a Republican." For this show of solidarity with the Grand Old Party, he lost the decent opinion of the reformers and gained the presidency. He might have achieved both, but that would have required moral courage, something he had not been told about.

Give a sissy a gun and he will kill everything in sight. TR's slaughter of the animals in the Badlands outdoes in spades the butcheries of that sissy of a later era, Ernest Hemingway. Elks, grizzly bears, blacktail bucks are killed joyously while a bear cub is shot, TR reports proudly, "clean through . . . from end to end" (the Teddy bear was yet to be invented). "By Godfrey, but this is fun!" TR was still very much the prig, at least in speech: "He immortalized himself along the Little Missouri by calling to one of his cowboys, 'Hasten forward quickly here!' " Years later he wrote: "There were all kinds of things of which I was afraid at first, ranging from grizzly bears to 'mean' horses and gunfighters; but by acting as if I was not afraid I gradually ceased to be afraid."

There is something strangely infantile in this obsession with dice-loaded physical courage when the only courage that matters in political or even "real" life is moral. Although TR was often reckless and always domineering in politics, he never showed much real courage, and despite some trust-busting, he never took on the great ring of corruption that ruled and rules in this republic. But then, he was born a part of it. At best, he was just a dude with the reform play. Fortunately, foreign affairs would bring him glory. As Lincoln was the Bismarck of the American states, Theodore Roosevelt was the Kaiser Wilhelm II, a more fortunate and intelligent figure than the Kaiser but every bit as bellicose and conceited. Edith Wharton described with what pride TR showed her a photograph of himself and the Kaiser with the Kaiser's inscription: "President Roosevelt shows the Emperor of Germany how to command an attack."

I once asked Alice Longworth just why her father was such a war-lover. She denied that he was. I quoted her father's dictum: "No triumph of peace is quite as great as the supreme triumph of war." A sentiment to be echoed by yet another sissy in the next generation: *"Meglio un giorno da leone che cento anni da pecora."* "Oh, well," she said, "that's the way they all sounded in those days." But they did not all sound that way. Certainly Theodore, Senior, would have been appalled, and I doubt if Eleanor really approved of Uncle Teddy's war-mongering.

As president, TR spoke loudly and carried a fair-sized stick. When Colombia wouldn't give him the land that he needed for a canal, he helped invent Panama out of a piece of Colombia; and got his canal. He also installed the United States as the policeman of the Western Hemisphere. In order to establish an American hegemony in the Pacific, TR presided over the tail-end of the slaughter of more than half a million Filipinos who had been under the illusion that after the Spanish-American War they would be free to set up an independent republic under the leadership of Emilio Aguinaldo. But TR had other plans for the Philippines. Nice Mr. Taft was made the governor-general and one thousand American teachers of English were sent to the islands to teach the natives the sovereign's language.

Meanwhile, in the aftermath of the Boxer Rebellion, TR's "open-door policy" to China had its ups and downs. In 1905 the Chinese boycotted American goods because of American immigration policies, but the United States was still able to establish the sort of beachhead on the mainland of Asia that was bound to lead to what TR would have regarded as a bully fine war with Japan. Those of us who were involved in that war did not like it all that much.

In 1905, the world-famous Henry James came, in triumph, to Washington. He was a friend of Secretary of State John Hay and of Henry Adams. "Theodore Rex," as James called the president, felt obliged to invite the Master to the White House even though TR had denounced James as "effete" and a "miserable little snob"—it takes one to know one—while James thought of TR as "a dangerous and ominous Jingo." But the dinner was a success. James described the president as a "wonderful little machine . . . quite exciting to see. But it's really like something behind a great plate-glass window on Broadway." TR continued to loathe "the tone of satirical cynicism" of Henry James and Henry Adams while the Master finally dismissed the president as "the mere monstrous embodiment of unprecedented and resounding noise."

Alice Longworth used to boast that she and her father's viceroy Taft were the last Westerners to be received by the Dowager Empress of China. "We went to Peking. To the Forbidden City. And there we were taken to see this strange little old lady standing at the end of a room. Well, there was no bowing or scraping for us. So we marched down the room just behind the chamberlain, a eunuch, like one of those in that book of yours, *Justinian*, who slithered on his belly toward her. After he had announced us, she gave him a kick and he rolled over like a dog and slithered out." What had they talked about? She couldn't recall. I had my impression that she rather liked the way the empress treated her officials.

In the years before World War II, Alice was to be part of a marital rectangle. The heart having its reasons, Alice saw fit to conduct a long affair with the corrupt Senator William Borah, the so-called lion of Idaho, who had once roared, "I'd rather be right than president," causing my grandfather to murmur, "Of course, he was neither." In 1940, when the poor and supposedly virtuous Borah died, several hundred thousand dollars were found in his safety deposit box. Where had the money come from? asked the press. "He was my friend," said Senator Gore, for public consumption, "I do not speculate." But when I asked him who had paid off Borah, the answer was blunt. "The Nazis. To keep us out of the war." Meanwhile, Alice's husband, the Speaker of the House Nicholas Longworth, was happily involved with Mrs. Tracy (another Alice) Dows.

Rather late in life, Alice Longworth gave birth to her only child. In *The Making of Nicholas Longworth*, by Longworth's sister Clara de Chambrun, there is a touching photograph of Longworth holding in his arms a child whose features are unmistakably those of a lion's cub. "I should have been a grandmother, not a mother," Alice used to say of her daughter. But then, she had as little maternal instinct toward her only child as TR had had paternal instinct for her. When Nicholas Longworth died in 1931, Alice Dows told me how well Alice Longworth had behaved. "She asked me to go with her in the private train that took Nick back to Ohio. Oh, it was very moving. Particularly the way Alice treated me, as if *I* was the widow, which I suppose I was." She paused; then the handsome, square-jawed face broke into a smile and she used the Edwardian phrase: "Too killing."

When Alice Dows died she left me a number of her books. Among them was *The Making of Nicholas Longworth*, which I have just read. It is a loving, quite uninteresting account of what must have been a charming, not very interesting man. On the page where Alice Dows makes her appearance "one evening at Mrs. Tracy Dows's home . . . ," she had placed a four-leaf clover—now quite faded: nice emblem for a lucky lot.

In the electronic era, letter-writing has declined while diaries are kept only by those ill-educated, crazed, lone killers who feel obliged to report, in clinical detail, just how crazed and solitary they are as they prepare to assassinate political leaders. Except for Christopher Isherwood, I can think of no contemporary literary figure who has kept, for most of a lifetime, a journal. *The Diaries of Anaïs Nin* were, of course, her fiction. Fortunately, the preelectronic Roosevelts and their friends wrote countless letters and journals and books, and Mr. McCullough has done a good job of selection; one is particularly grateful for excerpts from the writings of Elliott Roosevelt, a rather more natural and engaging writer than his industrious but not always felicitous older brother. Mr. McCullough's own style is easy to the point of incoherence. "The horse he rode so hard day after day that he all but ruined it," sounds more like idle dictation than written English. But, all in all, he has succeeded in showing us how a certain world, now lost, shaped the young Theodore Roosevelt. I think it worth noting that Simon and Schuster has managed to produce the worst set of bound galleys that I have ever read. There are so many misspellings that one has no sense of TR's own hit-or-miss approach to spelling, while two pages are entirely blank.

Now that war is once more thinkable among the thoughtless, Theodore Roosevelt should enjoy a revival. Certainly, the New Right will find his jingoism appealing, though his trust-busting will give less pleasure to the Honorable Society of the Invisible Hand. The figure that emerges from the texts of both Mr. McCullough and Mr. Morris is both fascinating and repellent. Theodore Roosevelt was a classic American sissy who overcame—or appeared to overcome—his physical fragility through "manly" activities of which the most exciting and ennobling was war.

As a politician-writer, Theodore Roosevelt most closely resembles Winston Churchill and Benito Mussolini. Each was as much a journalist as a politician. Each was a sissy turned showoff. The not unwitty Churchill—the most engaging of the lot—once confessed that if no one had been watching him he could quite easily have run away during a skirmish in the Boer War. Each was a romantic, in love with the nineteenth-century notion of earthly glory, best personified by Napoleon Bonaparte, whose eagerness to do in *his* biological superiors led to such a slaughter of alpha-males that the average French soldier of 1914 was markedly shorter than the soldier of 1800—pretty good going for a fat little fellow, five foot four inches tall—with, to be fair, no history of asthma.

As our dismal century draws to a close, it is fairly safe to say that no matter what tricks and torments are in store for us, we shall not see *their* like again. Faceless computer analysts and mindless cue-card readers will preside over our bright noisy terminus.

The New York Review of Books
August 13, 1981

THE SECOND

AMERICAN REVOLUTION

Future generations, if there are any, will date the second American Revolution, if there is one, from the passage of California's Proposition 13 in
1978, which obliged the managers of that gilded state to reduce by more
than half the tax on real estate. Historically, this revolt was not unlike the
Boston Tea Party, which set in train those events that led to the separation of England's thirteen American colonies from the crown and to the
creation, in 1787, of the First Constitution. And in 1793 (after the addition of the Bill of Rights) of the Second Constitution. And in 1865 of the
Third Constitution, the result of those radical alterations made by the
Thirteenth, Fourteenth, and Fifteenth amendments. Thus far we have
had three Constitutions for three quite different republics. Now a Fourth
Constitution—and republic—is ready to be born.

The people of the United States (hereinafter known forever and eternally as We) are deeply displeased with their government as it now malfunctions. Romantics who don't read much think that all will be well if
we would only return, somehow, to the original Constitution, to the
ideals of the founders, to a strict construction of what the Framers (nice
word) of the First Constitution saw fit to commit to parchment during
the hot summer of 1787 at Philadelphia. Realists think that an odd
amendment or two and better men in government (particularly in the

Oval Office, where too many round and square pegs have, in recent years, rattled about) would put things right.

It is taken for granted by both romantics and realists that the United States is the greatest country on earth as well as in the history of the world, with a government that is the envy of the lesser breeds just as the lifestyle of its citizens is regarded with a grinding of teeth by the huddled masses of old Europe—while Africa, mainland Asia, South America are not even in the running. Actually, none of the hundred or so new countries that have been organized since World War II has imitated our form of government—though, to a nation, the local dictator likes to style himself the president. As for being the greatest nation on earth, the United States's hegemony of the known world lasted exactly five years: 1945 to 1950. As for being envied by the less fortunate (in a *Los Angeles Times* poll of October 1, 1980, 71 percent of the gilded state's citizens thought that the United States had "the highest living standard in the world today"), the United States has fallen to ninth place in per-capita income while living standards are higher for the average citizen in more than eight countries.

Although this sort of information is kept from the 71 percent, they are very much aware of inflation, high taxes, and unemployment. Because they know that something is wrong, Proposition 13, once a mere gleam in the eye of Howard K. Jarvis, is now the law in California and something like it has just been enacted in Massachusetts and Arkansas. Our ancestors did not like paying taxes on their tea; we do not like paying taxes on our houses, traditionally the only form of capital that the average middle-class American is allowed to accumulate.

Today, thanks to the efforts of the National Taxpayers Union, thirty state legislatures have voted in favor of holding a new constitutional convention whose principal object would be to stop the federal government's systematic wrecking of the economic base of the country by requiring, somewhat naïvely, a balanced federal budget and, less naïvely, a limitation on the federal government's power to print money in order to cover over-appropriations that require over-borrowing, a process (when combined with a fifteen-year decline in industrial productivity) that has led to double-digit inflation in a world made more than usually dangerous by

the ongoing chaos in the Middle East from which the West's oil flows—
or does not flow.

Even the newspapers that belong to the governing establishment of
the republic are beginning to fret about that national malaise which used
to trouble the thirty-ninth Oval One. Two years ago, *The New York Times*
printed three articles, more in sorrow than in anger, on how, why, where,
when did it all go wrong? "The United States is becoming increasingly
difficult to govern," the *Times* keened, "because of a fragmented, inefficient system of authority and procedures that has developed over the last
decade and now appears to be gaining strength and impact, according to
political leaders, scholars and public interest groups across the country."

Were this not an observation by an establishment newspaper, one
would think it a call for a Mussolini: "difficult to govern . . . inefficient
system of authority. . . ." Surely, We the People govern, don't we? This
sort of dumb sentiment is passed over by the *Times*, which notes that
"the national political parties have continued to decline until they are little more than frameworks for nominating candidates and organizing Congress and some state legislatures." But this is all that our political parties
have ever done (honorable exceptions are the first years of the Republican party and the only years of the Populists). The Framers did not want
political parties—or factions, to use their word. So what has evolved over
the years are two pieces of electoral machinery devoted to the acquiring
of office—and money. Since neither party represents anything but the interests of those who own and administer the country, there is not apt to
be much "choice" in any election.

Normally, *The New York Times* is perfectly happy with any arrangement of which the *Times* is an integral part. But a series of crazy military
adventures combined with breathtaking mismanagement of the economy
(not to mention highly noticeable all-out corruption among the politicos)
has thrown into bright relief the failure of the American political system.
So the thirty-ninth Oval One blames the people while the people blame
the lousy politicians and wish that Frank Capra would once more pick up
the megaphone and find us another Gary Cooper (*not* the second lead)
and restore The Dream.

Serious establishment types worry about the Fragmentation of Power.

"Our political system has become dominated by special interests," said one to the *Times*, stars falling from his eyes like crocodile tears. After all, our political system is—and was—the invention of those special interests. The government has been from the beginning the *cosa nostra* of the few and the people at large have always been excluded from the exercise of power. None of our rulers wants to change this state of affairs. Yet the heirs of the Framers are getting jittery; and sense that something is going wrong somewhere. But since nothing can ever be their fault, it must be the fault of a permissive idle electorate grown fat (literally) before our eyes, which are television. So give the drones less wages; more taxes; and put them on diets.

But the politician must proceed warily; if he does not, that 71 percent which has been conned into thinking that they enjoy the highest standard of living in the world might get suspicious. So for a while the operative word was "malaise" in political circles; and no effort was made to change anything. Certainly no one has recognized that the principal source of all our problems is the Third Constitution, which allows the big property owners to govern pretty much as they please, without accountability to the people or to anyone else, since for at least a century the Supreme Court was perhaps the most active—even reckless—part of the federal machinery, as we shall demonstrate.

There is more than the usual amount of irony in the fact that our peculiar Constitution is now under siege from those who would like to make it either more oppressive (the Right-to-Lifers who want the Constitution to forbid abortion) or from those sly folks who want to make more and more money out of their real estate shelters. But no matter what the motive for change, change is now very much in the air; and that is a good thing.

This autumn, the counsel to the president, Mr. Lloyd N. Cutler, proposed some basic changes in the Constitution.* Although Mr. Cutler's approach was tentative and highly timid (he found no fault at all with the Supreme Court—because he is a partner in a Washington law firm?), he does think that it is impossible for a president to govern under the present Constitution because the separation of powers has made for a stalemate

*Foreign Affairs, Fall 1980.

between executive and legislative branches. Since "we are not about to revise our own Constitution so as to incorporate a true parliamentary system," he proceeded to make a number of suggestions that would indeed give us a quasi-parliamentary form of government—president, vice-president, and representative from each congressional district would all be elected at the same time for a four-year term (Rep. Jonathan Bingham has such a bill before the House); half the Cabinet to be selected from the Congress where they would continue to sit—and answer questions as in England; the president would have the power, once in his term, to dissolve the Congress and hold new elections—and the Congress would have the power, by a two-thirds vote, to call for a new presidential election; et cetera. Mr. Cutler throws out a number of other notions that would involve, at most, amendments to the Constitution; he believes that a new constitutional convention is a "non-starter" and so whatever change that is made must originate in the government as it now is even though, historically, no government has ever voluntarily dissolved itself.

Mr. Cutler also suffers from the malaise syndrome, contracted no doubt while serving in the Carter White House: "The public—and the press—still expect the president to govern. But the president cannot achieve his overall program, and the public cannot fairly blame the president because he does not have the power to legislate and execute his program." This is perfect establishment nonsense. The president and the Congress together or the president by himself or the Supreme Court on its own very special power trip can do virtually anything that they want to do as a result of a series of usurpations of powers that have been taking place ever since the Second Constitution of 1793.

When a president claims that he is blocked by Congress or Court, this usually means that he does not want to take a stand that might lose him an election. He will then complain that he is stymied by Congress or Court. In 1977, Carter could have had an energy policy *if* he had wanted one. What the president cannot get directly from Congress (very little if he knows how to manage those princes of corruption), he can often obtain through executive order, secure in the knowledge that the House of Representatives is not apt to exercise its prerogative of refusing to fund the executive branch: after all, it was nearly a decade before Congress turned off the money for the Vietnam war. In recent years, the presidents have nicely put Congress over a barrel through the impounding of money appropriated for projects displeasing to the executive. Impounded funds combined with the always vast Pentagon budget and the secret revenues of the CIA give any president a plump cushion on which to rest his Pharaonic crook and flail.

Obviously, a president who does not respect the decent opinion of mankind (namely, *The New York Times*) can find himself blocked by the Court and impeached by Congress. But the Nixon misadventure simply demonstrated to what extremes a president may go before his money is turned off—before the gates of Lewisberg Federal Penitentiary, like those to Hell or Disneyland, swing open.

Carter could have given us gas rationing, disciplined the oil cartels, encouraged the development of alternative forms of energy. He did none of those things because he might have hurt his chances of reelection. So he blamed Congress for preventing him from doing what he did not want to do. This is a game that all presidents play—and Congress, too. Whenever the Supreme Court strikes down a popular law which Congress has been obliged to enact against its better judgment, the Supreme Court gets the blame for doing what the Congress wanted to do but dared not. Today separation of powers is a useful device whereby any sin of omission or commission can be shifted from one branch of government to another. It is naïve of Mr. Cutler to think that the president he worked for could not have carried out almost any program *if he had wanted to*. After all, for eight years Johnson and Nixon prosecuted the longest and least popular war in American history by executive order. Congress's sacred and exclusive right to declare war was ignored (by Congress as well as by the presidents) while the Supreme Court serenely fiddled as Southeast Asia burned. Incidentally, it is startling to note that neither Congress nor the Court has questioned the *principle* of executive order, even in the famous steel seizure case.

What *was* the original Constitution all about? I mean by this, what was in the document of 1787 as defended in the Federalist Papers of 1787–1788 by Madison, Hamilton, and Jay? Currently, Ferdinand Lundberg's *Cracks in the Constitution* is as good a case history of that Constitution (and its two successors) as we are apt to get this troubled season. Lundberg is the latest—if not the last—in the great line of muckrakers (TR's contemptuous phrase for those who could clean with Heraclean zeal the national stables which he, among others, had soiled) that began with Steffens and Tarbell. Luckily for us, Lundberg is still going strong.

The father of the country was the father if not of the Constitution of the convention that met in May 1787, in Philadelphia. Washington had been troubled by the civil disorders in Massachusetts in particular and by the general weakness of the original Articles of Confederation in general. From Mount Vernon came the word; and it was heard—and obeyed—all around the states. Quick to respond was Washington's wartime aide Alexander Hamilton, who knew exactly what was needed in the way of a government. Hamilton arrived at Philadelphia with a scheme for a president and a senate and a supreme court to serve for life—while the state governors would be appointed by the federal government.

Although neither John Adams nor John Jay was present in the flesh at Philadelphia, Jay's handiwork, the constitution of New York State (written with Gouverneur Morris and R. J. Livingston), was on view as was that of John Adams, who wrote nearly all of the Massachusetts state constitution; these two charters along with that of Maryland were the basis of the convention's final draft, a curious document which in its separation of powers seemed to fulfill not only Montesquieu's cloudy theories of separation of powers but, more precisely, was a mirror image of the British tripartite arrangement of crown, bicameral legislature, and independent judiciary. Only the aged Franklin opted for a unicameral legislature. But the other Framers had a passion for England's House of Lords; and so gave us the Senate.

Lundberg discusses at some length just who the Framers were and where they came from and how much money they had. The state legislatures accredited seventy-four men to the convention. Fifty-five showed up that summer. About half drifted away. Finally, "no more than five men provided most of the discussion with some seven more playing fitful supporting roles." Thirty-three Framers were lawyers (already the blight had set in); forty-four were present or past members of Congress; twenty-one were rated rich to very rich—Washington and the banker Robert Morris (soon to go to jail where Washington would visit him) were the richest;

"another thirteen were affluent to very affluent"; nineteen were slave owners; twenty-five had been to college (among those who had *not* matriculated were Washington, Hamilton, Robert Morris, George Mason—Hamilton was a Columbia dropout). Twenty-seven had been officers in the war; one was a twice-born Christian—the others tended to deism, an eighteenth-century euphemism for agnosticism or atheism.

All in all, Lundberg regards the Framers as "a gathering of routine politicians, eyes open for the main chance of a purely material nature. . . . What makes them different from latter-day politicians is that in an age of few distractions, many—at least twenty—were readers to varying extents in law, government, history and classics."

Lundberg does not accept the traditional American view that a consortium of intellectual giants met at Philadelphia in order to answer once and for all the vexing questions of how men are to be governed. Certainly, a reading of the Federalist Papers bears out Lundberg. Although writers about the Constitution like to mention Locke, Hume, Montesquieu, and the other great savants of the Enlightenment as godfathers to the new nation, Montesquieu is quoted only four times in the Federalist Papers; while Hume is quoted just once (by Hamilton) in a passage of ringing banality. Locke is not mentioned. Fans of the Framers can argue that the spirit of Locke is ever-present; but then non-fans can argue that the prevailing spirit of the debate is that of the never mentioned but always felt Hobbes. There is one reference each to Grotius, Plato, and Polybius. There are three references to Plutarch (who wrote about great men) and three to Blackstone (who showed the way to greatness—or at least the higher solvency—to lawyers). God is mentioned three times (in the Thank God sense) by Madison, a clergyman's son who had studied theology. Jesus, the Old and New Testaments, abortion, and women's rights are not alluded to. The general tone is that of a meeting of the trust department of Sullivan and Cromwell.

Lundberg quotes Merrill Jensen as saying, "Far more research is needed before we can know, if ever, how many men actually voted for delegates to the state conventions [which chose the Framers]. An old guess that about 160,000 voted—that is, not more than a fourth or fifth of the total adult (white) male population—is probably as good as any. About 100,000 of these men voted for supporters of the Constitution and about 60,000 for its opponents." It should be noted that the total population of the United States in 1787 was about 3,000,000, of which some 600,000 were black slaves. For census purposes, each slave would be counted as three fifths of a person within the First Republic.

The Framers feared monarchy and democracy. In order to prevent the man who would be king from assuming dictatorial powers and the people at large from seriously affecting the business of government, the Framers devised a series of checks and balances within a tripartite government that would, they hoped (none was very optimistic: they were practical men), keep the people and their passions away from government and the would-be dictator hedged 'round with prohibitions.

In the convention debates, Hamilton took on the romantic notion of the People: "The voice of the people has been said to be the voice of God; and however generally this maxim has been quoted and believed, it is not true in fact. The people are turbulent and changing; they seldom judge or determine right. Give therefore to [the rich and wellborn] a distinct, permanent share in the government." The practical old Tory Gouverneur Morris took the same view, though he expressed himself rather more serenely than the fierce young man on the make: "The rich will strive to establish their dominion and enslave the rest. They always did. They always will. The proper security against them is to form them into a separate interest." Each was arguing for a Senate of lifetime appointees, to be chosen by the state legislatures from the best and the richest. It is curious that neither envisioned political parties as the more natural way of balancing economic interests.

Since Hamilton's dark view of the human estate was shared rather more than less by the Framers ("Give all power to the many, they will oppress the few. Give all power to the few, they will oppress the many"), the House of Representatives was intended to be the principal engine of the tripartite government. Like the British Parliament, the House was given (in Hamilton's words) "The exclusive privilege of originating money bills. . . . The same house will possess the sole right of instituting impeachments; the same house will be the umpire in all elections of the President. . . ." And Hamilton's ultimate defense of the new Constitution (*Federalist Paper* No. 60) rested on the ingenious way that the two houses of Congress and the presidency were chosen: "The House of Representatives . . . elected immediately by the people, the Senate by the State legislatures, the President by electors chosen for that purpose by the people, there would be little probability of a common interest to cement these different branches in a predilection for any particular class of electors."

This was disingenuous: the electoral franchise was already so limited in the various states that only the propertied few had a hand in electing the House of Representatives and the state legislatures. Nevertheless, this peculiar system of government was a success in that neither the mob nor the dictator could, legally at least, prevail. The turbulent "democratic" House would always be reined in by the appointed senators in combination with the indirectly elected president and his veto. The Constitution gave the oligarch, to use Madison's word, full possession of the government—the object of the exercise at Philadelphia. Property would be defended, as George Washington had insisted that it should be. Since Jefferson's teeth were set on edge by the word property, the euphemism "pursuit of happiness" had been substituted in the Declaration of Independence. Much pleased with this happy phrase, Jefferson recommended it highly to the Marquis de Lafayette when he was Rights of Man-ing it in France.

The wisest and shrewdest analysis of how the House of Representatives would evolve was not provided by the would-be aristo Hamilton but by the demure James Madison. In *Federalist Paper* No. 59, Madison tried to set at ease those who feared that popular gathering in whose horny hands had been placed the national purse. Madison allowed that as the nation increased its population, the House would increase its membership. But, said he with perfect candor and a degree of complacency, "The people can never err more than in supposing that by multiplying their representatives beyond a certain limit they strengthen the barrier against the government of the few. Experience will forever admonish them that . . . they will counteract their own views by every addition to their representatives. The countenance of the government may become more democratic, but the soul that animates it will be more oligarchic" because "the greater the number composing [a legislative assembly] the fewer will be the men who will in fact direct their proceedings." Until the present—and temporary—breakdown of the so-called lower House, this has proved to be the case.

By May 29, 1790, the Constitution had been ratified by all the states. The need for a bill of rights had been discussed at the end of the convention but nothing had been done. Rather than call a second convention, the Bill of Rights was proposed—and accepted—as ten amendments to the new Constitution. A principal mover for the Bill of Rights was George Mason of Virginia, who had said, just before he left Philadelphia, "This government will set out [commence] a moderate aristocracy: it is at present impossible to foresee whether it will, in its operation, produce a monarchy, or a corrupt, tyrannical [oppressive] aristocracy: it will most probably vibrate some years between the two, and then terminate in the one or the other." The words in brackets were supplied by fellow Virginian—and notetaker—Madison. As the ancient Franklin observed brightly, sooner or later every republic becomes a tyranny. They liked reading history, the Framers.

But the wild card in the federal apparatus proved not to be the predictable Congress and the equally predictable presidency whose twistings and turnings any reader of Plutarch might have anticipated. The wild card was the Supreme Court.

Lundberg calls attention to the following language of Article III of the Constitution.

> *The Supreme Court shall have appellate jurisdiction, both as to law and fact,* with such exceptions, and under such regulations as the Congress shall make."
>
> *The preceding twelve words [he continues] are emphasized because they are rarely alluded to in discussions about the Court. They bring out that, under the Constitution, the Supreme Court is subject to regulation by Congress, which may make exceptions among the types of cases heard, individually or by categories. Congress, in short, is explicitly empowered by the Constitution to regulate the Court, not vice versa.*

Certainly, the Court was never explicitly given the power to review acts of Congress. But all things evolve and it is the nature of every organism to expand and extend itself.

In 1800, the outgoing Federalist President John Adams made a last-minute appointment to office of one William Marbury. The incoming

Republican President Jefferson ordered his secretary of state Madison to deny Marbury that office. Marbury based his right to office on Section 13 of Congress's Judiciary Act of 1789. Federalist Chief Justice John Marshall responded with marvelous cunning. In 1803 (*Marbury* v. *Madison*) he found unconstitutional Section 13, the work of Congress; therefore, the Court was unable to go forward and hear the case. The partisan Jefferson was happy. The equally partisan Marshall must have been secretly ecstatic: he had set a precedent. In passing, as it were, Marshall had established the right of the Supreme Court to review acts of Congress.

The notion of judicial review of the Executive or of Congress was not entirely novel. Hamilton had brought up the matter in 1787 (*Federalist Paper* No. 78). "In a monarchy [the judiciary] is an excellent barrier to the despotism of the prince; in a republic it is a no less excellent barrier to the encroachments and representations of the representative body." But the other Framers did not accept, finally, Hamilton's view of the Court as a disinterested umpire with veto power over the legislative branch. Yet Hamilton had made his case most persuasively; and he has been much echoed by subsequent upholders of judicial review.

Hamilton believed that the judiciary could never be tyrannous because it lacked real power; he does admit that "some perplexity respecting the rights of the courts to pronounce legislative acts void because contrary to the Constitution, has arisen from an imagination that the doctrine would imply a superiority of the judiciary to the legislative power. It is urged that the authority which can declare the acts of another void must necessarily be superior to the one whose acts must be declared void." Since this is true and since the Constitution that Hamilton is defending does *not* give judicial review to the Supreme Court, Hamilton does a most interesting dance about the subject. The Constitution is the "fundamental law" and derives from the people. If the legislative branch does something unconstitutional it acts against the people and so a disinterested court must protect the people from their own Congress and declare the act void.

Nor does this conclusion by any means suppose a superiority of the judicial to the legislative power. It only supposes that the power of the people is su-

perior to both, and that where the will of the legislature, declared in its
statutes, stands in opposition to that of the people, declared in the Consti-
tution, the judges ought to be governed by the latter rather than the former.

This is breathtaking, even for Hamilton. He has now asserted that a court of life appointees (chosen from the rich and wellborn) is more interested in the rights of the people than the House of Representatives, the only more or less democratically elected branch of the government. But Hamilton is speaking with the tongue of a prophet who knows which god he serves. The future in this, as in so much else, was what Hamilton had envisaged, constitutional or not. Characteristically, by 1802, he had dismissed the Constitution as "a frail and worthless fabric."

Marshall was most sensitive to the charge of judicial usurpation of congressional primacy; and during the rest of his long tenure on the bench, he never again found an act of Congress unconstitutional. But Marshall was not finished with republic-shaping. Although he shared the Framers' passion for the rights of property, he did not share the admittedly subdued passion of certain Framers for the rights of the citizens. In 1833, Marshall proclaimed (speaking for a majority of his Court in *Barron* v. *City of Baltimore*) that the Bill of Rights was binding only upon the federal government and not upon the states. In order to pull off this caper, Marshall was obliged to separate the amendments from the Constitution proper so that he could then turn to Article VI, Paragraph 2, where it is written that this Constitution (pre–Bill of Rights) "shall be the supreme law of the land . . . any thing in the Constitution or laws of any state to the contrary not withstanding." Apparently, the first ten amendments were not an integral part of "this Constitution."

The result of Marshall's decision was more than a century of arbitrary harassment of individuals by sheriffs, local police, municipal and state governing bodies—to none of whom the Bill of Rights was held to apply. As for the federal government, the Supreme Court was only rarely and feebly willing to enforce the rights of citizens against it. It is startling to think that the Supreme Court did not seriously begin to apply the Bill of Rights to the states until the 1930s despite the Fourteenth Amendment (1868), which had spelled out the rights of citizens. Gradually, over the last thirty years, an often grudging court has doled out to the people of the United States (including Mr. Brown) most of those rights which George Mason had wanted them to have in 1793.

Fifty-four years after *Marbury* v. *Madison*, the Supreme Court found a second act of Congress unconstitutional. In order to return property to its owner (the slave Dred Scott to his master Dr. Emerson), the Supreme Court declared unconstitutional the Missouri Compromise; and made inevitable the Civil War. It was ironic that the Court which Hamilton had so Jesuitically proposed as a defender of the people against a wicked legislature should, in its anxiety to protect property of any kind, have blundered onto a stage where it had neither competence nor even provenance. (Article IV: "The Congress shall have power to dispose of and make all needful rules and regulations respecting the territory or other property belonging to the United States. . . .") But the wild card had now been played. Judicial review was a fact. The Court was now ready—give or take a Civil War or two—to come into its unconstitutional own.

In 1864, the Court struck down the income tax, denying Congress its absolute power to raise revenue; and not until the passage of the Sixteenth Amendment (1913) did Congress get back its right, in this instance, to raise taxes—which it can never *not* have had, under the Constitution. But as Lundberg says, "The Court had gained nearly eighteen years of tax-free bliss for its patrons although it was shown to be out of harmony with the thinking of the country as well as that of the framers, previous courts, and legal scholars—and the Constitution."

From March 9, 1865 (when the management of the reigning Republican party became almost totally corrupt), to 1970, ninety acts of Congress were held void in whole or in part. Most of these decisions involved property, and favored large property owners. As of 1970, the Court had also managed to overrule itself 143 times. Plainly, the Constitution that the justices keep interpreting and reinterpreting is a more protean document than the Framers suspected. "The trouble with the Constitution of the United States," wrote the *London Chronicle* a century ago, "is that nobody has ever been able to find out what it means." Or, put another way, since everybody knows what it means, much trouble must be taken to distort the meaning in order to make new arrangements for the protection of property.

Lundberg takes the position that, by and large, the Court's behavior is the result of a tacit consensus among the country's rulers: that two per-cent of the population—or one percent, or sixty families, or those *active* members of the Bohemian Club owns most of the wealth of a country that is governed by the ruler's clients in the three branches of govern-ment. On those occasions when their Congress is forced by public opin-ion to pass laws that they do not want enacted, like the income tax of 1864, they can count either on their president's veto or on the Court's in-vocation of the Constitution to get Congress off the hook. The various courts are so devised, Lundberg writes, as to "rescue the legislatures and executives from their own reluctant acts."

Except for the passing of the Sixteenth Amendment, Congress has made only two serious attempts to reclaim its constitutional primacy over the Court (as opposed to a lot of unserious attempts). The first was in 1868. The House Judiciary Committee, fearful that the Court would strike down a number of reconstruction acts, reported a bill requiring that two thirds of a court's judges must concur in any opinion adverse to the law. This bill passed the House but died in the Senate. In the same year, the House did manage to pass a law (over presidential veto) to limit certain of the Court's appellate powers. On March 19, 1869, the Court unanimously bowed to Congress, with a sideswipe to the effect that al-though the Constitution did vest them with appellate powers, the clause that their powers were conferred "with such exceptions and under such Regulations as Congress shall make" must be honored.

This is one of the few times that Congress has asserted directly its constitutional primacy over a Court that for the next seventy years took upon itself more and more the powers not only to review any and all acts of Congress but to make law itself, particularly when it came to prevent-ing the regulation of corporations or denying rights to blacks. During the last forty years, although the Court has tended to stand aside on most economic matters and to intervene on racial ones, the Court's record of self-aggrandizement has been equaled only by that of the Johnny-come-lately wild card, the president.

The first fifteen presidents adjusted themselves to their roomy constitu-tional cage and except for an occasional rattling of the bars (the Alien and

Sedition Acts) and one break-out (the Louisiana Purchase) they were fairly docile prisoners of Article II. In 1860, the election of the sixteenth president caused the Union to collapse. By the time that Abraham Lincoln took office, the southern states had organized themselves into what they called a confederacy, in imitation of the original pre-Constitution republic. As Lincoln himself had declared in 1847, any state has the moral and, implicitly, constitutional right to govern itself. But permissive Congressman Lincoln was not stern President Lincoln. Firmly he put to one side the Constitution. On his own authority, he levied troops and made war; took unappropriated money from the Treasury; suspended habeas corpus. When the aged Chief Justice Taney hurled the Constitution at Lincoln's head, the president ducked and said that, maybe, all things considered, Congress ought now to authorize him to do what he had already done, which Congress did.

Lincoln's constitutional defense for what he had done rested upon the oath that he had sworn to "preserve, protect and defend the Constitution" as well as to see to it "that the law be faithfully executed." Lincoln proved to be a satisfactory dictator; and the Union was preserved. But the balances within the constitution of the Second Republic had been forever altered. With the adoption of the Thirteenth, Fourteenth, and Fifteenth amendments extending the vote to blacks (and, by 1920, to women and, by 1970, to eighteen- to twenty-year-olds) while ensuring, yet again, that no state can "deprive any person of life, liberty, or property without the process of law; nor deny to any person within its jurisdiction the equal protection of the laws," the Bill of Rights was at last, officially at least, largely applicable to the people who lived in the states that were again united.

Needless to say, the Supreme Court, often witty if seldom wise, promptly interpreted the word "person" to mean not only a human being but a corporate entity as well. During the next fifty years, the Court continued to serve the propertied interests against any attack from the other branches of government while ignoring, as much as possible, the rights of actual persons. Any state that tried to curb through law the excesses of any corporation was sure to be reminded by the Court that it had no such right.

But the Third Republic had been born; the electorate had been expanded; and civil rights were on the books if not engraved in letters of fire upon the hearts of the judiciary. Although the presidents pretty much confined themselves to their constitutional duties, the memory of Lincoln was—and is—a constant stimulus to the ambitious chief magistrate who knows that once the nation is at war his powers are truly unlimited, while the possibilities of personal glory are immeasurable.

At the turn of the century Theodore Roosevelt nicely arranged a war for his president, McKinley, who did not particularly want one. In 1917 Wilson arranged a war which neither Congress nor nation wanted. Since then the presidents have found foreign wars irresistible. With the surrender of Japan in 1945, the last official war ended. But the undeclared wars—or "police actions"—now began with a vengeance and our presidents are very much on the march. Through secret organizations like the CIA, they subvert foreign governments, organize invasions of countries they do not like, kill or try to kill foreign leaders while spying, illegally, on American citizens. The presidents have fought two major wars—in Korea and Vietnam—without any declaration of war on the part of Congress.

Finally, halfway through the executive's war in Vietnam, the sluggish venal Congress became alarmed—not to mention hurt—at the way they had been disregarded by Johnson Augustus. The Senate Committee on Foreign Relations began to ask such questions as, by what inherent right does a president make war whenever he chooses? On March 8, 1966, the president (through a State Department memorandum) explained the facts of life to Congress: "since the Constitution was adopted there have been at least 125 instances in which the President has ordered the armed forces to take action or maintain positions abroad without obtaining prior Congressional authorization, starting with the 'undeclared war' with France (1798–1800). . . ." Congress surrendered as they had earlier when the inexorable Johnson used a murky happening in the Tonkin Bay to ensure their compliance to his war. It was not until many thousands of deaths later that Congress voted to stop funds for bombing the Indochinese.

How did the president break out of his cage? The bars were loosened by Lincoln, and the jimmy that he used was the presidential oath, as prescribed by the Constitution: "I do solemnly swear that I will faithfully execute the Office of President of the United States, and will to the best of my ability, preserve, protect, and defend the Constitution of the United States." Lincoln put the emphasis on the verb "defend" because he was faced with an armed insurrection. Later presidents, however, have zeroed in on the verb "execute"—as broad a verb, in this context, as any president on the loose could wish for. From this innocuous-seeming word have come the notions of inherent executive power and executive privilege, and that astonishing fact with which we have been obliged to live for half a century, the executive order.

Congress and Court can be bypassed by an executive order except on very odd occasions such as Truman's unsuccessful seizure of the steel mills. When Wilson's request to arm merchant American ships was fili-bustered to death by the Senate in 1917, Wilson issued an executive or-der, arming the ships. Later, still on his own, Wilson sent troops to Russia to support the czar; concluded the armistice of 1918; and introduced Jim Crow to Washington's public places. In 1936 Franklin Roosevelt issued a secret executive order creating what was later to become, in World War II, the OSS, and then in peacetime (sic) the CIA. This vast enter-prise has never been even moderately responsive to the Congress that obediently funds it. The CIA is now the strong secret arm of the presi-dent and no president is about to give it up.

For all practical purposes the Third Republic is now at an end. The president is a dictator who can only be replaced either in the quadren-nial election by a clone or through his own incompetency, like Richard Nixon, whose neurosis it was to shoot himself publicly and repeatedly in, as they say, the foot. Had Nixon not been helicoptered out of the White House, men in white would have taken him away. The fact that we are living in an era of one-term presidents does not lessen, in any way, the formidable powers of the executive.

The true history of the executive order has yet to be written. As of De-cember 31, 1975, the presidents had issued 11,893 executive orders. The Constitution makes no allowances for them. In fact, when an order wages war or spends money, it is unconstitutional. But precedents can al-ways, tortuously, be found for the president to "execute his office." In 1793, Washington proclaimed that the United States was neutral in the war between England and France, in contravention of the treaty of 1778 which obliged the United States to come to France's aid. In 1905 the Senate declined to approve a treaty that Theodore Roosevelt wanted to make with Santo Domingo. Ever brisk and pugnacious, TR made an agreement on his own; and a year later the Senate ratified it. In 1940 Franklin Roosevelt gave England fifty destroyers that were not his to give. But three years earlier, the Supreme Court had validated the principle of the executive *agreement* (*U.S.* v. *Belmont*); as a result, the executive agreement and the executive order are now for the usurper president what judicial review has been for the usurper Court.

Law by presidential decree is an established fact. But, as Lundberg notes, it is odd that there has been no effective challenge by Congress to this usurpation of its powers by the executive. Lundberg quotes the late professor Edward S. Corwin of Princeton, a constitutional scholar who found troubling the whole notion of government by decree: "It would be more accordant," wrote Corwin in *Court Over Constitution*, "with American ideas of government by law to require, before a purely executive agreement to be applied in the field of private rights, that it be supplemented by a sanctioning act of Congress. And that Congress, which can repeal any treaty as 'law of the land or authorization, can do the same to executive agreements would seem to be obvious." Obvious—but ignored by a Congress more concerned with the division of the contents of the pork barrel than with the defense of its own powers.

Between a president ruling by decrees, some secret and some not, and a Court making policy through its peculiar powers of judicial review, the Congress has ceased to be of much consequence. Although a number of efforts were made in the Congress during the Fifties to put the president back in his cage and to deflect the Court from its policymaking binges, nothing substantive was passed by a Congress which, according to Lundberg, "is no more anxious to restrict the president than it is to restrict the Supreme Court. Congress prefers to leave them both with a free hand, reserving the right at all times to blame them if such a tactic fits the mood of the electorate." When Congress rejected Carter's energy program, it was not blocking a president who might well have got around it with an executive order. Congress was simply ducking responsibility for a gasoline tax just as the president had ducked it by maliciously including them in the process. Actually, Congress does, from time to time, discipline presidents, but it tends to avoid collisions with the principle of the executive order when wielded by the lonely Oval One. So does the Supreme Court. Although the Court did stop President Truman from seizing the steel mills in the course of the Korean (by executive order) War, the Court did not challenge the principle of the executive order per se.

Since the main task of government is the collection of money through taxes and its distribution through appropriations, the blood of the Third Republic is the money-labor of a population which pays taxes to support an executive establishment of some ten million people if one includes the armed forces. This is quite a power base, as it includes the Pentagon and the CIA—forever at war, covertly or overtly, with monolithic Communism. "Justice is the end of government," wrote Madison (*Federalist Paper* No. 52). "It is the end of civil society. It ever has been and ever will be pursued until it is obtained, or until liberty be lost in the pursuit." Time to start again the hard pursuit.

It was the wisdom of Julius Caesar and his heir Octavian to keep intact the ancient institutions of the Roman republic while changing entirely the actual system of government. The new dynasty reigned as traditional consuls, not as kings. They visited regularly their peers in the Senate—in J.C.'s case once too often. This respect for familiar forms should be borne in mind when We the People attend the second constitutional convention. President, Senate, House of Representatives must be kept as familiar entities just as their actual functions must be entirely altered.

Thomas Jefferson thought that there should be a constitutional convention at least once a generation because "laws and institutions must go hand in hand with the progress of the human mind. As that becomes more developed, more enlightened, as new discoveries are made, new truths disclosed, and manners and opinions change with the change of circumstances, institutions must advance also, and keep pace with the times. We might as well require a man to wear still the coat which fitted him as a boy, as a civilized society to remain ever under the regimen of their barbarous ancestors." Jefferson would be amazed to see how the boy's jacket of his day has now become the middle-aged man's straitjacket of ours. The amended Constitution of today is roomier than it was, and takes into account the national paunch; but there is little freedom to move the arms because, in Herder's words, "The State is happiness for a group" and no state has ever, willingly, spread that happiness beyond the group which controls it. The so-called "iron law of oligarchy," noted by James Madison, has always obtained in the United States.

Ten years ago Rexford Guy Tugwell, the old New Dealer, came up with Version XXXVII of a constitution that he had been working on for some years at the Center for the Study of Democratic Institutions at Santa Barbara. Tugwell promptly makes the mistake that Julius Caesar and family did not make. Tugwell changes names, adds new entities. Yet the old unwieldy tripartite system is not really challenged and the result is pretty conventional at heart because "I believe," said Tugwell, explaining his new arrangements, "in the two-party system." One wonders why.

The Framers wanted no political parties—or factions. It was their view that all right-minded men of property would think pretty much alike on matters pertaining to property. To an extent, this was—and is—true. Trilateral Commissions exist as shorthand symbols of this meeting of minds and purses. But men are hungry for political office. Lincoln felt that if the United States was ever destroyed it would be by the hordes of people who wanted to be office-holders and to live for nothing at government expense—a vice, he added dryly, "from which I myself am not free."

By 1800 there were two political parties, each controlled by a faction of the regnant oligarchy. Today, despite close to two centuries of insurrections and foreign wars, of depressions and the usurpations by this or that branch of government of powers not accorded, there are still two political parties, each controlled by a faction of the regnant oligarchy. The fact that the country is so much larger than it was makes for an appearance of variety. But the substance of the two-party system or non-system is unchanged. Those with large amounts of property control the parties which control the state which takes through taxes the people's money and gives a certain amount of it back in order to keep docile the populace while reserving a sizable part of tax revenue for the oligarchy's use in the form of "purchases" for the defense department, which is the unnumbered, as it were, bank account of the rulers.

As Walter Dean Burnham puts it, "The state is primarily in business to promote capital accumulation and to maintain social harmony and

legitimacy." But expensive and pointless wars combined with an emphasis on the consumption of goods at the expense of capital creation has
called into question the legitimacy of the oligarchy's government. Even
the dullest consumer has got the point that no matter how he casts his
vote for president or for Congress, his interests will never be represented
because the oligarchy serves only itself. It should be noted that this
monomania can lead to anomalies. In order to buy domestic tranquillity,
Treasury money in the form of transfer-payments to the plebes now accounts for some 70 percent of the budget—which cannot, by law, be cut
back.

In the 1976 presidential election, 45.6 percent of those qualified to
vote did not vote. According to Burnham, of those who did vote, 48.5 percent were blue-collar and service workers. Of those who did not vote,
75 percent were blue-collar and service workers. The pattern is plain.
Nearly 70 percent of the entire electorate are blue-collar and service
workers. Since only 20 percent of this class are unionized, natural interest requires that many of these workers belong together in one party. But
as 49 percent of the electorate didn't vote in 1980, the "two-party system"
is more than ever meaningless and there is no chance of a labor party—
or of any party other than that of the status quo.

The regnant minority is genuinely terrified of a new constitutional
convention. They are happier with the way things are, with half the electorate permanently turned off and the other half mildly diverted by presidential elections in which, despite a semblance of activity, there is no
serious choice. For the last two centuries the debate has been going on
as to whether or not the people can be trusted to govern themselves. Like
most debates, this one has been so formulated that significant alternative
ideas are excluded at the start. "There are nations," said Herzen, "but not
states." He saw the nation-state as, essentially, an evil—and so it has
proved most of the time in most places during this epoch (now ending)
of nation-states which can be said to have started, in its current irritable
megalomaniacal form, with Bismarck in Germany and Lincoln in the
United States.

James Madison's oligarchy, by its very nature, cannot and will not
share power. We are often reminded that some 25 percent of the population are comprised of (in Lundberg's words) "the super-annuated, the

unskilled, the immature of all ages, the illiterate, the improvident propagators, the mentally below par or disordered" as well as "another 25 percent only somewhat better positioned and liable at any turn or whirligig of circumstances to find themselves in the lower category." As Herzen, in an unhappy mood, wrote, "Who that respects the truth would ask the opinion of the first man he meets? Suppose Columbus or Copernicus had put to the vote the existence of America or the movement of the earth?" Or as a successful movie executive, in a happy mood, once put it: "When the American public walks, its knuckles graze the ground."

The constant search for external enemies by the oligarchy is standard stuff. All dictators and ruling groups indulge in this sort of thing, reflecting Machiavelli's wisdom that the surest way to maintain one's power over the people is to keep them poor and on a wartime footing. We fought in Vietnam to contain China, which is now our Mao-less friend; today we must have a showdown with Russia, in order to. . . . One has already forgotten the basis for the present quarrel. No. Arms race. That's it. They are outstripping us in warheads, or something. On and on the propaganda grinds its dismal whine. Second to none. Better to die in Afghanistan than Laguna. We must not lose the will. . . .

There are signs that the American people are beginning to tire of all of this. They are also angry at the way that their money is taken from them and wasted on armaments—although they have been sufficiently conned into thinking that armaments are as good as loafers on welfare and bureaucrats on the Treasury teat are bad. Even so, they believe that too much is being taken away from them; and that too little ever comes back.

Since Lundberg began his career as an economist, it is useful to quote him at length on how the oligarchy operates the economy—acting in strict accordance with the letter if not the spirit of the three constitutions.

> The main decision that Congress and the President make that is of steady effect on the citizenry concerns appropriations—that is, how much is to be spent up to and beyond a half-trillion dollars and what for. The proceeds are supposed to come from taxes but here, in response to citizen sensitivity, the government tends to understate the cost. Because the government has taken to spending more than it takes in, the result is inflation—a steady rise in the prices of goods and services.

*The difference between what it spends and what it takes in the govern-
ment makes up by deviously operating the money-printing machine, so that
the quantity of money in circulation exceeds the quantity of goods and services. Prices therefore tend to rise and money and money-values held by
citizens decline in purchasing value. . . .*

*All that the government has been doing in these respects is strictly con-
stitutional. For the Constitution empowers it, first, to lay taxes without limit
(Article I, Section 8, Paragraph 1). It is empowered in the very next paragraph to borrow money on the credit of the United States—that is, the taxpayers—also without limit. . . . As to inflation, Paragraph 5 empowers the
government, through Congress and the President, not only to coin money
but to "regulate the value thereof." In other words, under the Constitution
a dollar is worth whatever Congress and the President determine it to be by
their fiscal decisions, and for nearly three decades officials, Republican and
Democratic alike, have decreed that it be worth less. . . .*

When Congress and president over-appropriate, the Treasury simply
prints

*. . . short-term notes and bonds and sends these over to the Federal Reserve
Bank, the nation's central bank. In receipt of these securities, the Federal
Reserve simply credits the Treasury with a deposit for the total amount. The
Treasury draws checks against these deposits. And these checks are new
money. Or the Treasury may simply offer the securities for sale in the open
market, receiving therefore the checks of buyers.*

Since there is no legal way to control either president or Congress under
the current system, it is inevitable that there would be a movement for
radical reform. The National Taxpayers Union was organized to force the
federal government to maintain a balanced budget. In order to accom-
plish this, it will be necessary to change the Constitution. So the National Taxpayers Union has called for a new constitutional convention. To
date, thirty state legislatures have said yes to that call. When thirty-four
state legislatures ask for a new convention, there will be one. As Professor Gerald Gunther of Stanford Law School recently wrote:

The convention delegates would gather after popular elections—elections where the platforms and debates would be outside congressional control, where interest groups would seek to raise issues other than the budget, and where some successful candidates would no doubt respond to those pressures. Those convention delegates could claim to be legitimate representatives of the people. And they could make a plausible—and I believe correct—argument that a convention is entitled to set its own agenda. . . .*

Those who fear that Milton Friedman's cheerful visage will be swiftly hewn from Dakota rock underestimate the passion of the majority not to be unemployed in a country where the gap between rich and poor is, after France, the greatest in the Western world. Since the welfare system is the price that the white majority pays in order to exclude the black minority from the general society, entirely new social arrangements will have to be made if that system is to be significantly altered.

Predictably, the oligarchs and their academic advisers view with alarm any radical change. The Bill of Rights will be torn to shreds, they tell us. Abortion will be forbidden by the Constitution while prayers will resonate in the classrooms of the Most Christian Republic. The oligarchs think that the people are both dangerous and stupid. Their point is moot. But we do know that the oligarchs are a good deal more dangerous to the polity than the people at large. Predictions that civil rights would have a rocky time at a new convention ignore the reality that the conglomeration of groups attending it will each have residual ethnic, ideological, religious, and local interests whose expression they will not want stifled. It is by no means clear that civil liberties would be submerged at a new convention; and there is no reason why the delegates should not decide that a Supreme Court of some sort should continue to act as protector of the Bill of Rights—a better protector, perhaps, than the court that recently separated a Mr. Snepp from his royalties.

The forms of the first three republics should be retained. But the

---

*"Constitutional Roulette: The Dimensions of the Risk" in *The Constitution and the Budget*, edited by W. S. Moore and Rudolph G. Penner (American Enterprise Institute for Public Policy Research, Washington and London, 1980).

presidency should be severely limited in authority, and shorn of the executive order and the executive agreement. The House of Representatives should be made not only more representative but whoever can control a majority will be the actual chief of government, governing through a Cabinet chosen from the House. This might render it possible for the United States to have, for the first time in two centuries, real political parties. Since the parliamentary system works reasonably well in the other industrially developed democracies, there is no reason why it should not work for us. Certainly our present system does not work, as the late election demonstrated.

Under a pure parliamentary system the Supreme Court must be entirely subservient to the law of the land, which is made by the House of Representatives; and judicial review by the Court must join the executive order on the junk-heap of history. But any parliamentary system that emerged from a new constitutional convention would inevitably be a patchwork affair in which a special niche could, and no doubt would, be made for a judicial body to protect and enforce the old Bill of Rights. The Senate should be kept as a home for wise men, much like England's House of life-Lords. One of the Senate's duties might be to study the laws of the House of Representatives with an eye to their constitutionality, not to mention rationality. There should be, at regular intervals, national referenda on important subjects. The Swiss federal system provides some interesting ideas; certainly their cantonal system might well be an answer to some of our vexing problems—particularly, the delicate matter of bilingualism.

The present Constitution will be two hundred years old in 1987—as good a date as any to finish the work of the second constitutional convention, which will make possible our Fourth Republic, and first—ah, the note of optimism!—civilization.

The New York Review of Books
February 5, 1981

THE NATIONAL
SECURITY STATE

Every now and then, usually while shaving, I realize that I have lived through nearly one third of the history of the United States, which proves not how old I am but how young the Republic is. The American empire, which started officially in 1898 with our acquisition of the Philippines, came to a peak in the year 1945, while I was still part of that army which had won us the political and economic mastery of two hemispheres. If anyone had said to me then that the whole thing would be lost in my lifetime, I would have said it is not possible to lose so much so quickly without an atomic catastrophe, at least. But lose it we have.

Yet, in hindsight, I can see that our ending was implicit in our beginning. When Japan surrendered, the United States was faced with a choice: Either disarm, as we had done in the past, and enjoy the prosperity that comes from releasing so much wealth and energy to the private sector, or maintain ourselves on a full military basis, which would mean a tight control not only over our allies and such conquered provinces as West Germany, Italy, and Japan but over the economic—which is to say the political—lives of the American people. As Charles E. Wilson, a businessman and politician of the day, said as early as 1944, "Instead of looking to disarmament and unpreparedness as a safeguard against war, a thoroughly discredited doctrine, let us try the opposite: full preparedness according to a continuing plan."

The accidental president, Harry Truman, bought this notion. Although Truman campaigned in 1948 as an heir to Roosevelt's New Deal, he had a "continuing plan." Henry Wallace was onto it, as early as: "Yesterday, March 12, 1947, marked a turning point in American history, [for] it is not a Greek crisis that we face, it is an American crisis. Yesterday, President Truman . . . proposed, in effect, America police Russia's every border. There is no regime too reactionary for us provided it stands in Russia's expansionist path. There is no country too remote to serve as the scene of a contest which may widen until it becomes a world war." But how to impose this? The Republican leadership did not like the state to be the master of the country's economic life while, of the Democrats, only a few geopoliticians, like Dean Acheson, found thrilling the prospect of a military state, to be justified in the name of a holy war against something called Communism in general and Russia in particular. The fact that the Soviet Union was no military or economic threat to us was immaterial. It must be made to appear threatening so that the continuing plan could be set in motion in order to create that National Security State in which we have been living for the past forty years.*

What is the National Security State? Well, it began, officially, with the National Security Act of 1947; it was then implemented in January 1950 when the National Security Council produced a blueprint for a new kind of country, unlike anything that the United States had ever known before. This document, known as NSC-68 for short, and declassified only in 1975, committed—and still, fitfully, commits—us to the following program: First, never negotiate, ever, with Russia. This could not last forever; but the obligatory bad faith of U.S.-U.S.S.R. meetings still serves the continuing plan Second, develop the hydrogen bomb so that when the Russians finally develop an atomic bomb we will still not have to deal with that enemy without which the National Security State cannot exist. Third, rapidly build up conventional forces. Fourth, put

*For those interested in the details, I recommend H. R. Shapiro's *Democracy in America*, the only political history of the United States from British shires to present deficits. Needless to say, this masterly work, fourteen years in the making, is published privately by Manhattan Communication, 496 LaGuardia Place, Suite 406, New York, NY 10012. The present volume is only half the whole and lacks scholarly apparatus (index, bibliography) but not scholarship.

through a large increase in taxes to pay for all of this. Fifth, mobilize the entire American society to fight this terrible specter of Communism. Sixth, set up a strong alliance system, directed by the United States (this became NATO). Seventh, make the people of Russia our allies, through propaganda and CIA derring-do, in this holy adventure—hence the justification for all sorts of secret services that are in no way responsible to the Congress that funds them, and so in violation of the old Constitution.

Needless to say, the blueprint, the continuing plan, was not openly discussed at the time. But, one by one, the major political players of the two parties came around. Senator Arthur Vandenburg, Republican, told Truman that if he really wanted all those weapons and all those high taxes to pay for them, he had better "scare hell out of the American people." Truman obliged, with a series of speeches beginning October 23, 1947, about the Red Menace endangering France and Italy; he also instituted loyalty oaths for federal employees; and his attorney general (December 4, 1947) published a list of dissident organizations. The climate of fear has been maintained, more or less zealously, by Truman's successors, with the brief exception of Dwight Eisenhower, who in a belated fit of conscience at the end of his presidency warned us against the military-industrial complex that had, by then, established permanent control over the state.

The cynicism of this coup d'etat was breathtaking. Officially we were doing nothing but trying to preserve freedom for ourselves and our allies from a ruthless enemy that was everywhere, monolithic and all-powerful. Actually, the real enemy were those National Security Statesmen who had so dexterously hijacked the country, establishing military conscription in peacetime, overthrowing governments that did not please them, and finally keeping all but the very rich docile and jittery by imposing income taxes that theoretically went as high as 90 percent. That is quite an achievement in a country at peace.

We can date from January 1950 the strict governmental control of our economy and the gradual erosion of our liberties, all in order to benefit the economic interest of what is never, to put it tactfully, a very large group—defense spending is money but not labor intensive. Fortunately, all bad things must come to an end. Our huge indebtedness has made the maintenance of the empire a nightmare; and the day Japan stops buying our Treasury bonds, the troops and the missiles will all come home to a highly restless population.

Now that I have defined the gloomy prospect, what solutions do I have? I shall make five proposals. First, limit presidential election campaigns to eight weeks. That is what most civilized countries do, and all democratic ones are obliged to do. Allow no paid political ads. We might then entice that half of the electorate which never votes to vote.

Second, the budget: The press and the politicians constantly falsify the revenues and the disbursements of the federal government. How? By wrongly counting Social Security contributions and expenditures as a part of the federal budget. Social Security is an independent, slightly profitable income-transferring trust fund, which should be factored out of federal revenue and federal spending. Why do the press and the politicians conspire to give us this distorted view of the budget? Because neither they nor their owners want the public to know how much of its tax money goes for a war that does not exist. As a result Federal Reserve chairman Alan Greenspan could say last March, and with a straight face, that there are only two options for a serious attack on the deficit. One is to raise taxes. The other is to reduce the entitlement programs like Social Security and Medicare. He did not mention the defense budget. He did not acknowledge that the so-called entitlements come from a special fund. But then, he is a disciple of Ayn Rand.

In actual fact, close to 90 percent of the disbursements of the federal government go for what is laughingly known as "defense." This is how: In 1986 the gross revenue of the government was $794 billion. Of that amount, $294 billion were Social Security contributions, which should be subtracted from the money available to the National Security State. That leaves $500 billion. Of the $500 billion, $286 billion go to defense; $12 billion for foreign arms to our client states; $8 billion to $9 billion to energy, which means, largely, nuclear weapons; $27 billion for veterans' benefits, the sad and constant reminder of the ongoing empire's recklessness; and, finally, $142 billion for interest on loans that were spent, over the past forty years, to keep the National Security State at war, hot or cold. So, of 1986's $500 billion in revenue, $475 billion was spent on National Security business. Of that amount, we will never know how much was "kicked back" through political action committees and so-called soft

money to subsidize candidates and elections. Other federal spending, incidentally, came to $177 billion in 1986 (guarding presidential candidates,
cleaning the White House), which was about the size of the deficit, since
only $358 billion was collected in taxes.

It is obvious that if we are to avoid an economic collapse, defense
spending must be drastically reduced. But it is hard to reduce a budget
that the people are never told about. The first politician who realizes why
those politicians who appear to run against the government always win,
could not only win himself but be in a position to rid us of the National
Security State—which is what people truly hate. "Internal Improve-
ments" was the slogan of Henry Clay's popular movement. A neo-Clayite
could sweep the country if he wanted seriously to restore the internal
plant of the country rather than invade Honduras or bob expensively
about the Persian Gulf or overthrow a duly elected government in Nica-
ragua while running drugs (admittedly, the CIA's only margin of profit).

Third, as part of our general retrenchment, we should withdraw from
NATO. Western Europe is richer and more populous than America. If it
cannot defend itself from an enemy who seems to be falling apart even
faster than we are, then there is nothing that we, proud invaders of
Grenada, can effectively do. I would stop all military aid to the Middle
East. This would oblige the hardliners in Israel to make peace with the
Palestinians. We have supported Israel for forty years. No other minority
in the history of the United States has ever extorted so much Treasury
money for its Holy Land as the Israeli lobby, and it has done this by making a common cause with the National Security State. Each supports the
other. I would have us cease to pay for either.

Fourth, we read each day about the horrors of drug abuse, the murder of policemen, the involvement of our own government in drug running, and so on. We are all aware that organized crime has never been
richer nor the society more demoralized. What is the solution? I would
repeal every prohibition against the sale and use of drugs, because it is
these prohibitions that have caused the national corruption, not to mention most of the addiction. Since the American memory has a span of
about three days, I will remind you that in 1919 alcohol was prohibited
in the United States. In 1933 Prohibition was repealed because not only
had organized crime expanded enormously but so had alcoholism. What

did not work then does not work now. But we never learn, which is part of our national charm. Repeal would mean that there is no money for anyone in selling drugs. That's the end of the playground pusher. That's the end of organized crime, which has already diversified and is doing very nicely in banking, films, and dry cleaning. Eventually, repeal will mean the end of mass drug addiction. As there will always be alcoholics, there will always be drug addicts, but not to today's extent. It will be safe to walk the streets because the poor will not rob you to pay for their habit.

Fifth, two years ago I described how the American empire ended the day the money power shifted from New York to Tokyo and we became, for the first time in seventy-one years, a debtor nation. Since then, we have become the largest debtor country in history. I suggested a number of things that might be done, some of which I've again mentioned. But, above all, I see our economic survival inextricably bound up with that of our neighbor in the Northern Hemisphere, the Soviet Union. Some sort of alliance must be made between us so that together we will be able to compete with Japan and, in due course, China. As the two klutzes of the north, each unable to build a car anyone wants to drive, we deserve each other. In a speech at Gorbachev's anti-nuclear forum in Moscow, I quoted a Japanese minister of trade who said that Japan would still be number one in the next century. Then, tactlessly he said that the United States will be Japan's farm and Western Europe its boutique. A Russian got up and asked, "What did he say about us?" I said that they were not mentioned but, if they did not get their act together, they would end up as ski instructors. It is my impression that the Russians are eager to be Americans, but, thanks to the brainwashing of the National Security State's continuing plan, Americans have a built-in horror of the Evil Empire, which the press and the politicians have kept going for forty years. Happily, our National Security State is in the red, in more ways than one. Time for a change?

The Nation
June 4, 1988

N . B .

Shortly before I gave this talk to the National Press Club, I spoke to the American-Arab Anti-Discrimination League in Washington (March 13, 1988). I used the same text, giving the history of the National Security State. Then instead of suggesting some things that might be done to help free ourselves from our masters, I addressed the thousand Arab-Americans on problems of specific interest to them. In the audience was the most dreaded of *The New Republic*'s secret agents, code name: Weasel, who, despite a shoulder-length gray fright wig, was easily identified by his tiny ruby-red rabid eyes. Later he characterized my remarks on the National Security State as "cheap patrician rant"—whatever that is; I've never heard a patrician rant the way I do, and at such cost: He characterized what follows not, surprisingly, as "anti-Semitic" but as "nativist," and accused me of now cheating the Arabs as I had once cheated the Jews. This is plainly code, meant to be understood only by the initiate. The Weasel knows. Here is what I said.

> It has been my fate—or, perhaps, function—to give warnings long before the politicians and the press are able to absorb them. After all, they are in place to give a rosy view of the National Security State, and they give good value for their salaries. Since I'm not paid, I can ruminate; and share my findings.
>
> I am here today because I said much of what I've said just now in New York City at the Royale Theatre, on January 11, 1986. I also passed on the news that the American empire had officially died the previous year when we became, after seventy-one years, a debtor nation, and the money power had gone from New York to Tokyo. I was predictably attacked by the press that serves the National Security State. I was also attacked by those simple Jesus Christers who have been taught all their lives to fear and loathe communism, whatever it may be, and I was also attacked by that not-so-simple Israel lobby which never ceases to demonize the Soviet Union in order to make sure that half the federal revenue goes to defense, out of which the state of Israel, the lobby's sole preoccupation, is financed. I was promptly attacked by that small group of Israel Firsters, who call themselves neoconser-

vatives. I hated my country, they said, because I had criticized that National Security State in which, like a prison, we have all been obliged to live—and go broke—for forty years.

I responded to my critics with characteristic sweetness, turning the other fist as is my wont. I said that as much as I hated what our rulers have done to my country, it was not us, the country, who were at fault. I then added, while we're on the subject of our respective homelands, I'm not so keen about yours, which is Israel. Until then, no one had really challenged the lobby in so public a way. Congress and president and press are all more or less bought or otherwise intimidated by this self-described "sexy" lobby. While the sins and errors of Israel are openly debated in Israel itself, there has been only fearful silence in bravery's home and freedom's land. Well, I lanced the boil. Naturally, I was called an anti-Semite, usually with the adjective "frenzied" or "virulent" attached.

Now, at the risk of hurting more feelings, I must tell you that I regard monotheism as the greatest disaster ever to befall the human race. I see no good in Judaism, Christianity, or Islam—good people, yes, but any religion based on a single . . . well, frenzied and virulent god, is not as useful to the human race as, say, Confucianism, which is not a religion but an ethical and educational system that has worked pretty well for twenty-five hundred years. So you see I am ecumenical in my dislike for the Book. But, like it or not, the Book is there; and because of it people die; and the world is in danger.

Israel had the bad luck to be invented at a moment in history when the nation-state was going out of style. These two clumsy empires, the Soviet Union and the United States, are now becoming unstuck. Only by force can the Soviets control their Armenians and Muslims and Mongols, and only by force can we try to control a whole series of escalating race wars here at home, as well as the brisk occupation of the southern tier of the United States by those Hispanics from whom we stole land in 1847. The world, if we survive, will be one not of nations but of international cartels, of computerized money hurtling between capitals, of countries making what contributions they can to a more or less homogeneous world economy. Simultaneously, armies and flags and centralized administration will give way to a regionalism that is interdependent with everyone else on earth.

Is this possible? Well, Switzerland is a splendid small-scale model of what the world could be. Four languages, four races, four sets of superstitions about one another—all live most harmoniously in a small area where they make a fortune out of those of us who haven't learned that we are living in a post–national security world. When we finally stop giving to Israel the money that Japan so reluctantly lends us, peace will have to be made. If a cantonal system is set up, some areas of Palestine will be Orthodox Jewish; others Shiite Muslim; others secular Jewish and/or Muslim and/or Christian. In any event, the Great Bronze Age realtor in the sky will finally have to accept that none of those desirable rental properties between the Nile and the Euphrates can ever again include in the lease a discrimination clause.

So what shall we celebrate this joyous Sunday? The slow but highly visible collapse, due to bankruptcy, of the National Security Council-68 state and its ramshackle empire. Once we Americans are free of this dangerous state and its imperial burden we may not have heaven on earth, but we will certainly have lessened the current hell, and got our country back.

MONOTHEISM AND
ITS DISCONTENTS

The word "radical" derives from the Latin word for root. Therefore, if you want to get to the root of *anything* you must be radical. It is no accident that the word has now been totally demonized by our masters, and no one in politics dares even to use the word favorably, much less track any problem to its root. But then a ruling class that has been able to demonize the word "liberal" is a master at controlling—indeed stifling—any criticism of itself. "Liberal" comes from the Latin *liberalis*, which means pertaining to a free man. In politics, to be liberal is to want to extend democracy through change and reform. One can see why that word had to be erased from our political lexicon.

Meanwhile, the word "isolationist" has been revived to describe those who would like to put an end to the National Security State that replaced our Republic a half-century ago while extending the American military empire far beyond our capacity to pay for it. The word was trotted out in the presidential election of 1992 to describe one Pat Buchanan, who was causing great distress to the managers of our National Security State by saying that America must abandon the empire if we are ever to repair the mess at home. Also, as a neo-isolationist, Buchanan must be made to seem an anti-Semite. This is not hard to do. Buchanan is a classic Archie Bunker type, seething with irrational prejudices and resentments, whose origin I'll get to presently.

The country is now dividing, as it did a half-century ago, between those who think that America comes first versus those who favor empire and the continued exertion of force everywhere in the name of democracy, something not much on display here at home. In any case, as the whole world is, more or less, a single economic unit in which the United States is an ever smaller component, there are no isolationists today. But the word games go on and the deliberate reversals of meaning are always a sign that our corporate masters are worried that the people are beginning to question their arrangements. Many things are now coming into focus. *The New York Times* promptly dismissed Buchanan as a minor irritant, which was true, but it ignored his potentially major constituency—those who now believe that it was a mistake to have wasted, since 1950, most of the government's revenues on war.

Another candidate, Jerry Brown, alarmed the *Times* even more than Buchanan did. There was the possibility that he could be elected. More important, he might actually change our politics in the sense of who pays for whom. In a sudden frenzy, the *Times* compared him to Perón—our Jerry?—a dangerous demagogue whose "sharp-edged anger . . . resonates among a variety of Americans." Plainly, the ownership of the country is frightened that the current hatred of politicians, in general, may soon be translated into a hatred of that corporate few who control the many through Opinion, as manufactured by the *Times*, among others.

Now to the root of the matter. The great unmentionable evil at the center of our culture is monotheism. From a barbaric Bronze Age text known as the Old Testament, three antihuman religions have evolved—Judaism, Christianity, and Islam. These are sky-god religions. They are, literally, patriarchal—God is the omnipotent father—hence the loathing of women for 2,000 years in those countries afflicted by the sky-god and his earthly male delegates. The sky-god is a jealous god, of course. He requires total obedience from everyone on earth, as he is in place not just for one tribe but for all creation. Those who would reject him must be converted or killed for their own good. Ultimately, totalitarianism is the only sort of politics that can truly serve the sky-god's purpose. Any movement of a liberal nature endangers his authority and that of his delegates on earth.

One God, one King, one Pope, one master in the factory, one father-leader in the family at home.

The founders of the United States were not enthusiasts of the sky-god. Many, like Jefferson, rejected him altogether and placed man at the center of the world. The young Lincoln wrote a pamphlet *against* Christianity, which friends persuaded him to burn. Needless to say, word got around about both Jefferson and Lincoln and each had to cover his tracks. Jefferson said that he was a deist, which could mean anything or nothing, while Lincoln, hand on heart and tongue in cheek, said he could not support for office anyone who "scoffed" at religion.

From the beginning, sky-godders have always exerted great pressure in our secular republic. Also, evangelical Christian groups have traditionally drawn strength from the suppressed. African slaves were allowed to organize heavenly sky-god churches, as a surrogate for earthly freedom. White churches were organized in order to make certain that the rights of property were respected and that the numerous religious taboos in the New and Old Testaments would be enforced, if necessary, by civil law. The ideal to which John Adams subscribed—that we would be a nation of laws, not of men—was quickly subverted when the churches forced upon everyone, through supposedly neutral and just laws, their innumerable taboos on sex, alcohol, gambling. We are now indeed a nation of laws, mostly bad and certainly antihuman.

Roman Catholic migrations in the last century further reinforced the Puritan sky-god. The Church has also put itself on a collision course with the Bill of Rights when it asserts, as it always has, that "error has no rights." The last correspondence between John Adams and Thomas Jefferson expressed their alarm that the Jesuits were to be allowed into the United States. Although the Jews were sky-god folk, they followed Book One, not Book Two, so they have no mission to convert others; rather the reverse. Also, as they have been systematically demonized by the Christian sky-godders, they tended to be liberal and so turned not to their temple but to the A.C.L.U. Unfortunately, the recent discovery that the sky-god, in his capacity as realtor, had given them, in perpetuity, some parcels of unattractive land called Judea and Samaria has, to my mind, unhinged many of them. I hope this is temporary.

In the First Amendment to the Constitution the Founders made it clear that this was not to be a sky-god nation with a national religion like that of England, from whom we had just separated. It is curious how little understood this amendment is—yes, everyone has a right to worship any god he chooses but he does *not* have the right to impose his beliefs on others who do not happen to share in his superstitions and taboos. This separation was absolute in our original Republic. But the sky-godders do not give up easily. During the Civil War, they actually got the phrase "In God We Trust" onto the currency, in direct violation of the First Amendment, while "Under God" was added to the Oath of Allegiance under Eisenhower.

Although many of the Christian evangelists feel it necessary to convert everyone on earth to their primitive religion, they have been prevented—so far—from forcing others to worship as they do, but they *have* forced—most tyrannically and wickedly—their superstitions and hatreds upon all of us through the civil law and through general prohibitions. So it is upon that account that I now favor an all-out war on the monotheists.

Let us dwell upon the evils they have wrought. The hatred of blacks comes straight from their Bad Book. As descendants of Ham (according to Redneck divines), blacks are forever accursed, while Saint Paul tells the slaves to obey their masters. Racism is in the marrow of the bone of the true believer. For him, black is forever inferior to white and deserves whatever ill fortune may come his way. The fact that some monotheists can behave charitably means, often, that their prejudice is at so deep a level that they are not aware it is there at all. In the end, this makes any radical change of attitude impossible. Meanwhile, welfare has been the price the sky-godders were willing to pay to exclude blacks from their earthly political system. So we must live—presumably forever—with a highly enervating race war, set in train by the One God and his many hatreds.

Patriarchal rage at the thought of Woman ever usurping Man's place at the helm, in either home or workplace, is almost as strong now as it ever was, while the ongoing psychopathic hatred of same-sexuality has made the United States the laughingstock of the civilized world. After all, in most of the First World, monotheism is weak. Where it is weak or nonexistent, private sexual behavior has nothing at all to do with those not involved, much less with the law. At least when the Emperor Justinian, a sky-god man, decided to outlaw sodomy, he had to come up with a good *practical* reason, which he did. It is well known, Justinian declared, that buggery is a principal cause of earthquakes, and so must be prohibited. But our sky-godders, always eager to hate, still quote Leviticus, as if that loony text had anything useful to say about anything except, perhaps, the inadvisability of eating shellfish in the Jerusalem area.

We are now, slowly, becoming alarmed at the state of the planet. For a century, we have been breeding like a virus under optimum conditions, and now the virus has begun to attack its host, the earth. The lower atmosphere is filled with dust, we have just been told from our satellites in space. Climate changes; earth and water are poisoned. Sensible people grow alarmed; sky-godders are serene, even smug. The planet is just a staging area for heaven. Why bother to clean it up? Did not the sky-god tell his slaves to "be fruitful and multiply, and replenish the earth, and subdue it, and have dominion . . . over every living thing that moveth upon the earth"? Well, we did just like you told us, massa. We've used everything up. We're ready for heaven now. Or maybe Mars will do.

Ordinarily, as a descendant of the eighteenth-century Enlightenment, which shaped our Republic, I would say live and let live and I would try not to "scoff"—to use Lincoln's verb—at the monotheists. But I am not allowed to ignore them. They won't let me. They are too busy. They have a divine mission to take away our rights as private citizens. We are forbidden abortion here, gambling there, same-sex almost everywhere, drugs, alcohol in a dry county. Our prisons are the most terrible and the most crowded in the First World. Our death-row executions are a source of deep disgust in civilized countries, where more and more we are regarded as a primitive, uneducated, and dangerous people. Although we are not allowed, under law, to kill ourselves or to take drugs that the good folk think might be bad for us, we are allowed to buy a handgun and shoot as many people as we can get away with.

Of course, as poor Arthur (There Is This Pendulum) Schlesinger, Jr., would say, these things come in cycles. Every twenty years liberal gives way to conservative, and back again. But I suggest that what is wrong

now is not cyclic but systemic. And our system, like any system, is obey-
ing the second law of thermodynamics. Everything is running down; and
we are well advanced along the cold, dusty road to entropy. I don't think
much of anything can be done to halt this progress under our present
political-economic system. We lost poor Arthur's pendulum in 1950
when our original Constitution was secretly replaced with the apparatus
of that National Security State, which still wastes most of our tax money
on war or war-related matters. Hence deteriorating schools, and so on.

Another of our agreed-upon fantasies is that we do not have a class
system in the United States. The Few who control the Many through
Opinion have simply made themselves invisible. They have convinced us
that we are a classless society in which anyone can make it. Ninety percent of the stories in the pop press are about winners of lotteries or poor
boys and girls who, despite adenoidal complaints, become overnight millionaire singers. So there is still hope, the press tells the folks, for the
99 percent who will never achieve wealth no matter how hard they work.
We are also warned at birth that it is not polite to hurt people's feelings
by criticizing their religion, even if that religion may be damaging everyone through the infiltration of our common laws.

Happily, the few cannot disguise the bad times through which we are
all going. Word is spreading that America is now falling behind in the civilization sweepstakes. So isn't it time to discuss what we all really think
and feel about our social and economic arrangements?

Although we may not discuss race other than to say that Jesus wants
each and every one of us for a sunbeam, history is nothing more than the
bloody record of the migration of tribes. When the white race broke out
of Europe five hundred years ago, it did many astounding things all over
the globe. Inspired by a raging sky-god, the whites were able to pretend
that their conquests were in order to bring the One God to everyone, particularly those with older and subtler religions. Now the tribes are on the
move again. Professor Pendulum is having a nervous breakdown because
so many different tribes are now being drawn to this sweet land of liberty
and, thus far, there is no indication that any of the new arrivals intends
ever to read *The Age of Jackson*. I think the taking in of everyone can
probably be overdone. There may not be enough jobs for very many more

immigrants, though what prosperity we have ever enjoyed in the past was usually based on slave or near-slave labor.

On the other hand, I think Asians and Hispanics are a plus culturally, and their presence tends to refocus, somewhat, the relentless white versus black war. Where I *am* as one with friend Pendulum is that the newcomers must grasp certain principles as expressed in the Declaration of Independence and the Bill of Rights. Otherwise, we shall become a racially divided totalitarian state enjoying a Brazilian economy.

To revert to the unmentionable, religion. It should be noted that religion seemed to be losing its hold in the United States in the second quarter of this century. From the Scopes trial in '25 to the repeal of Prohibition in '33, the sky-godders were confined pretty much to the backwoods. Then television was invented and the electronic pulpit was soon occupied by a horde of Elmer Gantrys, who took advantage of the tax exemption for religion. Thus, out of greed, a religious revival has been set in motion and the results are predictably poisonous to the body politic.

It is usual, on the rare occasions when essential problems are addressed, to exhort everyone to be kinder, gentler. To bring us together, O Lord, in our common humanity. Well, we have heard these exhortations for a couple of hundred years and we are further apart than ever. So instead of coming together in order that the many might be one, I say let us separate so that each will know where he stands. From the *one, many*, and each of us free of the sky-god as secular lawgiver. I preach, to put it bluntly, confrontation.

Whether Brown and Buchanan knew it or not, they were revealing two basic, opposing political movements. Buchanan speaks for the party of God—the sky-god with his terrible hatred of women, blacks, gays, drugs, abortion, contraception, gambling—you name it, he hates it. Buchanan is a worthy peddler of hate. He is also in harmony not only with the prejudices and superstitions of a good part of the population but, to give him his due, he is a reactionary in the good sense—reacting against the empire in favor of the old Republic, which he mistakenly thinks was Christian.

Brown speaks for the party of man—feminists can find another noun if they like. Thomas Paine, when asked *his* religion, said he subscribed only to the religion of humanity. There now seems to be a polarizing of the country of a sort that has never happened before. The potential fault line has always been there, but whenever a politician got too close to the facts of our case, the famed genius of the system would eliminate him in favor of that mean which is truly golden for the ownership, and no one else. The party of man would like to re-establish a representative government firmly based upon the Bill of Rights. The party of God will have none of this. It wants to establish, through legal prohibitions and enforced taboos, a sky-god totalitarian state. The United States ultimately as prison, with mandatory blood, urine, and lie-detector tests and with the sky-godders as the cops, answerable only to God.

For once, it's all out there, perfectly visible, perfectly plain for those who can see. For the first time in 140 years, we now have the outline of two parties. Each knows the nature of its opposite, and those who are wise will not try to accommodate or compromise the two but will let them, at last, confront each other.

Jefferson's famous tree of liberty is all that we have ever really had. Now, for want of nurture—the blood of tyrants and of patriots—it is dying before our eyes. Of course, the sky-god never liked it. But some of us did—and some of us do. So, perhaps, through facing who and what we are, we may achieve a nation not under God but under man—or should I say our common humanity?

The Nation
July 13, 1992

BLACK TUESDAY

According to the Koran, it was on a Tuesday that Allah created darkness. Last September 11, when suicide pilots were crashing commercial airliners into crowded American buildings, I did not have to look to the calendar to see what day it was: Dark Tuesday was casting its long shadow across Manhattan and along the Potomac River. I was also not surprised that despite the seven or so trillion dollars that we have spent since 1950 on what is euphemistically called "defense," there would have been no advance warning from the FBI or CIA or Defense Intelligence Agency.

While the Bushites have been eagerly preparing for the last war but two—missiles from North Korea, clearly marked with flags, would rain down on Portland, Oregon, only to be intercepted by our missile-shield balloons—the foxy Osama bin Laden knew that all *he* needed for his holy war on the infidel were fliers willing to kill themselves along with those random passengers who happened to be aboard hijacked airliners.

The telephone keeps ringing. In summer I live south of Naples, Italy. Italian newspapers, TV, radio want comment. So do I. I have written lately about Pearl Harbor. Now I get the same question over and over: Isn't this exactly like Sunday morning, December 7, 1941? No, it's not, I say. As far as we *now* know, we had no warning of Tuesday's attack. Of course, our government has many, many secrets that our enemies always seem to know about in advance but our people are not told of until years later, if at all. President Roosevelt provoked the Japanese to attack us at Pearl Harbor. I describe the various steps he took in a book, *The Golden Age*. We now know what was on his mind: coming to England's aid against Japan's ally, Hitler, a virtuous plot that ended triumphantly for the human race. But what was—is—on bin Laden's mind?

For several decades there has been an unrelenting demonization of the Muslim world in the American media. Since I am a loyal American, I am not supposed to tell you *why* this has taken place, but then it is not usual for us to examine why *anything* happens; we simply accuse others of motiveless malignity. "We are good," G.W. proclaims, "They are evil," which wraps that one up in a neat package. Later, Bush himself put, as it were, the bow on the package in an address to a joint session of Congress where he shared with them—as well as with the rest of us somewhere over the Beltway—his profound knowledge of Islam's wiles and ways: "They hate what they see right here in this Chamber." I suspect a million Americans nodded sadly in front of their TV sets. "*Their* leaders are self-appointed. They hate our freedoms, our freedom of religion, our freedom of speech, our freedom to vote and assemble and disagree with each other." At this plangent moment what American's gorge did not rise like a Florida chad to the bait?

Should the forty-four-year-old Saudi Arabian bin Laden prove to be the prime mover, we still know surprisingly little about him. The six-foot seven-inch Osama enters history in 1979 as a guerrilla warrior working alongside the CIA to defend Afghanistan against the invading Soviets. Was he anti-Communist? Irrelevant question. He wants no infidels of any sort in the Islamic world. Described as fabulously wealthy, Osama is worth "only" a few million dollars, according to a relative. It was his father who created a fabulous fortune with a construction company that specialized in building palaces for the Saudi royal family. That company is now worth several billion dollars, presumably shared by Osama's fifty-four brothers and sisters. Although he speaks perfect English, he was educated entirely at Jiddah. He has never traveled outside the Arabian Peninsula. Several siblings lived in the Boston area and have given large sums to Harvard. We are told that much of his family appears to have disowned him and many of his assets in the Saudi kingdom have been frozen.

Where does Osama's money now come from? He is a superb fund-raiser for Allah but only within the Arab world; contrary to legend, he has taken no CIA money. He warned the Saudi king that Saddam Hussein was going to invade Kuwait. Osama assumed that after his own victories as a guerrilla against the Russians, he and his organization would be used by the Saudis to stop the Iraqis. To Osama's horror, King Fahd sent for the Americans: thus were infidels established on the sacred soil of Mohammed. "This was," he said, "the most shocking moment of my life." "Infidel," in his sense, does not mean anything of great moral consequence—like cheating sexually on your partner; rather it means lack of faith in Allah—the one God—and in his prophet Mohammed.

Osama persuaded four thousand Saudis to go to Afghanistan for military training by his group. In 1991, Osama moved on to Sudan. In 1994, when the Saudis withdrew his citizenship, Osama was already a legendary figure in the Islamic world and so, like Shakespeare's Coriolanus, he could tell the royal Saudis, "I banish you. There is a world elsewhere." Unfortunately, that world is us.

In a twelve-page "declaration of war," Osama presented himself as the potential liberator of the Muslim world from the great Satan of modern corruption, the United States.

Osama's organization blew up two of our embassies in Africa, and put a hole in the side of an American warship off Yemen, Clinton lobbed a missile at a Sudanese aspirin factory, and so on to the events of Black Tuesday. G. W. Bush was then transformed before our eyes into the cheerleader that he had been in prep school. First he promised us not only "a new war" but a "secret war" and, best of all, according to the twinkle in his eye, "a very long war." Meanwhile, "this administration will not talk about any plans we may or may not have . . . We're going to find these evildoers and we're going to hold them accountable," along with the other devils who have given Osama shelter.

As of the first month of 2002, the Pentagon Junta pretends that the devastation of Afghanistan by our high-flying air force has been a great victory (no one mentions that the Afghans were not an American enemy—it was like destroying Palermo in order to eliminate the Mafia). In any case, we may never know what, if anything, was won or lost (other than much of the Bill of Rights).

A member of the Pentagon Junta, Rumsfeld, a skilled stand-up comic, daily made fun of a large group of "journalists" on prime-time TV. At great, and often amusing, length, Rummy tells us nothing about our losses and their losses. He did seem to believe that the sentimental Osama was holed up in a cave on the Pakistan border instead of settled in a palace in Indonesia or Malaysia, two densely populated countries where he is admired and we are not. In any case, never before in our long history of undeclared unconstitutional wars have we, the American people, been treated with such impish disdain—so many irrelevant spear carriers to be highly taxed (those of us who are not rich) and occasionally invited to participate in the odd rigged poll.

When Osama was four years old I arrived in Cairo for a conversation with Nasser, to appear in *Look* magazine. I was received by Mohammed Heikal, Nasser's chief adviser. Nasser himself was not to be seen. He was at the Barricade, his retreat on the Nile; he had just survived an assassination attempt. Heikal spoke perfect English; he was sardonic, worldly. "We are studying the Koran for hints on birth control." A sigh.

"Not helpful?"

"Not very. But we keep looking for a text." We talked off and on for a week. Nasser wanted to modernize Egypt. But there was a reactionary, religious element . . . Another sigh. Then a surprise. "We've found something very odd, the young village boys—the bright ones that we are educating to be engineers, chemists, and so on, are turning religious on us."

"Right wing?"

"Very." Heikal was a spiritual son of our eighteenth-century Enlightenment. I thought of Heikal on Dark Tuesday when one of his modernized Arab generation had, in the name of Islam, struck at what had been, forty years earlier, Nasser's model for a modern state. Yet Osama seemed, from all accounts, no more than a practicing, as opposed to zealous, Muslim. Ironically, he was trained as an engineer. Understandably, he dislikes the United States as symbol and as fact. But when our clients, the Saudi royal family, allowed American troops to occupy the Prophet's holy land, Osama named the fundamental enemy "the Crusader Zionist Alliance."

Thus, in a phrase, he defined himself and reminded his critics that he is a Wahabi Muslim, a Puritan activist not unlike our Falwell/Robertson zanies, only serious. He would go to war against the United States, "the head of the serpent." Even more ambitiously, he would rid all the Muslim states of their Western-supported regimes, starting with that of his native land. The word "Crusader" was the giveaway. In the eyes of many Muslims, the Christian West, currently in alliance with Zionism, has for a thousand years tried to dominate the lands of the Umma—the true believers. That is why Osama is seen by so many simple folk as the true heir to Saladin, the great warrior king who defeated Richard of England and the Western crusaders.

Who was Saladin? Dates 1138–1193. He was an Armenian Kurd. In the century before his birth, Western Christians had established a kingdom at Jerusalem, to the horror of the Islamic Faithful. Much as the United States used the Gulf War as pretext for our current occupation of Saudi Arabia, Saladin raised armies to drive out the Crusaders. He conquered Egypt, annexed Syria, and finally smashed the Kingdom of Jerusalem in a religious war that pitted Mohammedan against Christian. He united and "purified" the Muslim world and though Richard Lionheart was the better general, in the end he gave up and went home. As one historian put it, Saladin "typified the Mohammedan utter self-surrender to a sacred cause." But he left no government behind him, no political system because, as he himself said, "My troops will do nothing save when I ride at their head. . . ." Now his spirit has returned with a vengeance.

The Bush administration, though eerily inept in all but its principal task, which is to exempt the rich from taxes, has casually torn up most of the treaties to which civilized nations subscribe—like the Kyoto Accords or the nuclear missile agreement with Russia. The Bushites go about their relentless plundering of the Treasury and now, thanks to Osama, Social Security (a supposedly untouchable trust fund), which, like Lucky Strike green, has gone to a war currently costing us $3 billion a month. They have also allowed the FBI and CIA either to run amok or not budge at all, leaving us, the very first "indispensable" and—at popular request—

last global empire, rather like the Wizard of Oz doing his odd pretend-magic tricks while hoping not to be found out. Meanwhile, G.W. booms, "Either you are with us or you are with the Terrorists." That's known as asking for it.

To be fair, one cannot entirely blame the current Oval One for our incoherence. Though his predecessors have generally had rather higher IQs than his, they, too, assiduously served the 1 percent that owns the country while allowing everyone else to drift. Particularly culpable was Bill Clinton. Although the most able chief executive since FDR, Clinton, in his frantic pursuit of election victories, set in place the trigger for a police state that his successor is now happily squeezing.

Police state? What's that all about? In April 1996, one year after the Oklahoma City bombing, President Clinton signed into law the Anti-Terrorism and Effective Death Penalty Act, a so-called conference bill in which many grubby hands played a part, including the bill's cosponsor, Senate Majority leader Dole. Although Clinton, in order to win elections, did many unwise and opportunistic things, he seldom, like Charles II, ever said an unwise one. But faced with opposition to antiterrorism legislation that not only gives the attorney general the power to use the armed services against the civilian population, neatly nullifying the Posse Comitatus Act of 1878, it also, selectively, suspends habeas corpus, the heart of Anglo-American liberty. Clinton attacked his critics as "unpatriotic." Then, wrapped in the flag, he spoke from the throne: "There is nothing patriotic about our pretending that you can love your country but despise your government." This is breathtaking since it includes, at one time or another, most of us. Put another way, was a German in 1939 who said that he detested the Nazi dictatorship unpatriotic?

There have been ominous signs that our fragile liberties have been dramatically at risk since the 1970s when the white-shirt-blue-suit-discreet-tie FBI reinvented itself from a corps of "generalists," trained in law and accounting, into a confrontational "Special Weapons and Tactics" (a.k.a. SWAT) Green Beret–style army of warriors who like to dress up in camouflage or black ninja clothing and, depending on the caper, ski masks. In the early Eighties an FBI super-SWAT team, the *Hostage 270 Rescue Team*, was formed. As so often happens in United States–speak, this group specialized not in freeing hostages or saving lives but in murderous attacks on groups that offended them, like the Branch Davidians—evangelical Christians who were living peaceably in their own compound at Waco, Texas, until an FBI SWAT team, illegally using army tanks, killed eighty-two of them, including twenty-five children. This was 1993.

Post Tuesday, SWAT teams can now be used to go after suspect Arab Americans or, indeed, anyone who might be guilty of terrorism, a word without legal definition (how can you fight terrorism by suspending habeas corpus since those who want their corpuses released from prison are already locked up?). But in the post–Oklahoma City trauma, Clinton said that those who did not support his draconian legislation were terrorist co-conspirators who wanted to turn "America into a safe house for terrorists." If the cool Clinton could so froth, what are we to expect from the overheated post-Tuesday Bush?

Incidentally, those who were shocked by Bush the Younger's shout that we are now "at war" with Osama should have quickly put on their collective thinking caps. Since a nation can only be at war with another nation-state, why did our smoldering if not yet burning bush come up with such a war cry? Think hard. This will count against your final grade. Give up? Well, most insurance companies have a rider that they need not pay for damage done by "an act of war." Although the men and women around Bush know nothing of war and less of our Constitution, they understand fund-raising. For this wartime exclusion, Hartford Life would soon be breaking open its piggy bank to finance Republicans for years to come. But the mean-spirited *Washington Post* pointed out that under U.S. case law, *only* a sovereign nation, not a bunch of radicals, can commit an "act of war." Good try, G.W. This now means that we the people, with our tax money, will be allowed to bail out the insurance companies, a rare privilege not afforded to just any old generation.

Although the American people have no direct means of influencing their government, their "opinions" are occasionally sampled through polls. According to a November 1995 CNN-*Time* poll, 55 percent of the people believe "the federal government has become so powerful that it poses a threat to the rights of ordinary citizens." Three days after Dark Tuesday, 74 percent said they thought, "It would be necessary for Americans to give up some of their personal freedoms." Eighty-six percent favored guards and metal detectors at public buildings and events. Thus, as the

police state settles comfortably in place, one can imagine Cheney and
Rumsfeld studying these figures, transfixed with joy. "It's what they always wanted, Dick."

"And to think we never knew, Don."

"Thanks to those liberals, Dick."

"We'll get those bastards now, Don."

It seems forgotten by our amnesiac media that we once energetically
supported Saddam Hussein in Iraq's war against Iran and so Saddam
thought, not unnaturally, that we wouldn't mind his taking over Kuwait's
filling stations. Overnight our employee became Satan—and so remains,
as we torment his people in the hope that they will rise up and overthrow
him—as the Cubans were supposed, in their U.S.-imposed poverty, to
have dismissed Castro for his ongoing refusal to allow the Kennedy
brothers to murder him in their so-called Operation Mongoose. Our imperial disdain for the lesser breeds did not go unnoticed by the latest educated generation of Saudi Arabians, and by their evolving leader, Osama
bin Laden, whose moment came in 2001 when a weak American president took office in questionable circumstances.

The New York Times is the principal dispenser of opinion received
from corporate America. It generally stands tall, or tries to. Even so, as of
September 13 the *NYT*'s editorial columns were all slightly off-key.

Under the heading "Demands of Leadership" the *NYT* was upbeat,
sort of. It's going to be okay if you work hard and keep your eye on the
ball, Mr. President. Apparently Bush is "facing multiple challenges, but
his most important job is a simple matter of leadership." Thank God. Not
only is that *all* it takes, but it's *simple*, too! For a moment . . . The *NYT*
then slips into the way things look as opposed to the way they ought to
look. "The Administration spent much of yesterday trying to overcome
the impression that Mr. Bush showed weakness when he did not return
to Washington after the terrorists struck." But from what I could tell no
one cared, while some of us felt marginally safer, that the national silly-
billy was trapped in his Nebraska bunker. Patiently, the *NYT* spells it out
for Bush and for us, too. "In the days ahead, Mr. Bush may be asking the
nation to support military actions that many citizens, particularly those
with relations in the service, will find alarming. He must show that he

knows what he is doing." Well, that's a bull's-eye. If only FDR had got letters like that from Arthur Krock at the old *NYT.*

Finally, Anthony Lewis thinks it wise to eschew Bushite unilateralism
in favor of cooperation with other nations in order to contain Tuesday's
darkness by *understanding its origin* (my emphasis) while ceasing our provo-
cations of cultures opposed to us and our arrangements. Lewis, unusually
for a *New York Times* writer, favors peace now. So do I. But then we are
old and have been to the wars and value our fast-diminishing freedoms
unlike those jingoes now beating their tom-toms in Times Square in favor
of all-out war for other Americans to fight.

As usual, the political columnist who has made the most sense of all
this is William Pfaff in the international *Herald Tribune* (September 17,
2001). Unlike the provincial war lovers at *The New York Times*, he is appalled by the spectacle of an American president who declined to serve
his country in Vietnam, howling for war against not a nation or even
a religion but one man and his accomplices, a category that will ever
widen.

> *Pfaff: The riposte of a civilized nation: one that believes in good, in human
> society and does oppose evil, has to be narrowly focused and, above all, in-
> telligent.*
>
> *Missiles are blunt weapons. Those terrorists are smart enough to make
> others bear the price for what they have done, and to exploit the results.*
>
> *A maddened U.S. response that hurts still others is what they want: It
> will fuel the hatred that already fires the self-righteousness about their crim-
> inal acts against the innocent.*
>
> *What the United States needs is cold reconsideration of how it has ar-
> rived at this pass. It needs, even more, to foresee disasters that might lie in
> the future.*

War is the no-win all-lose option. The time has come to put the good
Kofi Annan to use. As glorious as total revenge will be for our war lovers,
a truce between Saladin and the Crusader-Zionists is in the interest of
the entire human race. Long before the dread monotheists got their
hands on history's neck, we had been taught how to handle feuds by none

other than the god Apollo as dramatized by Aeschylus in *Eumenides* (a polite Greek term for the Furies who keep us daily company on CNN). Orestes, for the sin of matricide, cannot rid himself of the Furies who hound him wherever he goes. He appeals to the god Apollo who tells him to go to the UN—also known as the citizens' assembly at Athens—which he does and is acquitted on the ground that blood feuds must be ended or they will smolder forever, generation after generation, and great towers shall turn to flame and incinerate us all until "the thirsty dust shall never more suck up the darkly steaming blood . . . and vengeance crying death for death! But man with man and state with state shall vow the pledge of common hate and common friendship, that for man has oft made blessing out of ban, be ours until all time." Let Annan mediate between East and West before there is nothing left of either of us to salvage.

The awesome physical damage Osama and company did to us on Dark Tuesday is as nothing compared to the knockout blow to our vanishing liberties—the Anti-Terrorism Act of 1996 combined with the recent requests to Congress for additional special powers to wiretap without judicial order; to deport lawful permanent residents, visitors, and undocumented immigrants without due process; and so on. As I write, U.S. "Concentration Camp X-Ray" is filling up at marine base Guantanamo Bay, Cuba. No one knows whether or not these unhappy residents are prisoners of war or just plain evildoers. In any case, they were kidnapped in Afghanistan by U.S. forces and now appear to be subject to kangaroo courts when let out of their cages.

This is from a pre-Osama text: "Restrictions on personal liberty, on the right of free expression of opinion, including freedom of the press; on the rights of assembly and associations; and violations of the privacy of postal, telegraphic, and telephonic communications and warrants for house searches, orders for confiscations as well as restrictions on property, are also permissible beyond the legal limits otherwise prescribed." The tone is familiar. Clinton? Bush? Ashcroft? No. It is from Hitler's 1933 speech calling for "an Enabling Act" for "the protection of the People and the State" after the catastrophic Reichstag fire that the Nazis had secretly lit.

Only one congresswoman, Barbara Lee of California, voted against the additional powers granted the president. Meanwhile, a *New York Times*–CBS poll noted that only 6 percent now opposed military action while a substantial majority favored war "even if many thousands of innocent civilians are killed." Simultaneously, Bush's approval rating has soared, but then, traditionally, in war, the president is totemic like the flag. When Kennedy got his highest rating after the debacle of the Bay of Pigs, he observed, characteristically, "It would seem that the worse you fuck up in this job the more popular you get." Bush, father and son, may yet make it to Mount Rushmore though it might be cheaper to redo Barbara Bush's look-alike, George Washington, by adding two strings of Teclas to his limestone neck—in memoriam, as it were.

Finally, the physical damage Osama and friends can do us—terrible as it has been thus far—is as nothing as to what he is doing to our liberties. Once alienated, an "unalienable right" is apt to be forever lost, in which case we are no longer even remotely the last best hope of earth but merely a seedy imperial state whose citizens are kept in line by SWAT teams and whose way of death, not life, is universally imitated.

Since V-J Day 1945 ("Victory over Japan" and the end of World War II), we have been engaged in what the historian Charles A. Beard called "perpetual war for perpetual peace." I have occasionally referred to our "enemy of the month club": each month we are confronted by a new horrendous enemy at whom we must strike before he destroys us. I have been accused of exaggeration, so here's the scoreboard from Kosovo (1999) back to Berlin Airlift (1948–49). You will note that the compilers, Federation of American Scientists, record a number of our wars as "ongoing," even though many of us have forgotten about them. We are given, under "Name," many fanciful Defense Department titles like *Urgent Fury*, which was Reagan's attack on the island of Grenada, a month-long caper that General Haig disloyally said could have been handled more efficiently by the Provincetown police department. (Question marks are from compilers.)

Perpetual War for Perpetual Peace
2002

CURRENT OPERATIONS

Name	Locale
Joint Guardian	Kosovo
Allied Force/Noble Anvil	Kosovo
Determined Force	Kosovo
Cobalt Flash	Kosovo
Shining Hope	Kosovo
Sustain Hope/Allied Harbour	Kosovo
Provide Refuge	Kosovo
Open Arms	Kosovo
Eagle Eye	Kosovo
Determined Falcon	Kosovo & Albania
Determined Effort	Bosnia-Herzegovina
Joint Endeavor	Bosnia-Herzegovina
Joint Guard	Bosnia-Herzegovina
Joint Forge	Bosnia-Herzegovina
DELIBERATE FORCE	Bosnian Serbs
Quick Lift	Croatia
Nomad Vigil	Albania
Nomad Endeavor	Taszar, Hungary
Able Sentry	Serbia-Macedonia
Deny Flight	Bosnia-Herzegovina

Dates	U.S. Forces Involved
11 Jun 1999–TDB 200?	
23 Mar 1999–10 Jun 1999	
08 Oct 1998–23 Mar 1999	
05 Apr 1999–Fall 1999	
16 Oct 1998–24 Mar 1999	
15 Jun 1998–16 Jun 1998	
Jul 1995–Dec 1995	
Dec 1995–Dec 1996	
Dec 1996–20 Jun 1998	
20 June 1998–Present	6,900
29 Aug 1995–21 Sep 1995	
03 Jul 1995–11 Aug 1995	
01 Jul 1995–05 Nov 1996	
Mar 1996–Present	
05 Jul 1994–Present	
12 Apr 1993–20 Dec 1995	2,000

Name	Locale
Decisive Endeavor/Decisive Edge	Bosnia-Herzegovina
Decisive Guard/Deliberate Guard	Bosnia-Herzegovina
Deliberate Forge	Bosnia-Herzegovina
Sky Monitor	Bosnia-Herzegovina
Maritime Monitor	Adriatic Sea
Maritime Guard	Adriatic Sea
Sharp Guard	Adriatic Sea
Decisive Enhancement	Adriatic Sea
Determined Guard	Adriatic Sea
Provide Promise	Bosnia

SOUTHWEST ASIA

Name	Locale
[none] (air strike)	Iraq
[none] (cruise missile strike)	Iraq
[none] (cruise missile strike)	Iraq
DESERT STRIKE	Iraq
DESERT THUNDER	Iraq
DESERT FOX	Iraq
Shining Presence	Israel

Dates	*U.S. Forces Involved*
Jan 1996–Dec 1996	??
Dec 1996–20 Jun 1998	??
20 Jun 1998–Present	
16 Oct 1992–Present	
16 Jul 1992–22 Nov 1992	??
22 Nov 1992–15 Jun 1993	??
15 Jun 1993–Dec 1995	11,700
Dec 1995–19 Jun 1996	??
Dec 1996–Present	??
03 Jul 1992–Mar 1996	1,000

Dates	*U.S. Forces Involved*
26 Jun 1993–13 Jan 1993	
13 Jan 1993–17 Jan 1993	
17 Jan 1993–26 Jun 1993	
03 Sep 1996–04 Sep 1996	
Feb 1998–16 Dec 1998	
16 Dec 1998–20 Dec 1998	
Dec 1998–Dec 1998	

Name	Locale
Phoenix Scorpion IV	Iraq
Phoenix Scorpion III	Iraq
Phoenix Scorpion II	Iraq
Phoenix Scorpion I	Iraq
Desert Focus	Saudi Arabia
Vigilant Warrior	Kuwait
Vigilant Sentinel	Kuwait
Intrinsic Action	Kuwait
Desert Spring	Kuwait
Iris Gold	SW Asia
Pacific Haven/Quick Transit	Iraq > Guam
Provide Comfort	Kurdistan
Provide Comfort II	Kurdistan
Northern Watch	Kurdistan
Southern Watch	Southwest Asia/Iraq
Desert Falcon	Saudi Arabia

OTHER OPERATIONS

Name	Locale
Korea	Korea
New Horizons	Central America

Dates	U.S. Forces Involved
Dec 1998–Dec 1998	
Nov 1998–Nov 1998	
Feb 1998–Feb 1998	
Nov 1997–Nov 1997	
Jul 1996–Present	
Oct 1994–Nov 1994	
Aug 1995–15 Feb 1997	
01 Dec 1995–01 Oct 1999	
01 Oct 1999–Present	
?? 1993–Present	
15 Sep 1996–16 Dec 1996	
05 Apr 1991–Dec 1994	42,500
24 Jul 1991–31 Dec 1996	??
31 Dec 1996–Present	1,100
1991–Present	14,000
1991–Present	

Dates	U.S. Forces Involved
Ongoing	
Ongoing	

Name	Locale
Sierra Leone NEO	Sierra Leone
MONUC [UN PKO]	DR Congo
Resolute Response	Africa
Gatekeeper	California
Hold-the-Line	Texas
Safeguard	Arizona
Golden Pheasant	Honduras
Alliance	U.S. southern border
Provide Hope I	Former Soviet Union
Provide Hope II	Former Soviet Union
Provide Hope III	Former Soviet Union
Provide Hope IV	Former Soviet Union
Provide Hope V	Former Soviet Union

COUNTERDRUG OPERATIONS

Name	Locale
Coronet Nighthawk	Central/South America
Coronet Oak	Central/South America
Selva Verde	Colombia
Badge	Kentucky

Dates	*U.S. Forces Involved*
May 2000	
Feb 2000–Ongoing	
Aug 1998–Present	
1995–Present	
1995–Present	
1995–Present	
Mar 1988–Present	
1986–Present	
10 Feb 1992–26 Feb 1992	
15 Apr 1992–29 Jul 1992	
1993?–1993?	
10 Jan 1994–19 Dec 1994	
06 Nov 1998–10 May 1999	

Dates	*U.S. Forces Involved*
1991–Present	
Oct 1977–17 Feb 1999	
1995–Present	
1990–Present?	

Name	Locale
Ghost Dancer	Oregon
Greensweep	California
Grizzly	California
Wipeout	Hawaii
Ghost Zone	Bolivia
Constant Vigil	Bolivia
Support Justice	South America
Steady State	South America
Green Clover	South America
Laser Strike	South America
Agate Path	CONUS
Enhanced Ops	CONUS

COMPLETED OPERATIONS

Name	Locale
Silent Promise	Mozambique/South Africa
Fundamental Response	Venezuela
Stabilize	Timor
Avid Response	Turkey
Strong Support [Fuerte Apoyo]	Central America

Dates	U.S. Forces Involved
1990–Present?	
Jul 1990–Aug 1990	
1990–Present?	
1990–Present	
Mar 1990–1993?	
199?–??	
1991–1994	
1994–Apr 1996	
199?–199?	
Apr 1996–Present	
1989–???	
???–Present	

Dates	U.S. Forces Involved
Feb 2000–? Apr 2000	
20 Dec 1999–Early 2000	
11 Sep 1999–Nov 1999	
18 Aug 1999–Sep 1999	
Oct 1998–10 Feb 1999	5,700

Name	*Locale*
Infinite Reach	Sudan/Afganistan
Shepherd Venture	Guinea-Bissau
[none]	Asmara, Eritrea NEO
Noble Response	Kenya
Bevel Edge	Cambodia
Noble Obelisk	Sierra Leone
Guardian Retrieval	Congo (formerly Zaire)
Silver Wake	Albania
Guardian Assistance	Zaire/Rwanda/Uganda
Assurance/Phoenix Tusk	Zaire/Rwanda/Uganda
Quick Response	Central African Republic
Assured Response	Liberia
Zorro II	Mexico
Third Taiwan Straits Crisis	Taiwan Strait
Safe Border	Peru/Ecuador
United Shield	Somalia
Uphold/Restore Democracy	Haiti
Quiet Resolve/Support Hope	Rwanda
Safe Haven/Safe Passage	Cuba > Panama
Sea Signal/JTF-160	Haiti > Guantanamo, Cuba
Distant Runner	Rwanda NEO
Korean Nuclear Crisis	North Korea

Dates	U.S. Forces Involved
20 Aug 1998–20 Aug 1998	
10 Jun 1998–17 Jun 1998	130
05 Jun 1998–06 Jun 1998	130
21 Jan 1998–25 Mar 1998	
Jul 1997–Jul 1997	
May 1997–Jun 1997	
Mar 1997–Jun 1997	
14 Mar 1997–26 Mar 1997	
15 Nov 1996–27 Dec 1996	
15 Nov 1996–27 Dec 1996	
May 1996–Aug 1996	
Apr 1996–Aug 1996	
Dec 1995–02 May 1996	
21 Jul 1995–23 Mar 1996	
1995–30 Jun 1999	
03 Jan 1995–25 Mar 1995	4,000
19 Sep 1994–31 Mar 1995	21,000
22 Jul 1994–30 Sep 1994	2,592
06 Sep 1994–01 Mar 1995	
18 May 1994–Feb 1996	
09 Apr 1994–15 Apr 1994	
10 Feb 1993–Jun 1994	

Name	*Locale*
[none]	Liberian NEO
Provide Relief	Somalia
Restore Hope	Somalia
Continue Hope	Somalia
Provide Transition	Angola
Garden Plot	Los Angeles, CA
Silver Anvil	Sierra Leone NEO
GTMO	Haiti > Guantanamo, Cuba
Safe Harbor	Haiti > Guantanamo, Cuba
Quick Lift	Zaire
Victor Squared	Haiti NEO
Fiery Vigil	Philippines NEO
Productive Effort/Sea Angel	Bangladesh
Eastern Exit	Somalia
DESERT STORM	Southwest Asia
Desert Shield	Southwest Asia
Imminent Thunder	Southwest Asia
Proven Force	Southwest Asia
Desert Sword/Desert Sabre	Southwest Asia
Desert Calm	Southwest Asia
Desert Farewell	Southwest Asia

Dates	U.S. Forces Involved
22 Oct 1992–25 Oct 1992	
14 Aug 1992–08 Dec 1992	??
04 Dec 1992–04 May 1993	26,000
04 May 1993–Dec 1993	??
03 Aug 1992–09 Oct 1992	
May 1992	4,500
02 May 1992–05 May 1992	
23 Nov 1991	
1992	
24 Sep 1991–07 Oct 1991	
Sep 1991	
Jun 1991	
May 1991–Jun 1991	
02 Jan 1991–11 Jan 1991	
02 Aug 1990–17 Jan 1991	
Nov 1990–Nov 1990	
17 Jan 1991–28 Feb 1991	
24 Feb 1991–28 Feb 1991	555,000
01 Mar 1991–01 Jan 1992	
01 Jan 1992–1992?	

Name	Locale
Steel Box/Golden Python	Johnston Island
Sharp Edge	Liberia

COLD WAR ERA

Name	Locale
Classic Resolve	Philippines
Hawkeye	St. Croix, U.S. Virgin Islands
Nimrod Dancer	Panama
JUST CAUSE	Panama
Promote Liberty	Panama
ERNEST WILL	Persian Gulf
PRAYING MANTIS	Persian Gulf
Blast Furnace	Bolivia
EL DORADO CANYON	Libya
Attain Document	Libya
Achille Lauro	Mediterranean
Intense Look	Red Sea/Gulf of Suez
URGENT FURY	Grenada
Arid Farmer	Chad/Sudan
Early Call	Egypt/Sudan

Dates	*U.S. Forces Involved*
26 Jul 1990–18 Nov 1990	
May 1990–08 Jan 1991	

Dates	*U.S. Forces Involved*
Nov 1989–Dec 1989	
20 Sep 1989–17 Nov 1989	
May 1989–20 Dec 1989	
20 Dec 1989–31 Jan 1990	
31 Jan 1990–??	
24 Jul 1987–02 Aug 1990	
17 Apr 1988–19 Apr 1988	
Jul 1986–Nov 1986	
12 Apr 1986–17 Apr 1986	
26 Jan 1986–29 Mar 1986	
07 Oct 1985–11 Oct 1985	
Jul 1984–Jul 1984	
23 Oct 1983–21 Nov 1983	
Aug 1983–Aug 1983	
18 Mar 1983–Aug 1983	

Name	Locale
U.S. Multinational Force [USMNF]	Lebanon
Bright Star	Egypt
Gulf of Sidra	Libya/Mediterranean
RMT (Rocky Mountain Transfer)	Colorado
Central America	El Salvador/Nicaragua
Creek Sentry	Poland
SETCON II	Colorado
EAGLE CLAW/Desert One	Iran
ROK Park Succession Crisis	Korea
Elf One	Saudi Arabia
Yemen	Iran/Yemen/Indian Ocean
Red Bean	Zaire
Ogaden Crisis	Somalia/Ethiopia
SETCON I	Colorado
Paul Bunyan/Tree Incident	Korea
Mayaguez Operation	Cambodia
New Life	Vietnam NEO
Frequent Wind	Evacuation of Saigon
Eagle Pull	Cambodia
Nickel Grass	Mideast
Garden Plot	USA Domestic
Red Hat	Johnston Island

Dates	*U.S. Forces Involved*
25 Aug 1982–01 Dec 1987	
06 Oct 1981–Nov 1981	
18 Aug 1981–18 Aug 1981	
Aug 1981–Sep 1981	
01 Jan 1981–01 Feb 1992	
Dec 1980–1981	
May 1980–Jun 1980	
25 Apr 1980	
26 Oct 1979–28 Jun 1980	
Mar 1979–15 Apr 1989	
06 Dec 1978–06 Jan 1979	
May 1978–Jun 1978	
Feb 1978–23 Mar 1978	
1978–1978	
18 Aug 1976–21 Aug 1976	
15 May 1975	
Apr 1975	
29 Apr 1975–30 Apr 1975	
11 Apr 1975–13 Apr 1975	
06 Oct 1973–17 Nov 1973	
30 Apr 1972–04 May 1972	
Jan 1971–Sep 1971	

Name	Locale
Ivory Coast/Kingpin	Son Tay, Vietnam
Graphic Hand	US Domestic
Red Fox [Pueblo incident]	Korea theater
Six Day War	Mideast
CHASE	various
Powerpack	Dominican Republic
Red Dragon	Congo
[NONE]	Chinese nuclear facilities
Cuban Missile Crisis	Cuba, Worldwide
Vietnam War	Vietnam
Operation Ranch Hand	Vietnam
Operation Rolling Thunder	Vietnam
Operation Arc Light	Southeast Asia
Operation Freedom Train	North Vietnam
Operation Pocket Money	North Vietnam
Operation Linebacker I	North Vietnam
Operation Linebacker II	North Vietnam
Operation Endsweep	North Vietnam
Operation Ivory Coast/Kingpin	North Vietnam
Operation Tailwind	Laos
Berlin	Berlin
Laos	Laos

Dates	U.S. Forces Involved
20 Nov 1970–21 Nov 1970	
1970–1970	
23 Jan 1968–05 Feb 1969	
13 May 1967–10 Jun 1967	
1967–1970	
28 Apr 1965–21 Sep 1966	
23 Nov 1964–27 Nov 1964	
15 Oct 1963–Oct 1964	
24 Oct 1962–01 Jun 1963	
15 Mar 1962–28 Jan 1973	
Jan 1962–1971	
24 Feb 1965–Oct 1968	
18 Jun 1965–Apr 1970	
06 Apr 1972–10 May 1972	
09 May 1972–23 Oct 1972	
10 May 1972–23 Oct 1972	
18 Dec 1972–29 Dec 1972	
27 Jan 1972–27 Jul 1973	
21 Nov 1970–21 Nov 1970	
1970–1970	
14 Aug 1961–01 Jun 1963	
19 Apr 1961–07 Oct 1962	

Name	Locale
Congo	Congo
Taiwan Straits	Taiwan Straits
Taiwan Straits	Quemoy and Matsu Islands
Blue Bat	Lebanon
Suez Crisis	Egypt
Taiwan Straits	Taiwan Straits
Korean War	Korea
Berlin Airlift	Berlin

In these several hundred wars against Communism, terrorism, drugs, or sometimes nothing much, between Pearl Harbor and Tuesday, September 11, 2001, we tended to strike the first blow. But then we're the good guys, right? Right.

Dates	U.S. Forces Involved
14 Jul 1960–01 Sep 1962	
23 Aug 1958–01 Jan 1959	
23 Aug 1958–01 Jun 1963	
15 Jul 1958–20 Oct 1958	
26 Jul 1956–15 Nov 1956	
11 Aug 1954–01 May 1955	
27 Jun 1950–27 July 1953	
26 Jun 1948–30 Sep 1949	

STATE OF THE UNION, 2004

In the 1960s and '70s of the last unlamented century, there was a New York television producer named David Susskind. He was commercially successful; he was also, surprisingly, a man of strong political views which he knew how to present so tactfully that networks were often unaware of just what he was getting away with on their—our—air. Politically, he liked to get strong-minded guests to sit with him at a round table in a ratty building at the corner of Broadway and 42nd Street. Sooner or later, just about everyone of interest appeared on his program. Needless to say, he also had time for Vivien Leigh to discuss her recent divorce from Laurence Olivier, which summoned forth the mysterious cry from the former Scarlett O'Hara, "I am deeply sorry for any woman who was not married to Larry Olivier." Since this took in several billion ladies (not to mention those gentlemen who might have offered to fill, as it were, the breach), Leigh caused a proper stir, as did the ballerina Alicia Markova, who gently assured us that "a Markova comes only once every hundred years or so."

I suspect it was the dim lighting on the set that invited such naked truths. David watched his pennies. I don't recall how, or when, we began our "States of the Union" programs. But we did them year after year. I would follow whoever happened to be president, and I'd correct his "real" State of the Union with one of my own, improvising from questions that

David would prepare. I was a political pundit because in a 1960 race for the House of Representatives (upstate New York), I got more votes than the head of the ticket, JFK; in 1962, I turned down the Democratic nomination for U.S. Senate on the sensible ground that it was not winnable; I also had a pretty good memory in those days, now a-jangle with warning bells as I try to recall the national debt or, more poignantly, where I last saw my glasses.

I've just come across my "State of the Union" as of 1972. Apparently, I gave it fifteen times across the country, ending with Susskind's program. Questions and answers from the audience were the most interesting part of these excursions. As I look back over the texts of what we talked about, I'm surprised at how to the point we often were on subjects seldom mentioned in freedom's land today.

In 1972, I begin: "According to the polls, our second principal concern today is the breakdown of law and order." (What, I wonder, was the first? Let's hope it was the pointless, seven-year—at that point—war in Southeast Asia.) I noted that to those die-hard conservatives, "law and order" is usually a code phrase meaning "get the blacks." While, to what anorexic, vacant-eyed blonde women on TV now describe as the "liberal elite," we were pushing the careful—that is, slow—elimination of poverty. Anything more substantive would have been regarded as communism, put forward by dupes. But then, I say very mildly, we have only one political party in the United States, the Property Party, with two right wings, Republican and Democrat. Since I tended to speak to conservative audiences in such civilized places as Medford, Oregon; Parkersburg, West Virginia; and Longview, Washington, there are, predictably, a few gasps at this rejection of so much received opinion. There are also quite a few nods from interested citizens who find it difficult at election time to tell the parties apart. Was it in pristine Medford that I actually saw the nodding Ralph Nader whom I was, to his horror, to run for president that year in *Esquire*? Inspired by the nods, I start to geld the lily, as the late Sam Goldwyn used to say. The Republicans are often more doctrinaire than the Democrats, who are willing to make small—very small— adjustments where the poor and black are concerned while giving aid and comfort to the anti-imperialists. Yes, I was already characterizing our crazed adventure in Vietnam as imperial, instead of yet another proof of our irrepressible, invincible altruism, ever eager to bring light to those who dwell in darkness.

I should note that in the thirty-two years since this particular State of the Union, our political vocabulary has been turned upside down. Although the secret core to each presidential election is who can express his hatred of African-Americans most subtly (to which today can be added Latinos and "elite liberals," a fantasy category associated with working film actors who have won Academy Awards), and, of course, this season it's the marriage-minded so-called gays. So-called because there is no such human or mammal category (sex is a continuum) except in the great hollow pumpkin head of that gambling dude who has anointed himself the nation's moralist-in-chief, William "Bell Fruit" Bennett.

Back to the time machine. In some ways, looking at past States of the Union, it is remarkable how things tend to stay the same. Race-gender wars are always on our overcrowded back burners. There is also—always—a horrendous foreign enemy at hand ready to blow us up in the night out of hatred for our Goodness and rosy plumpness. In 1972, when I started my tour at the Yale Political Union, the audience was packed with hot-eyed neocons-to-be, though the phrase was not yet in use, as the inventors of neoconnery were still Trotskyists to a man or woman or even "Bell Fruit," trying to make it in New York publishing.

I also stay away from the failing economy. "I leave to my friend Ken Galbraith the solving of the current depression." If they appear to know who Galbraith is, I remark how curious that his fame should be based on two books, *The Liberal Hour*, published a few years before the right-wing Nixon criminals tried to hijack the election of 1972 (Watergate was bursting open when I began my tour), and *The Affluent Society*, published shortly before we had a cash-flow problem.

In the decades since this State of the Union, the United States has had more people, per capita, locked away in prisons than any other country, while the sick economy of '72 is long forgotten as worse problems—and deficits—beset us. For one thing, we no longer live in a nation, but in a Homeland. In 1972, "roughly 80 percent of police work in the United States has to do with the regulation of our private morals. By that I mean controlling what we smoke, eat, put in our veins—not to mention trying to regulate with whom and how we have sex, with whom and how we gamble. As a result our police are among the most corrupt in the Western world."

I don't think this would get the same gasp today that it did back then. I point out police collusion with gamblers, drug dealers, prostitutes, and, indeed, anyone whose sexual activities have been proscribed by a series of state legal codes that were—are—the scandal of what we like to call a free society. These codes are often defended because they are very old. For instance, the laws against sodomy go back 1,400 years to the Emperor Justinian, who felt that there should be such laws because, "as everyone knows," he declared, "sodomy is a principal cause of earthquake."

Sodomy gets the audience's attention. "Cynically, one might allow the police their kinky pleasures in busting boys and girls who attract them if they showed the slightest interest in the protection of persons and property, which is what we pay them to do." I then suggested that "we remove from the statute books all penalties that have to do with private morals— what are called 'victimless crimes.' If a man or a woman wants to be a prostitute, that is his or her affair. Certainly, it is no business of the state what we do with our bodies sexually. Obviously, laws will remain on the books for the prevention of rape and the abuse of children, while the virtue of our animal friends will continue to be protected by the SPCA." Relieved laughter at this point. He can't be serious—or is he?

I speak of legalizing gambling. Bingo players nod. Then: "All drugs should be legalized and sold at cost to anyone with a doctor's prescription." Most questions, later, are about this horrific proposal. Brainwashing on the subject begins early, insuring that a large crop of the coming generation will become drug addicts. Prohibition always has that effect, as we should have learned when we prohibited alcohol from 1919 to 1933; but, happily for the busy lunatics who rule over us, we are permanently the United States of Amnesia. We learn nothing because we remember nothing. The period of Prohibition called the "Noble Experiment" brought on the greatest breakdown of law and order that we have ever endured—until today, of course. Lesson? Do not regulate the private lives of people, because if you do they will become angry and antisocial, and they will get what they want from criminals, who work in perfect freedom because they know how to pay off the police.

What should be done about drug addiction? As of 1970, England was the model for us to emulate. With a population of 55 million people, they had only 1,800 heroin addicts. With our 200 million people we had nearly a half-million addicts. What were they doing right? For one thing, they turned the problem over to the doctors. Instead of treating the addict as a criminal, they required him to register with a physician, who then gives him, at controlled intervals, a prescription so that he can obtain his drug. Needless to say, our society, based as it is on a passion to punish others, could not bear so sensible a solution. We promptly leaned, as they say, on the British to criminalize the sale and consumption of drugs, and now the beautiful city of Edinburgh is one of the most drug-infested places in Europe. Another triumph for the American way.

I start to expand. "From the Drug Enforcement Administration to the FBI, we are afflicted with all sorts of secret police, busily spying on us. The FBI, since its founding, has generally steered clear of major crime like the Mafia. In fact, much of its time and energies have been devoted to spying on those Americans whose political beliefs did not please the late J. Edgar Hoover, a man who hated commies, blacks, and women in, more or less, that order. But then the FBI has always been a collaborating tool of reactionary politicians. The bureau also has had a nasty talent for amusing presidents with lurid dossiers on their political enemies." Now in the year 2004, when we have ceased to be a nation under law but instead a homeland where the withered Bill of Rights, like a dead trumpet vine, clings to our pseudo-Roman columns, Homeland Security appears to be uniting our secret police into a single sort of Gestapo with dossiers on everyone to prevent us, somehow or other, from being terrorized by various implacable Second and Third World enemies. Where there is no known Al Qaeda sort of threat, we create one, as in Iraq, whose leader, Saddam Hussein, had no connection with 9/11 or any other proven terrorism against the United States, making it necessary for a president to invent the lawless as well as evil (to use his Bible-based language) doctrine of pre-emptive war based on a sort of hunch that maybe one day some country might attack us, so, meanwhile, as he and his business associates covet their oil, we go to war, leveling their cities to be rebuilt by other business associates. Thus was our perpetual cold war turned hot.

My father, uncle, and two stepbrothers graduated from the U.S. Military Academy at West Point, where I was born in the cadet hospital. Although I was brought up by a political grandfather in Washington, D.C., I was well immersed in the West Point ethos—Duty, Honor, Country— as was David Eisenhower, the president's grandson, whom I met years later. We exchanged notes on how difficult it was to free oneself from that world. "They never let go," I said. "It's like a family."

"No," he said, "it's a religion." Although neither of us attended the Point, each was born in the cadet hospital; each went to Exeter; each grew up listening to West Pointers gossip about one another as well as vent their political views, usually to the far right. At the time of the Second World War, many of them thought we were fighting the wrong side. We should be helping Hitler destroy Communism. Later, we could take care of him. In general, they disliked politicians, Franklin Roosevelt most of all. There was also a degree of low-key anti-Semitism, while pre–World War II blacks were Ellisonian invisibles. Even so, in that great war, Duty and Honor served the country surprisingly well. Unfortunately, some served themselves well when Truman militarized the economy, providing all sorts of lucrative civilian employment for high-ranking officers. Yet it was Eisenhower himself who warned us in 1961 of the dangers of the "military-industrial complex." Unfortunately, no one seemed eager to control military spending, particularly after the Korean War, which we notoriously failed to win even though the cry "The Russians are coming!" was heard daily throughout the land. Propaganda necessary for Truman's military buildup was never questioned . . . particularly when demagogues like Senator McCarthy were destroying careers with reckless accusations that anyone able to read *The New York Times* without moving his lips was a Communist. I touched, glancingly, on all this in Nixonian 1972, when the media, Corporate America, and the highly peculiar president were creating as much terror in the populace as they could in order to build up a war machine that they thought would prevent a recurrence of the Great Depression, which had only ended in 1940 when FDR put billions into rearmament and we had full employment and prosperity for the first time in that generation.

I strike a few mildly optimistic notes. "We should have a national health service, something every civilized country in the world has. Also, improved public transport (trains!). Also, schools which do more than teach conformity. Also, a cleaning of the air, of the water, of the earth before we all die of the poisons set loose by a society based on greed." Enron, of course, is decades in the future, as are the American wars of aggression against Afghanistan and Iraq.

In the end, we may offer Richard Nixon a debt of gratitude. I'm in a generous mood. "Through Nixon's awesome ineptitude we have seen revealed the political corruption of our society." (We had, of course, seen nothing yet!) What to do? I proposed that no candidate for any office be allowed to buy space on television or in any newspaper or other medium: "This will stop cold the present system, where presidents and congressmen are bought by corporations and even by foreign countries. To become president, you will not need thirty, forty, fifty million dollars to smear your opponents and present yourself falsely on TV commercials." Were the sums ever so tiny?

Instead, television (and the rest of the media) would be required by law to provide prime time (and space) for the various candidates.

"I would also propose a four-week election period as opposed to the current four-year marathon. Four weeks is more than enough time to present the issues. To show us the candidates in interviews, debates, uncontrolled encounters, in which we can see who the candidate really is, answering tough questions, his record up there for all to examine. This ought to get a better class into politics." As I reread this, I think of Arnold Schwarzenegger. I now add: Should the candidate happen to be a professional actor, a scene or two from Shakespeare might be required during the audition . . . I mean, the primary. Also, as a tribute to Ole Bell Fruit, who favors public executions of drug dealers, these should take place during prime time as the empire gallops into its Ben-Hur phase.

I must say, I am troubled by the way I responded to the audience's general hatred of government. I say we are the government. But I was being sophistical when I responded to their claims that our government is our enemy with that other cliché, *you* are the government. Unconsciously, I seem to have been avoiding the message that I got from one end of the country to the other: We hate this system that we are trapped in, but we don't know who has trapped us or how. We don't even know what our cage looks like because we have never seen it from the outside. Now, thirty-two years later, audiences still want to know who will let them out of the Enron-Pentagon prison with its socialism for the rich and free enterprise for the poor. So . . . welcome to Imperial America.

The Nation
September 13, 2004

GORE VIDAL was born in 1925 at the United States Military Academy at West Point. His first novel, *Williwaw*, written when he was nineteen years old and serving in the army, appeared in the spring of 1946. Since then he has written twenty-three novels, five plays, many screenplays, short stories, well over two hundred essays, and a memoir.

JAY PARINI is an American writer and academic. Among his works of fiction and criticism are *The Last Station*, *John Steinbeck*, and *Benjamin's Crossing*. Parini is Gore Vidal's literary executor and a regular contributor to various journals and newspapers, including *The Chronicle of Higher Education* and *The Guardian*. In 1976, he cofounded *New England Review*, and he has taught at Middlebury College since 1982. He lives in Vermont.